Praise for

INTO THE AMAZON

"Larry Rohter has written a masterful biography of Cândido Rondon, one of the most extraordinary characters to emerge out of the Americas in the last century and a half. A heroic figure of epic proportions, Rondon is synonymous with the exploration of the Brazilian Amazon. But he was much more than that. One part John Muir, one part Alexander von Humboldt, and one part Mahatma Gandhi, Rondon also left behind a rare personal legacy of humanism that feels both hugely relevant and sorely lacking today, with the fate of the Amazon and its Indigenous inhabitants hanging in the balance as never before. *Into the Amazon* is beautifully written, impressively researched, and makes for compelling reading. Larry Rohter has performed a great service by bringing Rondon, unsung for too long outside of Brazil, to a much wider audience. ¡Viva Rondon!"
—Jon Lee Anderson, author of *Che: A Revolutionary Life*

"*Into the Amazon* is an unparalleled gift to anyone who wants to understand the rainforest, Brazil, early environmentalism, or the struggle for Indigenous land rights. Larry Rohter's rigorous and eloquent account of Cândido Rondon's life provides a window into the colonization of the Amazon and a portrait of a soldier whose vision for human decency and nature protection is only gaining in relevance as we navigate the twin crises of climate change and biodiversity loss."
—John W. Reid, coauthor of *Ever Green: Saving Big Forests to Save the Planet*

INTO THE AMAZON

INTO THE AMAZON

THE LIFE OF
Cândido Rondon,
TRAILBLAZING EXPLORER,
SCIENTIST, STATESMAN,
AND CONSERVATIONIST

LARRY ROHTER

W. W. NORTON & COMPANY
Independent Publishers Since 1923

Copyright © 2023 by Larry Rohter
First American Edition 2023
First published as a Norton paperback 2024

Previously published in Portuguese as Rondon: Uma Biografia in 2019.

For information about permission to reproduce selections from this book,
write to Permissions, W. W. Norton & Company, Inc., 500 Fifth Avenue,
New York, NY 10110

For information about special discounts for bulk purchases, please contact
W. W. Norton Special Sales at specialsales@wwnorton.com or 800-233-4830

Manufacturing by Lakeside Book Company
Book design by Brooke Koven
Production manager: Anna Oler

Library of Congress Control Number: 2024934543

ISBN 978-1-324-07620-9 pbk.

W. W. Norton & Company, Inc., 500 Fifth Avenue, New York, N.Y. 10110
www.wwnorton.com

W. W. Norton & Company Ltd., 15 Carlisle Street, London W1D 3BS

1 2 3 4 5 6 7 8 9 0

For my children, Sonia and Eric,
in honor of their Brazilian heritage

What does your average Brazilian know of Rondon? That he was of Indian origin and dedicated his life to their regeneration and dignity. That today he is old and blind, and that in the heart of our Western jungle there is an immense tract of land christened Rondônia—in homage to Rondon. But that's all. Who was this man, how did he live during the years that prepared him for greatness? What is the weave of facts, inheritances and influences responsible for the full tapestry of his personality?

—RACHEL DE QUEROZ, 1957

Life consists with wildness. The most alive is the wildest. Not yet sub-dued to man, its presence refreshes him. One who pressed forward incessantly and never rested from his labors, who grew fast and made infinite demands on life, would always find himself in a new country or wilderness, and surrounded by the raw material of life. He would be climbing over the prostrate stems of primitive forest-trees. Hope and the future for me are not in lawns and cultivated fields, not in towns and cities, but in the impervious and quaking swamps.

—HENRY DAVID THOREAU, 1851

CONTENTS

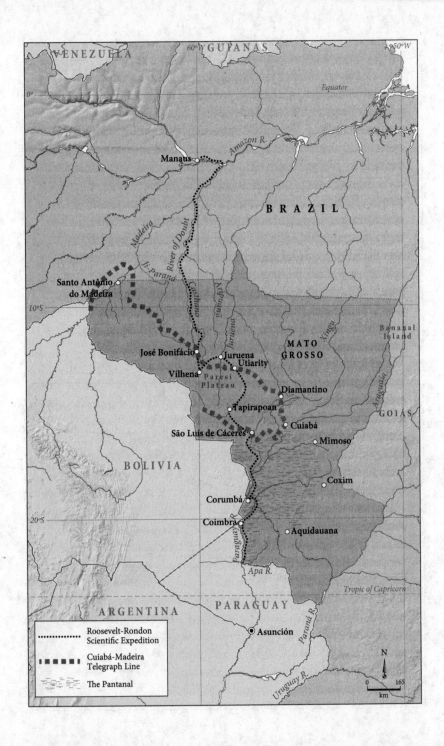

VENEZUELA

GUIANAS

60°

50°W

Equator

0°

Manaus

Amazon R.

BRAZIL

Madeira

River of Doubt

Ji-Paraná

Santo Antônio
do Madeira

10°S

José Bonifácio

Castanho

N'Ourena

Juruena

MATO
GROSSO

Xingu

Bananal
Island

Vilhena

Paresi
Plateau

Juruena
Utiarity

Diamantino

Araguaia

GOIÁS

Tapirapoan

Cuiabá

São Luís de Cáceres

Mimoso

BOLIVIA

Coxim

Corumbá

Coimbra

20°S

Aquidauana

Paraguay R.

Apa R.

Tropic of Capricorn

ARGENTINA

PARAGUAY

Paraná R.

Asunción

Uruguay R.

N

·········· Roosevelt-Rondon
Scientific Expedition

▬ ▬ ▬ Cuiabá-Madeira
Telegraph Line

The Pantanal

0   165
km

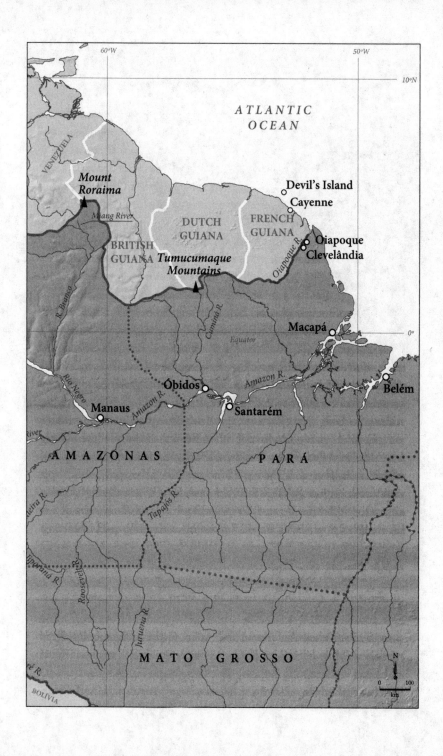

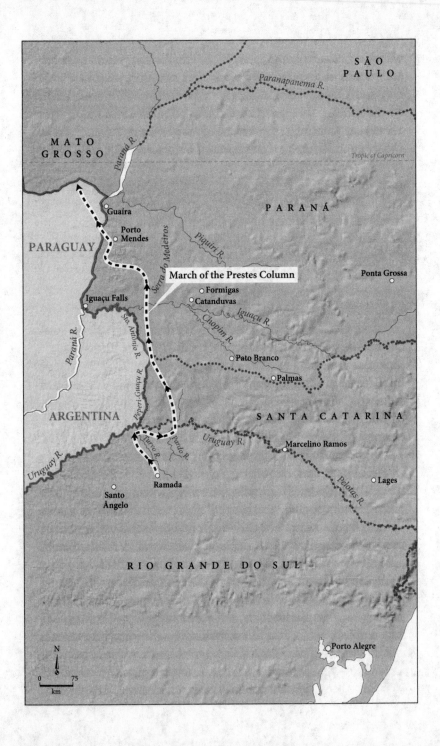

INTRODUCTION

EARLY ON THE afternoon of Sunday, April 26, 1914, a group of nineteen weary and bedraggled men—three of them Americans, the rest Brazilians—arrived at the confluence of two majestic rivers deep in the Amazon jungle. It had taken them two rain-soaked months to arrive there, and they were jubilant at reaching the end of their journey and the ordeal it had become. Behind them lay a succession of almost unimaginable trials and privations that had resulted in the deaths of three of their group, prostrated many with illness, and forced all of them to endure long periods of hunger. Ahead loomed worldwide acclaim for the feat they had accomplished: navigating and mapping a previously unknown tropical river nearly one thousand miles long, called the River of Doubt.

To commemorate the occasion, expedition members drove a wooden obelisk six feet high into the spongy ground the next morning and gathered around it for a series of photographs, with the expedition's two leaders standing on either side of the hand-hewn column. One of them, for whom the river was being renamed, was perhaps the most celebrated man in the world: Theodore Roosevelt, former president of the United States, a Nobel Peace Prize winner and prolific author whose accounts of his adventures were international best sellers. Hat in hand, eyeglasses fogged in the intense humidity, Roosevelt seemed visibly haggard and gaunt in the photographs: his clothes hung loosely from his body and he held on to the obelisk to steady himself.

To Roosevelt's left stands the other leader of the expedition, a forty-eight-year-old Brazilian Army colonel of Indigenous descent named Cândido Mariano da Silva Rondon. Several inches shorter than Roosevelt and dozens of pounds lighter, Rondon poses casually, almost nonchalantly, in his simple olive military garb, his hands thrust into his jacket pockets, with an impassive expression on his lean, copper-colored face. Unlike Roosevelt, a newcomer to the Amazon, Rondon had already spent nearly a quarter century exploring the world's largest tropical forest and its many rivers. So this was not the first time he had survived a harrowing expedition, and any relief he felt at having shepherded Roosevelt and his twenty-four-year-old son Kermit safely through this ordeal was tempered by the knowledge that he would soon have to plunge back into the jungle and resume the construction of a 1,200-mile telegraph line cutting through the Amazon, much of it across terrain inhabited only by hostile or uncontacted Indian tribes.

A few months earlier, the Roosevelt-Rondon Scientific Expedition, the official designation for the unusual binational undertaking, had traveled overland for several hundred miles along the path of the still-unfinished line, on their way to the headwaters of what was about to be rechristened the Rio Roosevelt. As the explorers made their way across savanna, highlands, and arduously cleared jungle, Roosevelt was astonished by the scale and audacity of the work he saw and, on returning to the United States, would proclaim Rondon's project one of the two greatest technological and engineering wonders of the age. "I never saw, nor know of, a project equal to the Strategic Telegraph Lines Commission headed by Col. Rondon," he said. "America can present to the world as cyclopean achievements, to the North the opening of the Panama Canal; in the South, the work of Rondon—scientific, practical and humanitarian."[1]

By any measure—number of expeditions, distances traversed, degree of difficulty, information gathered—Cândido Rondon is the greatest explorer of the tropics in recorded history, with a list of accomplishments that eclipses those of celebrated figures such as Henry Stanley, David Livingstone, or Sir Richard Francis Burton. After his five-month journey with Roosevelt, he continued to lead missions into the most remote reaches of the Amazon and Orinoco basins for another fifteen years. All told, Rondon participated in more than a score of expeditions through Brazil's northern wilderness, traveling more than twenty-five thousand miles by foot, over water, and on horse or mule as he surveyed his country's hitherto-unknown territory, mapped its borders, built roads and bridges, founded settlements, and made the initial, peaceful contact with dozens of Indigenous groups.

Rondon, however, was not simply a man of action. Trained as an astronomer and engineer, he was purged from the Brazilian Army at age sixty-five for political reasons and immediately shifted his focus from the practical to the theoretical, promoting scientific awareness of the Amazon and its peoples. During the course of his long life— Rondon was born the month Abraham Lincoln was assassinated and died just before his ninety-third birthday, shortly after the Soviets launched *Sputnik 1* into outer space—the commission bearing his name published over one hundred scientific papers, addressing disciplines as varied as anthropology, astronomy, biology, botany, ecology, ethnology, geology, herpetology, ichthyology, linguistics, meteorology, mineralogy, ornithology, and zoology. Scientists under Rondon's direction discovered and cataloged scores of new animal, plant, and mineral species, and to this day, Rondon remains the largest single contributor of specimens to the National Museum in Rio de Janeiro.

Unlike many other explorers—and in sharp contrast to international rubber consortiums, which dominated the economy of the Amazon in his time—Rondon was concerned about the human inhabitants of the region as well as its plant and animal life. Many of his own scientific papers either documented the languages of the Indigenous peoples of the area, some of whose blood flowed through his veins, or sought to explain their cultures, cosmology, rites, social structure, and religion. Always an innovator and early adopter of new technologies, he pioneered the use of film and sound recordings in anthropological fieldwork. Fully a decade before the 1922 release of Robert Flaherty's *Nanook of the North*, generally considered the first feature-length ethnographic documentary film, the Rondon Commission already included a staff cinematographer and was producing films about the Indigenous peoples of the Amazon and recording their music. Claude Lévi-Strauss, the great French theoretician of structural anthropology, would cite Rondon's work in his own groundbreaking 1955 study of the Amazon, *Tristes tropiques*, visiting the same villages Rondon had written about forty years earlier.

Rondon was also one of the most effective global campaigners for Indigenous rights during the first half of the twentieth century. As the founder and longtime director of the Brazilian government's Indian Protection Service, or SPI, he fought to defend Brazil's Indigenous peoples from the onslaught of ranchers, miners, loggers, and rubber tappers who coveted their land, and battled the intellectual and political leaders openly calling for their extermination on "scientific" grounds. On his own expeditions, Rondon adhered to a policy of absolute nonviolence in his dealings with tribal groups: the SPI's motto was "Die if you must, but kill never." As early as 1925, Albert Einstein, astonished by the notion of a "pacifist general" during a visit to Brazil, nominated Rondon for the Nobel Peace Prize as a way to honor those peaceful efforts, and when Rondon died in 1958, the International Red Cross saluted him as the "most important apostle of non-violence in modern times after Gandhi."[2]

In modern Brazilian history, the telegraph lines Rondon constructed resonate in the national psyche as an inspiring feat of national integration in the same way that the building of the Transcontinental Railroad was celebrated in the United States. Rondon is thus a central figure in Brazil's transition from a haphazardly organized empire to a modern republic. His public life spanned an extraordinary seventy years, beginning in the 1880s with involvement in the abolitionist movement. In the decades that followed he would help overthrow the emperor of Brazil, Pedro II, reject offers to become Brazil's military dictator, lead troops that quashed a military revolt against civilian rule, mediate a conflict between Colombia and Peru, help convince Brazil to support the Allies during World War II, and establish his country's first national parks. At the age of ninety-two, infirm and nearly blind, his last public act was to endorse construction of the new capital of Brasília, situated in territory he had explored and helped incorporate into the Brazilian nation six decades earlier. He was a soldier and a scientist, and also a statesman. In Brazil he is a national hero, whose face has appeared on currency and whose name graces streets, squares, museums, airports, government buildings, cities, counties, and even a state, called Rondônia.

Yet for all his significant achievements, Rondon has never been the subject of a comprehensive biography in English. To this day, he also does not have an entry in the authoritative *Oxford Atlas of Exploration* (which does, in contrast, contain entries for young Britons who later rode motorcycles across the Amazon on roads Rondon so laboriously carved out of the jungle) and is absent from the American *National Geographic Expeditions Atlas*, which ascribes the triumphs of the Roosevelt-Rondon Scientific Expedition to Roosevelt alone.

Why such a glaring discrepancy between the magnitude of Rondon's achievements and their lack of international recognition? Most obviously, as a glance at any photograph of Rondon immediately reveals, he does not conform in the least to the physical image the Anglo-Saxon world has cultivated of the great explorer. Contemporaries like Amundsen, Nansen, Peary, Shackleton, and Byrd were familiar European types, generally tall, physically imposing, and often blond or at least fair skinned. Rondon was, instead, short and wiry, a mestiço of mixed European and Amerindian descent like millions of other Brazilians, with a splash of African blood for good measure, and stereotypically Indigenous features, coloring, and physique.

Rondon's mission and objectives also differed from those of other explorers of his time. Many of them, especially the British, French, and Germans active in Africa and Asia in the decades before World War I, were advancing their countries' colonialist enterprises. Others, like Charles Darwin, Henry Walter Bates, and Alfred Russel Wallace, were motivated by scientific curiosity and had little interest in the politics of empire. Still another group was impelled almost entirely by a sheer love of adventure and the testing of one's manhood.

Though Rondon recognized that he was building on the scientific work of great naturalists like Alexander von Humboldt, his primary inspiration lay elsewhere. He was engaged first and foremost in an exercise in nation building meant to thwart European imperialism.

Nor was he an outsider testing himself in some "exotic" locale among "savage" races. Instead, he was a son of the Amazon frontier, working among people whose background and upbringing were often similar to his own. Indeed, while still a boy he would say that when he grew up he hoped to knit the harsh wilderness surrounding them into the fabric of the Brazilian state. Later, his optimism about the importance of scientific and material progress found an intellectual home in Auguste Comte's philosophy of Positivism, which became the driving force in his life.

But clearly the widespread racism of the era in which Rondon operated is a major factor—if not the principal one—in both his exclusion from the pantheon of great explorers and the international refusal to recognize his stature. As late as 1929, the *New York Times* was still referring to Rondon as "Colonel Roosevelt's guide,"[3] as if Rondon were playing Tonto to Roosevelt's Lone Ranger, and was not a distinguished scientist who spoke four European languages and half a dozen Indigenous tongues fluently. Roosevelt himself did not share this condescending, bigoted view. But given the cramped, sharply defined racial categories that existed in the United States in the early twentieth century, there was no place to accommodate a figure as brilliant and unorthodox as Rondon. A French-speaking Indigenous scientist, intellectual, and military officer? The notion seemed preposterous at the time, so Rondon was consigned to the subsidiary role of helper, guide, and scout, if mentioned at all.

But Rondon's biggest barrier to acceptance actually lay in London. During the Victorian and Edwardian eras, the Royal Geographical Society was the ultimate arbiter of all questions related to exploration and cartography, and Rondon's relationship with the RGS was anything but cordial. At the time, the society ran a training program to prepare English explorers for what its textbook described as "travel in savage countries," a category that included Brazil. The course was based on concepts of eugenics and "scientific racism," and promoted a strict racial hierarchy. In the terminology then employed by members of the British colonial service, a mestiço like Rondon was considered simply a "wog," and thus not to be taken seriously or respected, much less treated as a colleague.

Rondon was written about admiringly in books and magazine profiles published in Italy and Germany, and enjoyed cordial relationships with his peers elsewhere in continental Europe, especially French and Scandinavian explorers, scientists, and geographers. The Swedish explorer Algot Lange, for instance, described him in 1914 as "full of verve and virile force," said his "integrity and value are indisputable," and cited him as proof "that Indian blood mixed with white creates splendid men."[4] But the English explorer Percy Fawcett, a graduate of the RGS course, and the immensely popular adventure writer Arnold Henry Savage-Landor despised Rondon and repeatedly disparaged him in private correspondence and public writings, often in highly offensive racial terms. They believed he had ambitions far above his station; he in turn considered them incompetent poseurs, mere dilettantes, and openly said as much.

This rift grew especially pronounced after 1910, when the Brazilian government created the Indian Protection Service, with Rondon in charge. In that capacity Rondon more than once declined to issue travel permits or provide material assistance for RGS-supported expeditions, because the proposed undertakings would encroach unnecessarily on Indian sovereignty, deplete much-needed Brazilian government resources, or duplicate work Brazilians had already done themselves. To Savage-Landor, Fawcett, and other scions of the English establishment, it seemed intolerable that this little brown man should stand in their way.

Rondon might have fared better among the English elite had he been born into Brazil's hereditary aristocracy. But his background and early upbringing were decidedly humble. He was an orphan, born into poverty in a backward corner of Brazil where even a basic education and cultural refinements like books, music, and the theater were often unattainable luxuries. Despite those obstacles, he rose to become a marshal of the Brazilian Army, acquiring a deep knowledge of the arts and sciences along the way, driven by an insatiable intellectual curiosity and an unrelenting desire for self-improvement. Eventually, he became that rarity who was as comfortable in the cafés and salons of Rio de Janeiro as in the Amazon jungle, able to move easily between the worlds of science and shamanism. In reality, Rondon was a true-to-life Brazilian version of Horatio Alger, hero of popular American dime novels of that era. But this narrative did not impress English toffs raised on Victorian values and prejudices.

Viewed from the twenty-first century, Rondon is an inspiring and towering figure—a man of his era in some respects, but very much ahead of his time in others. He had, of course, his share of personal flaws. He was relentless in pursuit of his goals, expecting the men he commanded to be equally committed, and would not hesitate to punish them if they fell short of his exacting standards. To others, he sometimes seemed detached and distant, formal and fastidious. Most importantly, Rondon's fervent embrace of Positivism and the idealism it engendered, which began in adolescence but endured his entire life, blinded him to some of the most obvious political and social realities and contradictions of Brazilian life, and limited his effectiveness as a political figure. Had he not been so rigid a believer in Auguste Comte's secular faith, he might have been able to achieve much more for the causes he cherished, especially that of Brazil's Indigenous peoples.

But at a purely personal level, Rondon embodied the best of both modern and old-fashioned virtues. He was intensely and genuinely patriotic, adhered to traditional codes of honor, bravery, and chivalry, and repeatedly demonstrated a moral rectitude that, enhanced by a character both ascetic and abstemious, impressed those who regularly came into contact with him. The poet Paul Claudel, who during World War I served as France's ambassador to Brazil, once likened Rondon to "a figure from the Gospels," describing him as "pure, upright and without blood on his hands."[5] At the same time, Rondon's espousal of tolerance, cultural diversity, and nonviolence, his rationalism, and his recognition of the innate dignity of all human life and respect for the natural world and its ecosystems make him a very contemporary figure.

On his many expeditions, Rondon always kept extensive diaries and journals, in which he revealed most clearly his aspirations for himself, for his country, and for humanity. He often included his Positivist-inspired personal credo, based on "sympathy for all beings, towards whom one feels brotherhood" and the conviction that eventually "everything converges towards Love and the Common Good." By relying on science, arts, and industry, he reminded himself, it would someday be possible to "transform the Earth into Paradise, for all mankind, without distinction of race, belief, nation—banishing the specters of war, misery and disease." That day might be far off, but each human being had "the means to transform and improve himself,"[6] thereby gradually advancing civilization. Throughout his long and eventful life, beginning in the farthest outback of empire, that is precisely what Cândido Rondon always struggled to achieve. He was the man who came from nothing and gave everything he had to Brazil.

— PART I —

*Cândido Mariano Evangelista da Silva, around 1890, newly graduated
from the Superior War College with degrees in astronomy and military
engineering, a few months before he appended Rondon as a surname.*
(ACERVO DO MUSEU DO ÍNDIO/FUNAI—BRASIL)

I

Beyond the End of the World

I N HIS FINAL years, he would be celebrated throughout Brazil as "the Peace General." But the man whom the world would come to know as Rondon was born barely twenty-five miles from the main front of the most devastating conflict in the history of independent Latin America. Brazil and its neighbor Paraguay were at that moment just a few months into a bloody confrontation that would last five years, eventually drawing Argentina and Uruguay into the war, and leave an estimated four hundred thousand people dead and a million more wounded, homeless, or displaced. Paraguayan troops had invaded Mato Grosso, one of the biggest, poorest, and most isolated provinces of the much-larger Empire of Brazil, late in 1864. By early the next year, they had advanced to Coxim, just south of the hamlet of Mimoso, where Cândido Mariano Evangelista da Silva was born.

Because Mato Grosso—the name means "thick forest" or "dense jungle" in Portuguese—was so remote and backward, Rondon could never be sure of his birth date. Out on Brazil's western frontier in those days, the national government's administrative services were minimal, including the registration of births, deaths, and marriages. When Rondon enrolled in Brazil's military academy in the mid-1880s, he gave his date of birth as April 30, 1865. But later, as an officer, he asked that the date be changed to May 5, based on a belated discovery of Roman Catholic Church records in which a priest recalled baptizing the infant Cândido Mariano

3

on August 5, about three months after his birth. Other church records, though, suggest he may have been born as early as March 21, the start of autumn in the Southern Hemisphere. Eventually May 5 came to be the accepted birth date, and today it is a minor Brazilian holiday known as National Communications Day, commemorating the remarkable feat for which Rondon is best known: overseeing the installation of thousands of miles of telegraph lines across inhospitable terrain, enabling communication for the first time over vast distances.

In 1865, Brazil was a sprawling, ungainly country, held together by little more than the Portuguese language and the popularity of the only monarchy in the Western Hemisphere. Emperor Pedro II, known as "the Magnanimous," was an enlightened and relatively progressive sovereign, deeply interested in science and culture, opposed to slavery—then still legal in Brazil—and painfully aware of the economic and social backwardness of his realm. But the slavocrat plantation owners who dominated the country's political elite often thwarted his reformist impulses. These owners of sugar and coffee estates, who spent most of their time in the capital, had little interest in the development or welfare of faraway provinces like Mato Grosso, whose inhabitants they disdained as uncivilized and publicly compared to wild animals.[1]

Among the planter elite, prejudice against the country's Indigenous population—several million strong when the Portuguese arrived in 1500, but reduced by disease, bloodshed, and plunder to under one million by the middle of the nineteenth century—was particularly virulent. Africans, many of the plantation owners believed, could at least be made productive through forced labor once enslaved. But Indians? They ferociously resisted capture and encroachments on their ancestral lands and, when apprehended, would often refuse to work, seemingly willing themselves to die rather than cooperate. In 1852, William Herndon, an American naval officer traveling in the Amazon, summed up the sentiment about Indians he heard from the Brazilian elite: "The best use to which an Indian can be put is to hang him," he was repeatedly told, because "he makes a bad citizen and a worse slave."[2]

Rondon's early life was one of hardship. His father, Cândido Mariano da Silva, was an itinerant peddler of European, Indigenous, and African descent who died five months before Rondon's birth, just as the conflict with Paraguay was beginning. As with Rondon's birth date, the cause of his father's death cannot be precisely determined: many local accounts say he died of smallpox, but others cite malaria, or even suggest he died fighting in the War of the Triple Alliance—the only time Brazilians have waged war on their own soil. Given the chaotic circumstances and unhealthy conditions prevailing in Mato Grosso at that time, any of those causes is plausible.

Rondon's mother, Claudina Maria de Freitas Evangelista, was of Indigenous descent, with ancestry from the Bororo and Terena tribes, the two most important Indigenous groups in central Mato Grosso. The Bororo were nomadic hunters who are believed to have originated in Bolivia and made their way east into the southern Amazon and its neighboring wetlands shortly before the arrival of the Portuguese. Some Bororo communities were warlike, spurning contact with European civilization, but others were friendly, working as guides for Spanish and Portuguese colonizers, who began penetrating the region in the seventeenth century. For their part, the Terena are part of the Arawak group, who gradually migrated south from the Caribbean and also settled on the southern edge of the Amazon, where they farmed, foraged, and early on established a collaborative relationship with newly arriving Europeans.

Claudina Evangelista belonged to the branch of the Bororo whose territory extended to the Araguaia River, the easternmost of the major tributaries feeding the Amazon watershed. Also known as the Coroado, or "Crowns," because of the elaborate feathered headdresses they used in their rituals and ceremonies, the southeastern Bororo originally had a reputation as fearsome combatants. But by the time Claudina Evangelista was born, around 1840, the group's original lands had already been significantly reduced in size and its nomadic culture was under siege.

The Evangelista clan had been the dominant family in Mimoso ever since the settlement's founding. In the early nineteenth century, one of Rondon's maternal great-grandfathers, José Lucas

Evangelista, and his wife, Joaquina, received a royal land grant for services to the crown, presumably for helping subdue hostile tribes. On those thirty-two thousand acres (about fifty square miles) the couple raised cattle and horses. They also reared at least eight children, including Rondon's grandfather João, who in turn fathered ten children with Maria Constança de Freitas, who was of Terena descent; Rondon's mother, Claudina, was their youngest. Because José and Joaquina had many descendants, their original grant had been carved up into many much smaller parcels by the time Rondon was born. In addition, flooding reduced the total arable area by about half, so none of the members of the extended Evangelista clan could be considered landed gentry, or even prosperous.

Mimoso was by no means a traditional Bororo village. Its residents, however, like their ancestors, were excellent hunters, using both guns and bow and arrow, and also adept fishermen, whether with bow and arrow, harpoon-like spears, nets, or poison. Indeed, the Bororo refer to themselves as the Orarimogodogue, *orari* being their word for a type of succulent, boldly striped catfish. But these "catfish people" had also learned to grow corn, cassava, beans, and rice on small plots around their simple thatched-palm houses. Eventually settling in the area between the São Lourenço and Cuiabá Rivers, they also became expert cattle herders.

Rondon always spoke fondly of his mother, though his memories were blurry: she died when he was only two and a half years old. With no older sibling to care for him, he was handed over to a maternal grandfather, the widower João Lucas Evangelista, and his godmother and great aunt, Antônia Rosa da Silva, with whom he would spend the next four years. They both spoke fluent Portuguese, but Rondon would also have heard Bororo and Terena spoken.

Even today, Mimoso remains a tiny, out-of-the-way place with an edge-of-the-world feeling, consisting of little more than a few adobe houses strung out along a pockmarked two-lane road leading to a large metallic structure resembling a flying saucer, erected as a memorial to Rondon on the exact site of his birth. To the north lies Morro Redondo, an imposing mesa that hampers easy contact with the center of Mato Grosso, while immediately to the south and west are the northernmost limits of the vast inland swamp that Brazilians call the Pantanal, where some of Rondon's greatest feats of exploration and engineering occurred.

The Pantanal, an area the size of Great Britain or the state of Washington, is the world's largest marshland. Although today an angler's and bird-watcher's paradise, attracting an international clientele to its high-priced eco-lodges, it was nearly impassable during Rondon's childhood, effectively blocking Mimoso and points north from communication with settlements and fortifications to the south. In the rainy season, when the Pantanal expands to approximately eighty-one thousand square miles, it could be traversed only by boat, and teemed with caimans, poisonous water snakes, and piranhas; during the dry season, when it contracts to about fifty-four thousand square miles, jaguars, wolves, anacondas, and feral peccaries also posed a danger.

Explorers have always been fascinated by the region's mixture of peril and beauty. In the 1880s, the German scientist Karl von den Steinen twice crossed the Pantanal on his way to the heart of the Amazon, and pronounced himself "enchanted" by what he saw. "Almost everything is swamp, though the high crowns of the trees give the false impression of a beautiful meadow," he wrote during an 1884 expedition that took him near Mimoso. "The eternal aspect of this inexhaustible vegetation . . . simply intoxicates us."[3]

For the inhabitants of the Pantanal and other former war zones, Brazil's victory over Paraguay in 1870 brought neither peace nor prosperity. With the war's end, many demobilized soldiers and deserters from both sides remained in the devastated areas. Unable to find work, some sold their weapons, which led to a sudden flood of guns and ammunition into Mato Grosso. The result was a surge of banditry, violence, and cattle rustling. With barely two thousand soldiers, police, and national guardsmen responsible for an area larger than France, Italy, and Germany combined, the citizenry had no other choice but to band together in self-defense.

Nevertheless, Rondon would remember his years in Mimoso as a kind of tropical idyll. He and his playmates swam or hunted with slingshots, using animal calls to lure prey closer. The region was rich in wildlife and the air filled with a cacophony of sound from monkeys and hundreds of species of birds that flourished in the Pantanal. In the shallows, the *tuiuiú*, a type of stork with a black head, red collar, and white body, searched for food, while overhead, flocks of macaws, toucans, and cormorants filled the skies. In dugout canoes, local residents with their fishing rods and harpoons competed with the giant otter for tasty freshwater fish. On land, armadillos, capybaras, and anteaters roamed, and were hunted for food.

"We would climb up on the washstands where the washerwomen beat and rubbed the clothes, singing," he recalled nostalgically decades later. "Making the washstand into a trampoline, we threw ourselves into the water as quickly as we could, in a competition of agility. Other times, mounting calves we ourselves had tamed, we rode out into the fields to harvest watermelons . . . tapping them lightly with the knuckles of our hands" to determine which were the most ripe. "What a delight it was to extract the pulp, pink and juicy, by the handful!"[4]

At night, in the absolute darkness of a place with no electricity until well into the twentieth century, Rondon would stare fascinated at the sky, picking out the stars, constellations, and planets that lit up the heavens. The Milky Way was speckled with formations visible only south of the equator that bore the names of the animals Indigenous peoples discerned there: the Toucan, for example, and the Dourado, or Swordfish, plus Lobo the wolf and Musca the fly. Bororo and Terena mythology and cosmology, transmitted in stories told by family and neighbors, helped him identify these constellations. When Rondon enrolled at the military academy some years later, he would choose to specialize in astronomy.

By the time he was six, Rondon could already ride, shoot, set traps, hunt, fish, and track. He knew which berries, fruits, and mushrooms were edible, and which were not. From local Indigenous folklore, he learned about the medicinal qualities of the roots, bark, and leaves of certain trees and plants. He was a genuine backwoodsman, shaped and strengthened by life on the frontier, with skills he would use later in life. But in a place where raising cattle was just about the only way to earn a decent livelihood, a life as a cowboy—driving herds to market, branding calves with their owner's mark, rescuing strays from caimans in the swamp, lassoing stubbornly recalcitrant bulls—seemed to loom in his future.

At the age of seven, though, his time in Arcadia came abruptly to an end. Rondon had already demonstrated a rare intelligence—in his memoir he remembers a local rancher who called him a "child prodigy"—and it was clear that if he remained in Mimoso, where instruction did not go past first grade, his future would be restricted. So he was sent off to the provincial capital of Cuiabá, some sixty-five miles away, to live with one of his father's brothers, Manoel Rodrigues da Silva, enroll in school, and begin what he called "a second childhood."[5]

Initially, Rondon's grandfather João Evangelista refused to allow young Cândido to leave. "Tell them that I can't send my grandson, that I have many cows out in the pastures that need tending,"[6] Rondon recalled him saying. This was a perfectly normal response on the frontier, reflecting both the economic value and necessity of child labor.

With the end of hostilities, normal navigation of the dense network of rivers that crisscrosses Mato Grosso had not just resumed but intensified, and so riverine commerce was booming. Steamboats had been introduced during the war, and now they plied the rivers, one of the busiest of which was the Cuiabá, which linked the eponymous provincial capital with Corumbá, the province's main business center, on the border with Bolivia. Mimoso was located fewer than eight miles from the Cuiabá River, and the nearest town, Melgaço, was a regular stop on the newly thriving Corumbá-Cuiabá route.

The steamboats carried both cargo and passengers, providing opportunities for river-dwelling clans like the Evangelistas to break away from a subsistence economy and earn some money. Von den Steinen and other travelers wrote that every time their paddleboats stopped to take on new passengers or refuel, they were besieged by vendors, many of them acculturated Indian clans, selling locally produced food, trinkets, and hides. Women and girls spent their time tending the gardens around their simple houses and preparing tasty homemade sweets for sale to passengers: guava jelly, cookies, dried sugarcane. Men—and boys once they reached the age of five—not only herded and butchered cattle but also hunted jaguars, caimans, and herons.

This revitalized river commerce brought Mimoso into the global marketplace. Though almost all the benefits flowed elsewhere, locally all hands, no matter how young, were valued for whatever contribution they could make. Not only was demand for beef upriver in Cuiabá being satisfied, markets in Europe and North America hungry for hides and feathers—even more lucrative than meat because they could be transformed into fashionable articles of clothing—had opened up.

To wear down João's reluctance, Rondon's uncle Manoel sent several emissaries to persuade him to let the boy leave for Cuiabá. The old man eventually gave in, but only after extracting a promise that young Cândido would be sent back to Mimoso once his schooling ended. Manoel won him over when he produced a letter that the boy's father had purportedly written on his deathbed. The original has vanished, but Rondon often quoted from it: "I'm thinking of this first child I am about to have," Cândido the elder wrote to Manoel. "I may die before he is born. Brother, if this happens, and if the child we are expecting is a boy, don't leave him in Mimoso. Send for him, save him from the sad ignorance to which Mimoso's children are condemned."[7]

Today, Cuiabá is the core of a thriving metropolitan area with more than a million residents, and prides itself as being the "World Capital of Agribusiness." But when Rondon arrived there in 1873, it was little more than a frontier outpost with a small, dispirited army garrison, composed largely of soldiers sent there as punishment. The Amazon basin has only two discernible seasons, rainy and dry, and since all but a couple of Cuiabá's streets were unpaved, the town was an absolute quagmire of mud during one season and enveloped in blinding clouds of dust during the other. Foreign explorers who used Cuiabá as a jumping-off point for their forays into the wilderness hated the town, and complained in their writings about almost everything: the weather, the food, the people and their lack of culture, the prices, the lodgings. As late as the mid-1920s, the British adventurer Percy Fawcett would grumble that it was an "impoverished and backward" place, "little better than a ghost town."[8]

Even to a Brazilian from the coast, Cuiabá seemed remote and isolated. Gen. Floriano Peixoto, a native of the northeastern seaboard who fought with distinction in the war against Paraguay and returned to Mato Grosso in 1884 to serve as the province's military governor, memorably put it this way: "At the end of the world there exists a river; at the end of this river there rises a hill; behind the hill stands Cuiabá."[9]

And since no telegraph line connected Cuiabá to the rest of Brazil, communications were very slow: mail traveled aboard steamboats at the same snail's pace as passengers and cargo. As a result, when the Paraguayan Army invaded Mato Grosso late in 1864 and began its drive on Cuiabá, more than a month elapsed before the imperial court in Rio de Janeiro heard the news, and then months more passed before national troops could reach the front. It was dangerous politically and militarily; precarious communication and transportation links threatened Brazil's sovereignty in the heart of the continent.

An insalubrious climate also hindered development in Cuiabá, which had become the provincial capital in 1835. Malaria, dengue, yellow fever, leishmaniasis, Chagas disease, and other tropical maladies were rampant, along with a high incidence of tuberculosis and leprosy. Shortly before Rondon arrived, nearly half of its sixteen thousand inhabitants had perished in an epidemic of smallpox, transmitted by soldiers returning from the War of the Triple Alliance. For that reason, Cuiabá was one of the imperial government's favorite destinations when it wanted to punish particularly irksome criminals or political troublemakers with internal exile. People in the capital called it "our tropical Siberia."[10]

Later, Cuiabá served as the base for many of Rondon's expeditions; and as an old man, he continued to return there to visit friends and relatives. No matter how much time he spent in Rio, he always presented himself as a native of Mato Grosso and tried to promote the interests of his home state. Cuiabá gave Rondon a much-needed sense of home, even though its residents and its economy embodied the destructive, despoliatory, get-rich-quick mentality he would spend his entire life fighting.

That was the case from the city's very beginnings. In the 1670s, *bandeirantes*, or "flag bearers," the Portuguese term for those who explored the South American interior in search of riches and Indians to enslave, first passed by the site, and noted its promising location at the confluence of two rivers. In 1718, bandeirantes found the first signs of gold where the Coxipó and the Cuiabá flowed together, and settled there to mine the ore. In 1722, a large gold deposit was discovered, attracting adventurers from all over Brazil, then still a Portuguese colony. Further forays into the interior turned up more gold, as well as silver and diamonds, bringing more prospectors. Harsh climate and hostile Indians notwithstanding, by the late eighteenth century, Cuiabá was a boomtown. A century later, though, the gold deposits had mostly been exhausted, the town had fallen back into somnolence and neglect, and the bandeirantes had vanished.

On his father's side, Rondon descended from those same marauders as well as the Indians they enslaved. The Rondons had come to Brazil from Spain in the late sixteenth century, when Philip II reigned over both Spain and Portugal and Brazil was administered as a Spanish colony. The earliest, according to family lore, was a general who, when Portuguese dominion over Brazil was restored in 1640, returned to Europe, leaving his sons in Brazil. In the eighteenth century, Gaspar da Silva Rondon, Cândido's great-great-grandfather, left São Paulo to seek the fabled spoils of Mato Grosso. Eventually, he married Francisca Leonarda, the daughter of a Guaná Indian chief and a Guaná princess named Nhauaçu.

Like the Terena, the Guaná had migrated from the Guyanas thousands of years earlier and eventually settled in the savanna extending across parts of what is now Paraguay, Argentina, and Brazil. Some of them became vassals of the Guaicurú tribe, but others found refuge near Roman Catholic missions in Mato Grosso in the eighteenth century, embraced a sedentary life based on agriculture, and gradually earned a reputation as "tame" Indians, meaning they were peaceful and open to acculturation.

Gaspar da Silva Rondon flourished in Mato Grosso, becoming

a successful rancher, and had four children with his Guaná wife. Their only daughter married Generoso Ponce, scion of a family that remained politically influential in Mato Grosso until well into the twentieth century. Their youngest son, Francisco, however, defied his parents' wishes and eloped with an older widow named Escolástica. They settled farther north, and had numerous children, one of whom, Maria Rosa Rondon, was the grandmother of Cândido.

She married José Mariano da Silva, who is almost a cipher in historical records. The most common surname in Brazil is da Silva, and the first name José is equally popular, so it is as if he were named John Smith. By the time Cândido Mariano was born, the surname Rondon, which appears nowhere on his birth records, had become a familiar and respected one in Mato Grosso. Members of this large clan would distinguish themselves as governors of Mato Grosso, bishops and priests, judges and businessmen. But Cândido Mariano belonged to perhaps its least affluent branch.

In 1872, Brazil conducted its first census, listing just under 10 million inhabitants. Its racial composition differed sharply from that of the United States: just under 3.8 million Brazilians were classified as white, while nearly 2 million were counted as Black, the majority of them slaves. Though likely undercounted, another 387,000 people were deemed pure-blooded Indians. But the largest group, at just over 3.8 million people, or nearly 40 percent of the known population, were mestiços. These multiracial individuals could either be of mixed white and Indian ancestry, known commonly in Brazilian Portuguese as *caboclos*; have both Black and white antecedents, in which case they were categorized as mulattoes; or be of mixed African and Amerindian descent, what Brazilians call *cafuzos*.

Rondon belonged to the mestiço group. His mixed race would remain one of the central facts of his life throughout his many decades as a public figure. Because of his appearance, his upbringing, and his geographic origins, other Brazilians always classified him as a "caboclo," a complex word with both racial and class connotations: the authoritative *Aurélio Dictionary of Brazilian Portuguese* provides more than a dozen meanings in contemporary usage, including not just mixed-race individuals but also pure-blooded Indians who have culturally assimilated into mainstream Brazilian society and poor rural whites who in English would be called "hillbillies."[11]

For better or worse, Rondon exhibited many of the physical markers Brazilians associate with the caboclos, among them copper-colored skin, glossy jet-black hair, and high cheekbones. He was also short, standing a mere five feet three inches as an adult, thereby conforming to another cultural stereotype. In addition, he was born in a poor rural settlement in Mato Grosso, which at that time largely functioned outside the Brazilian economy. It occupied a darkly exotic place in the Brazilian popular imagination, precariously situated at "the most distant edge of the civilized world"[12] and strongly associated with the "savagery," "barbarism," and backwardness that Brazilians regarded as antithetical to a glorious national destiny.[13]

Mato Grosso was Brazil's second-largest province, occupying nearly six hundred thousand square miles, or more than twice the size of Texas. But census takers were able to count only 60,417 residents in that vast area, not even a quarter of whom were literate and just over 10 percent of whom were enslaved. Rondon saw slaves daily on the streets of Cuiabá, leaving a lasting negative impression: abolitionism would become the first great public cause he embraced after reaching Rio de Janeiro and joining the army.

Cuiabá's streets were also full of free but unacculturated Indians visiting from the countryside. In 1846, the provincial government had established a General Directorate for Indians to handle all aspects of Indigenous affairs, and so it was not unusual for tribal people to come to the capital to seek medical care, request machetes and other tools, plead for protection from enemies, or simply ask for money. Punitive military expeditions against hostile tribes also left from Cuiabá, and so Indian scouts and guides hired by the army from friendly peoples would gather there, too. Though all of this seemed exotic to European explorers, who commented on it in their travel diaries, to the child Cândido Mariano it was just a feature of daily life.

In his classes, the youngster proved an unusually adept student. He excelled in every subject, showing a particular aptitude for mathematics, the sciences, and geography. During his first year in

Cuiabá, he was enrolled at a private institution, but then transferred to a public school; his uncle could no longer afford the tuition and the school was unwilling to offer its mixed-race pupil a scholarship.

From the start, Rondon would have seemed an anomaly. Even the majority of people in Mato Grosso who could claim European descent were uneducated and illiterate, as were most Indigenous people. Rondon, by contrast, outperformed classmates of more privileged backgrounds, making him even more unusual. He evidently showed leadership qualities, too, because he was designated proctor of his class by the end of his first semester in public school.

Early on, though, Rondon was involved in a confrontation that later caused him great remorse. An army unit had brought a young Bororo boy, given the patriotic name Américo, to town to be educated. Américo taunted Rondon, calling him a half-breed and mocking him for being descended from the bandeirantes who had plagued the Bororo. One day, during recess, Rondon decided that enough was enough. "You are going to pay for this," he warned Américo.[14]

After classes, Rondon would recall, "I, the descendant of Bororos, their future defender, gave the little Bororo boy, my classmate, a thorough thrashing."[15] The colonel in charge of the garrison where the boy was lodged immediately complained to Rondon's teacher: Américo had been beaten so badly that "it was necessary to apply a poultice" to relieve his aches and bruises.

Rondon was unrepentant. "He insulted me," he remembered responding to his teacher. "I didn't do anything in the school, but outside, I had to beat him up." The teacher replied, "Well, the one who's going to get a thrashing now is you."[16] He then took a ruler and delivered a dozen whacks, "cruel and right on target," to the palms of his star pupil's hands. Rondon, silent and unflinching, was determined not to show any weakness, but, he said, "nothing like this ever happened again."[17]

In contrast to his happy early years in Mimoso, Rondon described his "second childhood" in Cuiabá as "solitary and sad."[18] His uncle Manoel, owner of a general store, had been widowed two years before Rondon's arrival, and Rondon's presence was meant to alleviate some of his loneliness. Obliged to help tend store after classes,

Rondon spent more time around adults than with other children. Aside from customers, the only visitors to Manoel's house—store in front, living quarters in back—were three sisters of his deceased wife and their husbands.

With classes, homework, and working in the store, "I didn't have much time to play,"[19] Rondon later lamented. Occasionally, he accompanied his uncle on excursions to the nearby countryside to buy provisions, like the fried fish and cassava flour that formed the foundation of the local diet. And sometimes he stole away for a bit of recreation. "My biggest source of amusement was to go to the Areão Grande beach, right in front of my uncle's house" on the banks of the river that gave Cuiabá its name. "There I would swim after performing my favorite gymnastic trick, walking on my hands"[20] down to the river's edge. Before long, Rondon could easily swim the five hundred yards to the other side of the river—a skill that later came in handy on his Amazon expeditions.

By the time Rondon moved to Cuiabá, a large group of Guaná had settled on the far side of the Cuiabá River, directly across from Uncle Manoel's store. The young Rondon interacted with them on a regular basis, since they operated an informal ferry service across the river and also brought handmade goods into town that they hoped to trade: hammocks, pottery, foodstuffs, cotton clothing, homeopathic medicines, leather, and snakeskins. The Directorate of Indians officially classified them as "blended" because they seemed comfortable among "civilized" Brazilians and had even adopted aspects of Western dress. But the Guaná themselves clung resolutely to their Indigenous identity, preferring to live together in a village of their own and to celebrate traditional rites, rituals, and festivals; their chants and music could be heard across the river. Did Rondon feel any special affinity, knowing that he was descended from a Guaná princess? He never said, but the relationship between the Guaná and the little boy they encountered down on the riverbank or in his uncle's store became a very cordial one.

By 1878, at the age of thirteen, Rondon had already finished elementary school, passing his final exams with honors and earning special praise from the oral examiners. But instead of returning to

Mimoso, he enrolled in the local normal school, taking a three-year course to earn certification as a teacher, most likely in some remote rural settlement like Mimoso.

In November 1881, when he was sixteen, he completed the teacher-training course with distinction. But Rondon now had ambitions far beyond what anyone of his race and class had achieved; the promise to his grandfather about returning to Mimoso had been forgotten. Some of Rondon's classmates talked of joining the army in the hope of being able to study someday at the military academy in far-off Rio, and that, Rondon recalled, "inspired me."[21]

In the rigidly stratified class structure of Brazil's late imperial period, a poor boy with Rondon's aspirations could follow one of two paths: study at a Roman Catholic seminary or join the army. A priest's life did not appeal to him; though naturally ascetic and self-disciplined, Rondon was inquisitive, had wide-ranging interests, and, at that stage, rebelled at dogma of any sort. The army, on the other hand, offered a number of attractive possibilities: "In those good old times," Rondon would write seventy-five years later, "a simple private, dirt poor, could enroll in the Military School," subsist on a cadet's "paltry" pay, and "prepare to serve the Nation."[22] So the army it was.

Just before graduation, Rondon approached his uncle, who was both startled and dismayed when his nephew asked to be allowed to go to Rio de Janeiro. Rondon tried to calm Manoel, who was aghast at the cost, making clear that he wasn't asking for financial support, just "your consent." He explained that he would enlist as a common soldier and then apply for enrollment in the military academy. But Manoel still wasn't convinced, pointing out that his nephew knew nothing of soldiering. At a loss, he sought the counsel of Dr. Malhado, a customer who taught at the normal school.

Dr. Malhado had an ingenious idea. During the Paraguayan War, Manoel Rodrigues had held the rank of captain in the National Guard, and under imperial regulations, the sons of officers in the regular army or the National Guard were given precedence in nominations to the academy. So Uncle Manoel proposed to formally adopt his nephew, and Dr. Malhado would further facilitate Cândido Mariano's chances of qualifying for the academy immediately by writing a strong letter of recommendation.

But Cândido Mariano did not want to be adopted: "I can only have one father," he said, rather brusquely. "You are my uncle, an uncle who I cherish and esteem, but you will never be my father." And he stubbornly refused to accept a letter of recommendation. "If I can't get onto this path on my own, then I will renounce my plans and become a cowboy. And I guarantee you that I will be a good cowboy."[3]

Finally, Uncle Manoel, with great reluctance, agreed that his obstinate nephew could enlist in the Brazilian Army. Consequently, on November 26, 1881, a few days after graduating from normal school, Cândido Mariano Evangelista da Silva reported for duty to the Third Artillery and Cavalry Regiment at an encampment on the outskirts of Cuiabá. Less than a week later, the buck private boarded a steamboat bound for Rio de Janeiro. After spending his entire childhood and adolescence confined to a radius of just sixty miles—with its narrowly circumscribed opportunities—he was about to achieve his first ambition: to experience and explore the world beyond Mato Grosso.

II

The "Furry Beast" in the Imperial City

O N   H I S   O W N   at the age of sixteen, the new recruit set off on the long voyage to Rio de Janeiro. The trip took twenty-nine days, by riverboat and then by sea. The government paid for a standard soldier's berth: a hammock in steerage.

Over the next four decades, until the advent of reliable train service and, later, commercial aviation, Rondon would repeatedly travel either this route or an even longer, more cumbersome one north to Manaus and then down the Amazon. With no safe overland alternative east and south, due to hostilities between the Brazilian government and Indigenous peoples, his only choice was to board a small boat passing near his birthplace in Mimoso and cross the Pantanal on the Cuiabá River before heading on to the port of Corumbá, perched on a bluff above the Paraguay River, at Brazil's border with Bolivia.

But that was only a preliminary to a much longer voyage. After boarding a larger vessel in Corumbá, he traveled through three foreign countries to reach Rio, stopping in Asunción, capital of recently vanquished Paraguay; then Buenos Aires, Argentina; and finally in Montevideo, Uruguay, nearly 1,700 miles south of Cuiabá. Rondon's vessel then entered the Atlantic Ocean and turned north. From that point on, its stops were in Brazilian territory, including Santos, the booming port that served São Paulo and its flourishing coffee plantations. This convoluted, costly route from Cuiabá to Rio covered nearly 3,200 miles—more than twice the distance of a land journey.

Rio de Janeiro must have been a shock to Rondon, who had never been anywhere with a population of more than 16,000 people. Rio had become the capital of the Portuguese Empire in 1808, when the Portuguese royal family fled Lisbon before Napoleon's invading forces. Then in 1822, Brazil achieved independence from Portugal, and the city became the seat of government for the new Brazilian Empire. All of this stimulated rapid growth during the second half of the nineteenth century. Rondon arrived in Rio on December 31, 1881, a time of especially explosive expansion: in the eighteen years between censuses in 1872 and 1890, Rio's population almost doubled, to 522,000 people. The capital was still a compact and often dirty place, rife with disease, subject to epidemics of yellow fever, cholera, malaria, and other virulent tropical maladies, as well as smallpox, prompting pejorative nicknames like "Filthy Port" and "City of Death."

The emperor, his family, and most of the Brazilian elite lived north of downtown, or on country estates even farther to the north and west, where exposure to disease was thought to be diminished. Prosperous merchants and foreigners tended to live in the south, in the emerging districts near the military academy, where Rondon hoped to study. But the crowded downtown area, known as the Old City, bustled with activity: the nearby port disgorged sailors from all over the globe, stevedores hauled imported goods to stores along the chic shopping promenade of Rua do Ouvidor, vendors hawked food treats and handicrafts from street corners, and the poor were squeezed into squalid tenements on the fringes of the city center.

Slaves made up nearly one-third of Rio's population. While Rondon was accustomed to seeing enslaved people on the streets of Cuiabá, the scale and pervasiveness of the institution in Rio were far greater than anything in Mato Grosso. In fact, the Brazilian capital had a larger slave population than any city in the Western Hemisphere. Public floggings, though not as prevalent as in colonial times, could still be seen at designated whipping posts in public squares.

Rio's population was overwhelmingly of European or African descent, so Rondon's Amerindian lineage was unusual. Photographs of him as a smooth-cheeked adolescent newly arrived in the capital reveal what Brazilians call "an Indian face." In the 1872 census, only 923 of the capital's residents, or 0.3 percent of the total population, described themselves as being of Indigenous descent, a percentage that remained virtually unchanged in the 1890 census.

Rondon's arrival in Rio coincided with a period of tremendous intellectual and political ferment. The most pressing issue was the abolition of slavery. With the support of Pedro II, who opposed any form of human bondage, the Brazilian Congress in 1850 passed a law outlawing the importation of slaves, effectively putting an end to three hundred years of slave trading across the South Atlantic from places such as Angola and Benin. But because the plantation economy in Brazil remained heavily dependent on slave labor, the measure had the perverse effect of increasing the market value of enslaved people already in Brazil and of stimulating slave trading between provinces.

Slaves often tried to rebel or flee to the remote interior. Plantation owners and slave traders appealed to the army to quell these uprisings and capture runaways, but the military had become allied with civilian leaders of the antislavery movement. Rondon avidly consumed the abolitionist pamphlets and broadsides upon his arrival in the capital.

During Rondon's childhood, the abolitionists had further chipped away at the system of enslavement: in 1871, for instance, a new measure decreed that any child born to a slave mother was automatically free, and that slaves also had the right to purchase their manumission. But the army and its allies were unwilling to wait a generation for slavery to end, and chafed at new iniquities that were emerging. In 1885, while Rondon was enrolled at the military academy, another law would free slaves who were sixty years of age or older. In reality, this worked to the advantage of plantation owners, because they no longer had to care for workers whose usefulness had diminished with age, and it did not satisfy abolitionists, who opposed a piecemeal approach.

As soon as Rondon reported for duty in Rio, in the first days of 1882, his carefully crafted plan to attend the military academy went awry: his Mato Grosso secondary school diploma, he learned, was not valid in the capital, and he would have to return to school to obtain a local certificate. That would take three years or more, so instead of almost immediately becoming a cadet, as he had hoped, he would have to serve as a common soldier until he qualified for admittance to the academy. Rondon had traveled from Mato Grosso to the capital with several other would-be applicants, and this news was so discouraging that they gave up and went home.

But not Rondon: "I remained firm in my determination to overcome this difficulty,"[1] he would later recall. Examining alternatives, he soon learned that passing examinations in specific subject areas would suffice to meet the military academy's requirements. He decided to enroll in an extension program offered by the Colégio Pedro II, Brazil's most prestigious secondary school, and do its coursework simultaneously with his military service. Founded in 1837, the *colégio* operated under a charter that required it to "serve both the sons of the elite and of the destitute," with admission based purely on merit, "preparing students for commerce, industry and public administration."[2] To groom them for such careers, pupils were taught by instructors who included some of the country's leading scholars, attracted by generous salaries and minimal classroom loads for teachers.

It was too late to enroll for the 1882 school year, so Rondon was forced to wait twelve months to begin the *colégio*'s three-year extension program. He planned, however, to accelerate the process by taking just one year of courses, skipping the remainder of the usual classroom work before taking the final qualifying exams. The new friends he had made were convinced he was crazy and had no chance of succeeding: "Furry beast!" Rondon recalled them saying, using a pejorative nickname for anyone of mixed race from the hinterlands. "You think that with the mathematics of Cuiabá you're going to come out on top? You're going to flunk out for sure!" Rondon, though, was armed with unshakable confidence in his own abilities, convinced that his schooling in Mato Grosso had supplied him with "all the necessary preparation, which, though not recognized officially, was perfectly adequate."[3]

So whether out of sheer cussedness or a stubborn desire to make his way on his own merits, Cândido Mariano da Silva began his military life as a common soldier, at the lowest possible rung on the ladder. Like others of his rank, he was assigned to menial duties at the main barracks adjoining the imperial palace. This turned out to be a fortunate coincidence: Rondon was allocated to a unit under the command of Captain Hermes da Fonseca, a future president of Brazil who would do much to advance Rondon's career.

Privates in the Brazilian Army earned very little and lived in spartan conditions. Among the recruits, the joke was that horses in the stables nearby enjoyed a more nourishing diet, better medical care, and more comfortable quarters than they did. A good horse was expensive, but common soldiers were easily replaceable and the mortality rate among them was high.

Rondon's fellow recruits came from equally humble circumstances. Many could not read or write when they joined the military, or already suffered from malnutrition or serious diseases. Even worse, an official study conducted in 1884 revealed that more than half of the army's thirteen thousand men had been imprisoned, for offenses committed either in civilian life or during their time in the military. "It made me suffer greatly to be lodged with these recruits," Rondon wrote in his memoirs. "As a boy, I had only one dream in life, to study so as to properly serve mankind."[4] That did not prepare him for living with foul-mouthed recruits who lacked ambition and engaged in drunken behavior, gambling, and thievery.

In that kind of rough-and-tumble environment, Rondon's studiousness made him stand out, as did the beautiful handwriting he had learned at school in Cuiabá. Before long, he was working as a scribe for the garrison secretary, copying official orders and other documents. He had barely settled into that job, though, when he was reassigned to the quartermaster general's office, a few blocks from the barracks. Each morning he walked to his job, and soon developed a routine: midway between the barracks and his workplace stood a food stand, run by an emancipated slave, selling simple, cheap snacks, which Rondon eagerly consumed as a supplement to his meager soldier's breakfast whenever he could afford it.

Across the street from the barracks was the Quinta da Boa Vista estate, a former ranch once owned by the Jesuits that the king of Portugal had chosen as his residence when the royal family arrived in 1808. The king's son, Pedro I, and his family continued to live there after the country gained its independence, and his son, Pedro II, had hired a French landscape architect to beautify the grounds and expand its gardens. As a humble recruit, Rondon was often required to stand guard at the imperial palace or on the margins of the estate for hours at a time, a duty that continued even after he was promoted to clerk, and which he found extremely boring.

But some sections of the Quinta da Boa Vista were open to the public, and Rondon spent most of his off-duty hours there, for his own peace of mind and to distance himself from the seedy atmosphere of the barracks. The luxuriant gardens brought back memories of the exuberant landscape of his birthplace, and some of the wildlife he observed on the imperial grounds, especially the large flocks of birds, was very familiar. But the animals that most awakened his nostalgia for home, "my greatest amusement," were the agile, long-snouted tapirs that roamed the grounds: "Recumbent at the edge of a gully, with a stream of fresh water born between rocks, with the branches of trees supplying shade, I would forget myself, watching them bathe in the clear waters, shaking their hindquarters and splashing me. I felt happiness in those contacts with the kind of nature that I had always loved passionately."[5]

Beyond that, the gardens were quiet, shaded, and rambling, an ideal place to study. Rondon soon acquired the habit of "strolling under the leafy trees" of the palace grounds on "long and interminable walks,"[6] reading textbooks and memorizing information for the tests he would soon take. Toward the end of 1883, after a stressful, exhausting year juggling military duties with studies, he took the examinations and passed with distinction, earning the highest grade possible in mathematics. On December 4, 1883, he was accepted by the military academy for classes beginning at the end of the Southern Hemisphere summer, on March 1, 1884. His gamble—on his ability to telescope three years of coursework into one—had paid off.

The academy was situated on what was then the outskirts of the imperial capital, at the base of a small peninsula jutting out to sea.

The site was stunningly beautiful, wedged between the 1,300-foot-high Sugarloaf Mountain and the imposing Babylon Hill, and sheltered by a cove directly facing the mouth of Guanabara Bay and the South Atlantic Ocean, with a sandy beach and a magnificent view out to a placid seascape dotted with small islands. On overcast days the nearby mountains could sometimes be seen piercing the clouds that shrouded them, and late in the afternoon on clear days, the setting sun would reflect off the garnet crystals that flecked the sand on the beach, tinging them in shades of pink, scarlet, crimson, and vermilion—hence the name Praia Vermelha, or "Red Beach."

Contrasting sharply with the sublime natural surroundings, the main academy building resembled a grim Dickensian workhouse more than a school—an impression reinforced by the iron bars on its windows. One of Rondon's contemporaries recalled that on first seeing the academy, he couldn't be sure whether he was entering "a convent or a prison."[7] Inside, the situation was no better. Cadets were lodged in cramped dormitories and took their lessons in equally overcrowded classrooms. The heat, especially in summer, was often stifling. Supplies of fresh water were erratic, and in Rondon's time electricity had not yet been installed, so cadets had to study, wash their clothes, and perform their nightly ablutions by flickering gaslight.

Having spent his early childhood in the countryside, Rondon was inured to these discomforts. But for his more privileged classmates, Praia Vermelha represented hardship, and they grumbled about living conditions. The biggest source of complaint was the lack of sanitation. "As for our bathrooms, it's best just to say nothing,"[8] one of Rondon's contemporaries later wrote. In general, he continued, living quarters had "no comforts" and were "without hygiene."[9] The death rate among cadets was high enough that one of the academy clerks earned the mordant nickname "Bury Him" because "he was accustomed to daily dispatching documents relating to deaths in the following fashion: 'Bury him in accordance with the law.'"[10]

Reveille sounded at 6 a.m., but it was Rondon's habit to rise promptly at 4, so as to squeeze more into his day, a custom he retained for the remainder of his life. First, he went for a long swim, even when the sea was choppy or rain was falling, and then took a cold shower in the chilly dawn. By 5 he was back in his spartan accommodations, where he would cram in a full hour of study before his fellow students awoke, reading in the dark by the faint light of a whale-oil lamp in his small cubicle.

After classes, many of the more affluent cadets wandered off to nearby cafés or parks to discuss politics and literature or gossip about academy affairs. Rondon hardly ever joined them: he did not consume alcohol, and even if he had, he could not have afforded to pay for his own drinks, much less buy a round for colleagues, as etiquette demanded. Instead, he remained behind, even on weekends and holidays, studying in his quarters, at the cadets' library, or in common areas. Because he was so poor, he could not afford to buy textbooks, and took thorough notes in his classes or asked to borrow course material from classmates. It was, as Rondon later acknowledged, "a life apart" from that of the average cadet, "austere and difficult."[11]

Rondon's drive to excel academically was motivated by both pride and need. Students at the academy were divided into two groups, cadets and ensigns, based on classroom performance, with ensigns ranked higher. Not only was being an ensign considered the important first step to a distinguished military career, it also came with a sizable monthly stipend. And Rondon, as poor as he was, yearned for that extra money even more than most of his colleagues.

At times, though, his desire to shine overwhelmed good judgment. That, in turn, led others to want to cut him down to size. In a mechanical engineering course, for example, the professor, Manuel Amarante, who had fought with distinction in the war against Paraguay, asked the students to solve a practical problem. Rondon, wanting the top grade, devised a response that used a differential equation, which allowed him to demonstrate his mastery of calculus. He was stunned when the papers came back and he did not receive the highest mark. When he asked why, Amarante told him that the best solution to any engineering problem is the least complicated, and that his did not meet that standard.

Rondon should have stopped right there and let the issue slide, as he later admitted. Instead, he had a tantrum, and stormed angrily out of the classroom. As an additional protest, he took to turning in blank exam papers for the remainder of the semester, which of course earned him one zero after another—and eventually a failing average. Then, at the end of the term, he asked for a make-up oral exam before a departmental board, which Amarante for some reason granted him.

Word of Rondon's pigheadedness had gotten around, so many classmates came to witness the exam, as did the academy's commandant. Something in Rondon's demeanor must have displeased him, because several of Rondon's friends remember the commandant leaving in the middle of the exam, clearly irritated. "What this cadet needs is to be locked up in the brig," he remarked on the way out. "He's insubordinate and undisciplined."[12] But Amarante and the others were more forgiving: based on his performance in the oral exam, Rondon passed the course with honors, salvaging his grade point average and saving himself from possible expulsion or imprisonment. (Years later, Rondon's eldest daughter, Aracy, would marry Amarante's son Emmanuel, who had become one of Rondon's most trusted subalterns, while her sister Clotilde Teresa would marry another of Amarante's sons, João Estanislau.)

During the late imperial period, cadets were divided into two distinct social groups: those who frequented the court and those who did not. The latter were known in the slang of the time as "orange blossoms," and it was into this category that Rondon fell. "In general, orange blossoms belonged to that group of cadets with few financial resources or, in many cases, none whatsoever," a contemporary of Rondon's later recalled. "Almost always they had only the uniform on their back or some unfashionable hand-me-down piece of clothing barely in wearable condition."[13] In Rondon's case, it was a cheap celluloid dickey with a detachable collar and a snap-on tie.

About the only time Rondon socialized was at Carnival: in one of the earliest photographs of him, he is leaning on a telescope, next to a group of jovial classmates costumed as Oriental viziers and wizards. Normally, though, while his better-off classmates were spending their weekends flirting with socially prominent girls or attending the theater downtown, Rondon was at "Instructive Recreation," the name given to the lending library organized by cadets from the senior class.

"The monthly circulation of novels was extraordinary, with an equally large number of consultations of scientific works," one of Rondon's classmates recalled. "At this time there was no cadet who was not familiar" with masters of fiction such as Victor Hugo, Alexandre Dumas, and Jules Verne, read always in the original French, or popular Brazilian and Portuguese novelists of the era, such as José de Alencar, Eça de Queiroz, and Alfredo Taunay. "Among those also widely read were Comte, Spencer, Buchner, Bichat, Flammarion, Calvo, Teixeira de Freitas, Lafayette, Laffite, Lagrange, Bertand, Plato and so many of the other auxiliaries of human progress."[14]

The Academic Club, where cadets gathered to debate, also played an essential role in shaping Rondon's intellectual outlook and cultural preferences. Members "not only prepared various formal papers, to be discussed in public session, but also took note of important events taking place in Brazil or abroad." When, for example, Victor Hugo died in 1885, during Rondon's sophomore year at the academy, "the passion that many students felt for Victor Hugo," Rondon included, led the club to organize a commemoration "at which brilliant orators lectured."[15]

Attracted particularly to the sciences, Rondon also made a point of reading works of the great naturalists. Von Humboldt, whom he came to idolize, was at the top of his list, but he took a special interest in Europeans who had visited Brazil: von Martius, von Spix, von Langsdorff, Darwin, Wallace, Bates, Agassiz. He also buried himself in the studies and reports of eminent Brazilian travelers and scientists; a few years later, once he was earning a regular salary and could afford to buy books, the writings of these great explorers and thinkers were among the first he acquired for his personal library.

What saved Rondon from being considered a joyless, tiresome pedant, and ostracized by his classmates, was his athleticism. In the late imperial period, groups of cadets regularly competed with other teams from the posh social clubs frequented by sons of the aristocracy in sports like swimming, boating, sprinting, and rock climbing. Thanks to his upbringing, Rondon excelled in all of those activities, especially the aquatic events, and often was the star of the squads the academy sent to such competitions. He clearly regarded these contests as serious business: to hone his mountaineering skills, Rondon took to climbing Sugarloaf Mountain during his free hours, using ropes to scale the sheer rock cliff face. Because of Rondon, the cadets from Praia Vermelha more often than not won top honors in city meets, and this earned him respect from his classmates.

Nonetheless, as is so often the case in the military and other rigidly hierarchical organizations, plebes at the academy were systematically subjected to hazing. After their first night, all plebes, including those of Rondon's class, were required to attend a boisterous general assembly directed by the upperclassmen, at which the extensive "Code for Beasts" was announced to them, "constantly interrupted by witticisms, gibes and wisecracks, all more or less risqué" from the older cadets. One of the first articles proclaimed: "Animal and filth are synonyms for bicho," the Portuguese word for "beast." Another stated that "the bicho does not think, cannot reason, and acts by instinct; he does not live, he vegetates, and he is stupid by nature." And: "The bicho has only duties to fulfill on behalf of his illustrious upperclassmen masters."[16]

Nowhere in his writings did Rondon ever mention being hazed, or complain of being singled out for abuse because of his backwoods upbringing or Indigenous background. The only hint he may have suffered discrimination is suggested by a nickname bestowed on him: *bicho peludo*, which can mean "furry brute" or "hairy beast." That generic term was often applied to sloths, monkeys, the skunk-like *gambá*, and other exotic creatures native to the Amazon jungle, and to describe the *mapinguari*, a fetid, one-eyed, apelike creature, covered in matted red fur and with feet facing backward, that is a familiar, frightening figure in Amazonian mythology. Since Rondon had little body hair, never sported a beard, and was neither fierce nor particularly outgoing when he arrived at the academy, labeling him a "furry brute" seems an odd choice—unless it was meant to be a humorous but racially insensitive slight. The same applies to his other sobriquet: *bicho do mato*, the "beast from the forest."

Rondon had to endure these nicknames, given the survival-of-the-fittest environment prevailing in the barracks. If the recipient of any nickname took the situation seriously and tried to react, "he was doomed," recalled one of Rondon's contemporaries. "Many times he would then be stuck with it for good. And it wasn't unusual for the catcalls to be accompanied by a volley of old boots, sandals, etc."[17]

By tradition, however, more privileged cadets also had an obligation to financially assist their less fortunate classmates, who obviously included Rondon. "Responding to this, secret associations were organized," wrote one former cadet whose tenure at the academy overlapped with Rondon's. "During the first days of the month, in the depths of the night, without these needier colleagues sensing it, someone placed under the pillow of each of them an envelope containing money. . . . It was charity performed on the sly, absolutely averse to any kind of ostentation."[18]

In June 1885, midway through his second year, a curious episode nearly snuffed out Rondon's life; he survived only because affluent friends intervened. He was on his way to class when he fainted and fell down a flight of stairs. When he came to, he was not in a bed at the military hospital but in lodgings off academy grounds shared by two friends from Mato Grosso. Worried about his injuries, they had decided to care for him themselves rather than see him consigned to the infirmary, where he might end up on Bury Him's list.

For months, Rondon had been pushing himself to the edge of exhaustion and, to stretch his budget, eating sparingly, with the canteen's meager diet supplemented almost exclusively by beans and bread. "In that year of 1885, I often went down to the infirmary, with gastro-intestinal disturbances, the consequence perhaps of excessive work right after meals or of avitaminosis caused by previous food deficiencies,"[19] he wrote later. Perhaps, he and his friends thought, some enforced bed rest and a better diet would do him good.

But Rondon's condition grew worse, and a doctor from a nearby clinic was called in. "My state of weakness did not permit me any kind of intellectual effort," Rondon later recalled. "I spent hour after hour alone, counting the boards on the ceiling or the stains on the wall," sometimes drifting into fever dreams or hallucinations, "while my friends went to the Military School."[20] Despite the doctor's ministrations, Rondon continued to lose strength and weight: the situation looked so grim that his two friends took up a collection among other classmates so that Rondon could have a decent casket and a proper burial when he died.

Then something happened that, Rondon later wrote, left his doctor "open-mouthed." Rondon had been craving pineapple, and begged his friends to buy one. When they asked the doctor if that was medically advisable, he "shrugged his shoulders with the look of someone thinking 'why upset him if there is nothing more to do?'" So a pineapple was cut up and fed to Rondon in pieces, "which I savored with intense pleasure," he recalled. He fell asleep, and when he awoke "it was as if new life had been instilled in me."[21] He continued on that course of "treatment" for another few days, and when the doctor next came to visit, "he suspended all further medication, prescribing a diet of fruit and light meals." Against the odds, Rondon had pulled through.

Given the absence of medical records, it is impossible from a distance of more than 135 years to know what was afflicting Rondon. But the recuperative powers he ascribed to pineapple provide us with possible clues, or at least grounds for speculation. At first glance, it would seem likely that Rondon was suffering from one of the diseases historically common among soldiers and sailors on severely restricted diets, such as scurvy or beriberi. After all, pineapple is rich in vitamin C, and also contains significant amounts of manganese, thiamine, vitamin B6, and copper; lack of vitamin C is known to cause scurvy, and beriberi is a thiamine deficiency.

But Rondon's recovery, at least as he remembered it, was so rapid, so dramatic, that a physical source seems questionable. So could his problem have been psychosomatic? Freud had not yet developed his theories of behavioral medicine when Rondon fell ill, but it is clear that, in his intense desire to outshine his more privileged fellow students, he had subjected himself to a punishing physical and mental routine. The result was stress and anxiety, which we now know can generate physical maladies of exactly the type Rondon experienced.

Because of his illness, Rondon missed nearly six months of classes. In order not to be held back, he unwisely decided to take final exams with his classmates, as if he had not missed a single lecture. "However, my lack of strength betrayed me, my body did not obey the commands of the brain, and I lost my senses when it came time for the exam."[22] For the first time, he had to swallow an academic failure.

Even worse, under the academy's rules, cadets who failed final exams in their first or second year were supposed to be returned to the ranks. But Rondon's academic performance had been so distinguished that an exception was made. His failing test scores were simply expunged from his record, meaning that officially he never took the final exams at all, and he was allowed to do the year over. Since "I was already master of almost all of the syllabus," he subsequently devoted his own reading and studying to the third-year curriculum, so that he could remain a year ahead of coursework for the remainder of his time at the academy. "As a result, I became the tutor of my slower colleagues, sometimes working deep into the night to teach them the assignment."[23]

Rondon's grueling routine left little time for extracurricular activities beyond sports, with one significant exception: in 1887 he and other cadets founded a literary journal, called the *Magazine of the Academic Family.* The first issue appeared in November, when Rondon was twenty-two; he is listed on the masthead simply as Cândido Mariano da Silva. In many ways, the magazine was a typical student publication, with a mixture of poems, short stories, reviews, and essays typical of the era. But it was at times something much more: it became a vehicle to expound the virtues of republicanism, science, and rationality.

The magazine's first issue opened with an idealistic but almost Darwinian manifesto of purpose and objectives, signed by the four members of the editorial board, among them Rondon. "Under the irrepressible action of the biological law of adaptation," the new publication aimed "to take on characteristics adequate to the historical moment we are living through." Its program, they added, "can be reduced to the following: to cultivate art, science, philosophy and religion as much as possible, with full freedom for discussion, analysis and criticism, under the influence of the most rigorous moral discipline."[24]

Rondon's regular study group at the academy included three cadets affiliated with the magazine who would go on to become significant figures in Brazilian history: Euclides da Cunha, Augusto Tasso Fragoso, and Lauro Müller. They were in some ways a peculiar quartet, with markedly different personalities, backgrounds, and temperaments, and of the other three, Rondon was closest to da Cunha, regarded today as one of Brazil's greatest writers. The two first became acquainted when they were seated next to each other in a second-year course in analytic geometry, and quickly discovered a series of affinities. Da Cunha had also lost his mother at the age of three and was handed off to be raised by her relatives; his father, although still alive, had remarried and was largely absent from the boy's life. Nonetheless, like Rondon, da Cunha had a father figure—his grandfather—also named Manoel Rodrigues, like Rondon's uncle. Additionally, he and Rondon were the two shortest and scrawniest cadets in their year, each standing barely five feet three inches and weighing less than 120 pounds. Politically and philosophically, their views also aligned. Both were ardent abolitionists and republicans, deeply influenced by the teachings of their military superiors.

Even more than Rondon at his most volatile, da Cunha was habitually hotheaded and reckless, as shown by an incident early in 1889 that became famous in Brazilian history. To prevent the cadets from going to the Rio docks to greet a republican politician returning from Europe, a review of the troops by the minister of war was scheduled for the same hour. But as the cadets paraded past, da Cunha broke formation and tried to break his sword in half in protest; when that failed, he simply threw it to the ground in the direction of the minister and stalked off.

This caused a scandal, which the military academy and War Ministry covered up. Da Cunha was first hospitalized, supposedly with a case of "nerves" that had caused a breakdown, and then imprisoned. Under the harsh military regulations then in place, he could have theoretically been hanged. But Rondon and other cadets lobbied on his behalf, and he was spared, his punishment limited to expulsion from the academy.

Rondon's friendship with da Cunha continued after graduation. They worked in different regions of the country, so they rarely saw each other, but they corresponded, and when both were in Rio, they set aside time to meet and talk. In September 1890, when da Cunha married Ana Emília Ribeiro, the eighteen-year-old daughter of an influential military officer and politician, he wanted Rondon as his best man. Unfortunately, Rondon was on assignment in the interior. But when the couple's first son, Solon, was born in 1892, da Cunha asked Rondon to be his godfather, and Rondon accepted—a decision that would have serious repercussions years later.

During their years as cadets, Rondon relentlessly pursued the recognition he craved for his outstanding performance. More than anything, he wanted the coveted promotion to ensign, and when, after his first year back from illness, "I finished in second place, my response was irrepressible tears." The next year was similar: although "I was first on the list" for a promotion and the much-needed financial boost it would bring, he was told that "there were very few slots" available, and he again faced what he described as "deferred expectations."[25]

Rondon was unable to accept such a situation, and impetuously petitioned the commandant, "requesting that he arrange" the promotion Rondon felt should already be his. Almost immediately he was summoned to the office of the commandant, who was aghast at Rondon's audacity. "He explained that my application constituted a grave breach of discipline, worthy of imprisonment in the fortress of Santa Cruz, but that, knowing me, he would limit himself to an affectionate reprimand." As before, Rondon could not control his emotions: "Once again thick and silent tears bubbled from my eyes" as he endured the rebuke, then turned and marched out of the office, "erect and firm."[26]

When the promotion finally came through, on June 4, 1888, Rondon was ecstatic. His monthly salary immediately rose to a sum he later described as "a fortune in those days, especially for someone like me, accustomed to a stoic life."[27] The improvement in his material circumstances, though, also symbolized something far more significant: in less than seven years, he had gone from lowly foot soldier to the very top of his class at the military academy. This long-awaited honor validated his struggle to excel and all the sacrifices it demanded. But in his last year at the academy, these personal considerations were eclipsed by tumultuous historical events: Brazil's government was overthrown, with Rondon both eyewitness and participant.

III

The Republic

LATE IN 1888, the imperial government announced a sweeping reform of military education, perhaps hoping to dampen republican sentiment among the army's future officer corps. Plebes remained at Praia Vermelha, but ensigns like Rondon and other upperclassmen transferred to a newly established war college, near the emperor's palace and the garrison protecting him. During his last year there, Rondon studied advanced calculus, a course taught by Benjamin Constant Botelho de Magalhães, and also began learning German from Constant's Frankfurt-born son-in-law.

Rondon had first encountered Benjamin Constant during his second year at the academy, when he and Euclides da Cunha took analytic geometry together. Constant was probably the most admired instructor among the cadets, owing to his fierce embrace of abolitionism and an equally impassioned rejection of monarchism. But both of those ideas, he explained to the idealistic young military intellectuals gathered around him, were anchored in a philosophical system that could explain the past and guide Brazil and all mankind to an auspicious future: Positivism.

Rondon's exposure to Positivism and Constant's influence transformed his life. Within months, he had adopted Positivism as his personal and political creed, and would remain a fervent Positivist the rest of his life. He organized his family and raised his children in accordance with Positivist precepts. He uncomplainingly accepted

Positivist strictures that prevented him from holding elected office, and during his expeditions through the Brazilian wilderness, he unfailingly sought to apply Positivist principles in his dealings with the Indigenous peoples he met. It is no exaggeration to say that Positivism became the single most important influence on Rondon's life, that it shaped his worldview and gave him both physical and moral strength to endure the almost unimaginable hardships he would confront on his expeditions.

Like so many other intellectual and cultural influences on Brazilian society, Positivism originated in France. Reacting to the bloodshed and turmoil of the French Revolution, the social philosopher Auguste Comte, born in 1798, sought a new ideology capable of providing a peaceful, secular solution to the looming crisis brought on by Europe's first wave of industrialization. As a young man, he had worked as the private secretary of Henri de Saint-Simon, the father of utopian socialism, but Comte gradually concluded that the only solution to humanity's problems lay in science, not politics or religion, and came to reject socialism in any form. "The revolutionary principle," he would write, "consists in recognizing no other spiritual authority than individual reason, especially concerning essential questions."[1]

To deal with those questions, Comte devised a "Classification of the Sciences." Fundamental to all other sciences was mathematics, which was succeeded in importance by astronomy, physics, chemistry, and biology, in that order. At the apex, though, he created a brand-new science—devoted to the study of humankind itself, the most intricate and multifaceted of all disciplines. He called it sociology, and deemed it "the queen of the sciences."[2]

Human society initially existed, Comte also argued, in a "theological" state, dependent on supernatural explanations like religion to organize and elucidate the external world. Furthermore, within this phase three distinct levels could be discerned: the fetishistic was the most primitive and was succeeded by polytheistic and then monotheistic periods, the last of which was dominated by Christianity, Judaism, and Islam and prevailed throughout most of the world in the nineteenth century.

In the wake of the Enlightenment, though, some individuals and societies had already progressed to a second phase, which Comte called the "metaphysical" or "investigatory" stage. In these more advanced circumstances, reason and questioning predominated, and both religion and lay authority began to be critically examined. But only by fully developing and applying the sciences, especially sociology, Comte argued, could humanity hope to reach the final, ideal phase of existence. This, of course, was the "positivist" stage of history, in which humankind bowed to no higher power and rationalism would reign. But to reach that third stage, a society must inevitably pass through the two previous phases: no shortcuts were allowed.

Eventually, in his later years—and to the horror of some of his early supporters—Comte reframed his science-based philosophy as a secular faith, what he called "the Religion of Humanity," and wrote a "Catechism of Positive Religion" for his followers to study. His objective, he stated, was to reorganize society "without god or king through the systematic worship of Humanity,"[3] and to that end he created all the trappings of a conventional religion. This led Comte's critics, among them some who had earlier been sympathetic to Positivism in its purely philosophical form, to dismiss the Religion of Humanity as simply a form of "Catholicism without Christianity."

From a vantage point in the twenty-first century, Positivism seems a hodgepodge of half-baked ideas, a "labyrinthine synthesis of philosophy, science, sociology, politics and religion,"[4] as one modern critic describes it. Why did it have such appeal for Rondon and other young intellectuals at the end of Pedro II's long reign? One answer is that its doctrine was evolutionary, not revolutionary, offering the prospect of progress and social transformation without violence: the Brazilian historian José Murilo de Carvalho has for that reason described it as "Bolshevism for the middle class."[5] This was an important feature for peaceable Brazilians, especially for those of Rondon's teachers who, like Constant, had experienced the bloodshed of the Paraguayan War and emerged as pacifists. Comte's philosophy contrasted sharply with the contemporaneous Communism of Marx and Engels, which involved class struggle, presumably including that of the sort seen in the Paris Commune of 1871, still a vivid memory for Francophile Brazilian elites.

In addition, Positivism offered a rejoinder to theories of "scientific racism" that were gaining force and respectability in the second half of the nineteenth century throughout Europe and North America but were deeply insulting to countries like Brazil. The notion of a hierarchy of races was an old one, but the publication of Darwin's *On the Origin of Species* in 1859 provided new ammunition for those who believed that the "white" or "European" race was superior to all others. Darwin never mentioned *Homo sapiens* in that groundbreaking work, but to advocates of scientific racism, the advanced status of European civilization could only be the result of his process of natural selection. It followed, therefore, that "savage" and "inferior" races like Africans and Amerindians, being less fit, were doomed to extinction.

One of Positivism's underlying tenets, though, was a belief in the essential equality of all humans. Societies existed at markedly different levels of material and intellectual development, but this was due to cultural and historical factors, not biology. Or to put the issue in a specifically Brazilian context that would have resonated profoundly with Rondon: the Indians of Mato Grosso might be backward, but that was not because they belonged to an inherently "inferior" race. Rather, their society still functioned at the fetishistic level of the religious stage of history, but could advance dramatically through exposure to the sciences. Sociology and related disciplines like anthropology and ethnology could play a role in the process of lifting up both the Indian and the Afro-Brazilian, but that vital knowledge and progress could be diffused only once new roads, telegraph lines, and railways were built across the backward interior. And who was responsible for building this infrastructure? Military engineers like Rondon.[6]

Indeed, it was the duty of the Positivist elite, precisely because it was more rational and enlightened, to guide others out of ignorance. Thus, neither democracy nor a republic were ideal forms of government: strong hands and firm but wise rule were needed at the top. "There is nothing repugnant about a dictatorship, certain that it will be done for the good of the fatherland," Constant would write. "We need a progressive dictatorship with due respect for public liberties."[7]

In Europe and North America, Positivism proved to be merely another passing mid-nineteenth-century intellectual fad, and its influence ephemeral. John Stuart Mill, George Eliot, and Thomas Huxley were early devotees, but they and others balked at Comte's makeover of his philosophy into a full-fledged religion. The exception to that pattern was in Latin America, where even after Comte's death in 1857, Positivism would remain influential in places like Mexico and Chile. Nowhere, though, was it embraced with more fervor than in Brazil.

Rondon began his sixth and final year at the academy in March 1889 just as Brazil tumbled into a deep institutional crisis. On May 13, 1888, while her father was in Europe receiving medical treatment, Princess Isabel, heir to the throne, decreed the complete, immediate abolition of slavery. Republicans had long called for this, as had those monarchists desirous of a more equitable Brazil. But the "Golden Law," as it became known, infuriated the powerful slave-owning class: rural plantation owners suddenly lost the field hands they needed to grow sugar and coffee, and some in the urban upper class worried about losing servants essential to their comfortable lifestyle. Not only would both elite groups be forced now to pay their laborers, they would not be compensated for the loss of their "property."

Republicans, though gratified to be finally rid of an institution that was a drag on Brazil's economy and a stain on its global image, still called for far more sweeping change. The monarchy thus found its opponents emboldened and many of its most avid traditional supporters now alienated. Pedro II clearly misread the rapidly eroding political situation when he returned from Europe and remarked, in response to reports of plotting and anti-monarchical sentiment at the military academy, that teaching republicanism to the cadets "won't hurt—you may be able to convert them"[8] to the monarchist cause.

At the academy, the cadets were finding it difficult to focus on their classwork and drills. Energized but distracted, they gathered between classes and during meals and study sessions to debate the best course for Brazil's future. Describing that period, Rondon later wrote: "Our studies marched parallel to our social concerns, to the enthusiasm felt at the promise that life was offering us the organization of a better and more just society."⁹ By now not just a committed Positivist but also a fervent Francophile, he was anxious to see the ideals of the French Revolution—Liberty, Equality, and Fraternity—applied in Brazil, and felt the only path to achieving that was through "my participation in two civic movements intertwined by logic, the freeing of the slaves and the proclamation of the republic."¹⁰

Early in the school year, the superintendent of the academy, now thoroughly alarmed, summoned students to a special assembly and, seeking a middle ground, advised that it would be best for them personally and for the military as an institution if they stayed away from political meetings calling for the overthrow of the monarchy. If they insisted on participating in such events away from the academy, he added, they were strictly prohibited from wearing their uniforms.

In response, Rondon immediately rose from his seat. "I cannot possibly go anywhere unless I am in uniform," he declared, to the applause of his classmates. "You, as our commander, will have to do whatever you deem to be your duty."¹¹ After some thought, the commandant issued a directive forbidding cadets from attending any political meetings whatsoever. But Rondon and his republican friends simply flouted the order, some of them even jumping the walls of the war college after the commandant instituted an early curfew.

As an upperclassman, Rondon had the right to live outside the barracks and, thanks to his enlarged stipend, could actually afford to do so. Accordingly, he moved with several of his friends into a "republic," a student hostel common throughout Latin America. The new lodgings were in one of the imperial capital's most prestigious neighborhoods, only a few blocks from the war college itself and close to a palace where two of the emperor's grandsons lived. Like Rondon, most of his new roommates were from distant, disdained, or ignored corners of the empire, and all later had distinguished careers as state governors, members of Congress, generals, or presidential aides. All of them were united in their adulation of Benjamin Constant, with whom they spent as much time as possible.

By mid-October, the monarchy's situation was growing untenable. On October 23, at a banquet at Praia Vermelha to welcome a just-arrived Chilean naval delegation, republicans and monarchists clashed openly in front of the foreign visitors. Constant was one of the orators, delivering a fierce rebuttal to allegations of military insubordination, accusing the imperial government of wanting merely "an Army of Janissaries," slavishly loyal to the emperor. But that would not happen, Constant argued, because "under the uniform of each soldier beats the heart of a citizen and a patriot."[12] The cadets, Rondon among them, applauded wildly and led several minutes of loud cheers for their "master." The minister of war was so offended that he stormed out before Constant could finish his speech, serenaded by jeers and cadets shouting "Long Live the Republic . . . of Chile!"[13]

On the night of Saturday, November 9, 1889, matters came to a head. Two events took place in Rio de Janeiro, and Rondon attended both; the first was an extravagant imperial ball, sponsored by the royal family in honor of their Chilean visitors and to commemorate Princess Isabel's twenty-fifth wedding anniversary. It was held on Fiscal Island, a customs collection site. For this fête, the chief minister, in charge of the preparations, had spared no expense or luxury. He ordered the island strung with lanterns and covered with an artificial forest of palm trees; the interior of the French Gothic–style lighthouse tower at the center of the island was lavishly decorated.

The ball's five thousand invitees included members of the court, senators and deputies, the diplomatic corps, military officials, and the cream of civilian high society; everyone arrived in formal dress, the men with their medals and the women festooned with jewels. As two orchestras played waltzes, polkas, mazurkas, and Brazilian tunes at opposite ends of the small island, the guests gorged themselves on pheasant, turkey, 1,800 pounds of shrimp and lobster, trays groaning with asparagus and truffles, 304 cases of imported wine, champagne, cognac, thousands of liters of beer, and chilled platters of sweets, ice cream, exotic tropical fruits, and other desserts.

The ball, intended to convince the press and the Brazilian people of the empire's permanence and splendor, instead trumpeted the imperial elite's extravagance and obliviousness to their imminent downfall. For Brazilians, to talk of "dancing at the Fiscal Island" is even today a phrase equivalent to "fiddling while Rome burns" or "rearranging the deck chairs on the *Titanic*." Several of the main conspirators in the plot to overthrow Pedro II attended, not just cadets like Rondon. But shortly after midnight, he and his friends slipped away from the event, which continued until dawn, and discreetly made their way to another gathering, this one at the nearby Military Club.

That meeting had already been underway for several hours by the time the cadets arrived in their blue dress uniforms and red capes. No consensus had yet been reached regarding the fate of the monarchy. Marshal Deodoro da Fonseca, the club's president, was absent, flattened by a fever contracted in Mato Grosso, so Constant was presiding over the debate, which grew more strident as the night wore on.

Constant was openly urging revolt, a startling position for a committed Positivist. Comte had always opposed violence and revolution in any form, but Constant had "refined" Positivist doctrine to include military intervention "in especially extreme cases." He argued that the conditions for it had been met in this instance, and that it was the duty of "citizen-soldiers" to rescue the country from "the lamentable state of affairs to which the policies of men without reason or discretion would reduce us."[14] At one point, Constant offered to resign from the army to protest the emperor's policies, rather than lead a revolt. The assembly vociferously rejected that idea, however, and the meeting ended with Constant promising to "reach a dignified result within eight days," which is to say, no later than November 17.

After that, the situation changed rapidly. On November 10, Constant visited da Fonseca, informed him that the military was ready to move, and asked that he lead the uprising, to which the marshal agreed, albeit reluctantly: in a letter to one of his relatives he had recently written that "Brazil's situation under a monarchy is bad, but without the monarchy it would be worse."[15] The next day, Rondon and fifty-six other cadets, most of them Positivists, signed a declaration promising to follow Constant "onto the field of armed resistance."[16] Also on November 11, Constant met at his home with leading civilian politicians and journalists and won their support.

On the afternoon of November 14, Rondon's friends and roommates the Leal brothers, Alexandre and Antônio, invited him to a birthday party that evening; when he demurred, they mentioned that Chiquita Xavier, the object of his affections for more than a year, would be there. Knowing a coup might begin at any moment, Rondon was still reluctant: "I felt myself divided," he wrote, "between my ardent desire to be at Chiquita's side and my worries about remaining alert."[17] Nonetheless, he went, dressed in civilian clothes, and was seated with Chiquita when a horse-drawn carriage arrived shortly after 10 p.m., summoning him and the Leal brothers. They raced back to their quarters, put on their uniforms, and made their way to the nearby headquarters of the Second Regiment.

He later recalled that "the barracks was crowded"[18] when they arrived, and guns were being distributed. Rondon was given his weapon of choice, a Nagant revolver, which he kept his entire life as a memento of that night. At 2 a.m., Benjamin Constant arrived, and immediately went into a conference room with other senior officers. The Positivist leader Raimundo Teixeira Mendes was also present, loudly demanding that the military "proclaim a dictatorship! Proclaim a dictatorship!" When Constant emerged from the meeting, he summoned Rondon and his friend Augusto Tasso Fragoso, and asked them to undertake a delicate, risky mission.

The army was ready to rise up, sure of support throughout the ranks, Constant told them, but it was not yet clear how the navy stood: Admiral Eduardo Wandenkolk, the naval commander, had been ambiguous, saying that he supported the rebels' objectives "up to a point." Constant asked Rondon and Fragoso to carry a sealed letter to the admiral with a crucial question: Will you allow our insurgent forces free passage when we move to depose the emperor? If the answer was yes, or if the navy was to remain neutral, then the cadets would return with that message, after first alerting a nearby infantry battalion that the uprising was on. But if the navy decided to remain loyal to the monarchy, then both Rondon and Fragoso would likely be arrested as rebels and imprisoned; theoretically they could even be court-martialed and, if found guilty, executed. That was the risk they were being asked to assume.

Just before 4 a.m., Rondon and Fragoso set out on horseback, Constant's letter in hand. As they galloped through the silent city, their horses' hooves pounded thunderously along the cobblestone, "but we advanced without obstacles." As they neared army headquarters, halfway to their destination, the two rebel emissaries slowed to a trot and rode as close as possible to an iron grating on the far side of the large parade ground in front of the building, shielding themselves behind foliage "so as not to be detected" as they passed. The headquarters, they saw, was "completely illuminated, as if to warn that the Government was watching,"[19] and this made them even more cautious; activity at that hour was a bad omen.

The Navy Club, where Admiral Wandenkolk was staying, was located downtown, a couple of miles from where Rondon had set off. His horse, already white with foam and sweating from the arduous ride, must have sensed his nervousness, for it suddenly slipped and swerved, and he had to steady it as he and Fragoso approached. They dismounted, knocked at the door three times, and waited tensely for what seemed "several minutes"[20] before getting any response. From inside they heard a guard utter a password, to which they replied with the counter-password that Constant had furnished them, repeating it three times. A narrow slot in the door opened, and they handed over Constant's letter to the navy commander. After that, Rondon and Fragoso waited anxiously to learn their fate—and Brazil's.

To their relief, after another long delay, the slot opened and they were handed a letter, addressed to Constant. No armed squadron emerged to arrest them. Relieved, they headed off to the infantry battalion's barracks, conveyed Constant's instructions to the captain in charge, then raced back to rebel headquarters, Wandenkolk's letter in hand. They arrived just as the sun was beginning to rise.

Exhausted as Rondon may have been after the long, tense ride, there was no time for sleep now that the navy's support was assured.

Benjamin Constant put Rondon in charge of an artillery unit, and ordered him to march his men, in the company of several other infantry and cavalry detachments, back to army headquarters, where the emperor's entire cabinet was now convened in emergency session. Constant's objective was to make an overwhelming show of force in order to avoid bloodshed and compel the government's capitulation; Rondon's artillery unit was part of that display.

It was morning now, and civilian onlookers and sunrise strollers, with their pet dogs and parasols, gathered at the parade grounds to watch as the confrontation unfolded. One of Rondon's friends even encountered Dr. Xavier and his daughters on a nearby street and advised them to head back home. The Xaviers, like a half-million other civilian residents of the imperial capital, had no idea that a military uprising was underway.

By the time Constant himself arrived at army headquarters, it was clear that his strategy was working. When the cabinet ordered the commander of loyalist forces inside headquarters, Gen. Floriano Peixoto, a hero of the war against Paraguay, to attack the rebels, he refused, saying, "Here we are all Brazilians, and I will not fire on my brothers."[21] Just after 9 a.m., the iron gates of army headquarters opened, and the loyalist troops emerged, to the cheers and embraces of their rebel comrades, accompanied by a twenty-one-gun salute. Cries of "Long live the Republic!" began to fill the air, to the bafflement of curious bystanders.

After Rondon and his unit arrived at the parade ground in front of army headquarters, Constant had ordered him to join his small group of bodyguards. Now Constant and da Fonseca triumphantly entered army headquarters and went directly to the room where the emperor's cabinet awaited them. With Rondon, the only nonwhite person in either group, standing next to him, his trusty Nagant in its holster, Constant told the ministers that they were now relieved of office, under arrest, and "at the disposal" of the new "revolutionary" regime. Rondon would always remember the way the chief minister looked at that moment: "He could not stop glaring at Benjamin Constant. . . . He had always foreseen that this fellow would bring the Monarchy crashing to the ground."[22]

Rondon would always refer to the proclamation of the United States of the Republic of Brazil that November 15 as the "Revolution of 1889." But most modern-day historians consider it a military coup. Yet regardless of its name, it remains the first and only example of a successful Positivist-led seizure of power.

Rondon accompanied Constant to his new office at the War Ministry, where a crowd of well-wishers and opportunists soon gathered. Miguel Lemos, head of the Positivist Apostolate of Brazil, came to offer his blessing to the new government, and Constant replied, his voice "thick with emotion" and near tears, that the new republic "could not have better counselors"[23] than Lemos and Teixeira Mendes. A new era, it seemed, was dawning, and at the age of twenty-four Rondon "had the honor" not only to be present at its creation but also to have played a small but vital role in its arrival.

— PART II —

*Lt. Col. Cândido Rondon with a child from the Paresi tribe
on the Mato Grosso plateau, around 1910. Tu fui ego eris.*
(ACERVO DO MUSEU DO ÍNDIO/FUNAI—BRASIL)

IV

"There Begins the Harshest of Backlands"

T HE EUPHORIA AMONG republicans at the birth of a new political order did not last long. By the beginning of 1890, barely
six weeks after overthrowing the emperor, they were already
quarreling among themselves and jockeying for advantage in the
new government. Cabinet members came and went. Among the
early casualties was Benjamin Constant, who stepped down as minister of war in March, moving to the far less powerful position of
minister of public instruction, posts and telegraphs in the vain hope
of implanting a Positivist system of education. By year's end he had
been forced from the government altogether, and in January 1891 he
died of malaria, just short of his fifty-fourth birthday. His successor
as minister of war, Admiral Wandenkolk, would last only a month
before being pushed aside by Floriano Peixoto, who would become
president by the end of 1891.

Though the Positivist faction within the army was clearly in
eclipse, the military itself was not. Instead, it was cementing its control, often through authoritarian means, and to Rondon's direct benefit. On January 4, 1890, he was promoted to second lieutenant in
the artillery branch, a typical posting for someone with his training
in mathematics, physics, and engineering. Barely two weeks later,
though, he was notified of an enviable upgrade to first lieutenant,
attached to the general staff, in recognition of "relevant services."[1]

This, of course, referred to Rondon's contributions to establishing the republic on November 15.

Rondon was not the only one so rewarded; all the other cadets and officers directly involved in the coup d'état were, too. And at the urging of Rondon and the rest of the editorial board of the *Academic Family* magazine, their cashiered friend, Euclides da Cunha, was restored to the officer corps. With a new regime trying to sort out its enemies from its friends, participation in the toppling of Pedro II was a distinction that put an entire cohort of young soldiers, not just Rondon, on a fast track. Not all would flourish as he did—da Cunha, for example, would get himself into political trouble again in 1894 and leave the army in 1896 to become a civil engineer—and many others would abandon Positivism. But they had a group identity even stronger than usual among graduates of the same class, and forged a deep sense of camaraderie that would endure over the next forty years.

On February 1, 1890, after Rondon received the raise that came with his promotions, ensuring some modest financial security, he and Chiquita Xavier announced their engagement, setting February 1, 1892, as a wedding date. None of Rondon's friends were surprised at the news, nor were Chiquita's parents. The relationship had clearly been a serious one from the start, and both Chiquita's mother and father liked Rondon and thought him destined for a distinguished career; the complicated question of his racial and class background seems to have been ignored.

Francisca Xavier was seven years younger than Rondon. Her father, Francisco José Xavier, was a distinguished physician specializing in tuberculosis treatment, and director of a hospital. On the side, Dr. Xavier also taught at the Colégio Pedro II, where he came to know Rondon: in 1883, he was Rondon's geography and Portuguese instructor, and in that capacity was one of the first to see Rondon's intellectual promise. He would become one of Rondon's most significant early advocates and allies.

Though Francisca was at first homeschooled by her parents, eventually the rector of the Colégio Pedro II took on the responsibility of tutoring the academically gifted young woman himself.

At that time, girls were not allowed to enroll in the school, but he did not want to see Francisca's talents wasted. At the age of sixteen, she enrolled in normal school, intending to become a teacher, but after accepting Rondon's proposal, she ended her studies, just before obtaining her certificate.[2]

Rondon was introduced to Chiquita by the Leal brothers, fellow cadets at the military academy. As Rondon told the story, the Leals had invited the entire Xavier family as their guests to attend military exercises scheduled for February 1887 at the academy parade ground. The Leals' father had recently become principal of the Colégio Pedro II, and the brothers knew that Professor Xavier had two attractive young daughters, Teresa and Francisca, and wanted their fellow cadets to meet them.

During a break in the maneuvers, the Leals brought the girls over to the cadets to make the formal introductions. Rondon hung back, circumspect and a bit shy, as was his nature around people he did not know. Seeing this, one of the brothers came over to him, and tried, fruitlessly, to get Rondon to come forward. "Introduce myself to Dr. Xavier's family!" Rondon jokingly protested. "Don't you know that I'm a beast of the wilds, that I only know how to read books and that, unless it's with my comrades, any kind of contact makes me die of embarrassment?"[3]

Only after his friends chided him on his rude behavior did Rondon relent, "quite begrudgingly." "This is the best student in the school," the Xavier sisters were told. But Rondon remained uncommunicative, and during the fifty-seven years he and Chiquita were married, she never ceased teasing him about that: "He remained silent in the face of the cordiality with which he was received, as prim as can be," she would complain playfully. "Then he fled, simply vanished." To which Rondon would reply that his bashfulness was due to having overheard Chiquita whisper to her sister: "Look how chunky he is!"[4]

Before long, though, Rondon shed his shyness and exploited every opportunity to spend time with the Xavier family, with or without the Leal brothers. His three-year courtship of Chiquita was decidedly old-fashioned, adhering to the stifling formality of the late imperial period. The couple spent no time alone: mostly he joined her family at their home or on picnics and other outings, and when she ventured outside the family quarters, her sister was with her as a chaperone. Sometimes the entire family would make the trip down to the city to see Rondon compete in an athletic event or military exercise, or would invite him to join them at concerts or plays. But those occasions, even with the limited contact they provided, were sufficient to allow Chiquita to gauge Rondon's character and suitability, and when he proposed early in 1890, she accepted without hesitation.

Unfortunately, Rondon and Chiquita would be forced to spend almost the entire first year of their engagement apart, their only communication being through letters and the occasional telegram. Just two days before Christmas 1889, as he was about to graduate from the war college and even before the announcement of his promotions, Rondon was assigned his first posting as an officer. As soon as the rainy season eased, he would join an engineering and construction unit installing a telegraph line from Cuiabá east to the state of Goiás and the Araguaia River, a project begun during the empire but stalled because of logistical and technical problems and confrontations with hostile Indigenous groups.

So on March 6, 1890, seen off by Chiquita and the rest of the Xavier family, Rondon left the port of Rio de Janeiro, and headed back toward his native region for the first time in almost a decade. He had departed Mato Grosso immersed in doubts about his future, fearful that failure might doom him to a life of insignificance. But now, after the usual month's journey by boat, he would be returning to Cuiabá in triumph, with a science degree and in the uniform of an officer of the Brazilian Army. "It is easy to gauge my emotions on seeing my native State again after such a long absence," Rondon wrote. "I had departed excited by a burning desire to succeed, and I was returning happy."[5]

The posting was perfect for Rondon, because connecting Mato Grosso and Goiás to the rest of Brazil, an aspiration since adolescence, activated both the scientific and the idealistic sides of his personality. But he was also attracted by the opportunity to learn from an older officer and fellow Positivist whom he admired deeply, Antônio Gomes

Carneiro. Nearly two decades older than Rondon, Gomes Carneiro was raised as a Catholic and, as a youth, aspired to be a priest: he studied first at seminaries in his home state of Minas Gerais, and later at a Benedictine monastery in Rio. But when the war with Paraguay began, he left, out of a sense of patriotism, and enlisted in the army as a common foot soldier. Sent to the front lines, he fought in several battles, was wounded three times, and was promoted twice.

Combat profoundly changed Gomes Carneiro. He abandoned his religious faith, and, when the war ended, he enrolled in the military academy. There, he excelled academically and, like so many of his contemporaries, fell under the spell of Auguste Comte. After graduation, promotions and honors came quickly: in 1881, at the age of thirty-four, he was chosen to accompany the emperor on an inspection tour. Soon after, Rondon met him at the military academy, where Gomes Carneiro was teaching engineering. He was promoted to the rank of major, and then, when he took command of the Araguaia telegraph project, to lieutenant colonel.

"He was truly my teacher in practical matters of the wilderness," Rondon would later write. Thanks to Gomes Carneiro's tutelage during two long reconnaissance missions they made together shortly after Rondon's arrival, "I was able to gain a thorough knowledge" of eastern Mato Grosso and of the skills needed to install a telegraph line. In addition, they forged a personal bond that kept them "tightly connected for the remainder of his life," Rondon recalled. Riding along on horseback as "commander and subaltern" through the untracked hinterland, Gomes Carneiro "would satisfy my ardent desire for knowledge, giving me the scientific and common names for all the plants, familiarizing me with the animals we came across, explaining to me the composition of rocks, slate and carbonates while he took measurements and carefully noted localities and geographic features"[6] in his field notebook.

The first 125 miles of the projected route of the Araguaia telegraph line were inhabited, if only sparsely, by Brazilians who had made their way inland from the coast, mostly ranchers and former slaves who stayed on after emancipation as poorly paid farmhands. In his 1872 novel, *Innocence*, Alfredo Taunay provides a description of the desolate region where he had served during the Paraguayan War. "There begins the harshest of backlands. . . . There the traveler finds no shelter, not even a ruined house or a thatched hut. He finds nothing to protect him from the cold of night or the storms that threaten or the rains that fall. Everywhere there is only the silence of an untouched land and virgin vegetation."[7]

Gomes Carneiro also made Rondon realize that the Positivist practice of nonviolence was the best method for approaching hostile tribes, for both practical and moral reasons. Rondon would later recall how his commander referred to Indigenous tribes as "our jungle brothers" and, in order to protect them from the depredations of white settlers and his own trigger-happy troops, directed that handbills be affixed to telegraph poles up and down the line with the following warning: "Henceforth, whosoever attempts to kill Indians or drive them from lands that are legitimately theirs will have to respond for that act to the chief of this commission."[8]

As the expedition moved eastward, the remaining 250 miles of the proposed line crossed territory inhabited by the Bororo. The tribe became ever more hostile as the crew advanced, uninvited and unwanted. This was not the heart of the Amazon, where nature itself, whether in the form of turbulent rivers or dangerous animals, was the principal cause for concern. As Gomes Carneiro knew from previous experience and quickly transmitted to Rondon, the real challenge in reaching the Araguaia lay in overcoming the fierce human resistance they were likely to face.

One day, out on a reconnaissance mission together, Rondon and Gomes Carneiro came across the embers of recently extinguished fires, a sure sign that Indians were nearby. That night, around midnight, asleep in their tent, they were awakened by the din of chattering birds and howling monkeys. "It was as if all the fauna around us were conferring among themselves,"[9] Rondon would recall, and the racket alarmed them. Some of the bird calls they identified were of species active only during the day, which meant that what they were hearing was actually the Bororo communicating with one another. And since the Bororo avoided combat at night, that suggested an attack would be coming at dawn.

What happened next so impressed Rondon that he would remember it until the end of his life. "I am of the firm opinion of never fighting with the Indians," Gomes Carneiro told him, even though the two of them had superior firepower. "Besides being unfair, it would compromise the results of the expedition. We have only one recourse: to break camp and leave."[10] So by the flickering light of a small fire in the middle of the night, undoubtedly observed by Bororo, they undid their tent, mounted their horses, and left, turning back in the blackness and galloping until they reached the nearest settlement around sunrise.

As was standard procedure on engineering projects deep in the interior, Gomes Carneiro divided the troops under his command into three sections. An advance team first scouted the terrain and chose the best route for the telegraph line. The "central squadron" was in charge of the actual construction: its members cleared a pathway, leveled hills, chopped down trees and trimmed their trunks into poles, attached porcelain insulators onto the wooden arms bolted to the poles, then raised the post, secured it into the ground, and, finally, strung the line from one pole to another. Once those tasks were completed, a rearguard team carried out a topographical assessment of the constructed line and determined its geographic coordinates.

As the junior officer in the squadron, Rondon was put in charge of the rearguard team. He had twenty soldiers under his command, and operated up to ten miles behind the main construction crew. Being out in the bush, far from supply lines, Rondon was forced to employ the frontiersman's skills he had acquired as a child. Those had not withered during his decade in Rio de Janeiro. When food ran low, for example, he knew how to extract sugar from the buriti palm, which he used to sweeten a tea made from a species of fern found in the fissures of the carbonate rocks that Gomes Carneiro had shown him; he also knew how to transform buriti sap into a refreshing beverage and even how to ferment it into a kind of wine.

Rondon's knowledge of regional plant and animal species meant that those under his command, most of whom were from coastal cities or farms, never had to go hungry. But there were times they resisted his offerings. When he came back from the hunt with game, they were delighted to eat the turkey-like jacu, or the equally tasty curassow. They could even accept the gray, pig-like tapirs that splashed in the shallows of rivers and swamps. "Frequently, though," Rondon would recall, "we were reduced to snakes and monkeys as sources of meat." And every now and then, "when our belts were tightened to their last notch," Rondon would shoot a wolf or a vulture, which, when cooked, produced "a dark foam with a nauseating smell."[11] In those cases, the soldiers balked, and reluctantly agreed to eat only after Rondon himself set the example.

Discomfort never bothered Rondon. What mattered to him was the realization that "the forest I had learned to love would never allow us to die of hunger."[12] This was a crucial insight that would affect the planning, organization, and execution of all his forays into the wilderness, including his celebrated expedition with Theodore Roosevelt. When possible, he decided, it was fine to carry lots of provisions, at least at the start of a mission. But when necessary, one should also be able to travel light and live off the land, armed with the specialized local knowledge that would make it possible to march through unexplored terrain, no matter how harsh.

But this was not the only difficult leadership test Rondon faced. Privates in the Brazilian Army at the dawn of the republic were drawn from the lowest levels of society. Many were illiterate, others suffered from malnutrition or disease, some had been forced into press gangs, and others were newly liberated slaves lacking other opportunities. This lack of motivation and reliability was a constant problem for the Brazilian Army and Navy in the late nineteenth century, and it would remain so well into the early decades of the twentieth century. One American scholar has described the army that Rondon entered as "a proto-penal institution" that served "as the primary institutional bridge between the State and the 'criminal' underworld in the late 1800s." Judges and local police routinely sentenced wrongdoers—or sometimes even innocent men who had the misfortune to be caught up in official dragnets—to six-year sentences in the military. In addition, children picked up off the streets were sometimes consigned to army orphanages, where they were inducted into the ranks just as soon as they reached the minimum age for military service. And each year about one thousand men were dragooned into the army as the result of conduct deemed "disorderly, immoral and violent."[13]

Not surprisingly, it was difficult to maintain discipline or esprit de corps in such circumstances, and officers frequently turned to corporal punishment to combat disorderliness and snuff out mutinies before they could take root. Since Rondon himself had begun his military career as a common soldier, he probably had a better understanding than most officers of how his troops thought and behaved. Certainly he did not fear the tough conditions they had to endure, and embraced them himself when he thought it necessary to set an example. But he also demanded a lot of his men, nearly as much as of himself, and when they balked at his orders, mutinied, or deserted their mission, he did not hesitate to have them tied up to posts or trees and whipped.

Rondon could never bring himself to call corporal punishment by its proper name. Instead he employed an obscure euphemism: "Count Lippe's procedure,"[14] named for an eighteenth-century Prussian military officer who helped reorganize, train, and "modernize" the Portuguese Army. His regulations, which Brazil adopted, authorized officers to inflict varying degrees of punishment on soldiers who committed crimes, including beating, caning, whipping, imprisonment, and even the execution by firing squad of deserters and others showing cowardice during wartime.[15] On missions to remote areas where state institutions did not yet exist, individual officers also were granted enormous authority over their men, and encouraged to exercise it.

Rondon recognized that corporal punishment was inhumane, and that it conflicted with his Positivist beliefs. But there were times, he also argued, that it was necessary to "act with greater energy" to safeguard his own life and maintain order and "the principle of authority" among unruly troops. Decades later, he would acknowledge to his closest aide and confidant, Benjamin Constant's nephew, Armando Amilcar Botelho de Magalhães, that such actions were "an affront to military regulations, which could not foresee such circumstances or the exceptional rules of discipline for detachments serving in the wilderness, where one cannot count on support from other military troops."[16]

Not long after completing the first stage of the mission, two developments suddenly elevated Rondon's status on the expedition. The first was that a major in charge of the advance team resigned his commission to run for a seat, successfully as it would turn out, in the constituent assembly of 1891 that would draw up Brazil's first republican constitution. Rondon appears to have distinguished himself as commander of the rearguard troops, because Gomes Carneiro immediately appointed him head of the advance team—a mere lieutenant replacing a major. But then came a second piece of news, which threatened to upset that plan: at the recommendation of Benjamin Constant, now education minister in the new government, the army general staff had decided to appoint Rondon a professor of astronomy and celestial mechanics at the military academy.

Rondon had mixed feelings about the proposed new assignment. It was a promotion, and to a prestigious, tenured job in the capital, where he would be able to spend long periods of time with Chiquita. Additionally, it offered the prospect of an entirely different kind of life, "calm and methodical," settled and secure, the type of sinecure that would allow him the freedom to follow whatever scientific pursuits he chose. All of that was enticing. But he was also enjoying the engineering and cartographic challenge of erecting the telegraph line, as well as the "thrilling" life of action that accompanied it.

Gomes Carneiro, though, was not of two minds: he was distressed at the prospect of losing such a talented and dedicated officer. He immediately protested in a telegram to the high command in Rio, the text of which survives and indicates his unhappiness: "Just received your telegram unfortunately cannot comply order this adjutant being indispensable suggest the following that he be withdrawn when mission concluded, remaining until then in function for which he nominated. Gomes Carneiro."[17]

"Agreed, having consulted Minister of War"[18] was the terse response from Rio, signed by none other than the vice president of the republic. Viewed in retrospect, all of this is quite remarkable. Rondon was barely twenty-five, yet here we see three of the most distinguished figures in the military, two of them leaders of the new republic, wrangling over the future of a mere lieutenant. It showcases the high esteem in which Rondon was held from the very beginning of his career as an officer, and the powerful patrons he had accumulated.

On November 28, 1890, an army circular decreed that Lt. Cândido Mariano da Silva would henceforth be "conceded permission to add to his name the surname 'RONDON.'"[19] In his memoirs, Rondon himself described this action as primarily a way of paying tribute to his uncle Manoel. "My heart overflowed with grateful affection" on returning to Mato Grosso, he stated, "towards he who at times played the role of my father and whose name—the name of my paternal grandmother—I now took on so as to honor him."[20] But Uncle Manoel's matronymic was Rodrigues, not Rondon.

Another explanation seems more likely. The surname da Silva has long been the most common in Brazil, and another Cândido Mariano da Silva was a well-known swindler. The name had thus acquired unsavory associations, and, theoretically, Rondon could have been dragged into legal proceedings and forced to prove that he and the con man were different people. He might also have had problems getting credit and been subjected to nasty gossip, an alarming prospect to a man of his rectitude.

Given that situation, it was much better to adopt an unusual surname like Rondon, which had the additional advantage of carrying considerable prestige in Mato Grosso. Taking the Rondon name allowed him to hint at family ties, however remote or nebulous, to a prestigious and influential clan that included governors, monsignors, and prosperous businessmen.

In March of 1891, after Rondon had spent almost a year on the Araguaia telegraph project and the line was nearly complete, the army high command in Rio finally demanded that Gomes Carneiro release him to begin duties at the military academy. This pleased Rondon immensely, not only because it brought him back to Chiquita. In addition to teaching, he learned, his responsibilities included research projects at the National Observatory, where he was reunited with his friends Fragoso, who accompanied him on the fateful midnight ride across Rio, and Hastímfilo de Moura, also part of Benjamin Constant's Positivist circle at the military academy.

Established by Pedro II in 1845 as the Imperial Observatory of Rio de Janeiro, the National Observatory had been led since 1881 by Louis Ferdinand Cruls, a Belgian astronomer and former teacher of Rondon's who specialized in geodesics but had also helped demarcate the precise boundaries of several Brazilian provinces. During his tenure, the observatory became one of the foremost centers of scientific research in Brazil: besides astronomy, its work encompassed meteorology and the measurement of time, and it was completing an ambitious forty-year study of Brazil's climate when Rondon began working there, contributing his superb mathematical skills.

Rondon, Fragoso, and Moura got along so well with their chief that he often invited them for meals and conversation at the family's residence, which adjoined the observatory. The Crulses' three-year-old son, Gastão, rushed around the house and was constantly underfoot as the adults discussed science, the arts, and politics at their informal salon. Rondon's friendship with the family endured long after Louis Cruls's death in 1908. Gastão grew up to become a prominent writer and a ceaseless booster of Rondon and his work. After achieving popular success in 1925 with *The Mysterious Amazon*, a science-fiction novel in the style of H. G. Wells, Gastão Cruls joined Rondon on one of his last Amazon expeditions, subsequently producing both a scientific-medical treatise and a second best seller, the nonfiction work called *The Amazon as I Saw It*, which helped to exalt Rondon's image even further in Brazil.

Early in 1892, Cruls was appointed director of an expedition to explore central Brazil's vast interior with the goal of determining the best location for a new national capital. He wanted all three of the young military officers on his staff to accompany him. But since Rondon was about to marry and had been granted leave for his honeymoon, the high command vetoed his participation and he missed out on a splendid adventure.

The group was in the field for nearly a year, and when the "Commission to Explore the Central Plateau" filed its report in 1893, it recommended a site about 125 miles east of the terminus of Rondon's telegraph line. For the next sixty years, the commission's document sat in a drawer, but in the 1950s the idea was revived. Rondon, by then the only still-living member of the observatory staff of the 1890s, lobbied hard for its implementation, and when he died in 1958, the construction of Brasília was finally underway.

With their wedding date fast approaching, Rondon and Chiquita had to make some important decisions. As a Positivist, Rondon harbored an anticlericalism that would only intensify as he aged. But to placate his fiancée and future in-laws, he agreed to a Roman Catholic ceremony. With a friar officiating, Gomes Carneiro as best man, and Benjamin Constant's widow, Maria Joaquina, as matron of honor, both the religious and a civil ceremony were held at the Xavier family's home, which was also the site of the wedding reception. The honeymoon lasted a full month, but the young couple did not go far: they spent their time in a little house near the Piedade train station.

More difficult was deciding what kind of life the newlyweds would lead afterward. "We began our life with both of us putting the general interest above personal considerations," Rondon wrote. Constructing the telegraph line, he felt, had been an important contribution to his country—and, if anything, the experience had even deepened his patriotism. But continuing as an army engineer and explorer would require Rondon to spend long periods away from Chiquita and the children they intended to have, or force Chiquita to spend long periods in the backlands, away from her parents, her sister, and the only world she knew.

The alternative was for Rondon to adopt a more fixed and stable routine, centered on his work at the military academy and the National Observatory. "I could see, outlined before me, a future in which I would lead a tranquil life with the family I hoped to start and at my academic career,"[21] he wrote. Though not especially enthusiastic about the teaching component of his duties, he was delighted by the opportunity to do meaningful research, serve the nation, and advance human knowledge.

But pursuing a career in science was a risky choice for Rondon or, for that matter, any other young Brazilian intellectual intent on having an impact on national life. Even within the army, prestige accrued mainly to those in a combat—rather than administrative or technical—role. Positivists such as Rondon gravitated toward engineering and other technical functions, not the surest path to glory and promotions, which he, like any other ambitious young officer, also sought.

In addition, Positivist teaching discouraged innovative scientific inquiry. "For the Positivist, science was a goal already achieved, and the world had been completely understood," the Brazilian social scientist Simon Schwartzman has noted. "Thus, there could no longer be space for questioning, doubt or experiments. All that remained was the need to move into action, to convince the unbelievers. Within such a framework, where would one place the idea of a laboratory, a research center, or a university interested in broadening the frontiers of knowledge?"[22]

Throughout his long life, Rondon wrestled with the dilemma embodied in this position, and never really resolved it. By nature, he had a supple and inquisitive mind, ideally suited for scientific work and the hypothesizing that goes with it. His meticulously annotated field notebooks, compiled over a period of forty years and filled with page after page of observations, measurements, and speculation, belie the Positivist notion that, thanks to Comte's genius, science was now a settled matter. So do the scores of reports that the Rondon Commission published, filled with theories and new discoveries, in fields from astronomy to zoology. But at the same time, his enduring faith in Positivism, and his personal loyalty to its leaders, pulled him in the opposite direction. Clearly, Rondon allowed some cognitive dissonance in his thinking, because the two points of view that he embraced were fundamentally incompatible.

In the end, confronted with a choice between an academic existence spent largely in classrooms and laboratories and one dominated by action and challenges in the field, Rondon opted for the latter: "I decided to change paths after mature reflection, exchanging ideas"[23] with Chiquita, he wrote. She acquiesced in this decision, he claimed, encouraging him to do what he thought would best serve the nation. Relinquishing his academic appointment, he asked to return to the wilderness. And so, shortly after the honeymoon ended, Rondon once again headed back to Mato Grosso, accompanied by nineteen-year-old Chiquita, on her first trip to the Brazilian frontier.

Rondon's decision quickly reaped him rewards. Not long after he resumed work on the Araguaia line, Gomes Carneiro was reassigned to the far south, to quell one of the many rebellions that broke out in the first years of the republic. As his successor, Gomes Carneiro suggested Rondon, who, though not next in the chain of command, had shown a remarkable aptitude for the commission's tasks. After the recommendation was approved, Gomes Carneiro left for the south and, on February 9, 1894, was killed in combat. For the third time, Rondon had lost a beloved father figure. But because of Gomes Carneiro's intervention, Rondon, at the age of twenty-seven, received a command for the first time, and would be elevated to captain before 1892 ended. Rondon's future seemed assured. A decade would pass, however, before he would be promoted again.

V

Burdensome Tasks and Forced Obedience

BACK IN THE wilderness again, Rondon had a twofold assignment. First he had to repair the same telegraph line built under
Gomes Carneiro's command. During the October-to-March
rainy season, storms and high winds had snapped the thin cable,
which the federal government had forced the construction team to
use so as to save money; frequent flooding had also weakened sup-
ports and made poles lean at perilous angles or even collapse. Rondon had to string heavier wire along the original route and make
sure the poles were sturdier and secured deeper in the ground. This
proved a valuable lesson: for the rest of his career, Rondon always
insisted on top-grade materials for construction, even if bureaucrats
in Rio de Janeiro complained about the cost.

Despite its initial construction problems, the telegraph line had
an instantaneous impact on the frontier. The strategic importance
of reliable communications links was obvious in the military realm,
but the benefits of the line's construction for commercial and other
economic activities were immediately apparent as well: banks were
able to open new branches and issue lines of credit, while local merchants could more quickly replenish their shelves. Cattle ranches
and maté tea plantations, which produced the frontier's two most
important commodities, became more efficient and prosperous:
their owners, now linked to a global market, were able to order capital equipment from distant manufacturers or instantly check prices

anywhere. Since regular telephone service between Mato Grosso and the cities of the coast would not be installed until the 1960s, the telegraph would retain its importance for decades and constitute the most reliable link to the outside world. To grateful residents of his home state, Rondon was not just a hero, but an avatar of progress—which, as a Positivist, made him particularly proud.

As Rondon's career was beginning to blossom, his family was also growing. Ten months after he and Chiquita married, their first child was born and named Heloisa Aracy, in honor of Benjamin Constant's youngest daughter. Chiquita and the baby remained at his base of operations in Cuiabá while he explored the interior, and on April 29, 1894, a second child—their only son—was born there: Bernardo Tito Benjamin, known simply as Benjamin, after Rondon's mentor, Benjamin Constant.

Left alone in Cuiabá, Chiquita was unable to adjust to frontier life. She could ride a horse well enough and learned other useful skills, but missed the basic necessities of a comfortable life, which were hard to obtain in Cuiabá. Even more, she worried about the children's health, especially the infant, Benjamin. Shortly after his birth, it was decided that she, Aracy, and Benjamin would return to live in Rio; Rondon would accompany them on the voyage and then return to Mato Grosso alone.

On the morning of their departure date in late June, with the family's baggage already aboard the vessel that would take them down the Paraguay River to Buenos Aires, Rondon got a report of a crisis at Quebra-Pote, or "Break the Jug," the closest of his construction camps. Soldiers had risen up against their commanding officers, chased them off, and then celebrated with "a most unrestrained orgy, almost all of them in a state of drunkenness." Rondon had promised his wife to accompany her, and if he were to keep that commitment, "the time available in which to act was extremely limited," he recognized. "On the other hand, how could I leave, allowing the Commission to fall into indiscipline?"[1]

Reluctantly, Rondon ordered that a horse be saddled for him. "Though fearing it would be impossible for me to return in time, my wife accepted that decision." So he galloped off to the encampment and immediately ordered the bugler to sound the call for assembly. Out of habit, even the most inebriated soldiers obeyed; fearful officers who had fled into the bush also reappeared. Once they were assembled, Rondon "severely admonished" both the enlisted men and their commanders, considered by Rondon to be cowards. "An officer cannot abandon his post," he chastised them. "If necessary, you die there."[2]

For the mutinous soldiers, the punishment went beyond a mere tongue-lashing. Rondon sent a squad "into the bush, in search of tree branches," and when they returned, "the soldiers, each in turn, were whipped."[3] When the floggings were finished, Rondon jumped on his horse, galloped back to the port, and boarded the ship just in time.

"I returned embittered," he wrote. "It deeply pained me to have been forced to resort to Count Lippe's procedure. I gave myself over to resentful reflections on the fact of undisciplined men still in the stage of 'forced obedience' always being sent to me to work in the Commission."[4]

As he and his family journeyed south, the weather turned cooler, and by the time they arrived in Buenos Aires, it was the height of the Southern Hemisphere winter. Anxious about Benjamin, barely two months old, Chiquita did not want to linger in the Argentine capital. Accordingly, Rondon booked passage on the first vessel leaving for points north: a cargo ship hauling cattle to Europe for slaughter, with an intermediate stop in Rio. The accommodations were basic, the bellowing of livestock and the stink of their manure constant, and the only other passengers were a group of French Salesian priests on their way home. But the vessel had a capable Russian doctor who tended to Benjamin's needs, and the family arrived in Rio intact.

Chiquita's father had managed to find lodgings for her and the children near the Xavier family's own home, in Cascadura, at the time a semirural railway junction on the far northern outskirts of the capital. Trains offered quick transportation to the city center, while a few farms and ranches provided a bucolic atmosphere that suited Rondon just fine. He described the property as a *chácara*, a kind of small farm, with its own orchard, and the time he spent getting his wife and children settled there as "a delightful interval."⁵ For the remainder of the century, until a promotion ensured him a bigger salary and larger quarters, Cascadura would be their home in Rio.

Rondon was under orders to return quickly to Mato Grosso, so he did not linger in the capital. This time, his journey was entirely overland: first by railway, and then astride his loyal mule, Barétia, to Cuiabá along the telegraph line, with a brief stopover at an army base in Goiás. It was a strenuous but necessary itinerary, because Rondon had received new reports of incidents of insubordination in his construction brigade, which were put down by force, and he wanted to arrange with local commanders for reinforcements, if needed, along the way.

Arriving at the site where the telegraph line was being repaired, Rondon was disconcerted by what he found. "Everything had been resolved by the time I arrived," he wrote, "but the soldiers' attitude was one of open indiscipline."⁶ This reflected what was happening countrywide: in September 1893, dissident elements in the navy had risen up against the government and bombarded the capital. The rebels, who included the same Admiral Wandenkolk to whom Rondon had galloped across Rio to deliver a message in November 1889, eventually fled south, where they made common cause with regional separatists and supporters of the former monarchy. In March of 1894, the uprising was finally quelled, with a brutality extraordinary for Brazil: nearly three hundred insurrectionists, civilian and military, holed up at the Santa Cruz fortress were summarily executed, and more than one hundred other soldiers were court-martialed, sentenced to hard labor, and immediately transported to Mato Grosso, where they were assigned to units like Rondon's telegraph-construction team.

These survivors of the carnage at Santa Cruz were the worst of the troops Rondon had to deal with when he returned to Mato Grosso in the waning months of 1894. "Construction of the telegraph line required burdensome tasks to which the soldiers did not want to submit," he complained, calling the recalcitrants "bad elements."⁷ Mass desertions were common, as former rebels and other malingerers preferred to escape into the wilderness, in territory full of hostile Indians, rather than labor under Rondon's command. He responded by sending contingents to hunt down the deserters and bring them back to camp for corporal punishment and more forced labor under the vigilant gaze of armed sentries.

This soon led to a direct confrontation. As a fervent supporter of the republic, Rondon had little sympathy for the vanquished rebels: he had even petitioned the president's office to be reassigned to fight them in the south, but was told that his work was too valuable. In addition, he was still grieving about Gomes Carneiro's death, and made no secret of his grudge against the rebels.

For their part, the rebels banished to Mato Grosso were determined to continue resisting the central government and all who supported it. Not long after their arrival, the former insurrectionists joined another disgruntled group of soldiers and plotted to assassinate Rondon. They planned to strike on payday, murder Rondon and all the other officers, seize the construction unit's money-laden strongbox, distribute the cash inside, and then escape to neighboring Bolivia.

Unfortunately for the plotters, some twenty common soldiers fled before the uprising and, after being captured, revealed the murder plan. Rondon decided to punish only the chief conspirator. He summoned his men and told them that since Mato Grosso had no military court, he would apply the law of the frontier. The ringleader was tied to the flagpole in front of Rondon's tent and held there for a week, through broiling sun, heavy rain showers, and chilly nights. He quickly broke down, "passing the nights bawling at the top of his lungs,"[8] but Rondon was unmoved. The punishment ended only when Rondon realized that the other soldiers were starting to feel sorry for the plotter, who was immediately expelled from the telegraph unit and sent to a penal brigade.

Rondon mistakenly thought this would quell the rebellion, but the malingering and the assassination plots continued. Once again, he wrote, "I was forced to go against my religious principles and resort to Count Lippe's procedure."[9] During one of these floggings, something terrible happened that scarred Rondon's psyche and nearly derailed his career: As a soldier, naked to the waist, was being caned with a bamboo switch, it snapped and punctured his lung. Although Rondon immediately ordered the punishment stopped, it was too late. An infection soon developed, the soldier fell ill, first with peritonitis and then sepsis, and, without access to proper medical care, died a few days later.

One of Rondon's colleagues, a fellow captain named Távora, in charge of an infantry battalion, sent Rondon a letter criticizing his conduct. "He complained of disciplinary measures and work methods he considered detrimental to the soldiers," Rondon wrote. This rankled Rondon, for two reasons. One was a simple question of protocol: an officer of equal rank, he argued, should not address him directly, but should adhere to "proper ethics" and register any complaint through the commandant of the military district or the directorate of engineering. The second, more important, rationale was that Távora's disapproval of Rondon's actions was simply unrealistic, given the conditions on the frontier: "I resorted to the only means of maintaining discipline in the wild among men removed from their duties in Rio precisely because they were insubordinate," Rondon later wrote in his diary. "It was in desperation that I was forced to make use of it." But in his letter responding to Távora, which does not survive, Rondon seems to have taken a much sharper tone. "My response was prideful, a reaction of equal intensity to the aggression against me,"[10] he wrote later. Távora's response was to forward a copy of Rondon's letter to the district commander, demanding a formal military inquiry.

In a confrontation of this sort, Távora had several advantages. Though both men held a captain's rank, Rondon had less seniority, so Távora stood slightly higher in the formal hierarchy and could argue that Rondon was being insubordinate. Additionally, and more crucially in an institution with a strong bureaucratic tradition, some of the soldiers who had been flogged had been loaned to Rondon's detachment; in a strictly formal sense, they remained assigned to the infantry battalion. Távora therefore could argue that Rondon had exceeded his authority in ordering the corporal punishment of infantry soldiers officially under another officer's command.

The members of an initial inquiry panel found this argument persuasive, and so an official court-martial was ordered, with formal charges placed against both Rondon and the soldiers who had administered the fatal flogging on his orders. Called on to testify under oath, "I argued that I had been forced to take exceptional measures by the unavoidable necessity of maintaining military discipline and order."[11] But the tribunal, meeting in Cuiabá, failed to reach a verdict and appealed to higher-ups in Rio de Janeiro. As a result, Rondon was summoned to the capital in January 1895 to undergo more questioning and investigation.

Rondon's fate now rested in the hands of Col. Belarmino de Mendonça, the adjutant general, or chief administrative officer, of the Brazilian Army. Mendonça had enlisted in the army as a patriotic fourteen-year-old after the outbreak of war with Paraguay and, like Rondon, served as a common soldier before being admitted to the military academy. He earned a degree in engineering as well, and was later put in charge of units building roads, railways, and military bases in the south. Later, he was elected to the Constitutional Assembly and then served a term in Congress. He returned to the army just months before Rondon's case landed in his lap.

Because Mendonça's experience was so similar to Rondon's, he was, perhaps, the ideal person to oversee the case, since he was likely to understand the disciplinary challenge presented by recalcitrant troops in the field. A new minister of war had just assumed his post while retaining a seat on the Supreme Military Tribunal, so he was distracted, overburdened, and likely to approve whatever decision Mendonça handed him.

Nevertheless, Rondon agonized over the soldier's death and, on temporary leave, spent much of his time reflecting on his own conduct and that of the others involved. He was in Cascadura with Chiquita and the children, but could find little pleasure in their company, with such a serious accusation hanging over him. If convicted, he faced the prospect of a reduction in rank at the very least, or dishonorable discharge from the army, or even a prison sentence.

His worry was unnecessary. When the War Ministry announced its decision, just before Rondon's thirtieth birthday, it was that the case should be "archived as unfounded."[12] Rondon was completely absolved, and could resume his duties immediately. Not only that, a statement was telegraphed to the district commander back in Mato Grosso to insert into the order of the day read to all soldiers and officers that Rondon should be "commended and thanked for services rendered."[13] This was an implicit rebuke to Távora and an endorsement of Rondon's harsh conduct.

By happenstance, Rondon's interlude in the capital coincided with profound changes at the government's highest levels. Brazil's first two presidents had been generals who favored a strongly centralized state and governed in a semi-authoritarian style, paying little heed to Congress, the press, or even their own cabinets. But on November 15, 1894, as Rondon was about to leave for Rio and his court-martial, Brazil swore into office its first civilian, popularly elected head of state for a four-year term. A lawyer born in São Paulo, Prudente de Morais had served first as that state's governor, and then as president of the Constitutional Assembly and president of the federal Senate. He was very much a creature of his state's emerging economic oligarchy, especially its powerful coffee growers, and intended to check the military's ascendancy.

For Rondon, the arrival of a new civilian-led administration had long-term implications. He had enjoyed personal relationships with previous presidents, and was able to communicate directly with them, entirely bypassing the chain of command. That access would now disappear: Rondon had no personal relationship with de Morais, and henceforth would have to navigate bureaucratic channels, often a slow, cumbersome process. This situation continued for the remaining thirty-five years of the First Republic: every time a new president and cabinet took office, Rondon would have to learn how to persuade and cajole him and his appointees. In the end, he became quite adept at bureaucratic politics, but it was not something he did naturally.

While waiting for the Ministry of War to decide his future, Rondon had found solace in Positivism. Just as Positivism was losing its relevance elsewhere, Comte's Brazilian followers had created two rival and bitterly competing factions. One group, known as the "philosophical Positivists" or "heterodox" bloc, embraced the Master's early, purely scientific doctrine, especially his focus on sociology as a discipline that would guide mankind to the ideal polity. The other, "orthodox" faction followed Comte's later teachings advocating a "religious Positivism" or a church that would contain a spiritual element but reject the supernatural and instead be based on logic and science.

Rondon sided with the orthodox group, led by Raimundo Teixeira Mendes and Miguel Lemos. They had created a Brazilian outpost of Comte's "Religion of Humanity," holding regular Sunday services at their headquarters in downtown Rio, complete with liturgy, sacraments, saints, and priests. Religious Positivists were supposed to live according to three main maxims, which Rondon often wrote out in his diaries, as if for inspiration. The first was to "live for others," meaning to put aside ego, ambition, and selfishness. The second was to "live openly," which, if followed correctly, would eliminate any need for secrecy, concealment, and subterfuge in human conduct. And finally, all Positivists were to "live for the Great Day," an era sometime in the future in which the precepts of Positivism would reign and a golden age of Progress be ushered in.[14] Since Comte coined the word "altruism," it is hardly surprising that all three maxims call for the sublimation of individuality to a collective good.

Once cleared of all charges, Rondon hurried back to Mato Grosso. The telegraph-construction schedule had not eased in his absence, and because Rondon had lost valuable time during his enforced absence, he had to resume his mission with even greater vigor. For the next two years, he would remain in the wilderness, with only telegrams and letters linking him to his family. Eventually, Chiquita learned Morse code, so she and Rondon could chat online for hours at a time after his workday was over and she had put the children to bed; they continued this practice for decades, leaving no record of their conversations behind.

In 1896, with a rail link completed from São Paulo to Aquidauana on the southern edge of the Pantanal in southwestern Mato Grosso, Rondon was ordered to begin studies to extend the telegraph line in that direction as well. Rondon enjoyed the work, which gave him an excuse to ride off into the countryside and observe the natural world around him. "I made extraordinary excursions, sometimes penetrating as far as 35 miles" from the rail line, he wrote. "Not only did this give me an exact idea of the terrain and the features of construction, but I also gathered data for future projects."[15]

This new assignment also put Rondon in regular contact with the engineering director of the railway, Austrian-born Leopold Weiss, and immediately, the son of the hinterlands and the European émigré were at odds. So when an economic crisis erupted in the capital in 1898, forcing budget cuts and a temporary curtailment of his surveying work, Rondon asked to be relieved of his duties, reassigned to the Ministry of War, and transferred to Rio de Janeiro.

Another factor—concerns about his family—also prompted his request. Chiquita and the children had traveled once again on the exhausting journey from Rio de Janeiro to Mato Grosso, where she had contracted both malaria and yaws, a painful, debilitating, and unsightly infection of the skin, bones, and joints. Benjamin, too, was often ill.

Rondon returned with his family to Rio de Janeiro in January 1899 and found the capital afflicted by both political and economic crises. President Manuel Campos Salles, a lawyer from São Paulo, had been inaugurated a few weeks earlier, and was confronting a raft of problems. Among these was a tense relationship with the armed forces. The previous president, de Morais, had just barely survived an assassination attempt by a foot soldier during a troop review in Rio ten days before leaving office; the minister of war stepped in the way, took the bullet, and died later that day.

But the assassination attempt was just one manifestation of a much larger problem. In 1896, a millenarian conflict that came to be known as the Canudos War had broken out in the arid backlands of Bahia, in the northeast. A self-proclaimed prophet named Antônio Conselheiro attracted thousands of poverty-stricken followers there, asserting that the republic and the progressive, Positivist-inspired measures it had promulgated—civil marriage and separation of church and state among them—were the work of the antichrist and a sign that the end-time was nearing. The federal government responded by sending thousands of troops to suppress the movement and demolish its settlement at Canudos.

But a first military campaign, in October 1896, was a spectacular failure. A second offensive and then a third, both early in 1897, yielded identical results. Only the fourth campaign, in October 1897, succeeded in quelling the rebellion, but at tremendous cost: In the end, an estimated twelve thousand soldiers were needed to subdue a motley band of peasants and former slaves. The death toll was estimated at twenty-five thousand people—including the colonel leading one of the government campaigns, five thousand government soldiers, and hundreds of prisoners, whose throats were slit. In the final assault Antônio Conselheiro himself was killed. The slaughter traumatized the nation and stained the reputation of the army, which came to be seen as both bloodthirsty and inept in combat.

Many of Rondon's classmates fought at Canudos, and he grieved for those who died. His former classmate and close friend Euclides da Cunha was there, too, as a journalist reporting on the fighting, and was harshly critical of the army's leadership and conduct. By the time Rondon returned to Rio, da Cunha was already at work on the enormously influential *Rebellion in the Backlands*, in which he condemned the government's behavior as "a crime, one that we must denounce."[16] Tellingly, despite Rondon's continuing loyalty to the government and army, da Cunha's fierce indictment, published in 1902, did not damage their friendship.

But it was the economic crisis that most directly affected Rondon and his work. The Campos Salles administration had inherited a large foreign debt and a high inflation rate, and was forced to renegotiate the terms of loans contracted with its foreign creditors, led by Great Britain. Repayment of a new £10 million loan, guaranteed by Brazilian customs proceeds, severely limited government revenues and forced adoption of an austerity budget. The new finance minister, a native of Mato Grosso, understood the importance of infrastructure projects in developing and integrating the frontier, but at the same time had to curtail inflationary deficit spending and pay Brazil's bills. He canceled scores of public works projects, including railways and telegraph lines.

Rondon would remain in the capital until the crisis passed, supervising the military's work on a detailed map of Mato Grosso, based in large part on his own data. He enjoyed this unexpected interlude with his family, but he would describe his new duties in his memoirs as "a fleeting assignment, an interim between the second and third stages of my life."[17]

The most significant development during Rondon's hiatus in Rio was his formal initiation into the Religion of Humanity. During his studies of the Positivist catechism out in the field, Rondon had read and absorbed the faith's "15 Universal Laws of Supreme Inevitability" as well as the laws of the seven sciences Positivism revered. The induction ceremony took place at the new Temple of Humanity just south of downtown Rio. As a latecomer to the faith, Rondon was too old for the sacrament of "admission," so he was instead a candidate for the next stage, which Positivists call "destination," when a believer chooses a career and takes a sacred vow to exercise it for the benefit of humanity.

Rondon's Positivist faith gave him a welcome spiritual anchor. He spent many hours at the Temple of Humanity—still standing today on Benjamin Constant Street—at Sunday services and also in conversation with other Positivists, especially Raimundo Teixeira Mendes, his spiritual adviser for the next thirty years. Even as an old man, he participated in Sunday worship service, and socialized afterward with other congregation members.

For Rondon, the Temple of Humanity was a refuge and a spiritual home. His sense of vocation was already intense, but the Positivist Church also provided fellowship to his family during his long absences. Teixeira Mendes was especially diligent in this respect: he and Lemos often accompanied Rondon to the port to see him off on his missions. But Lemos's health was already weakening, so it fell to Teixeira Mendes, practicing the altruism the church preached, to help Chiquita and the children when Rondon was away. The family moved from Cascadura to be close to him, and he became a kind of uncle to the children, who, following the birth of Clotilde Teresa, numbered three. "You inspire and constitute in my entire Family, beyond all our sentiments of supreme gratitude, a true spiritual Father," Rondon wrote in a letter to Teixeira Mendes in 1900, a few months after the arrangement went into effect.

Rondon had always felt tormented by his conflicting sense of duty to both country and family, and he shared his anguish with Teixeira Mendes. "I am sorry to find myself far from the surroundings where I have customarily known true happiness, and where I should constantly remain for the sake of educating my dear little children," he wrote his adviser from Mato Grosso. "But this is the only way in which I can make my small contribution to the Holy Crusade of which you are the energetic and wise propagandist and endearing Apostle."[18]

In reality, becoming a full-fledged member of the Positivist Church would require even more sacrifices and restrictions, which would become obvious only as Rondon's career flourished over the next two decades and he became a national hero. All new initiates, including Rondon, were required to take an oath promising to "consecrate all their activity and all their devotion to the incorporation of the proletariat into modern society, the summation of all Positivist action."[19] In concrete terms, this meant that no Positivist, no matter how prominent, was permitted to run for or hold political office, elective or appointed, or accept a teaching position, join a scientific or literary society, engage in journalism, or accept payment of any kind for anything he wrote.

The purpose of these limitations had to do with the Religion of Humanity's emphasis on altruism, and intended to keep its adherents closer to the proletariat by preventing them from rising into the moneyed and privileged classes. Such prohibitions, however, were "incompatible with their very objectives and completely irreconcilable with the Brazilian situation,"[20] the country's leading historian of Positivism, Ivan Lins, would later write. "Offering the ascetic austerity and inflexible rigidity of a monastic order, the statutes of the Positivist Church and Apostolate isolated its followers from the rest of the world and transformed their group into a giant cloister."[21]

This crippling innovation was a peculiarly Brazilian interpretation of Comte's doctrine, for the founder of Positivism meant for such restrictions to apply only to priests of the Positivist Church, not to ordinary believers. Many of Rondon's oldest friends, including da Cunha and Fragoso, refused to join the Positivist Church or broke altogether with the movement over this issue; they tried to get him to do the same, citing the example of Benjamin Constant and the two cabinet posts he had accepted. But Rondon would not budge: he fully accepted Comte's edict that "submission is the foundation of individual improvement."[22] That decision would have enormous consequences for him, nearly always negative, in the years to come.

VI

Article 44, Section 32

I N THE FIRST week of January 1900, Rondon was summoned to a meeting at army headquarters in Rio de Janeiro and assigned a new challenge, out in the field. After repeated attempts to build a telegraph line from Cuiabá to Corumbá, a strategic port and garrison on the border with Bolivia, and then south to Fort Coimbra on the border with Paraguay, the army was determined to try yet again, and decided that Rondon should command the operation.

As everyone in the military knew, this mission could wreck a promising career. The first attempt began in 1888, when Deodoro da Fonseca was ordered to start work on a link between the two border posts; that mission ended when the monarchy fell a year later. In 1892, another high-ranking officer began a preliminary study of the Cuiabá-to-Corumbá route, concluded it would be too expensive to build (in both monetary and human cost) and lobbied his superiors for reassignment. A year later, a military engineer who had built telegraph lines in the south undertook the project, but soon was stymied by what were described as "insurmountable"[1] logistical difficulties.

As a Mato Grosso native, Rondon understood the obstacles, felt coerced into taking the assignment, and resented it. "I accepted the commission under the conditions that you well know," he wrote to Teixeira Mendes. "I don't want to provoke the anger of a Ministry that was quite tactless with me in the organization of the task. I will, therefore, stick with this until I have a chance to leave and preserve my military self-esteem."[2] That would not take long, he assumed, "because I know from lengthy experience that our pretentious administrators do not take seriously anything they begin."

But Rondon was wrong. The project would end up consuming more than six years, such was its complexity. The biggest problem he faced was geographic: the most direct route from Cuiabá west to the border went straight across the Pantanal swamp, an area as large as Great Britain. That meant Rondon and his exploratory team would have to confront not just the usual tropical diseases, hostile tribes, and predatory wildlife, but also an unparalleled set of engineering challenges across a vast area with no real terra firma. A generation of very capable and experienced military engineers had failed to meet the challenge. Now, Rondon was expected to find answers, while simultaneously carrying out surveying projects that the authorities in far-off Rio envisioned as the prelude to construction of both a highway and a railroad parallel to the telegraph line.

To achieve all of this, Rondon was given a meager force of just fifty soldiers from an infantry battalion stationed in the neighboring state of Goiás to supplement his own small permanent unit. From his own experience, he knew this was not good news: the local commandant would surely transfer to Rondon's command the most troublesome, most incompetent soldiers or those most weakened by disease. Not only that, Rondon would have to go to Goiás himself, then quickly march the reinforcements across nearly five hundred miles of wilderness to the only telegraph station on the proposed line, which now sat abandoned, save for nineteen soldiers and a single junior officer stationed there as caretakers.

Beyond those material concerns, Rondon also had to engage in tactful lobbying and delicate diplomacy with local officials. In the decade since the monarchy ended, power in the Republic had become significantly decentralized: it was up to the chief executive of each state, still officially known as a "president," to decide how the federal laws, budgets, and edicts would be honored and enforced, if at all. "In this regime," Campos Salles said shortly after assuming power late in 1898, "true political strength . . . has migrated to the states."[3]

So, before setting out with his ill-suited squadron, Rondon, adhering to military protocol, traveled to Cuiabá to pay his respects to the commander of all troops in Mato Grosso. His main goal, however, was to meet with the state's governor, a retired navy admiral, and ensure he would not oppose the project. Though Rondon noted that the telegraph line was clearly "of immediate interest to the state," it was not at all uncommon during the First Republic for governors to sabotage undertakings that threatened their private commercial interests or those of their friends. "I argued for a monetary contribution from him," Rondon wrote in his diary, "since the amount of money made available to me" by the federal government "was minimal in comparison to the scale of the project."[4] The governor agreed, giving Rondon nearly the equivalent of the initial parcel the federal government had authorized, and also writing a letter ordering all state government agencies to aid the project whenever asked.

Rondon then turned his attention to obtaining the assent of the other power in the region: its Indigenous inhabitants, the Bororo. They lived along the São Lourenço River, and were perhaps even kinfolk of his mother, whose extended family lived just north of that area. This connection was potentially advantageous, but Rondon could not take it for granted. Once again, he followed protocol and rode alone on horseback to the village of Kejare to meet with Oarine Ecureu, or Yellow Swallow, leader of the largest settlement of the São Lourenço Bororo. There he was welcomed with warm embraces and ritual chants that translate as "Our great chief has arrived! Hail to the great chief of the Bororo!"[5] That evening he was honored with a banquet that lasted long into the night, filled with platters of freshly caught fish, storytelling, and ritual invocations in homage to the dead.

The next day, Rondon distributed gifts to everyone in the village, fulfilling one of his obligations as Pagmejera, the Chief of Chiefs. Already, the extra money that the governor had authorized was proving useful. Rondon was eager to press on with his mission and return to his men, but Yellow Swallow asked that he remain for two more days. Pleased at the presence of the Pagmejera, Kejare's residents wanted to pay further tribute to Rondon with a *bacororo*, a ceremony associated with a mythical figure of the same name who in Bororo cosmology presides over one of two Villages of the Dead. To do that properly, though, residents of the surrounding countryside had to be summoned. Once they arrived, there was much singing and dancing, which Rondon described as "light and graceful in movement." Once the rite was concluded, he could at last politely take his leave, promising, "Aregodo augai curimata," or "Goodbye, I am leaving, but will return."[6]

As the telegraph construction mission slowly advanced, Rondon's men, unaccustomed to the climate and terrain, faltered. He had set off with eighty-one troopers, but disease and faintheartedness soon took their toll. Seventeen soldiers deserted, and twice as many fell ill, mostly to malaria, and either died or were evacuated to Cuiabá. With his task force reduced to just thirty men, Rondon's situation turned dire. Like the commanders of the three previous efforts to build a Cuiabá-Corumbá line, he risked seeing his mission collapse, bringing with it personal failure and professional embarrassment.

In the end, the Bororo provided his salvation. Yellow Swallow and Baru, or Clear Sky, leader of a neighboring village, suddenly appeared, accompanied by dozens of their men. They were on a hunting trip, and had decided to visit the Pagmejera. Desperate, Rondon asked for their help in building the line.

There is no way of knowing exactly what Rondon, Yellow Swallow, and Clear Sky said to one another during that discussion in April 1900, which means we have no idea how Rondon convinced the Indians to provide their aid. They were conversing in Bororo, a language that none of Rondon's junior officers understood, and which, in any case, did not yet exist in written form.

But in view of what happened next, their conversation was clearly a watershed moment, one that ultimately ensured the success of Rondon's mission. Within days, Clear Sky returned with 120 Bororo, not just adult men capable of performing the arduous labor needed to construct the telegraph line, but also their women and children, and even their pets: dogs, monkeys, parrots. Yellow Swallow appeared a few days later with an even larger group, about 150 people. In other words, two entire Bororo communities, obeying the instructions of their leaders, showed up expressly to help their friend and kinsman Rondon. For the duration of the first phase of his mission, just over a year, they would travel with him and his men. As the line advanced across the Pantanal toward Corumbá, they would break camp and accompany Rondon's contingent whenever it moved to the next base of operations.

On Rondon's part, this was an extraordinary achievement on multiple levels. The most obvious and most significant was this: Rondon had upended the long-held notion among Brazil's elite—and elsewhere—that Indigenous peoples were always enemies of the spread of "order and progress" sponsored by "civilized" society and could never be collaborators in its expansion. Using purely peaceful means, however, Rondon had not merely ensured the goodwill of Indigenous tribes, he had somehow persuaded them to participate in "the Brazilian national project" by convincing them it would bring them benefits, too.

That same debate about the Indigenous people of Brazil would intensify and consume much of Rondon's energy in the next decade. Before Rondon, it was assumed that the only way to get Indians to abandon a hunter-gatherer lifestyle and labor in a productive, predictable fashion was through coercion. Had that not constantly been the case since Pedro Álvares Cabral landed in the south of Bahia in 1500? And even when compelled to work, Indians always did so halfheartedly, didn't they? Now Rondon—using only kind words, gifts of tools and trinkets, and other shows of friendship—had demonstrated that it was actually possible to enlist Indigenous peoples as partners in extending the most modern of technologies to the country's most remote hinterlands.

When Rondon successfully enlisted the Bororo's help to build the line, it was also a crucial step on a purely practical level. The Bororo lived outside a money economy, so they did not have to be paid a salary, as soldiers and local peasants did. Instead, it was possible to ensure their cooperation with strategically timed gifts. Nor did they need to be supplied with food or clothing; instead, they could live off the land, fishing and hunting, and provide Rondon's troops with food, folk-based medicinal remedies, and valuable pointers on local geography, wildlife, and plant lore. They even had their own pack animals to haul their few belongings. Given Rondon's shoestring budget, this was a godsend.

"The Indians quite easily subjected themselves to the military routine and the precise work"[7] the mission required, Rondon reported. After a second conversation with the two Bororo leaders that Rondon described as "long, full of friendly words and expressive figures of speech,"[8] it was agreed that the Indians would clear a pathway for the telegraph line, cutting down trees, clearing brush, and removing stumps. The teams designated for work would rotate from day to day so that the Bororo would be able to continue to hunt and fish, as was their habit. The only condition they imposed was that Rondon himself direct the Bororo work teams, and not a junior officer who did not speak their language.

Rondon's diaries suggest that his concern lay more with the behavior of his own troops than with that of the Bororo. So he called the two contingents together, and issued a tough new set of regulations, first in Portuguese and then in Bororo. After work, when the two groups withdrew to their own campsites, which were separate but within walking distance of each other, soldiers were absolutely prohibited from going into the Bororo encampment alone or even in groups without authorization. If the Bororo caught an enlisted man intruding, they were to bring him directly to Rondon, who would apply an appropriate punishment. Only in this way, Rondon knew, could he prevent his soldiers from stealing food and tobacco from the Bororo, and trying to have sex with the women and girls; he also wanted to keep alcohol away from the Indians and worried that too much close contact between his soldiers and the Bororo could spread diseases to which Indigenous peoples had no resistance.

But one night a few weeks into the collaboration, Rondon awoke to a sudden burst of yelling, followed by a procession of Indians, four of whom were carrying one of Rondon's soldiers above their heads. As a crowd gathered, Rondon excoriated the offender in two languages for his insubordination, and promised punishment in the morning. "Nobody slept" the remainder of the night, Rondon noted, and at daylight the Bororo were already gathering, "anxious to know the decision of the Pagmejera,"⁹ wondering whether he would really keep his promise. He did: Rondon ordered the soldier tied to a tree and left exposed to the sun for the day, with no water to slake his thirst. To torment him further, Rondon and the others took their meals in his presence but did not offer him food. In his diary, Rondon noted that "Yellow Swallow was exultant"¹⁰ at seeing justice actually done. Rondon had proved to be a man of his word, justifying the faith that Yellow Swallow and Clear Sky had shown in him and cementing their friendship.

When the two contingents finally separated, it was May 19, 1901, and the final telegraph station at Itiquira had just been inaugurated. Upon reaching the settlement in late April, Rondon's expedition, both soldiers and Indians, were greeted jubilantly by residents, thrilled that they could at last communicate instantly with the rest of the world. To celebrate, they organized a banquet, to which both the troopers and the Bororo were invited. To reciprocate the courtesy, Yellow Swallow and Clear Sky arranged another lavish *bacororo*, with many of the Bororo who had worked on the telegraph project dancing and singing late into the night, dressed in jaguar skins. The next morning, they returned to the wilderness, carrying their few belongings in wicker baskets strung across their shoulders.

The Bororo parted company with Rondon's expedition because the dry season, the best time for hunting, was about to arrive, and the expedition had reached the east bank of the Taquari River, which was the limit of what the Bororo considered their territory. On the other shore began the realms of the Terena and other peoples, and "there I will not go,"¹¹ Yellow Swallow told Rondon. Over there on the other side, Rondon would have to begin all over again, negotiating with each tribal group as the telegraph line moved to the south and west. But his dealings with the Bororo had provided him a template for how to secure the cooperation of Indigenous groups, and he would apply this technique again and again as construction advanced. In recognition of his achievement, Rondon was promoted to major on July 7, 1903.¹²

As Rondon's team moved southwest, toward Aquidauana, the terrain began to change, and he faced new challenges. Instead of the floodplain of the Pantanal, he and his men now began to encounter quicksand, which made installation of telegraph poles all the more difficult. Even with the aid of the Terena tribesmen he befriended, who knew the region and its idiosyncrasies, the process slowed nearly to a halt: instead of installing one hundred poles a day, Rondon and his men now had to be content with setting just a half dozen, and sometimes three hours were needed just to position a single pole. Whenever possible, Rondon favored beams made of *jacarandá*, a hardwood belonging to the rosewood family; these posts were now sharpened to a point at one end, hauled by canoe to the work site and then laboriously pushed through the quicksand until they struck clay. Only then could Rondon be sure the poles would not topple or tilt precariously.

In addition to the slow progress, mortal dangers were everywhere, robbing Rondon of some of his best and most dedicated men. Late in 1903, for example, Rondon was out on an inspection tour when he heard that a promising young officer, Lt. Francisco Bueno Horta Barbosa, was missing. Hurrying to the campsite where the lieutenant's men were waiting for his return, Rondon learned that Horta Barbosa had been in a canoe leading a reconnoitering mission when the waters began rising and he generously changed places with one of his men who could not swim. Mounting the soldier's mule, Horta Barbosa had ridden ahead of them. The others took refuge on a hummock and sent a request for help.

Eventually, the lieutenant's body was found—or rather, what remained of it. He had apparently been unseated from the mule when it began bucking, perhaps out of fear when it sensed a dangerous animal like a snake or caiman in the swamp. In any case, Horta Barbosa had fallen or been thrown into the water, where he was consumed by piranhas: all that was left of him was a skeleton with a pair of feet still encased in heavy, protective army boots.

Rondon was used to losing men, even inured to it, but this was different. Five members of the Horta Barbosa family had volunteered to work with him, and all were diligent officers, as well as loyal and dedicated Positivists. His relationship with them was almost paternal, and he dreaded having to tell the other four, and the Positivists in Rio, that Francisco had died. Back at the hum-mock, Horta Barbosa's men were startled to see their dignified commander break first into tears and then into sobs. That night, Rondon rode back to Aquidauana in pouring rain, "cold and hungry and sick at heart."[13]

When the route of the telegraph line eventually veered back into Bororo territory, Rondon was again able to call on his Indigenous friends for help. And just as before, luck played a part: Rondon's soldiers were ferrying supplies across a river when their main canoe capsized and sank, sending everything into the water. Shortly after, a Bororo hunting party happened by and, after conferring with the Pagmejera, went into action. The Indians swam to the bottom of the river and res-cued the telegraph wire, boxes of isolators, arms for the poles, and food supplies. "Everything was saved,"[14] Rondon gratefully reported. Not only that, the Bororo also transported the material on their shoulders for many miles to the primitive warehouse Rondon's men had built at their advance camp.

On another occasion, part of the route Rondon had selected for the telegraph line proved too swampy, and he had to find an alterna-tive. The only viable substitute was a stretch of ruggedly hilly ter-rain, and Rondon was preparing his men for the ordeal ahead when yet another Bororo hunting party appeared. After ritual embraces and declarations of friendship, Rondon explained his predicament, and the Bororo agreed to help. In water up to their waists, the hunt-ers carried the expedition's food supplies, baggage, and matériel to the foot of the rise, thereby sparing Rondon's men. Without the help of the Bororo, he wrote in his diary, "the Commission would have suffered delays or perhaps even failure, for the soldiers would have had to be diverted from their construction duties to resolve the innumerable problems that presented themselves."[15]

Because Rondon was himself a native of the Mato Grosso fron-tier, he was also able to enlist the help of friends and relatives to ease his work. For example, Miguel Evangelista, a maternal uncle, was put in charge of the expedition's cattle after earlier recruits failed to adequately tend the herd, allowing cows to lose weight and leav-ing them prone to disease. Rondon suspected, given the suspiciously high number of cattle that simply vanished from supposedly secure campsites, that some of the cattle herders colluded with local rustlers. All of that stopped after Uncle Miguel arrived.

Rondon also engaged some cousins from the Evangelista side of the family—childhood playmates and, like him, natives of Mimoso—as scouts. In addition, at one frontier ranch where he stopped, hoping to buy more cattle to feed his men, he discovered that the foreman there was a schoolmate from Cuiabá, who gave him a favorable price. And when the commission reached Coxim, he was surprised to learn that João Batista de Albuquerque, his favorite elementary school teacher during his days in Cuiabá, was now the town's leading businessman. Not only did Rondon know he would not be cheated, but Albuquerque, knowing Rondon's rectitude and reliability, furnished him with supplies in advance of payment even before a government letter of credit arrived, and vouched for Rondon to other local merchants. "I am not doing business with the government, which I will deal with only when payment is made in advance," Albuquerque told a fellow shop owner who warned him he would lose his shirt by accepting a promissory note. "I'm dealing with Cândido Mariano, and I trust only him."[16]

Other times, though, Rondon's status as a local boy who had made it beyond Mato Grosso actually complicated his assignment. The state remained a rough and frequently violent frontier region. As Rondon memorably put it in a letter to Teixeira Mendes, his spiritual adviser in Rio, "The law that reigns here in Mato Grosso is Article 44, Section 32"—.44 being the caliber of the Winchester rifle that Brazilian frontiersmen preferred and .32 being the caliber of the Colt revolver that many of them also carried.[17]

Rondon tried to steer clear of the local quarrels that often erupted into shootouts, ambushes, and outright warfare. But with cousins, uncles, and aunts scattered all over the state, his sense of obligation to family sometimes made it impossible to avoid such conflicts. His father's side was not the problem: Manoel, his paternal uncle and foster father, died in September 1903, and though Rondon deeply mourned his passing, his ties to other members of the Rondon and da Silva branches were distant. But the Evangelistas, his mother's people, were a different story. Rondon was eternally grateful to them for taking him in as an orphan, and they had become perhaps the most prominent family in Mimoso and the surrounding area. That meant they were deeply involved in disputes about land ownership and local politics.

The clashes that erupted in those years across Mato Grosso only intensified after Francisco Rodrigues Alves became president of Brazil late in 1902. Rodrigues Alves, from São Paulo, implemented policies that emphasized development in his home state, Rio, and Minas Gerais, essentially leaving outlying areas like Mato Grosso to their own devices. As a result, Mato Grosso fell into a state of undeclared civil war that pitted two strongmen and their militias against each other. Antônio Paes de Barros, who fought in the war against Paraguay as a teenager and went by the innocuous nickname Totó, drew much of his support from the owners of maté and sugar plantations in the southern part of the state. Cattle ranchers and the owners of rubber-extraction enterprises in the northern half of the state, on the other hand, tended to support his rival Generoso Ponce, a journalist turned politician who represented Mato Grosso in the national Senate and was very distantly related to Rondon through one of his father's great-grandmothers.

Both sides, however, were oligarchic and corrupt, often resorting to vote fraud and intimidation to maintain their authority, and were feared in the countryside for the brutality of their hired gunmen. In the beginning, Totó Paes, leader of the Republican Conservative Party, clearly had the upper hand, and used violence to preserve his advantage. In 1901, he had a son-in-law appointed chief of police in Cuiabá; in a notorious incident soon afterward, police arrested twenty-nine of Ponce's followers, slit their throats, and tossed their bodies into the river to be consumed by piranhas. Over the next two years, the state had four governors, and violence grew more severe throughout the countryside.

Initially, Paes courted Rondon, offering him a seat in the state assembly. Rondon courteously demurred, citing his Positivist beliefs, and tried to remain neutral as the conflict intensified. But both sides regarded him as a powerful potential ally, with connections to influential patrons in Rio de Janeiro and access to government funds, and continued, without success, to ask for his support. Then, in December 1905, Rondon was finally forced to take sides: he was visited by Francelino Evangelista, one of his many maternal uncles, who told him that a gunman loyal to Totó Paes had killed another uncle, Pedro Evangelista, during a gun battle near Mimoso. The family wanted Rondon, as its most powerful member, to intervene and prevent further bloodshed.

Rondon had just been summoned by the high command in Rio de Janeiro for consultations and was about to embark on another long trip to the capital. So he stopped to see Totó Paes while passing through Cuiabá. There, over lunch, with his uncle Francelino at his side, he negotiated a truce meant to put an end to the feud between the Evangelista clan and the governor's allies: Paes would send the state police to Mimoso to arrest Uncle Pedro's killer if the Evangelistas would promise not to take the law into their own hands by killing the gunman first.

When Rondon returned to Mato Grosso in April 1906, he was angered to learn that while the Evangelistas had kept their side of the bargain, the police were indeed dispatched to Mimoso, but not to arrest the murderer; instead, they tried to take Francelino Evangelista into custody. The result was a gun battle between the police and yet another of Rondon's uncles, Antônio Evangelista, and three of Rondon's cousins. The Evangelistas exchanged fire with the police until Uncle Francelino could escape into the bush, then stopped shooting and surrendered. Once the four men were disarmed, the police took them into the same thicket. After tying them up and beating them, they slit their throats, then burned Uncle Francelino's house to the ground.

With this, Rondon was driven decisively into Ponce's camp. "This grave misfortune disturbed my work plans," he later wrote, rather dispassionately, referring to the summary execution of his relatives. "I was unable to immediately begin the explorations"[18] to extend the line. Instead, from Corumbá he sent a pair of telegrams to Rio, one informing the War Ministry of the violence in Mimoso and another to the Justice Ministry requesting writs to protect Uncle

Francelino and two cousins. As soon as Rondon received an affirmative response from the national authorities, he summoned his uncle and cousins. He also received a telegram from his wife back home in Rio, who had read newspaper accounts of the conflict and was now "asking that I not get involved in the issue, for the sake of her peace of mind and that of the children."[19] But by then it was too late.

Late in April, Rondon set out for Cuiabá on horseback, accompanied by his imperiled kinfolk, a pair of lieutenants attached to the Telegraph Commission, and five soldiers. Along the way, they heard rumors that Totó Paes wanted to end the violence by negotiating an accord with Ponce and the opposition, but these were soon followed by vivid descriptions of mass jailings and raids on opposition strongholds. By mid-May, all of Mato Grosso was in rebellion against Paes.

On May 17, Ponce began a drive on Cuiabá, leading a force of some 500 men that, as it proceeded northeastward from Corumbá, eventually grew to more than 2,000 fighters. At the same time, another group of 1,200 supporting Ponce began to move on the state capital from the north. Both detachments were joined by criminals and other opportunists, which caused many of the governor's dwindling band of supporters to flee to the state capital, where some took refuge in the Telegraph Commission's office. Upon learning of Rondon's ties of blood and affection to the Evangelistas, they feared for their own lives, expecting Rondon to take revenge on them for his relatives who had been butchered in Mimoso. Rondon repeatedly reassured them that they would be spared, and their terror diminished.[20]

Totó Paes, meanwhile, sent a frantic plea to the government in Rio, asking that troops be sent to Mato Grosso to assist him. The army was slow in responding to his entreaties, in part because of the telegrams Rondon had sent assessing the worsening situation in his home state, and Congress refused to declare a state of siege. Receiving no answer, Totó Paes fled Cuiabá in late June, hoping to hold out until a federal detachment arrived. But rival forces had already seized two family plantations where he had hoped to seek refuge, so the governor had to hole up in a gunpowder factory south of the state capital. After he ignored a demand for surrender, Ponce's forces attacked the factory on July 6, captured Paes, then executed him and mutilated his body. In Mimoso, several of his followers were killed, in all likelihood by members of the Evangelista clan. The federal troops arrived in mid-July, too late to help.

With at least a semblance of order restored and his relatives no longer in danger, Rondon was able to focus again on the telegraph project. Construction had continued under the command of Lts. Antônio Pyrineus de Souza and Manuel Rabelo while he was away in Rio and then distracted by the local hostilities, but Rondon still needed to inspect the work before the line could be put into service. One final spur, northwest from Cuiabá to the old state capital, also remained to be built, so Rondon spent most of the rest of 1906 supervising its construction.

By year's end, the project that nearly everyone back in Rio assumed to be impossible was in fact complete. In fewer than seven years, aided by friendly Indians and working amid unending political turmoil, Rondon had managed to install 1,100 miles of telegraph lines and build seventeen new stations. His reputation was not only preserved but enhanced. At the age of forty-one, his ascent to national renown as the embodiment of a distinctly Brazilian can-do spirit was about to begin.

VII

"Correcting the World"

ARRIVING IN RIO de Janeiro early in 1907, Rondon discovered that his success was to be rewarded with another mission that had long thwarted the nation's leaders. President Afonso Pena, sworn into office just two months earlier, took a direct interest in Rondon's work and summoned him to the presidential palace to discuss a project that he hoped would ensure his own place in history. A lawyer and former cabinet minister, Pena, at fifty-nine, had as his presidential slogan "To govern is to populate." This meant encouraging immigration from Europe, the Middle East, and Japan, but also entailed opening up Brazil's vast interior for both newly arrived immigrants and native-born Brazilian settlers.

Pena was especially concerned about incorporating rubber-rich Acre, wrested from Bolivia in 1903, and the rest of the remote northwest into national life. At their meeting, Pena outlined the plan: build a telegraph line from Cuiabá all the way to the Madeira River and then on to Manaus and Acre; survey the region for mineral and other riches; map its natural features; catalog its plant and animal life; build roads and railways; and establish agricultural settlements. No Brazilian knew more about conditions in the wilderness than Rondon, so Pena wanted to know: "Do you think it is possible to execute a project along these lines?"

Inwardly, Rondon was thrilled to hear the president delineate such a far-reaching proposal, for, as he later admitted, Pena was expressing "a point of view that had always been my own." So he did not hesitate in his response: "It's just a matter of wanting to do it,"[1] he answered.

"Well, I want to," Pena replied. And with that, the deal was sealed: Rondon would lead the project, officially designated the Commission for the Strategic Telegraph Line from Mato Grosso to Amazonas, CLTEMA for short, but soon to be popularly known as the Rondon Commission. Rondon would also have the authority and budget to carry out the scientific investigations that both he and Pena considered essential to the enterprise's long-term success. If the bureaucracy resisted or showed even the slightest sign of foot-dragging, Pena added, Rondon's instructions were clear: "Bring the matter directly to me."[2]

So in mid-February, Rondon was detached from the Army Engineering Corps and transferred to the Ministry of Public Works. As chief of the new program, Rondon took command of dozens of military engineers and ordinary soldiers, and also a large number of civilians. They ranged from functionaries of the Division of Posts and Telegraphs to highly trained scientists. "I preferred the more arduous task"[3] to a conventional assignment, Rondon acknowledged, no doubt aware that the compensations for taking on a more risky effort were many: in his early forties and still a major, he was now unshackled from the encumbrances of the military hierarchy, subject to no authority but his own and the president's.

By midyear he was back in the field and ready to begin exploration and construction. As usual, Rondon put himself in charge of the most challenging aspect: "large-scale reconnaissance of the wilderness and preparatory studies to fix the path of the main line."[4] And as in the case of the Pantanal project, the most important part of that groundwork was gaining the assent of the Indigenous peoples who lived in the region through which the telegraph line would pass.

The northern half of the new telegraph line, which would have an overall length of more than one thousand miles, would traverse unexplored jungle with unknown inhabitants. But two main Indigenous groups lived along the line's southern section: the Paresi and the Nhambiquara. Dealing with them would be tricky, for the two tribes had a long history of mutual hostility, which had intensified in recent decades as they were squeezed into a smaller territory because of encroaching rubber tappers and ranchers. Rondon thus had to take care not to alienate one group by appearing too friendly toward the other; he needed the support of both, but the cultural and linguistic differences and enmity between the Paresi and the Nhambiquara were so extensive that he could not employ a uniform approach. Each group would have to be approached with a distinct set of tactics.

The specific details of how Rondon established peaceful contact with tribes considered hostile are often frustratingly sparse, even in his diaries, but fortunately that is not the case with the Paresi, his first objective. In the 1970s and 1980s, the Brazilian anthropologist Maria Fátima Roberto Machado interviewed several groups of mostly elderly Paresi, by then living in poor neighborhoods in Cuiabá and its outskirts. Some of them were still able to vividly recall Rondon first appearing in their villages more than six decades earlier, and others, immersed in the oral tradition of their people, knew stories about him handed down by parents and grandparents, or aunts and uncles. In some instances, the distinction between memory and legend was blurred, but altogether, the recollections provide a coherent account of how Rondon made the Paresi his friends and allies.

Because of Rondon's experiences with the Bororo and other peoples to their south, the Paresi already knew who he was long before he and his men first appeared in their territory. Word of the Pagmejera, the feats he had accomplished and his friendliness and generosity toward Native peoples, had spread among the Indigenous groups of the southern Amazon along trade and travel routes, and the Paresi were very curious to know more about him.

The initial contact occurred in the second half of 1907, and in typical fashion, Rondon's timing was perfect: he happened to ride into a large village just as an elaborate banquet was getting underway. The celebrants included visitors from several other nearby Paresi settlements and the mood was festive. Because Rondon was initially unaccompanied, his presence did not arouse alarm or suspicion.

Platters of meat, sweets, and drink were being passed around, and

Rondon tried everything he was offered, sharing it with others. A hammock was brought for him, and when groups of curious children gathered around, he let them jump into the hammock or sit on his lap—among them the village headman's daughter, who later took the name Maria Zozokoialô. Musicians played on nose and pan flutes for him as others sang, and he watched delightedly as the Paresi men and boys played a variety of soccer in which the ball was allowed only to be batted around with the head: not even feet could be used.

Maria Zozokoialô remembered Rondon jokingly asking her if he should go onto the field and join the game. "Oh no," she replied, to which he responded with laughter and a tousling of her hair. "You're too fat. You'll only hurt yourself."[5]

When it came time for the men to begin a ritual dance in which they periodically stamped their feet on the ground, Rondon observed for a while, taking careful notes until he figured out the rhythm, and then joined in. If his initial behavior, gentle and sociable, won him the affection of the Paresi, this act of respect for Paresi tradition and culture sealed a friendship that would last for more than fifty years, until Rondon's death. On future expeditions, he would often employ Paresi men as scouts and porters, and once the telegraph line was finished, handpicked Paresi were sent to school, trained in Morse code, and put in charge of stations in their territory.

As that first feast was taking place, a group of hunters returned to the village and were startled to see Rondon there, being treated as the guest of honor. Maria Zozokoialô recalled the leader of the hunting party asking her father about the stranger, and was startled by her father's response: "He is our new chief. . . . He has come to correct the world!"[6]

The Paresi's world had been disrupted ever since the first Portuguese explorers arrived late in the seventeenth century. In 1723, the explorer and slave hunter Antônio Pires de Campos published an account of his contacts over "many years" with the tribe, which he described as "not warlike, only defending themselves when they are threatened" and "tireless in cultivating their crops." "These people are so numerous that one cannot count their villages or settlements," he wrote. "Many times in one day's march one will pass by ten or a dozen villages, and in each one of these there will be ten or even 30 houses, some of which are 30 or even 40 paces wide, round like an oven and very tall."[7]

Barely 150 years later, that peaceful domain had all but vanished. When the German explorer Karl von den Steinen visited the southern edge of Paresi territory in the 1880s, "only a small relic remained" of the "great kingdom" Pires de Campos had described, he wrote, and "we cannot bring together anything more than the wreckage of what once had been!" The cause for this decline was obvious: "The hunting of slaves was followed by the exploitation of gold and diamonds, which was ruthlessly imposed on the Indians."[8]

Just as predictable was the tribe's hostile response. When von den Steinen checked government records in Cuiabá before heading to the region, he found reports warning that "it is not uncommon for these Indians to treacherously attack those who travel between Diamantino and Vila Maria." Other groups were described in official accounts as "enemies, rapacious, and practitioners of arson in the zone around the city of Mato Grosso,"[9] the old provincial capital. In such a state of mutual antagonism, made worse by a rubber boom that only gained full force after von den Steinen's expedition, it is no wonder the Paresi welcomed Rondon as their possible savior.

As the Paresi children remembered it decades later, Rondon stayed in their village for about two weeks. During that time he studied the Paresi language, compiling a glossary and grammar that the Rondon Commission later published, and carefully observed the customs and rituals of their daily life. He appears to have paid special attention to Paresi medical practices, for his diary is full of notations about plants and herbs with medicinal uses, and the children recalled him spending much time with the village's shaman and medicine man.

When Rondon asked the Paresi for permission to build a telegraph station at a location known as Ponte de Pedra, or Bridge of Stone, the Indians were astonished. In their cosmology, that exact location, a natural bridge of basalt at the end of a series of waterfalls and rapids, was the center of the world, the place where the Halíti, as the Paresi called themselves, had originated. It was also there that the mythical hero Wazare organized the world, distributing the surrounding land among the various Paresi clans and giving names to the places where they would live.

Now, Rondon had come to fulfill a function similar to Wazare's, "correcting" a world that had become disorderly, unstable, and threatening. He produced maps, which themselves seemed remarkable to a culture without writing, and in the presence of Paresi leaders decreed, much as Wazare had done at the dawn of time: "This here is yours, and that there, over that way, belongs to the whites."[10]

We do not know whether Rondon deliberately chose Ponte de Pedra as his center of operations because he already knew of the myth and wanted to make an overwhelming initial impression, or whether it was just serendipity that led him there. In all likelihood, he wanted to establish his base there simply because the location offered the best physical conditions and easy access to water. But there is no doubt that his decision had a powerful impact on the Paresi, who saw Rondon's decision to install himself at that holy spot as fulfillment of a divine prophecy.

Once Rondon had cemented his friendship with the Paresi, he acted, as best he could, as their protector. They expected and demanded this of him, for Paresi society was strongly hierarchical, with a father figure at the top. In years to come, he was regularly called on to intercede in Paresi affairs, even by telegraph when he was not in the region. But one incident in particular has passed into Paresi lore as an example of Rondon's beneficence and zeal on their behalf.

Not long after the first station on the telegraph line north from Cuiabá went into operation, white businessmen from the state capital and others, lured by the promise of profit, established ranches along the new route. One of them, a judge from nearby Diamantino, used Paresi workers to clear his fields but, Rondon heard, did not pay them. Instead, he pressed them into wage slavery—charging the workers exorbitant prices for the food they ate and the tools they used, so that costs far outstripped their meager wages. These Paresi had no notion of money or credit, and when Rondon learned of this exploitation, he became irate and immediately went to the rancher's homestead to confront him.

"You're not a judge, you're a piece of shit," he berated the judge, according to the Indians' account. Taken aback, the official tried to justify his actions, saying the Paresi could not leave until they repaid the debts they had contracted. But Rondon was having none of it. "They don't owe anything to anyone," he replied. "Whoever heard of an Indian in debt? Indians have free will, they live in freedom, they don't live like us. I have a mind to teach you a lesson. You're no authority whatsoever, you're not good enough for that."[11]

Rondon's tongue-lashing of the judge took place with many Paresi as witnesses. To provide some form of compensation to the enslaved Indians, Rondon also ordered the judge to slaughter several head of cattle and prepare a feast for the Paresi that very evening. The Indians needed to eat heartily, Rondon announced to all present, because first thing in the morning they were all leaving with him, as free men.

"He took those people who deserved it out of slavery," Maximiano Enoré, the source for this story, concluded nearly seventy years later. "When something was wrong, he put himself on the front line and set things right."[12]

On numerous other occasions, Rondon intervened to prevent powerful outsiders from forcing the Paresi to become their slaves, servants, or concubines. But this highly personal approach, typical at the time of both Brazilian society and Indigenous cultures, had obvious disadvantages. Rondon could not be everywhere at once, and the more distant he was from an abusive situation, the more difficult it was to exercise his authority. The well-being of entire tribal groups largely depended on the goodwill and moral scruples of individuals such as Rondon, or his subalterns—or the missionaries, whose motives he distrusted.

This clearly was not a workable long-term solution. Brazil was modernizing, and as the state extended its reach, settlers moved en masse to the interior. Rondon recognized this, and as a result began pushing for the creation of a new government agency specifically charged with overseeing Indigenous affairs. He began searching wherever he could for templates for such an entity: in his papers from the first decade of the twentieth century, for example, we find a copy of the organizational manual and federal statute governing the U.S. Bureau of Indian Affairs, forwarded to him by the Brazilian legation in Washington. But while Rondon marveled that the BIA commissioner himself was occasionally a Native American, he objected to several aspects of U.S. policy, such as restrictions on Indigenous languages, religions, and culture in schools, and thought the cultural, political, and social differences between Brazil and the United States too great for him to adapt an American model. That led him to investigate the policies of other Latin American countries with significant Indigenous populations: he was particularly interested in Mexico, since he had long admired Benito Juárez, the first Indigenous president of Mexico.

With the Paresi now an ally, Rondon intended to begin exploration of the Juruena River, whose headwaters he thought lay somewhere in their domains. Though the Juruena was known to be one of the two principal sources of the Tapajós River, which in turn is one of the main tributaries of the Amazon, its upper reaches were a mystery, one that Rondon thought could be solved with the help of his new friends. So in September 1907 he and his men set off on an old trail in the direction of a river he assumed to be the Juruena, with Paresi hunters accompanying them; along the way, they paused at Paresi villages that had been alerted to their passage and whose inhabitants greeted them ebulliently. In his diary, Rondon described the landscape as lush, and he marveled at the beauty of the magnificent waterfalls the explorers encountered as they made their way north.

But everything changed on October 10. The trail suddenly ended, and Rondon's scouts told him they had now reached the limit of Paresi territory. Such was their loyalty that Rondon's Paresi scouts were willing to continue with him. But the expedition's task now became much more difficult. Going forward, the explorers would have to use machetes and sickles to make their way through the luxuriant bush; they would also have to remain constantly alert to the possibility of ambush by the Nhambiquara. So Rondon gave his men a couple of days to celebrate Columbus Day and prepare for the challenge ahead, making camp on the bank of a previously unmapped stream.

Just hours after they resumed their march, they came across the first sign of the presence of the Nhambiquara: a pair of crude hunting shelters with arched entrances. Soon, two dogs went missing, never to be seen again. And when they came to a river that Rondon immediately named the Papagaio, because of the many parrots that flocked there, they found another sign: a rope footbridge across the stream. Continuing, sometimes in heavy rain, they eventually came to a ridge that Rondon took to be the watershed between the Papagaio and the river they were seeking. Reaching the top, with a grassy plain ahead of him, Rondon caught his first glimpse of a Nhambiquara tribesman: "We sighted in the middle of a great plain a completely naked Indian, who we presume must belong to this legendary tribe."[13]

Because the Nhambiquara had a fearsome reputation and were known to be hostile both to Europeans and to other Indigenous groups, Rondon had to adopt a very different strategy of engagement. Moving cautiously, not wanting to alarm the Nhambiquara hunter, Rondon could see that the man was loosening a beehive from a tree to harvest its honey, and that he was unarmed, having laid his bow and arrows and a club on the ground. It was only when the expedition's macheteros approached Rondon that the Nhambiquara became aware of their presence: "Upon hearing the noise, he turned around without showing any alarm and continued on his way."[14] Rondon hoped that the man, who surely had noted that Rondon and his soldiers were heavily armed, would return to his village and tell his kinfolk of the nonviolent encounter.

Despite the danger of ambush, Rondon reminded his men of their pledge of nonviolence and soldiered on, certain that Nhambiquara lookouts were tracking him now. Early the next morning, already on the march, he spotted a particularly majestic sucupira tree, with its distinctive purple flowers, and climbed to its top to get a better view. Off in the distance, down in a valley, was a silver ribbon of water that was very likely the Juruena. With a small advance party, he plunged into the bush, and before the morning was out, they heard the roar of a waterfall. As they reached it, they spotted an Indian trail, which they followed to a crystalline river, some 250 feet wide. "Our enthusiasm was indescribable," Rondon wrote. "We celebrated with a volley from my Winchester and from the two Colt 45's."[15]

After a trek of forty-eight days and 384 miles, Rondon and his men had finally reached the source of the Juruena. Now he had to decide whether to continue, or turn back: more than half his men were sick, and their pack animals were weakened from having no place to graze. But the new trail suggested that a Nhambiquara village was nearby, and he decided to forge ahead. As his men and animals rested, he mapped the vicinity, took astronomical readings, and rummaged through the expedition's supplies to ensure he still had a stock of items to offer the Nhambiquara as tokens of friendship. He was disappointed to discover that only two machetes could be spared, one brand-new and one used: machetes were, he wrote, "the pound sterling of the wilderness."[16] On October 22, the expedition, somewhat refreshed, headed out again.

A half mile from their campsite, the attack came. A Paresi scout named Domingos was in the lead of the exploration group, armed with a Winchester and riding a mule, followed by Rondon, also mounted and carrying the Remington rifle he often used for hunting, along with two of his subalterns, both with Colt double-action revolvers. Suddenly, he sensed something darting past his head, "quick and fleeting, as if it were a bird that had passed in front of me at the level of my eyes, extremely close."[17] Instinctively, he turned to follow the object's path and saw that it had lodged in the soil. It was an arrow, its shaft and fletching still quivering.

Rondon now turned his mule toward the attackers, but faced another salvo of arrows, one of which came in cheek-high and struck the edge of the pith helmet strung around his neck. He found himself staring directly at a pair of Nhambiquara warriors, whose eyes were as "hard, penetrating, as implacable as the points of their silent arrows."[18] He saw them preparing for another assault, and drew his Remington in response, but instead of aiming at them, he still had the presence of mind to fire into the air, hoping to scare them away.

A third arrow was already on its way, and struck Rondon in the chest. But in an amazing stroke of luck, it embedded itself in the leather bandolier strung across his torso, where he stored his bullets.[19] The Nhambiquara attackers, as well as the Paresi advance scout, saw that the arrow had hit Rondon and was now protruding from his chest. But the attackers also noticed that he did not fall, and so, amazed, they turned and disappeared back into the jungle. By now the rest of the expedition's advance team had arrived. With emotions running high, they wanted to pursue the "impudent" Nhambiquara and teach them a lesson. But Rondon made them turn around and head back to Paresi country.

"Faithful to my program of only penetrating the wilderness with peaceful intentions and never in a warlike fashion, I could not consent to the slightest reprisal," Rondon would later explain. "I had not come to conquer Indians through violence but to bring to the Juruena the knowledge indispensable to the construction of the telegraph line, as a means of summoning them to civilization." Nothing, he added, "could justify the kind of insistence that could degenerate into war with the inhabitants of the region." Avoiding hostilities, he argued, was not only a question of justice, "but also in the interest of future operations of the Commission."[20] So after examining and photographing the arrows the Nhambiquara had shot at them, Rondon began his retreat.

But when the advance party reached the main camp, and the other members of the expedition learned the details of the ambush, resistance to Rondon's pacifism became so intense that it bordered on insubordination. The men "argued about the shame that would fall upon us if we did not react by showing our superiority," he wrote. "I had great difficulty in making them understand that our mission had to be fraternal and peaceful."[21] In the end, he prevented rebellion only by insisting that the soldiers put themselves in the Nhambiquara's place.

"If someone invaded your house to kill and rob, what would you do?" he asked. "Without a doubt, we would kill them! So how come you want the Indians to behave differently?"[22]

Once the men's anger had cooled, Rondon ordered them to construct a raised platform, where gifts for the Nhambiquara were placed. Rondon left the usual tools and trinkets, but also ordered that each man rummage through his backpack and contribute at least one item to the pile.

Subsequent stages of the withdrawal, however, did not completely calm the troops or convince them that their commander's peaceful approach was correct. The Nhambiquara continued to harass the expedition. There were no more attacks on the explorers themselves, but the Nhambiquara directed fusillades of arrows into pack animals, which had to be abandoned. Later, Rondon would learn that the Nhambiquara assumed he and his men were part of a group of rubber tappers who had invaded the tribe's territory a few months earlier and killed several hunters. But when they saw Rondon emerge unscathed after being struck by a poison arrow, one that the Nhambiquara had themselves seen jutting from his chest, they were also hesitant to attack, believing that he had supernatural powers.[23]

After his Paresi scouts came across two more Nhambiquara hunting shelters, Rondon, hoping to avoid another ambush, decided to take a fifty-five-mile detour around the area. The explorers came upon a rudimentary rubber tapper's trail, and followed that. This was fortunate because, as Rondon later noted, both his men and their animals were growing famished and exhausted, and hacking a path through the jungle now seemed beyond their ability. "Even the strongest," he wrote, "were now worn out."[24] Stopping to rest or hunting for food seemed too dangerous, so Rondon decided to push on to the Papagaio River, where they would be much closer to Paresi territory and safety.

But when they arrived at the riverbank, on November 4, what they found only added to their distress. The canoe they had left there was gone: the Nhambiquara had evidently untied it and maliciously let it drift away downstream. "The level of disappointment was so high that it took from my dejected companions the last remnants of their courage and energy," Rondon wrote. To swim across the river "would be impossible for half-starved men drained by fatigue, ill, terrified by the possibility of an attack."[25]

Rondon knew he had to do something. As other members of the expedition lay spent on the riverbank, he fashioned several tree branches into a large circle, then attached a cowhide to form a crude improvised raft. To this he fastened a rope, then plunged into the water with a first load of cargo and swam across to the safe side of the river, hauling the raft by the rope, gripped between his teeth. After depositing the cargo on the other shore, he repeated the process until all the equipment was safely unloaded there. Then he began transporting the sickest and weakest of his companions on the same raft. Taking heart, those able to swim entered the water one by one and made their way to the other side. Three hours later, the crossing was complete: the men and their equipment had reached safety without anyone or anything being lost. The men cheered their commander, who in turn praised them for their bravery.

After surviving this grueling ordeal, the men's confidence returned. Once back in Paresi territory, Rondon's men could hunt and replenish their food stocks, and within a couple of days they encountered a friendly group of Paresi hunters, who promised to spread word that the expedition had returned from the land of the dreaded Nhambiquara. When the exploration team reached the first Paresi village, its members were received warmly and invited to feast on delicacies prepared especially for them. By month's end, following brief detours to the home villages of the Paresi scouts to say farewell and pay them with knives, machetes, scythes, and clothing, Rondon and his men were back at an army base north of Cuiabá, their initial mission finally completed.

Rondon would spend the early months of 1908 inspecting the construction work done on the first phase of the telegraph line. On orders from the commission's doctor, however, he took a brief, enforced rest after a bout of malaria and a near collapse while delivering a dedication speech for one of the new stations. But the problem of the Nhambiquara—and how to win their cooperation—was never far from his mind, and would remain so for the next five years. There was simply no alternative to an agreement with them: their territory blocked the only viable path for the telegraph line as it snaked its way to the north and west toward the Madeira River.

Yet the Nhambiquara seemed determined to hold themselves apart. Their language bore no relation to any other in the Amazon, and though they often lived near rivers, they hardly participated in the intertribal trade often conducted via water routes. Rondon estimated their population at around ten thousand, broken into more than a dozen different subgroups with distinct identities and customs. They owned few possessions and were focused on the spiritual: anthropologists would later describe them as having "an apparently simple material culture and an extremely complex cosmology."[26] The Paresi in particular regarded their Nhambiquara neighbors as backward, due to their habit of sleeping on the ground, sometimes out in the open, instead of using hammocks.

In the end, Rondon decided that a nonviolent but intimidating show of strength might be the most effective way to stave off future attacks and persuade the Nhambiquara to accept some form of peaceful coexistence. Accordingly, in late June of 1908 he assembled a new expedition, composed of 127 men and dozens of pack animals, and set off for the outpost at Aldeia Queimada, or "Burnt Village." This was a risky approach, and he knew it: for one thing, moving across the wilderness with such a large force created logistical challenges he usually preferred to avoid, and once the explorers left the savanna and entered the jungle, their pack animals had nowhere to graze.

But the expeditionaries themselves constituted the biggest source of danger. The larger the military unit deployed, the greater the likelihood of a chance encounter with a Nhambiquara hunting party—and an unwanted outburst of violence that might sabotage Rondon's long-term plan. Many of his men were strangers to the frontier and its ways, including fifty-two inexperienced recruits who would remain at the permanent operational base he hoped to build at the Juruena River; they might easily panic or blunder into conflict.

Rondon therefore implemented an intensive program of indoctrination in nonviolence as he and his men traversed the wilderness. In his order of the day on July 30, for example, he instructed his troopers that even if wounded in a confrontation with the Nhambiquara, they should take no reprisals. If they came to an abandoned village, nothing could be stolen or burned: everything had to be left intact in order to demonstrate the expedition's good intentions. Rondon also reiterated what he had said to his first exploration team, that as members of the Brazilian Army, they were the invaders, and the inhabitants of the region had every right to defend themselves.

Once the expedition crossed into Nhambiquara territory in August, he assumed that it would be constantly watched, so Rondon took additional precautions to avoid conflict. At night, he posted sentinels around the campsite and also ordered all soldiers not on guard duty to turn in their weapons, in order to avoid panicky responses to strange sounds in the jungle: the explorers could hear the haunting music of Nhambiquara playing their nose flutes, and strange animal calls by Indians communicating with one another in the dark. This frightened the soldiers, and "few slept," Rondon reported, but he continued to preach nonviolence. "Let us be vigilant, so as not to give in to the impulses of military pride that exalt courage and thereby make us forget about prudence and, above all, kindness."[27]

The first test of Rondon's teachings came late in August, a month into the expedition, as they neared the Juruena, and the outcome was not exactly encouraging. Rondon was supervising a tree-felling for the construction of a canoe when he heard a commotion at the rear of the column, where sappers were clearing a trail. A terrified soldier shouted to him: "An Indian woman shot me with an arrow!"[28] Nhambiquara men had long hair, so the soldier had mistaken one of them for a woman. Rondon immediately ordered the cornet sounded, and after his troops gathered, he marched them back to the site of the encounter, to show them no Indians were still there. He went into the bush alone, and fired a shot in the air to summon the expedition's dogs. "That was enough to make all of them fire their weapons convulsively," he wrote, "and it was difficult for them to hear my order of 'cease fire!'"[29]

Rondon intensified his indoctrination while the men worked on building the new rear base on the banks of the Juruena. By September 7, Brazilian Independence Day, he was able to inaugurate the Juruena Central Detachment with a display of patriotic pomp that also demonstrated to the Nhambiquara the technological prowess of the Rondon Commission. A gramophone was produced and played the national anthem, which echoed through the river valley and, Rondon later learned, both fascinated and alarmed the Indians.

Rockets and fireworks shot into the sky, and powerful sticks of dynamite were also detonated, generating thunderous booms "ricocheting to the north and to the south."[30]

Rondon made a speech, largely directed at the fifty-two recruits who would remain behind to defend the new base. He warned them of dangers they would face, but once again emphasized the importance of never using violence. The success of the entire expedition, as well as the lives of their fellow explorers, he told them, depended on their restraint, even in the face of provocation.

Three days later, Rondon and his remaining forces headed out, with two Paresi scouts who had accompanied him the year before once again in the lead. Their task was twofold: gather the scientific and cartographic information necessary for the construction of the telegraph line and, if possible, make peaceful contact with the Nhambiquara, preferably the same group that had attacked them in 1907.

The initial signs were promising. Before long, they came upon a village whose residents had fled rather than offer resistance; a fire's embers were still glowing and pots full of porridge were left behind. Among other abandoned items, Rondon discovered that some of the gifts left the previous year had been found and were in use. Also, a Paresi scout on reconnaissance encountered a Nhambiquara hunter, who fled without a fight. At another abandoned site, the explorers found an arrow embedded in the walls of the main lodge, from which two bundles of corn hung. Rondon's men interpreted this as a hostile act, but Toloiri, the senior Paresi accompanying the expedition and Rondon's closest Paresi friend, said no, the symbolism was exactly the opposite: a gesture of thanks to acknowledge receipt of Rondon's gifts. And while the Nhambiquara left tracks around the improvised corrals where the expedition's oxen and donkeys were kept each night, none of the pack animals was shot or stolen this time.

But then two messengers arrived with a sheaf of telegrams for Rondon, all of them containing bad news. Discipline was breaking down back at the Juruena base. Worse, farther to the rear, work on the telegraph line was "paralyzed." In addition, resupply lines for food and construction equipment were not functioning properly. As a result, recruits were deserting en masse "so as to escape the tortures of hunger."[31] And alarmingly, the commission's line of credit had been suspended due to the national government's failure to pay Rondon's suppliers in Mato Grosso.

Rondon learned of all this misfortune after climbing to the top of a tall tree, where he had just spotted a bluish-tinged, unexplored plateau in the distance. He was eager to map and gather scientific data from those highlands, which were vaguely designated in atlases as the "Northern Range" and about which even the Paresi knew little. But duty obligated him to return to the rear to address these unpleasant administrative problems. "Tremendous disappointment!"[32] he wrote. So he sent Lt. João Salustiano Lyra, his most trusted subaltern, and a small team ahead to check out the approaches to the escarpment, while the others buried supplies in the ground in the expectation of returning.

As for Rondon himself, he began preparing his responses to the many levels of bureaucracy that had to be either chastised, cajoled, or consulted: "The ministers, directors of Engineering and of Telegraphs, the president of the State and the military commander of the District."[33] The 1908 expedition, so promising at the outset, had come to an abrupt end: "Now it has become urgent to head back, so as to avoid the collapse of the giant undertaking" of the telegraph line itself, he wrote. A conciliation with the Nhambiquara, so vital to the commission's long-term success, had to be postponed yet again.

VIII

"Returning Immediately, through the Other Side"

FOR RONDON, EXPLORATION had always been about discovering limits—both geographic and personal—and then pushing past them. Each new expedition seemed more audacious and ambitious than the last, as if designed to test the threshold of human endurance. Beginning with his first foray into the Araguaia in 1890, he had always ratcheted up the physical challenge he would face in his next mission and recruited collaborators—whether civilian or military, Brazilians or foreigners—who shared his sense of enterprise, scientific curiosity, dedication, and patriotism. That attitude had served him well for almost twenty years, ensuring him a level of expertise unmatched anywhere in the world.

But in 1909, Rondon almost went too far. In his zeal to advance the telegraph line and fulfill the tasks entrusted to him, he subjected himself and his men to a level of danger and physical and mental exhaustion that surpassed anything they had ever experienced and which they could not sustain. In the end, they were saved only by an encounter in the jungle so unlikely that the word "serendipity" vastly understates its improbability.

The year began innocuously. Rondon had been separated from his family for more than two years, but on February 23 they reunited in Corumbá, where Chiquita and the children—there were six now, following the births of Marina Sylvia in 1903, Beatriz Emilia in 1905, and Maria de Molina in 1907—had just arrived after the long boat trip from Rio de Janeiro. It was a joyous occasion, but one also tinged with worry for Chiquita. Ever since a Nhambiquara arrow struck Rondon in 1907, she had wanted him to travel with more protection, fearing he might be attacked again. Specifically, she wanted him to wear an arrow-proof armored vest. Rondon agreed, on one condition: that all other members of any expedition he commanded also receive the same protection. Government officials quickly vetoed that proposal as too expensive, as Rondon knew they would, and so Chiquita had to give up the idea. But Rondon did acquiesce to his wife's insistence that he buy an uncharacteristically luxurious new saddle to lessen his discomfort.

With his family on its way back to Rio after a six-week interlude together, Rondon, somewhat melancholy and still feeling weak from the malaria that troubled him throughout 1908, began in mid-April to organize another push into the wilderness. The preparations took several weeks: 500 oxen and 160 mules left from Cuiabá, but all except 50 perished from hunger or disease on the way to Rondon's base camp at Aldeia Queimada, forcing him to seek replacements as best he could. And in May, riding out to visit the Paresi on his way north to base camp, he was saddened by even worse news. Rondon had hoped to convince his friend Toloiri to join him again as chief scout on the upcoming expedition, but arriving in Toloiri's village, he found his Paresi comrade stricken with pneumonia, and could not save his life.

The most serious challenges to Rondon's plans, however, were bureaucratic and political. On returning from the Juruena, he had submitted detailed expense reports for 1907 and 1908 to the ministry in Rio as required, hoping to accelerate full restoration of the commission's depleted line of credit. Six months passed before he was reimbursed. In the meantime, he put any thought of exploration on hold and made no further purchases of gifts for the Nhambiquara. Instead, he focused on getting his construction detachments in shape, improving logistics and communications between front and rear lines, and restoring cordial ties with local merchants.

After a month's illness, President Afonso Pena also succumbed to pneumonia, on June 14, leaving Rondon without a patron to protect him. Increasingly, grumbling was heard in the army about how his Amazon venture was sapping the military budget, while in Congress Rondon's project had become entangled in the acrimonious political debate that erupted as Pena grew more debilitated and his opponents sought to block the ascension of Vice President Nilo Peçanha, his constitutional successor. Voices in both the military and the legislative branch even began demanding that the telegraph line be defunded altogether.

On June 2, his credit line finally restored—and his own prestige enhanced by a promotion to lieutenant colonel—Rondon left Juruena. His plan was bold, but potentially risky. In order to operate at peak efficiency, he divided his expeditionary forces into two groups, with himself as leader of one and Capt. Manoel Pinheiro and Lt. Amilcar Botelho de Magalhães in charge of the other. Rondon's group, with Lyra second in command, would head northwest by land to find the headwaters of the Jaci-Paraná River and then descend its unexplored upper reaches; the other team, laden with supplies, would travel by boat to the Madeira, follow its course south to the mouth of the Jaci-Paraná, and ascend that river to a designated meeting place. Until the two parties encountered each other, Rondon and his team would have to supplement their supplies by foraging for food in a harsh wilderness that had never been properly mapped.

Rondon's group, forty-two men in all, was an odd mixture of veterans and rookies. Left without Toloiri's sage guidance, Rondon turned to a pair of Paresi scouts from another village; he was certain of their trustworthiness because of a just-concluded treaty of alliance between their people and the Brazilian state, which Rondon himself had brokered. He also selected several of his most experienced subalterns, as well as scientists from the National Museum who had accompanied him before, among them the botanist Frederico Carlos Hoehne and the zoologist Alípio de Miranda Ribeiro. There was also a motley, unseasoned crew of fourteen military recruits and eighteen locally hired farmhands serving as pack-animal herders, who had never been tested by a monthslong trek through the wilds.

While Rondon and this advance team explored the uncharted land ahead to determine the route of the telegraph line, most of the

600 men under his permanent command were tasked with erecting telegraph poles in already explored areas. As Rondon was proceeding north from Aldeia Queimada, some 250 of his men headed in the opposite direction; if all went well, they would eventually meet another construction crew of 350 men moving northwest from the line's starting point. The officers in charge of the two units would handle routine difficulties, but in the event of grave problems with engineering or Indians, messengers would be sent overland from Juruena, follow trails until they caught up with Rondon, then wait for an order that would be conveyed to the rear guard for implementation. It was a cumbersome and inefficient process, but until the telegraph line was completed, lower-ranking officers would have little autonomy, and ultimate authority would be concentrated in Rondon's own hands.

The start of the expedition was not auspicious. For more than a month, Rondon had been running a very high temperature, due to a continuing bout of malaria. In early May, visiting the Paresi, he wrote in his diary: "This fever just won't leave me; since April 28 it's been reappearing regularly, every night, in spite of the medicines taken." When June arrived, his situation still had not improved; this was unusual, and it worried him, even though he had confronted a similar problem in 1908. On the day the expedition departed, he confessed to his diary that "in spite of the medical precautions, my physical state continues not to inspire confidence."[1]

Nevertheless, he insisted on going, and once the expedition was underway, Rondon refused to allow Joaquim Tanajura, the expedition's doctor, to examine him, even though every other member had to submit to a thorough checkup, which resulted in several soldiers and civilians being sent back to Aldeia Queimada. But Rondon did not want to lose any more men or time, and assembled his remaining troops for a pep talk. "I'll go ahead alone if I have to," he declared, "but all those willing to go with me, take one step forward." Seeing that no one had backed out, he then barked, "Forward march!"[2]

So they continued. But Tanajura insisted that Rondon mount an ox and ride rather than walk, to save his energy. At first, Rondon reluctantly agreed, but because everyone else continued on foot, he wrote, "with every meter, my self-respect diminished." He soon dismounted, countering the doctor's objections by saying, "It is my duty to set an example," even though, he conceded, "I'm going to be sick as hell."³

A week later, Rondon caught sight of a first group of Nhambiquara. Passing through a bamboo forest, he glimpsed ten hunters in a clearing, who ignored him, slipping back into the dense growth. Two days later, the explorers reached a supply point where they had wrapped and buried provisions and equipment in the ground the year before, but immediately discovered, to their immense disappointment, that the Nhambiquara had been there first and destroyed as much as they could. Fortunately, the Indians had not known what to do with tinned cans of food, so these were salvaged. But both incidents reminded Rondon that going forward, he and his men would have to remain constantly vigilant in order to avoid the confrontations and attacks that had plagued earlier expeditions.

The imposing Serra do Norte mountain range loomed in the distance now, and that seemed to invigorate Rondon. The expedition came upon a deep valley with luxuriant grass—a rarity in the region—and was pleasantly surprised to find that some of the sickly cattle they abandoned the year before had not only survived but flourished, growing fat from grazing in the lush pastures. Rondon decided to set up a ranch at the location, and ordered a handful of his men to tend the animals and to plant cassava and vegetables there. Regarding the Nhambiquara, who he assumed were observing the expedition's every move, Rondon's instructions were simple: do not seek contact with them, and when, inevitably, they steal crops or livestock, attempt no reprisals. And if they approach you out of curiosity, try to "initiate a relationship of friendliness."

By the last day of June, Rondon's team was atop the Serra do Norte, and preparing to settle in for a long, pleasant stay as they mapped the area: up on the plateau wild game was plentiful, the soil fertile, and the weather cooler, which discouraged mosquitoes and energized the explorers. Rondon intended to construct another outpost here, and his men set cheerfully to work. Almost immediately, though, a messenger from the rear arrived with telegrams, letters, and handwritten messages that, read in a single sitting, soured Rondon's mood and indeed jeopardized his mission.

Back at Juruena, he was informed, two of his men had just perished from beriberi. From there, the news only worsened: he also learned of the death of President Afonso Pena, "the Telegraph Commission's great friend and protector,"[4] and a subsequent telegram sent from commission headquarters back in Rio alerted him that the telegraph project might possibly be disbanded altogether. Yet another message seemed to confirm that: military headquarters ordered Rondon to return promptly to the capital. As the messenger waited for a response, Rondon mulled over his situation and then dictated a brief reply for transmission to the high command: "Coming back immediately, through the other side."[5]

Rondon's clever, ambiguously misleading response is a classic example of *jogo de cintura*—a much-admired talent in Brazil for reacting quickly and skillfully, using deft footwork to avoid or extract oneself from an unpleasant situation. By appearing to obey an order without actually complying, Rondon lessened his risk of facing charges of insubordination when he eventually made his way back to the capital. By then, the political scenario might have become more favorable; certainly Rondon's allies in Congress and friends in the press would now have more time to fight on his behalf, in coordination with the commission's office in Rio. But at the same time, Rondon intensified the pressure on himself: the expedition now needed more than ever to deliver spectacular achievements in order to justify his defiance and expenditures.

All through July and well into August, as Rondon's health gradually returned to normal, the explorers assiduously mapped the entire basin of the Serra do Norte: at one point, Lyra, surveying to the west, advised Rondon he had stumbled on the "deepest and most profusely entangled forest he had ever seen."[6] As they worked, "all around us we found indications of Indians: beaten-down paths, hunters' blinds and other signs that we were near one or more lodges," while "to the northwest, we could see large plumes of smoke rising into the air."[7] Out hunting one day, two of his men shot a deer and then saw a pair of Indians, who apparently had been stalking the same prey and, frightened by the gunfire, jumped out from behind their blinds and dashed into the thicket. The explorers took the deer back to camp but, following the usual Rondon Commission protocol, left behind knives and machetes for the Indian hunters, "so that they might see that our interest was in trading for objects, not in taking what belonged to them."[8]

By mid-August, the expedition seemed to be discovering a new river every day. The region contained the headwaters of a tight network of streams, flowing away in various directions, at least one for every cardinal point of the compass. Many quickly widened and deepened, suggesting that they were significant tributaries of much larger rivers. On August 16, for example, Rondon laconically noted in his diary the specifications of a stream twelve meters wide, half a meter deep, and with a measured flow of one decimeter per second; it was the height of the dry season, and though some stretches of the river seemed dry, he perceived waterfalls ahead and decided to turn back. Rondon named the stream the River of Doubt, little imagining it would, only a few years later, present him with his greatest challenge as an explorer.

Atop the Serra do Norte, the mapping work had revealed an easily accessible valley heading due north and then off to the east. But the projected telegraph line had to follow a northwesterly course, into Lyra's "profusely tangled forest," and so the expedition headed in that direction. Almost immediately, the going became difficult: as they descended, the jungle thickened and the number of streams to be forded increased. Progress slowed, since the dense forest made it difficult for pack animals to find any kind of natural trail. To lighten the load, Rondon ordered all the expedition's "less necessary things" jettisoned.

After three months of haphazard encounters with Indigenous groups, the expedition finally began making solid contacts in early September. These were not Nhambiquara, but other tribes whose docility seemed to indicate they had never had contact with "civilized" people, and certainly not with the rapacious rubber tappers, who made enemies everywhere they went. Lyra and a Paresi scout were the first to stumble on such a group: two men and two women who withdrew into the thicket as the explorers approached their huts and then watched passively as Lyra examined the dwellings. The Paresi scout tried unsuccessfully to talk to them, then departed after depositing gifts on the ground and making friendly gestures.

On the way back to the expedition's campsite, they met a woman carrying a large basket of wild pineapples, accompanied by a small child, and once again tried to engage in conversation. After almost bumping into them, "she made no gesture of surprise or fright, only stepping to the side of the trail to indicate to the strangers the route they should follow."⁹ Encouraged by that response, the Paresi scout asked for directions to the "Big River," but could understand only one word of the woman's long and cordial reply: "water." Lyra, meanwhile, amused himself by taking her child in his arms and playfully teasing the tyke until it began to giggle. When they related these episodes to Rondon, he was delighted, for it suggested that the commission would encounter no hostility when construction teams returned to build the telegraph line.

The contacts with Indigenous groups became more frequent, and Rondon continued to do all he could to build their trust. A few days after Lyra's adventure, Rondon was out with the two Paresi scouts when they heard a very large group marching through the forest with their belongings, most likely an entire community looking for a new place to settle. Rondon's dogs charged, frightening the Indians, and as they fled in panic, a young boy was separated from his parents, trampled, and somehow left behind. The child seated himself calmly in Rondon's lap, talking incessantly all the while. Rondon decided it was best to leave the boy where he was, gave him a silver pocketknife, and left presents for the rest of the group as a sign of his peaceful intentions.

The rainy season began in October with Rondon and his men penetrating deeper into the jungle yet seemingly no closer to the river sighted from the Serra do Norte. Occasionally, they would find traces of an Indigenous trail, but Rondon, wary of an ambush, preferred to avoid these. After their tranquil interlude atop the Serra do Norte, his team was growing discouraged and fearful; one man deserted, and even the trusted Lyra urged Rondon to turn back, arguing for descending the River of Doubt, which he thought might be a tributary of the Jaci-Paraná.

Rondon, however, insisted on plunging ahead, ordering that pack animals be left behind and that every man carry only as much as he could transport on his back. That meant abandoning valuable scientific material—zoological and anthropological items collected for the National Museum, for example, as well as photographic plates—in order to speed up the march. After resting on Columbus Day, the caboclos, the mixed-race civilian backwoodsmen Rondon had hired as porters and muleteers, began constructing a large canoe. One third of the men, Rondon decided, would descend the nearby Pimenta Bueno River in the rough-hewn dugout. They were ordered to live off the land as best they could, to reduce the strain on provisions.

But soon it was clear that even more drastic measures were needed. On October 23, a team bringing supplies from the rear caught up with Rondon, but only two burros and two cows had survived, "and these so skinny and fatigued that they could barely remain upright."[10] Rondon's solution was to divide the expedition into three smaller groups. One would return to the rear base, recovering the animals, provisions, and scientific specimens abandoned along the trail. The second would explore the Jamari River, which, according to their maps, would eventually link up with the Pimenta Bueno. And the third, under Rondon's command, would continue overland to the northwest.

Rondon's ability to subsist on small amounts of food, and to go many hours between meals, sometimes made him oblivious to the needs of others, and so it was as stores began to run out. One day hunters shot a raccoon-like coati and brought it back to camp to prepare for lunch. But the expedition's zoologist immediately noticed that its coat was of an unusual color and pattern, suggesting it was probably a new species, and asked that it be completely preserved. Caught between the hunger of his men and his love of science, Rondon chose the latter, and lunch that day ended up being the usual nuts and wild fruit instead of a welcome piece of meat.

Meanwhile, back in Rio de Janeiro alarm was beginning to pervade press coverage of the expedition, no doubt adding to Chiquita's level of anxiety. On October 2, a Nhambiquara attack on a resupply team was reported in dramatically embellished form, so she fruit-lessly sought additional details from the commission's office in the capital. Because Rondon had now advanced so far beyond the last telegraph station, he was unable to send her any message assuring her that all was well, much less dispatch his daily, detailed letters.

Similarly, as the weeks passed and Rondon did not reappear, the members of the Botelho de Magalhães contingent grew increasingly concerned. They had arrived at the designated meeting point on the Jaci-Paraná in mid-September, and every night, promptly at 8 p.m., they sent signals into the sky in the hope that Rondon was nearby and they could draw his attention. When the evenings were clear, they would occasionally send a white weather balloon rising up above the trees as a kind of beacon. But the response was always a disappointing silence, rather than shouts of jubilation or a volley in return.[11]

As the main party advanced, its contacts with Indigenous groups gradually diminished, and then ceased altogether. In one sense this was a relief, since it meant Rondon no longer had to worry about hostile encounters where he might lose men or they might fire at Indians. But the underlying, ominous implication was not lost on the explorers: the terrain they were entering was so harsh, with moun-tains so impenetrable and a forest so primeval, that even the hardiest Indians made a point of avoiding it.

By mid-November, Rondon's compass showed they had reached a point eleven degrees south of the equator and sixty-three degrees west of the prime meridian. According to their maps, they were close to the headwaters of the Jaci-Paraná, and so when they came to a stream, they decided to descend it. After several days, they spotted on the riverbank two trees inscribed with initials in capital letters, surely representing the claim of a rubber tapper who had recently worked there. Upon reaching a small clearing five miles farther downstream they found more encouraging signs: several opened tins of condensed milk and canned fruit, as well as some broken crockery. The river had turned to the northeast, away from the direction they expected, but they decided to persist, convinced that this was merely a slight cartographic imprecision, and at night they began looking to the sky for the homing beacons launched by the main resupply team.

They would soon discover their mistake. On November 26, Lyra was chopping a path through the tangled brush when he heard a voice crying, "Help! I'm lost in this jungle!" Lyra was initially elated: he assumed they had finally met someone from the Botelho de Magalhães team. But that feeling quickly gave way to shock and bafflement. Before him, sobbing with emotion and exhaustion, stood a tall, gaunt stranger in rags with long, unkempt blond hair and blue eyes, "in the final stage of the physical misery to which a human being can be reduced after a long period of cruel suffering and terrible privations."[12]

The man's name was Miguel Sanka, and he was a twenty-four-year-old Hungarian-born adventurer who had made his way north to Manaus seeking his fortune. There, failing to find a clerical job, he signed on as an "administrator" at a rubber-tapping post, accepting a big advance on his wages in the form of provisions and equipment. Once out in the jungle, Sanka realized that the job he had been promised—that of a bookkeeper—actually was nothing of the sort, that he was now just another indentured worker. But he had no way to escape by going back the way he came: he knew from his journey upstream that a heavily armed security force maintained checkpoints on the river and that they beat and sometimes, according to what he was told, even shot any runaways they caught.

Sanka's situation only worsened when he came down with malaria. In a feverish state, he decided to flee his riverside hut, but became utterly lost. This was in the first days of July, he told Lyra, and so for almost five months he had been wandering through the jungle, without a compass to steer him or matches for a fire. Initially, following the sun, he headed westward with a fishing line, a machete, a hammock, and an almanac as his only belongings, hoping to reach Bolivia. After he abandoned that hope, he spent another month skirting the base of the Serra do Norte, gradually losing his strength and his grip on sanity, subsisting on a diet of coconuts, insect larvae, and Brazil nuts.

When Sanka reached Rondon's encampment and told his story, Rondon assumed he was still confused and hallucinating. Sanka claimed to have been working on the Urupá River, a branch of the Ji-Paraná, and to have traversed only one other river on the meandering zigzag route he had taken before encountering the expedition. That did not seem possible, for every map Rondon had consulted indicated that Sanka would have had to cross several major streams. Either Sanka was crazy, or all the existing maps, most dating to the eighteenth century and colonial times, were grievously wrong. But Sanka stuck to his story.

With a growing sense of dread, Rondon began to suspect that Sanka was indeed telling the truth. If so, the expedition was in grave danger. His men were already drained and weakened, their bodies infested with parasites that burrowed under their skin and invaded their stomachs. The rains were incessant. It was impossible, Rondon realized, to ask his troops to cross another rugged and unexplored stretch of jungle to get to a river that might not be where the maps said it was. There was also Sanka's welfare to consider: he, too, was in no condition for such a trek, nor could they abandon him. For lack of any alternative, the explorers would have to continue descending the same river, no matter where it took them.

This turned out to be the correct decision, and one that probably saved the lives of all involved. The maps were in fact horribly wrong. In reality, the Jaci-Paraná River was slightly more than one full degree of latitude from the location shown on the old maps. This meant that Rondon would have had to lead his exhausted men through seventy miles of dense jungle before they could reach a river that would eventually take them to the main resupply team.

With no prospect now of encountering Botelho de Magalhães downriver, and their food supplies all but exhausted, the exploration team was now forced to subsist on hearts of palm and whatever fish could be caught: Rondon and his men were running so low on essentials that they could not even give Sanka any of the salt he craved. Some took to fishing with dynamite just above waterfalls. When the stunned fish landed in the pools below, they were quickly scooped up and put in a basket. Once, however, hoping to augment his catch, an officer put several fish in his mouth while grabbing for others. But one was a piranha, and it bit off the tip of his tongue, causing severe bleeding; Dr. Tanajura was able to stanch the flow only by applying a type of jungle moss that Indigenous people used as a poultice.

Downriver, the two smaller teams dispatched at the end of October were waiting at the jungle headquarters of Sanka's employers when Rondon finally arrived there in December. Taking pity on Sanka's condition, Rondon insisted he be freed from his contract, and put him on the next boat to Manaus with other expedition members, where he could receive needed medical treatment. Rondon owed a great deal to Sanka: without their improbable meeting, Rondon and his men might not have survived.

Rondon's own health had worsened, too. His malaria returned, more debilitating than ever, and on January 1, his temperature rose to 105 degrees. For that reason, he headed directly for Manaus rather than wait for the arrival of Botelho de Magalhães and the resupply team that had remained on the Jaci-Paraná. On the way back to Rio, his malaria became so severe that he was taken off his ship at Salvador and hospitalized for several days. But he had survived the most severe test of his life, and had more than justified his bold decision to "return immediately through the other side."

As always after an expedition, Rondon conducted an inventory of accomplishments as the ship steamed home. All told, he and his exploration team had traveled 806 miles on land, paddled 707 miles by dugout canoe, and delineated the 200-mile extent of the Serra do Norte. At the same time, the telegraph-construction team had successfully completed 404 miles of new line. In all, Rondon had lost three men: two to disease and another who accidentally shot himself while cleaning his rifle.[13]

But Rondon's most enduring achievement in 1909 was to literally redraw the map of one of the most remote parts of the world. Everything cartographers thought they knew about the region between sixty and sixty-three degrees west longitude and nine and twelve degrees south latitude had proved wrong, and maps dating back to the first Iberian colonial expeditions, still in use in atlases around the world, had to be junked. This area, comprising more than twenty thousand square miles, larger than the Netherlands or Denmark, and including unknown rivers, mountains, plateaus, and prairies, is today known as Rondônia; and the imaginary circle of longitude at fifty-seven degrees west, near the point where the 1909 expedition began, became known as the Rondon Meridian—the only line of longitude named for a person.[14]

IX

"With Presents, Patience and Good Manners"

E XHAUSTED, SAPPED OF the physical and mental energy that had earned him a reputation as the toughest military officer of his generation, Rondon arrived in Rio de Janeiro on February 6, 1910. It was a Sunday, Carnival was underway, and after months of speculation in the press that he was dead, lost, or disabled, his return was so noteworthy that gaudily costumed revelers, singing newly composed Carnival songs celebrating Rondon's feats in the wilderness, came to the docks to greet him, some dressed as explorers, Indians, or jungle beasts.

Under strict orders from his doctors and the army high command to rest and regain his health, he spent most of the next twelve months at home in the capital with Chiquita and the children. But as his strength gradually returned, Rondon used his enforced absence from the field to fight for long-standing policy objectives. Once again, as he campaigned for creation of a new government agency to safeguard Brazil's Indigenous peoples, their lands, and their interests, he encountered fierce resistance. Yet he persisted, and for good reason: the word "genocide" had not been invented yet, but looking back, we can say that Rondon's efforts that year may have helped avert one.

After President Afonso Pena died in mid-1909, Nilo Peçanha succeeded him as a placeholder. The winner of a fiercely contested presidential election held on March 1, 1910, was Hermes da Fonseca,

Rondon's immediate superior back when he enlisted, but the new president would not be inaugurated until November 15. As a result, Peçanha spent most of 1910 serving as a largely impotent interim president. It was a year of continuous uncertainty and ceaseless political conflict, beginning with the election and ending with a military rebellion, when mutineers seized naval vessels and threatened to shell the capital.

For Rondon, the most important issue, even more than the annual battle for funding of the Telegraph Commission, was Indian policy. Curiously, what forced that question onto the national agenda in 1910 were issues not in the Amazon, where the largest number of tribes lived, but in São Paulo, where the economy was most dynamic and was rapidly modernizing. As in the Amazon, the debate centered on infrastructure needs. But this time, rather than telegraph lines, the focus of controversy was a proposed railway linking São Paulo and Mato Grosso, which was being sabotaged by the Kaingang tribe.*

His health still fragile, Rondon remained intent on crafting a national policy toward Indigenous peoples and did not go to São Paulo to deal with the Kaingang; instead, he sent Manuel Rabelo, a promising young officer who had participated in Rondon Commission expeditions since 1906. Thirteen years younger than Rondon, and of noble descent, Rabelo had enlisted in the army at fifteen, and immediately saw combat defending the republic. After enrolling in the military academy, he became a Positivist, and specialized in military engineering, graduating with honors in 1901. Rondon trusted him: he had already promoted Rabelo twice, and the two men would remain close friends and collaborators until Rabelo's death in 1945.

---

* During Rondon's life, the official orthography of Brazilian Portuguese underwent numerous changes, and these have continued into the twenty-first century. This is a phenomenon especially challenging as it relates to the names of Indigenous peoples and place names derived from Indigenous words. Thus: Manáos or Manaus? Bororo, Borôro, or Bororó? Kaingang or Caingang? Nhambiquara or Nambikwara? The practice followed throughout this book is to always use the spelling most favored today, except in cases when quoting directly from documents written before a change in orthography went into effect. Spelling errors in diaries have also been left intact.

São Paulo is today Brazil's most populous and prosperous state, but in the early twentieth century, growth was concentrated in the state's eastern and southern sections, especially around the state capital, also called São Paulo. In his book *Saudades do Brasil*, the French anthropologist Claude Lévi-Strauss describes how in 1935, arriving in the city and searching for maps in preparation for a scientific expedition along Rondon's telegraph line, "what you would find in the stores were maps fewer than 20 years old, in which the entirety of the west of the state was left blank, with just this mention: 'uncharted territory inhabited by Indians.'"[1]

The Kaingang dominated a large chunk of that territory, as well as parts of Argentina and the similarly unmapped upland interior of Brazil's three southernmost states: Rio Grande do Sul, Santa Catarina, and Paraná. A nomadic people, they had fled to the inland forests in colonial times, to escape slaving expeditions and the Jesuit missions that sprang up in Paraguay, Argentina, and southern Brazil in the seventeenth and eighteenth centuries as part of the Roman Catholic Church's plan to catechize and subdue Indigenous peoples. But by the nineteenth century, colonists and military expeditions began penetrating even those inland domains, moving both the Kaingang and their allies and ethnic cousins, the Xokleng, into settlements, threatening their traditional way of life.

After slavery was abolished in 1888, the new republican government began encouraging mass immigration from Europe, as a substitute source of labor on plantations and in factories, but also to "whiten" Brazil's population. Due to its climate and topography, which resembled that of Central Europe, the south was particularly appealing. Eventually, tens of thousands of colonists from Germany, Italy, and Poland settled there.

The newcomers were drawn by promises of "empty land," despite the fact that Indigenous peoples had lived there since long before Brazil became a Portuguese colony. Conflicts ensued, and the European settlers, especially the Germans, complained that the Brazilian government was not providing enough protection. The European colonists, of course, were better armed than the Kaingang, so the outcome was predictable.

The last remaining autonomous Indigenous groups interpreted the start of construction of the Northwestern Railroad between São Paulo and Mato Grosso as their death knell, and decided to resist. Construction of the main line had begun in June 1905 from Bauru, 175 miles northwest of the city of São Paulo, and the first 55-mile stretch was formally inaugurated fifteen months later, without incident. But as the project advanced farther into the interior, the Kaingang's hostility grew: construction crews were attacked and killed in hit-and-run raids, completed sections of track torn up, supplies and equipment intercepted and robbed, or destroyed.

Like the Mato Grosso–Amazonas telegraph line, the Northwestern Railroad was a strategic priority, so the authorities in Rio refused to be deterred. The railway's construction had first been proposed during the reign of Pedro II, immediately after the War of the Triple Alliance exposed Brazil's vulnerabilities, but it had taken nearly thirty years to raise money, propose a route, and survey the terrain. The final stations of the line were to be Corumbá and Ponta Porã, bordering Bolivia, places familiar to Rondon. The line would make it possible to haul raw materials such as minerals and timber from Mato Grosso to industrializing São Paulo. Giving in to the Kaingang was not an option, and since Rondon was the government's foremost expert on Indian affairs, resolving the impasse fell to him.

This was not an easy task. Because the Kaingang lived near São Paulo's rapidly encroaching coffee plantations, and were seen as standing in the way of Brazil's Positivist-inspired national ideals of "Order and Progress," public sentiment turned against them. To someone in São Paulo or Rio de Janeiro, a tribe in far-off Amazonas or Pará was an exotic, even romantic abstraction. Not so with the Kaingang: they were frequently vilified as "savages" or "barbarians" or, most often, as *bugres*, a highly pejorative word connoting "subhuman." The Kaingang felt the brunt of that prejudice as gangs of *bugreiros* hunted them down. "The Brazilians killed many women and children, the death rate that they inflicted on women being about twice that of the men," the anthropologist Jules Henry wrote in a classic study of the Kaingang. Living in small, family-centered groups, "the Kaingang have no idea of coming together and forming a solid unit against an outside aggressor. . . . Whoever pursues them constantly has them at his mercy, for they become panic-stricken and never turn to face their pursuers until they are brought to bay like hunted animals."[2]

Rondon's most outspoken adversary in the debate about Indian rights was the zoologist Hermann von Ihering, director of the Museu Paulista in São Paulo. A German native, von Ihering earned a medical degree in Berlin, migrated to Brazil in 1880, and settled in Rio Grande do Sul, initially serving as physician to a German settlement. But within three years, he began working as a traveling naturalist, collecting bird and other specimens for the National Museum in Rio de Janeiro. In 1894, he founded the Museu Paulista, conceived as a rival to the museum in the capital.

A decade later, von Ihering wrote a pamphlet in English, a classic exercise in scientific racism called *The Anthropology of the State of São Paulo*, for distribution at the Brazilian pavilion at the St. Louis World's Fair. He discussed the Indian tribes that inhabited São Paulo even before the arrival of the Portuguese, and saw their future in the bleakest of terms. Criticizing what he viewed as the Indigenous peoples' inability to adapt to a European-style polity or economy, von Ihering predicted that Brazil's Indians, whether already acculturated or resisting incorporation into the Brazilian nation, would soon be completely obliterated by the forces that modernity was unleashing.

"The present Indians of São Paulo do not represent an element of labour and progress," he wrote. "As in other parts of Brazil, no serious and continued labour can be expected of the civilised Indians, and as the savage Caingangs are obstructing the colonisation of the forest regions habited by them, no other result seems possible than that of their extermination."[3]

When rendered into Portuguese in 1906, the translator made an appalling mistake. In the original, von Ihering's remark about "extermination" of the Kaingang can be read as merely predicting an inevitable historical process. In Portuguese, however, that nuance was completely lost, and the phrase was translated so that it seemed he was encouraging the slaughter of Indigenous peoples who stood in the way of progress, that a genocide was the only solution: "It seems we have no alternative but to exterminate them" was the way it read.

Rondon's Positivist allies attacked the pamphlet as a "ruthless and barbaric theory . . . alien to our sentiments"[4] as Brazilians. But von Ihering's views found approval among the emerging São Paulo business class that provided financial support to his museum and to the newspapers and magazines that published his theories. He stepped up his attacks on Rondon and others who viewed Indigenous cultures benevolently, mocking what he called "the sentimental predilection" and "generous character of a people in love with the fate of primitive man."[5] He also criticized Rondon's decision to send Rabelo to conciliate the Kaingang as foolish and doomed to failure.

Rondon's peaceful methods did nothing to alleviate "the anarchy that currently characterizes the relationship between the national authorities and the fierce tribes," nor "come anywhere near the scientific aspect of the issue," von Ihering said, so a newer, tougher approach was needed. "The upward trajectory of our culture is in danger," he warned, "and it is necessary to put a stop to this abnormality. . . . If we wish to spare the Indians for humanitarian motives, it is necessary that, first of all, measures be taken so they no longer perturb the advance of colonization. . . . Above all, the white race should be protected against the red race. Any other kind of dogma simply is not appropriate."[6]

Deeply distressed by what it regarded as a governmental incursion into one of its traditional domains, the Catholic Church, with the Salesian order in the lead, also sharply opposed Rondon's campaign to create an Indian Protection Service. Since colonial times, the Church had taken primary responsibility for Brazil's Indigenous peoples, especially in the Amazon. Now a secularist government was proposing to strip the Church of one of its principal remaining raisons d'être: the care and evangelization of "heathen" peoples.

As Rondon opened one telegraph station after another, intending for them to serve as "poles of attraction" for Indigenous peoples, the Salesians were often the first to colonize nearby. They built schools there and in other parts of the state, especially along rivers flowing through tribal areas, and established farms and ranches where young Indian graduates of their schools could be put to work. In some respects, these were similar to the "reductions" the Jesuits had established throughout the interior of South America in the seventeenth and eighteenth centuries.

Rondon and his men sometimes visited the Salesian settlements while traveling in the hinterland, and were frankly disturbed by what they saw. They admired the grit, courage, and spirit of sacrifice of the Salesian brothers and priests—which in some ways resembled that of the Rondon Commission members—but the Salesian approach to dealing with Indigenous peoples could not have been more different.

In classes, students were forbidden to speak their native language. Many Salesian institutions were boarding schools, where children were separated from their parents for long periods of time. To Rondon and his men, all this seemed a recipe for cultural obliteration, meant to transform Indians into obedient Christians estranged from their own families, history, culture, and character. In addition, there were reports of sexual abuse of young Indians by the clerics, which were never proved but helped fuel Rondon's opposition to their presence.[7]

By 1910, questions concerning land tenure and ownership had also become an area of contention. In some cases, tribal groups that were poorly equipped to understand the concept of private property signed over to the Salesians deeds for large, fertile tracts of land that had always been collectively held; on other occasions, the state government ignored the long-standing presence of Indigenous peoples and simply gave deeds to the Salesians. Rondon had always opposed such land grabs by whites, and he was not about to make an exception for a group of foreign priests.

Additionally, many of the Indians working on Salesian plantations did not seem to be earning wages, just room and board. Instead, the profits their labor generated went to the Salesian order. So as Rondon and his fellow Positivists saw it, an Indian Protection Service was necessary to safeguard Indigenous peoples from just this type of exploitation under the guise of faith and benevolence.

The stage was set for an epic political battle, with Rondon's secular and religious opponents united in opposition to his objectives. Newspapers and magazines sympathetic to the Roman Catholic Church attacked Rondon, urging readers to complain to their elected representatives. Von Ihering even argued that Rondon's opposition to Roman Catholic proselytizing among Indigenous peoples violated Positivist doctrine. "As a Positivist, Col. Rondon is not in the least bit logical," he wrote, "in view of the fact that he excludes the teaching of religious Catechism from the Indians when, in the well-known opinion of Comte, the spirit must first pass through a theological phase."[8]

While this domestic debate was taking place, foreign pressure on Brazil to adopt a more humane policy toward its Indigenous peoples was mounting: at a 1908 meeting in Vienna of the International Congress of Americanists, Alberto Vojtěch Frič, a young, idealistic Czech ethnologist and botanist just returned from southern Brazil, denounced the activities of Indian hunters, citing specific massacres of the Kaingang and Xokleng in horrifically graphic detail.

This led to scathing headlines in the European press, duly noted by Brazilian diplomatic missions across the continent and relayed to the Foreign Ministry in Rio. Documents on file there show that this publicity generated fear that Brazil's international image could be permanently tarnished, which would discourage further colonization and bank lending.

The renowned Irish antislavery and human rights campaigner Roger Casement, a British diplomat based in Brazil, was by 1910 focusing Europe's attention on abuses of Indigenous peoples enslaved on rubber plantations in the Putumayo region of Peru, and Brazil feared being tarred with the same brush. So the Foreign Ministry quietly allied itself with Rondon: creating an Indian Protection Service under his direction would allow Brazil to trumpet abroad that it supported the humane treatment of its Indigenous peoples.

This strategy clearly was effective. In the years to come, the Brazilian government would publicize Rondon's work, especially his policy of nonviolence, earning international approbation. "Rondon is a very capable man I believe," Casement wrote to the Foreign Office in London in 1910. "It is a good thing to see that one of these republics is beginning to realise its duties and responsibilities towards the Indian tribes."[9] He praised Rondon as "protector of the native Indians"[10] and in 1912 even suggested a role for him overseeing Peruvian compliance with reforms to the Amazon rubber industry.

In lobbying for an Indian Protection Service, Rondon also allied himself with one of the most influential members of Congress, a deputy who held a seat during the entire forty years of the First Republic, José Bonifácio de Andrada e Silva, whose great-uncle and namesake had helped draw up Brazil's first constitution in 1823, fought for the gradual abolition of slavery and, when that failed to gain approval, proposed another measure to immediately outlaw the importation of slaves into Brazil.

But it was the original José Bonifácio's "Notes for the Civilizing of the Wild Indians of the Empire of Brazil" that most influenced Rondon. That document did not deny that tribal people were often violent in their dealings with whites, but argued that this was the fault of Europeans: "Under the pretext of making them Christians, we have inflicted many injustices and cruelties upon them," José Bonifácio wrote. "It is horrifying to reflect on the rapid depopulation of these wretched souls since our arrival in Brazil." His ultimate goal was still to "catechize and resettle" Indigenous peoples so as to "convert these barbarians into civilized men," but he wanted to use peaceful means to do so. "The Indians are a rich treasure for Brazil if we have the good sense and astuteness to make use of them," he argued. "We can win them over" by following the example of the Jesuits, who met Indigenous peoples "with the Gospel in one hand and with presents, patience and good manners in the other."[11]

José Bonifácio's "Notes" were doubly important to Rondon. First, they offered him a blueprint for dealing with Indigenous peoples, particularly in their emphasis on nonviolence. And second, in the fierce political quarrels over Indian policy that raged during the first two decades of the twentieth century, the original José Bonifácio would prove to be an invaluable ally: anytime Rondon was accused of favoring impractical ideas that stood in the way of Brazil's progress, he simply pointed to the Patriarch of Independence and quoted from the "Notes" to show that his new proposals were part of a long, illustrious Brazilian tradition of humaneness and generosity, drawing on Bonifácio's ideas while simultaneously gaining cover and legitimacy from them.

Lobbying in the American sense of the word has always been viewed with suspicion in Brazil, but Rondon had to do it to prevail against von Ihering, the Salesians, and other opponents. In May of 1910, the Rondon Commission opened a new headquarters on the busiest street in downtown Rio on the first floor of a private house. The Central Office functioned as Rondon's personal base of operations when he was in the capital: in his office, his desk faced a portrait of José Bonifácio, with a photograph of Benjamin Constant on the wall behind him and a bust of Napoleon nearby. During Rondon's long absences, the staff continued to advance his agenda and keep him informed of political developments in the capital.

To run the new operation, Rondon turned to Botelho de Magalhães, a thirty-year-old lieutenant with an exceptional republican and Positivist pedigree. A nephew of Benjamin Constant and son of a general, he joined the Rondon Commission in 1908, after earning a degree in military engineering at the academy. His illustrious surname undoubtedly helped open doors everywhere in the capital, but his absolute loyalty made him especially valuable as Rondon's trusted surrogate in Rio.

"Through the Central Office, it would be possible to refute the criticisms of the inefficiency of the Commission and its excessive spending, now and then reported by the national press," the Brazilian scholar Luciene Cardoso wrote in a study of the Rondon Commission's foothold in the capital. "This new agency would act in the coordination of releasing information about the work of the Rondon Commission, through the publishing of technical-scientific reports on the activities undertaken and the publication of articles in various newspapers."[12] And in what Rondon saw as a logical extension of its stated mission, the Central Office would also advocate for creation of an Indian Protection Service.

In addition, the office made it a priority to acquire the best scientific devices, almost all of them imported from Germany or England:

prism binoculars made by Zeiss, state-of-the-art theodolites, precision compasses, Graphophones and cylinders for audio recordings in the field, and so on. At Rondon's insistence, the commission created a new department to obtain and learn how to use equipment for registering visual images. The new division, under the command of Lt. Luiz Thomaz Reis, was called the Photography and Cinematography Sector and from its start existed for both scientific and public relations purposes.

"Via photography and cinematography, one can obtain an idea of the wilderness without setting foot there, without feeling the inconveniences of the climate, the mosquitos, the ticks and other even more disagreeable things,"[13] Botelho de Magalhães wrote decades later. Soon, Brazilian newspapers, magazines, and cinemas were flooded with photographic and film images of Indigenous peoples at their daily routines and in friendly interactions with the Rondon Commission; sometimes, reinforcing the notion that these "savages" were actually fellow citizens, the Indians were photographed wrapped in, raising, or saluting the Brazilian flag.

In the end, Rondon got much of what he wanted. In one of Nilo Peçanha's last significant acts in office, with Rondon and José Bonifácio de Andrada e Silva flanking him, the president formally announced the creation of the Indian Protection Service (abbreviated as SPI in Portuguese) on September 7, 1910, Brazilian Independence Day. Rondon's doctrine of nonviolence toward Indigenous people, which he had been practicing in the field for twenty years, was now official government policy, encoded in the phrase "Die if you must, but kill never," and Rondon himself was appointed director of the new government agency.

These were significant gains, but Rondon was not granted full autonomy. Rather than functioning as a freestanding agency, the SPI was created as a division of the Ministry of Agriculture, Industry and Commerce, which had been established as a full-fledged cabinet office only a few months earlier. That meant that Rondon would ultimately have to report to the sitting minister, Rodolfo da Rocha Miranda, a prominent coffee grower from São Paulo, on issues relating to Indigenous affairs.

The federal government's complicated, and potentially contradictory, objectives in creating the SPI were evident in its new official designation: Service for the Protection of Indians and Placement of National Workers. This title associated Indigenous peoples with Brazil's labor force, and reduced them to the same status as other marginalized groups, such as caboclos and freed slaves.

Rondon did not necessarily oppose these objectives; as a Positivist, he, too, wanted the "jungle-dwellers" to enjoy the full benefits of Brazilian citizenship and Western civilization, including eventual participation in a money economy. But he always envisioned that assimilation process as gradual and voluntary, with each tribal group choosing its own pace.

In an exchange of letters with Miranda published in the country's leading newspapers before the government decreed the creation of the SPI, Rondon made clear that he would agree to take command of the agency only if the government met certain conditions. His seventeen stipulations were meant to ensure that his view of the agency's purpose and agenda prevailed. "Above all," he insisted that Indigenous groups retain "formal possession of the lands on which they live, returning to the remaining tribes the same territory usurped from them whenever possible, or a sufficient extension to be determined by the Government through friendly accords with them, always employing fraternal processes."[14]

As regards "the catechism of indigenous peoples, including their incorporation into our society by the assimilation of our work methods and art forms as well as the adoption of our habits," Rondon wrote, taking direct aim at the Roman Catholic Church, "I judge that to be a problem that cannot be addressed at the present moment. . . . As a Positivist and member of the Positivist Church of Brazil, I am convinced that our indigenous peoples should incorporate themselves into the West, but without any effort to force them to do so through theologizing."[15]

Miranda, quite progressive in his views, readily endorsed Rondon's conditions. However, he left the cabinet at the end of 1910, and was succeeded by another representative of São Paulo coffee-growing interests, who took a more narrow and legalistic view of Indigenous issues. The conflict between Rondon's emphasis on purely voluntary "attraction" and the insistence of others in government on mandatory "absorption" was thus baked into the Indian Protection Service from the very start, and remains a perennial problem, even today.

With the political terrain shifting again, Rondon needed new allies. On November 15, 1910, Peçanha was replaced by Marshal Hermes da Fonseca, the first military officer to be elected Brazil's president. Though da Fonseca had known Rondon for more than twenty-five years and was the first to recognize his extraordinary personal qualities, Rondon was not automatically guaranteed his support. As war minister, for instance, da Fonseca had sometimes been slow to pay the Rondon Commission's bills and also expressed reservations about the telegraph line's strategic value; he thought construction of railroads yielded better results, and was especially enthusiastic about finishing a railway through the rubber-producing areas along the new border with Bolivia.

The new president's qualms were encouraged by José Joaquim Seabra, a powerful, well-connected lawyer who had become rich representing foreign companies, and openly opposed the telegraph line. A decade older than Rondon, the wily Seabra, known as "J. J." and "the Fox," had served a pair of earlier administrations in three different cabinet posts (Justice, Interior, and Foreign Affairs), and was a consummate political wheeler-dealer. In Hermes da Fonseca's cabinet, he was appointed to the supremely lucrative post of minister of public works, with control over all government contracts, and immediately began undermining Rondon.

Seabra argued that Rondon was spending too much of the public's money on a project of dubious value, and demanded that the Telegraph Commission be dissolved. Rondon told the story of how Seabra one day gave the president a stack of decrees to be signed and how da Fonseca, leafing rapidly through the pile, noticed Rondon's name on one document. "Upon checking what it dealt with," namely, disbanding the Telegraph Commission, "he reiterated that he would not sign this document."[16]

This sparring between the president and his powerful cabinet minister continued for two years, until Seabra left to become governor of his home state. Although he never quite succeeded in shutting down the commission entirely, he had some success in reducing its number of employees, shrinking their salaries, and cutting the commission's budget.

Rondon had always envisioned the creation of an Indian Protection Service as part of a much larger effort to fight racism toward Brazil's Indigenous peoples and raise consciousness about their plight. After two decades spent waiting each year for budget committees in the Senate and Chamber of Deputies to approve appropriations for telegraph construction, the creation of the SPI now obliged Rondon to redouble his activities. The bureaucratic battle with J. J. Seabra was only a taste of problems to come. For the remainder of his military career, and even beyond, Rondon would constantly have to conduct rearguard actions on two fronts to defend the institutions he had built. Win or lose, there would never be a respite.

X

Mariano's Tongue

B Y EARLY 1911, a year after his return to Rio de Janeiro, Rondon had fully recovered, and he was once again fit enough to return to Mato Grosso. The telegraph project had proceeded with Rondon supervising from afar during his time in the capital. He communicated with the commission's work crews through telegrams and letters, offering advice and direction when technical and personnel problems occurred. Growing impatient at being confined to the capital, he was eager to return to the field, especially now that his authority and autonomy had been strengthened.

So in March 1911, Rondon and Chiquita, six months pregnant with their seventh and last child, Branca Luiza, took the train to a European-style spa in Minas Gerais. After a relaxed stay there, he wrote, "I felt myself ready to resist the buffeting of life in the wilds" and "began to prepare for my trip to Mato Grosso."[1] As was the case with each of his six other children, Rondon would not be present for Branca's birth, on June 8.

Before leaving Rio, Rondon undertook one last campaign to strengthen government and public support for the Telegraph Commission project and the Indian Protection Service. In April, he delivered a pair of lectures that became prestigious social events: speaking at the Palácio Monroe, an imposing Beaux-Arts structure that eventually became the home of the Brazilian Congress, Rondon's audience included President da Fonseca as well as most of his cabinet and influential members of Congress. With abundant press coverage guaranteed, the lectures offered the most favorable platform imaginable for Rondon to expound his positions.

The nationwide drama surrounding the 1909 expedition was also a factor in generating intense interest in Rondon. He had been exploring the wilds of the remote interior for twenty years, but none of his other missions had excited the Brazilian public in quite the same way. Doubts that had preoccupied the nation when Rondon and his men were presumed missing or dead now had answers. Rondon had become a national hero, but some questions remained: Just who is this man? What is he like?

Read more than a century later, the lectures are a curious mixture of swashbuckling adventure narrative and fatiguing technical data, undoubtedly aimed at the engineers and geographers in his audience. To twenty-first-century ears, this may seem an odd format, but in an era before television or radio, it was edifying, entertaining, and, judging by the press coverage the lectures received, quite effective.

Indirectly, Rondon was responding to complaints that his projects wasted money that the government, still hamstrung financially, could ill afford. He discussed in some detail how telegraph lines were laid and dangled the prospect of immense riches that the Brazilian nation could exploit if rational and well-regulated development of the northern wilderness were only allowed to continue. These included not only the gold, silver, and diamonds pioneers had mined two hundred years earlier, he intimated, but also metals and minerals vital to modern industry that his expeditions had cataloged: iron, copper, tin, aluminum, nickel, cobalt, molybdenum, manganese, tungsten, zinc.

Along with hints of this bonanza, he pleaded, somewhat contradictorily, for better treatment of the Indigenous peoples who had been living in the region since long before Brazil was colonized. He described the suffering and poverty the Rondon Commission had encountered on its expeditions, and appealed to his listeners to discount the negative images of Indigenous peoples that others were propagating.

"Observing those scenes of deep and generalized affliction, many thoughts occurred to me regarding the ideas I have so many times seen expressed about the character, temperament and moral nature of the poor Indian," he continued. "Our prideful ignorance has made us write much nonsense and evil with respect to them. But certainly nothing is more false than affirming that they are insensitive and indifferent to the suffering of others."[2]

In truth, Rondon added, Indigenous peoples could even stake a claim to moral superiority over "civilized" man, whose depredations on lands not their own were infinite. Indians were thus the victims, not the aggressors. "Unfortunately, all business dealings between Indians and civilized people are done in the manner of the hunt immortalized in fables," he said. "The civilized always play the role of the lion," and "from that conflict, vengeance and carnage result."[3]

On May 15, Rondon delivered a third lecture, this time at the Salão Germania in São Paulo, which was heavily attended and widely covered in the press. This was a frontal assault on an enemy stronghold, for Rondon knew that sympathizers of von Ihering, members of the local business elite, and leaders of the German immigrant community would attend. The tone of this lecture was therefore somewhat different from the two in Rio, with less exposition and more open advocacy. Taking veiled swipes at the von Ihering camp, it was a full-throated call to recognize the Indian not just as a human being but as a fellow countryman.

"Among you, Brazilians who live in the comfort and security of the big cities, only every now and then does the remote and muffled echo of the cries of desperation and pain of these other Brazilians make themselves heard, filling the most distant and untamed corners of our beloved fatherland,"[4] he proclaimed before going on to strike a nationalist note aimed at recent European immigrants. "Thus the amorphous wave of outsiders can continue to grow, threatening to inundate and smother the last vestiges of our nationality."[5]

In other parts of the lecture, Rondon disputed von Ihering's contention that Indigenous peoples were irredeemably savage, backward, ignorant, and warlike. "I have been working among them for 20 years," he said, "and have found them everywhere with hearts open to the most noble sentiments of mankind, of a lucid intelligence and quick to learn everything taught to them, indefatigable in the roughest toil, and friends who are constant and faithful to those who treat them with kindness and justice."[6]

But Rondon reserved his most passionate remarks for the lecture's end. He chastised his fellow Brazilians for failing in their moral obligations as citizens of a modern state, founded on values of equality and justice, and contrasted that with the dismal and degraded conditions to which Indians were permanently condemned: "If they accept white society, they are reduced to the worst form of slavery—that of slaves whose lives are of no interest to their masters—and if they take to the bush, they are harassed and exterminated by iron and fire.

"Where is our justice as a cultured and civilized people?" he continued. "Where is our sentiment of fairness as a mature people who have grown up in the shadow of admirable Roman institutions? Where is our kindness as men shaped by the infusion of chivalrous and Catholic values, that we have arrived at this monstrous iniquity of denying the right to life and property, on Brazilian soil only to those Brazilians with the most legitimate claim to nationality?"[7]

Rondon's remarks instantly provoked controversy, especially because he spoke in an official capacity, but he did not linger in São Paulo to gauge their impact. Boarding a train the next day, he headed for what he called a "zone of conflict" in the western part of the state, where Rabelo and his men had spent the better part of a year trying to win over the Kaingang. Rabelo thought he was making progress, having gained a truce of sorts, but then surveying teams sent by the state government as part of advance work for a railway bridge across the Paraná River began "killing the Kaingang population and devastating their villages," Rondon noted. "Of course, tremendous retaliation against the invaders erupted."[8]

After conferring with Rabelo and his team, Rondon decided that a base, not a fort, should be built at a site where various trails between distant Kaingang settlements converged. The men cleared a forested area two hundred yards by three hundred yards and in the center erected small thatched huts. These would serve as dwellings for Rabelo and his men—never more than twelve at a time, so as not to seem threatening—and to store supplies, gifts, and food. Around the perimeter of the cleared area, Rondon ordered a barbed-wire fence installed, and had it buttressed by the trunks of felled trees. At night, the edge of the base was constantly illuminated by kerosene lamps, but he directed that the interior be kept totally dark.

The idea was to display a confidence bordering on indifference, but never a sign of aggression. The Kaingang contingent could gather at will around the perimeter of the SPI base at night and bellow war whoops, blow horns, and bang its lethal clubs against tree trunks. But it would be to no effect: "What certainly astonished them," Rondon observed, "was that we neither lowered our guard nor showed the slightest sign of fear, even on the occasion of their brashest threats."[9]

A single sentry remained on duty throughout the night, with shifts rotating every few hours, but beyond that, "there was only one more man, to keep the gramophone playing, with one disc after another purposely chosen to convey the impression of many people awake, laughing and relaxing without concern."[10]

By day, Rondon's approach was completely different. Along the paths that zigzagged through the forest, he erected small platforms protected with palm leaves and left presents for the Kaingang: machetes, knives, bolts of cloth, beads and other trinkets, "arranged in such a way that the Indians understood these were gifts voluntarily and very calculatingly offered."[11] It was crucial to convey that impression, Rondon explained, since it would defeat his purpose if the Kaingang believed he was responding out of fear and paying them some sort of tribute.

After the Kaingang became less timid and began accepting the presents, he ordered Rabelo to clear an additional area around the base and grow crops such as corn and squash, planted "with things arranged in such a fashion that our benevolent intent was clear."[12] In his diary, he added this note: "The difficulty lies in discovering how to make that kind of offer, giving them at the same time the certainty that they expose themselves to no risk accepting it."[13]

This nonviolent approach, which Rabelo continued, soon began to yield results: early in 1912, Rondon would learn by telegram, the first Kaingang visited the rudimentary base, seeking an alliance with this new group of *civilizados* that had demonstrated a peaceful intent. Then a Kaingang group was persuaded to ride a train to the state capital, where they were showered with gifts and promises. Over the next three years, several other Kaingang communities moved to the cleared area around Rabelo's base, now a full-fledged SPI "Attraction Post," with a school and clinic, and construction of the railroad was completed. Ultimately, this would prove a disastrous decision for the Kaingang, for Rondon could not continue to protect them from incursions by coffee growers and ranchers. But in the immediate context of the 1910 debate about extermination, the fledgling SPI's alleviation of hostilities with the Kaingang was a defeat for von Ihering and his allies, seeming to validate everything Rondon had been saying.

As midyear approached, Rondon was well on his way to Cuiabá and from there a return to the jungle and construction of his Amazon telegraph line. "Our wilderness life has begun," he noted with undisguised pleasure on June 4. "We slept on the ground, on layers of saddle padding, with my rubber poncho, lined with red flannel, as a blanket."[14] After an absence of nearly eighteen months, Rondon was back in the world where he felt most comfortable.

Rondon's principal concern was still the Nhambiquara, who continued to reject the Telegraph Commission's efforts to establish a friendly relationship. For instance, while opening a trail one day, one of his adjutants and a scientist from the National Museum were ambushed. The officer, a fervent Positivist and a favorite of Rondon's, was struck by two arrows, including one that punctured his lung, and the scientist was "gravely wounded." But, adhering to Rondon's credo of nonviolence, neither reacted, so both were praised in citations Rondon wrote.[15]

On his way north to deal with the Nhambiquara, Rondon stopped at various Bororo villages to visit old friends and listen to their needs and complaints, once again enjoying the role of the Pagmejera. "I distributed presents widely," he wrote from one village, "ordered a cow to be slaughtered for a banquet and, at night, held a session for the awed Indians to watch slides to the sound of a gramophone." He also made a short detour to Mimoso, where his uncle Francelino

Evangelista had organized "visits and more visits" with "all the relatives who consider me chief of the family, or rather, the clan." En route, with Francelino's approval, he even accepted an invitation to visit the family of the assassinated former governor Totó Paes, attempting to assuage the political differences of 1906 that caused the execution of four Evangelistas.[16]

Aware of Rondon's newly expanded authority, which could potentially cripple the Roman Catholic Church's missionary activities among Indigenous peoples, the Salesians also sought to make amends. When Rondon arrived in Cuiabá, the bishop there, Francisco de Aquino Correia, a Salesian who had often wrangled with Rondon, organized a reception for him, where a young Bororo student recited a poem that Correia had composed in Rondon's honor.[17] But Rondon was not impressed by the flowery, transparently obsequious versification. As he traveled from one Salesian mission to another, he noted the highly regimented lifestyle the Salesians imposed on their charges, including the requirement that students attend mass. He was also deeply offended by the Salesians' practice of taking title to land the government had allocated to the Bororo, his mother's people, for their own use and collective ownership.

After devoting most of the year to Indigenous issues, Rondon formally reassumed command of the Telegraph Commission on October 12, 1911. This reunited him with many of the officers and scouts who had accompanied him in the past, including his uncle Miguel Evangelista. But there were several newcomers. Two in particular—one a military officer, the other a civilian—would come to play vital roles in Rondon's work over the next three decades: Lt. Luiz Thomaz Reis, known as "Rondon's cinematographer," and the anthropologist and ethnologist Edgar Roquette-Pinto. The presence of both men demonstrated the Rondon Commission's increasing emphasis on scientific research, always using the latest technological tools.

One of Brazil's most promising young intellectuals, Roquette-Pinto had studied medicine in his native Rio. But immediately on graduation in 1905 he joined the anthropology department of the National Museum, where he soon felt an irrepressible desire to venture out into the field. Since his duties included the classification and labeling of the items the Rondon Commission brought back from its explorations, he got to know Rondon and began to pester him for a job on an expedition. "The poetry of those remote lands seeped into my thoughts," he wrote. "To listen to the master was to hear the beckoning voice of the wilderness, to feel the rustling of distant forests."[18] Rondon liked the young man, detected his promise, and eventually persuaded Roquette-Pinto's superiors at the museum to allow him to join the expedition in 1912.

Rondon's decision to bring Roquette-Pinto and Reis along proved fortuitous, for in April 1912, five years of patient effort finally came to fruition. Rondon was out with his uncle Miguel and a Paresi scout named Belarmino, exploring an area of brush and small streams, when they came across an Indian trail and decided to follow it. A few minutes later, they nearly collided with five unarmed Nhambiquara. After "making it understood that we wished to visit them in their villages," Rondon wrote, the Indians responded with "signals for us to follow them."[19]

Uncle Miguel opposed accepting the invitation, telling Rondon it could only be the prelude to an ambush. Belarmino sided with Uncle Miguel after the Nhambiquara indicated that they wanted to travel with the three outsiders sandwiched between one of their number in the lead and four in the rear. To put his companions at ease, Rondon suggested to the Nhambiquara that they go in front, with the armed explorers following on their mules. The Nhambiquara did not like this idea at all, for they too feared an ambush. Eventually, Rondon negotiated a compromise: three of the Indians would go in front, with Rondon and Belarmino immediately behind them, followed by two more Indians, with Uncle Miguel bringing up the rear.

The atmosphere of mutual suspicion and distrust began to dissipate only after the entire group made its way through a dense patch of jungle and emerged into another clearing. This was the Indians' village, and as Rondon approached, he was met by the village headman, who was carrying a bowl filled with a slightly fermented pineapple beverage. Rondon never liked to drink liquor, but on this ceremonial occasion he made an exception and, responding to the gestures of Indian men around a fire, joined them there.

As the day wore on, Rondon noted other encouraging signs. The chief told men returning from the hunt to deposit their bows and arrows outside the village itself, an order clearly designed to reassure the visitors, and through gestures communicated to Rondon that the five men he encountered on the trail had also been armed but left their weapons in the bush so as not to appear threatening. When night fell, Rondon, Uncle Miguel, and Belarmino were installed in a comfortable cabana warmed by a fire. "We slept," Rondon wrote, "though warily, since these Indians were unknown to us."[20] In the morning, women and children appeared for the first time, another sign of growing confidence, "curious to see the strange guests."

When Rondon decided it was time to resume his reconnaissance, the Nhambiquara expressed a desire to accompany him. Taking the outsiders by the hand, with other men holding the reins of their burros, the Indians led Rondon and his group to a second village, where an old woman was already preparing the pineapple beverage in anticipation of their arrival. On their way back to the point of first contact, still guided by the Nhambiquara, they were escorted to two other villages. At the last, where the men were out hunting, the barking of dogs startled the women and children, who fled into the bush. But the Nhambiquara accompanying Rondon called out to their frightened kinfolk, "assuring them of our friendly intentions."[21]

This was the breakthrough Rondon had been yearning for. He invited the Nhambiquara to return with him to his encampment, sending Belarmino ahead to alert the others, so as to avoid any incidents. "They joined in our sparse supper, showing themselves content, as if at one of their own banquets," he observed. "After dark, there was dancing. . . . And so it was, there in those woods, fraternizing with the Indians, that I spent my wife's birthday, the 14th of April."[22]

When the Nhambiquara finally decided to return to their villages and departed amid avowals of friendship by both sides, Rondon could scarcely have been more content. But within the hour, the new relationship was put to the test. The late-arriving leader of a distant settlement suddenly appeared to complain of an encounter with one of Rondon's muleteers. A party of Nhambiquara hunters had crossed paths with him along a riverbank, and the muleteer had panicked and fled, firing his rifle into the air and accidentally wounding one of the Nhambiquara. The chief had a simple question: What did Rondon intend to do to make things right?

This was a challenge Rondon could not afford to fail. If he could not mollify the chief, news would spread that he was not a man of his word, and all the progress that had just been achieved would be undone. So Rondon, hampered by being limited to sign language combined with the occasional word from Portuguese or Paresi, treaded carefully. First, he apologized for the wounding of the tribesman, stressing that it was inadvertent. Then he offered a particularly generous distribution of gifts as a payment of blood money. And finally he promised that such a thing would not happen again, now that a friendship had been sealed, and that if by chance it did, Rondon would personally punish the wrongdoer. The chief seemed satisfied with this, for contacts with other Nhambiquara villages continued, and even intensified.

With the danger of Nhambiquara attacks now eased, the pace of telegraph construction picked up, and several new stations opened during the remainder of 1912. On January 28, 1913, Rondon headed back to his work on the telegraph line. He would spend much of the first half of that year trying to establish peaceful contact with another tribe, the Parintintin, and stitching together an alliance among those peoples who were now friendly to Rondon but who harbored long-standing grudges against one another—Paresi and Nhambiquara, for example. "To harmonize these tribes," he wrote, "would be another victory for the Indian Service or, rather, the defeat of selfishness by love."[3]

Rondon's method was to ride into a village of one Indigenous group accompanied by a white adjutant and a member of an enemy tribe. Since Rondon was the Chief of Chiefs, village leaders allowed their foe to enter the village with him—albeit "uncomfortably, at first." Gifts were exchanged ritualistically, and each encounter ended with Rondon offering presents to both sides. If things went well, the visitor would then invite his hosts to visit "his own village to drink corn liquor and eat sweets."[4] Since neither side wanted to anger Rondon, such visits could be made without fear.

Cessation of hostilities among rival tribes was part of Rondon's larger plan: to transform Indigenous peoples into custodians of the telegraph line, and bring them a step closer to the Brazilian state. In pursuit of that objective, in 1913 he negotiated an accord with the Corarini tribe whereby that group agreed to leave its traditional homeland, move to the Juruena, and "take charge of the upkeep" of a 245-mile stretch of the line in return for official title to the new territory they would inhabit. The Uaimaré and Caxiniti, subgroups of the Paresi, came to similar understandings with the commission that year: each agreed to become caretakers of 125 miles of the telegraph line, which Indian groups had begun to call "Mariano's tongue" in honor of Rondon. To further deepen that commitment, Rondon also sought volunteers among Indigenous groups to be trained as telegraph operators.[25]

Rondon's other endeavor that year was upgrading existing telegraph stations, so that each could serve as the nucleus for a new settlement. He was incapacitated, though, by another bout of malaria in July, "with a fever of more than 104 degrees, which forced me to stop on my way and wait until it ended."[26] Nonetheless, work continued. At the new José Bonifácio station, for example, he planted 129 cashew trees transported from the Northeast, as well as a grove of eucalyptus trees originally from Australia, and coconut palms brought from Bahia; a century later, all three species abound throughout the region. At other stations he introduced cattle, chickens, and established "Agricultural Schools" where local tribal peoples could learn new forms of farming and husbandry.

On October 4, Rondon was at the Barão de Melgaço station when he received a stack of telegrams from the Ministries of War, Public Works, and Foreign Affairs. He was wanted immediately in the capital: Theodore Roosevelt, former president of the United States, was embarking by ship for Rio de Janeiro that very day, and the Brazilian government had agreed to organize an excursion into Brazil's unmapped interior for him, with Rondon as his escort and chaperone. The most celebrated adventure of Rondon's remarkable career was about to begin.

— PART III —

Principal members of the Roosevelt-Rondon Scientific Expedition at the
confluence of the River of Doubt and the Rio Aripuanã, April 27, 1914.
From left to right: George Cherrie, João Salustiano Lyra, Dr. José Antônio
Cajazeira, Theodore Roosevelt, Cândido Rondon, and Kermit Roosevelt.
Note that Kermit is wearing a Brazilian military uniform, since all of his own
clothing had been consumed by termites and other insects.
(ACERVO DO MUSEU DO ÍNDIO/FUNAI—BRASIL)

XI

"The Greatest Number of Unforeseen Difficulties"

I
N THE ANNALS of exploration, the Roosevelt-Rondon Scientific Expedition of 1913–14 ranks as one of the great feats of modern times. For five months, a team composed at its peak of more than one hundred men, both Brazilians and Americans, few of whom spoke each other's language, made its way across South America's great heartland, across savanna, swamp, plateau, desert, and jungle. They traveled by land and on rivers, on foot and by horse and mule, by truck, steamboat, barge, launch, and canoe, moving supplies, pack animals, and boats across more than 2,500 miles. They confronted disease, wild animals, unanticipated geographic hazards, hostile Indian tribes, and the deepest, darkest recesses of their own souls.

Perhaps just as remarkable was the expedition's command structure. In marked contrast to the usual pattern of exploration in Africa, Asia, and even North America, the Roosevelt-Rondon Scientific Expedition did not have a white man of European descent solely in charge, making all decisions and issuing orders, with anonymous, subordinate "native guides" doing all the heavy lifting and getting none of the credit. Even though Theodore Roosevelt was one of the world's most celebrated figures at the time, he mostly deferred to his Brazilian counterpart, recognizing that Rondon and his men, whether military or civilian, white, Black, or Indian, had the experience and local knowledge essential to their party's survival.

Yet for all its heroic achievements, the Roosevelt-Rondon expedition was hastily organized and haphazardly planned, with its itinerary changed several times before the exploration team even set out. Crucial supplies were omitted, while many superfluous items later had to be jettisoned. It was marked by cultural tensions, with the two commanders and their retinues pursuing different objectives and different exploration strategies. Under instructions to leave a positive impression on his distinguished foreign visitor but at the same time grievously short of money, Rondon in particular was forced to improvise and reduce expenses. All these hurdles make the expedition's contributions to geographic and scientific knowledge even more remarkable.

The difficulties began with Roosevelt's conception of what an expedition in the Amazon might actually entail. After leaving the White House in March 1909, a still-vigorous fifty-year-old, Roosevelt was restless and eager for a respite from American politics. His resulting African safari, which lasted nearly a year, from April 1909 to early in 1910, was meticulously planned in consultation with the renowned English naturalist, explorer, and big game hunter Frederick Selous, author of such books as *Travel and Adventure in South-East Africa* and *A Hunter's Wanderings in Africa*. While he was still in the White House, Roosevelt began an extensive correspondence, seeking advice from British colonial authorities and naturalists and other experts at scientific organizations like the American Museum of Natural History and the Smithsonian Institution on every conceivable subject—what kind and quantity of tinned food to bring, what clothes to pack, what books to read in advance, what weapons were the most effective, and so on.

So by the time Roosevelt arrived at the port of Mombasa, in today's Kenya, on April 21, 1909, he was well equipped and prepared for the adventure ahead. Initially concerned that he was "not fit for the hard work of the genuine African explorer type"[1] due to his "sedentary" years in the White House, he now "worried that he would be mistaken for a 'Cook's tourist,'"[2] so fancy were his accommodations. The first phase of his journey into the interior was on a special train supplied by the governor of British East Africa, and

Roosevelt's daylight hours were mostly spent sitting with Selous on a specially constructed bench attached to the cowcatcher at the front of the locomotive; at breakfast and dinner, abundant repasts were served in the dining car.

Traveling by railway allowed the Roosevelt party to stop whenever and wherever it wanted and to make leisurely hunting forays into the bush and to places like Mount Kenya and Lake Naivasha without having to worry about supply lines; Roosevelt also made occasional rail trips back to Nairobi to resupply, deliver specimens, and check on mail. After reaching Lake Victoria, a new phase began, and the Roosevelt group—which had now swelled to more than three hundred with porters, bearers, and runners included—traveled overland from the lake north across the equator, following a well-trodden route to Lake Albert and the headwaters of the White Nile. On reaching the Nile, Roosevelt and his comrades boarded a comfortable steam-wheeler that took them first to Khartoum, where his wife, Edith, awaited him, and then on to Cairo and a series of speaking engagements in Europe.

The African safari, largely paid for by $95,000 in grants from Andrew Carnegie and other magnates, proved such a pleasant experience that it whetted Roosevelt's appetite for another, more rigorous adventure, more like his youthful days in the wilds of the Dakotas when he worked as a cowboy. Politics delayed that dream, as he chose to run, unsuccessfully, in the 1912 election against both William Howard Taft and Woodrow Wilson. While campaigning, he was shot in the chest by a would-be assassin. So as 1913 dawned, Roosevelt found himself in a situation similar to that of 1909—restless for adventure and disenchanted with politics—but now four years older and various pounds heavier.

Roosevelt once again began to contemplate an escape to the wilderness. This time, though, he focused on the New World, remembering his exploits in Cuba during the Spanish-American War. Roosevelt had recently met a Roman Catholic priest named John Augustine Zahm, who pressed him to collaborate in a tropical American expedition. A member of the Order of the Holy Cross, Zahm had trained as a scientist and written a pair of travel books about South America: *Up the Orinoco and down the Magdalena* in 1910 and *Along the Andes and down the Amazon* in 1912. Encouraged by Zahm's enthusiasm, persistence, and apparent knowledge of the region, Roosevelt acquiesced, and delegated to Zahm the bulk of the responsibilities for organizing an expedition.

Unfortunately, Father Zahm was no Selous, as events subsequently demonstrated; more poseur than true explorer, his South American books were conventional travelogues of journeys in heavily explored areas. Roosevelt was himself sidetracked by other obligations, beginning with looming deadlines for three books he had contracted to write. In addition, in traveling to South America he hoped to combine two very different purposes. The first was to deliver lucrative lectures in the major capitals of the southern half of the continent, on topics like "Essential Virtues of a Democracy" and "Character and Civilization." The second was to undertake serious scientific work in the wilderness. He had combined political and scientific tasks before, in 1909 and 1910, but the speeches were given after the African safari ended, allowing Roosevelt time to compose them while in the wild. Now the sequence was reversed.

Writing the lectures was a particularly delicate task, in view of the unpopularity of the Monroe Doctrine in Latin America and Roosevelt's own reputation as a "Big Stick" imperialist who had carved off a piece of Colombia to build the Panama Canal. Roosevelt did not want to provoke additional controversy with anything he said while in the Southern Hemisphere, so he vetted his speeches with envoys of each country he planned to visit. While he waited for input, rather than prepare for the South American expedition, he went off on a hunting trip to the Grand Canyon with his sons Archie and Quentin and his cousin Nicholas Roosevelt. He "took a personal interest in the preparations" for the Arizona excursion "to make sure it went off without a hitch," but "no such attention to details would characterize the South American trip, which Roosevelt seemed to think would be far less physically demanding."[3]

Left alone to supervise the exploration's logistics, Zahm made a series of curious decisions. For instance, while buying equipment in New York, he met a forty-four-year-old salesman named Anthony

Fiala, a former chemist, cartoonist, Spanish-American War veteran, and member of two polar expeditions—one of which had been marooned in the ice for two years and had to be rescued by a relief party. Fiala implored Zahm to let him join Roosevelt's group, and Zahm promptly agreed. It is unclear why he assumed that an Arctic explorer would know anything about the Amazon, but Fiala was put in charge of procuring the mountain of gear and supplies for the trip.[4]

Later, Roosevelt would express regret for not having paid closer attention to provisioning. In a letter to John Keltie, secretary of the Royal Geographical Society, on February 25, 1915, he acknowledged "the lack of preparation" before the expedition set off, but shifted the blame for "this rather absurd lack of forethought" to a combination of what he called "certain traits of Brazilian character" and Zahm's misjudgments. "If I could have had Kermit make the preparations for me, Fiala bringing down from New York what Kermit advised," he wrote, "we would have made the journey with far fewer accidents, with more comfort and in two weeks less time."[5] He instead chose not to draw on his son's experience in the Brazilian interior.

When it came time to choose the naturalists who would do the hard scientific work of the expedition, Roosevelt took a much more methodical approach. He already knew that his son Kermit, a veteran of the African safari and both a crack shot and a capable taxidermist, would participate. (Roosevelt's wife, Edith, insisted on it, for she worried about her husband's health and his ability to withstand strenuous conditions.) Kermit had been in Brazil since graduating from Harvard in 1912, working as an engineer, first for the Brazil Railway Company and then for the Anglo-Brazilian Iron Company, supervising the construction of railroads, trestles, and bridges. The plan was to pick him up when the rest of the American group stopped in Salvador on its way to Rio de Janeiro. With Kermit's announcement of his engagement to Belle Wyatt Willard, the daughter of the U.S. ambassador to Spain, now imminent, it was an ideal opportunity for father and son to travel together before Kermit's assumption of marital duties. "I had to go," Roosevelt later admitted to a friend. "It was my last chance to be a boy."[6]

For the more technical slots, though, Roosevelt relied on the judgment of his friends Frank Chapman, curator of ornithology at the American Museum of Natural History, and Henry Fairfield Osborn, a paleontologist who was president of the museum's board of trustees. They recommended George Cherrie, a forty-eight-year-old ornithologist who had undertaken more than ten South American expeditions and written dozens of scientific papers, and Leo Miller, a much younger specialist in mammals and reptiles. Roosevelt interviewed Cherrie personally, and heartily endorsed his participation, but could not do the same with Miller, who was on an expedition in the Orinoco.

In Cherrie's case, Roosevelt was taken with not just the ornithologist's professional skills but also his candor. "Colonel, I think you should know a little bit about me before we start on this journey into the wilderness," Cherrie told Roosevelt at their interview. "I think you should know that I occasionally drink." Roosevelt, whose abstemious habits were well known, asked Cherrie what he drank. Well, that depended on what was on hand, the ornithologist replied. "How much do you drink?" was Roosevelt's next question. "All that I want," Cherrie replied. With that, Roosevelt guffawed and said, "Cherrie, just keep right on drinking!"[7]

Zahm was instructed to inform the Brazilian embassy in Washington about Roosevelt's intentions early in 1913. At first, Ambassador Domício da Gama and his staff found it implausible that an obscure middle-aged priest could be speaking for Roosevelt. But once Zahm's bona fides were established, thanks to a letter from Roosevelt, da Gama was intrigued, even delighted. Despite the "Roosevelt Corollary" to the Monroe Doctrine, the former president was viewed in Rio as friendly to Brazilian interests: after all, he had elevated the American diplomatic presence in Brazil from a legation to a full embassy, in recognition of the country's growing importance. "At the turn of the century, an embassy was still a diplomatic rarity found exclusively in the capitals of acknowledged world powers," wrote the historian E. Bradford Burns, noting that Washington then "counted only seven embassies, Rio de Janeiro none." And without the Roosevelt administration's support, the Third

Pan-American Conference would not have been held in Rio in 1906, another diplomatic feather in Brazil's cap.[8]

Zahm's correspondence with the Brazilian embassy in Washington, still on file in the Foreign Ministry archives in Rio, foreshadows problems to come. His tone was imperious, as if he and Roosevelt were doing the Brazilians a favor by deigning to visit their country. He assumed that the Brazilian government would bear all the costs of the expedition, and asked for a Brazilian military detachment to accompany and protect them. He wrote to Ambassador da Gama on September 25, 1913, declaring, "We shall be most grateful if you will have your Government make us provisions for the transportation of our boats, equipment and scientific corps from Cuyaba, or, if need be, from Corumba." He requested, also, "a special yacht or river cruiser" to "contribute materially to the comfort and pleasure of our journey."[9]

When da Gama informed the Foreign Ministry in Rio of Roosevelt's desire to visit Brazil as part of a speaking tour that would include Argentina, Uruguay, and Chile, the Brazilian government reacted with a mixture of enthusiasm and anxiety. If the trip went well, they knew it would generate positive publicity globally that could greatly benefit Brazil. As the Brazilian authorities saw it, if Roosevelt wrote a favorable account of his Amazon travels, it would encourage foreign investment and development there. This was no small consideration for a government almost totally dependent on coffee exports for foreign exchange, and deeply in debt to foreign creditors.

But Brazil's government had to be certain that every moment he spent on Brazilian soil was flawless. As the country's rulers knew better than anyone, this was no easy task in a nation with weak organizational skills, a precarious infrastructure, and a limited budget. "Recognizing the importance of the traveler and of the results of his excursion through our country, which will be the subject of a book and of articles in newspapers and magazines within and outside the United States, I dare to suggest that he be offered all the facilities for his voyage and the most ample and gracious hospitality among us," da Gama recommended in a cable sent on June 27, 1913. "A trip through the wilderness will complete this effect."[10]

And even though Roosevelt had lost the 1912 presidential election, he finished a strong second in a field of four. The American press was filled with speculation that he would run again in 1916, and many expected that this time he would win. Since the birth of the Brazilian republic, Brazilian foreign policy had been based on what Burns calls "an unwritten alliance" with the United States. Thus, strengthening personal ties with a once and perhaps future occupant of the White House offered an easy, relatively cost-free way for Brazil to cement that partnership and advance its other diplomatic goals.

Once the decision was taken to proceed, there was no doubt about who would lead Roosevelt through the wilderness. Lauro Müller, Rondon's old friend, classmate, and fellow editor at *The Academic Family* during their years together at the military academy, had become minister of foreign affairs in February 1912. Based on thirty years of friendship, and knowing the risks of the expedition, he deemed Rondon the only feasible candidate to accompany Roosevelt.

In his memoirs Rondon wrote that he agreed to take Roosevelt through the Amazon only "under the condition that the expedition not limit its activities to a series of excursions to hunt for big game,"[11] and that serious scientific work be undertaken. The archival evidence, however, tells a different story. Nothing in the official record or his diaries indicates how Rondon first learned of the plan for the expedition—whether by a telegram from the Foreign Ministry or in the news summaries the commission's office in Rio regularly telegraphed to him, known as "Rondon's newspaper." But on September 23, 1913, he sent a telegram from the Nhambiquara station, in essence volunteering for the task. He also suggested how it should be staffed and offered a possible itinerary, while laying down his own conditions for accepting the assignment: "The organization of the expedition will be under my care, and the Foreign Minister will place at my disposition the totality of the necessary funds," he wrote, adding: "I propose to prepare everything so that our illustrious guest will lack nothing for the duration of the expedition."[12]

It may be that the enthusiastic tone of the telegram was merely Rondon's obligatory nod to the hierarchical structure of the Brazilian military, meant to please his superiors. But even if that is the case, Rondon's wording indicates several important things. For instance, with Roosevelt due to land in Rio in barely a month, it is clear that the American and Brazilian sides had not yet decided on an itinerary. Nor was the precise degree of difficulty of any such journey into the wilderness clear: Rondon refers both to an "excursion" and an "expedition," which are two very different things.

When Rondon learned on October 4 that he had been chosen to lead the Roosevelt expedition, he immediately headed north to Manaus and then onward to Rio aboard a commercial steamer. "There was no time to lose,"[13] he wrote, since his vessel was racing Roosevelt's to reach Rio. Rondon also ordered canoes to be left at the headwaters of various rivers, so that no matter what itinerary was chosen, the necessary equipment and supplies would be there when the expedition arrived.

The same day, Roosevelt and his party, which included the exploration team, his wife, a private secretary, and a niece, departed from Brooklyn aboard the SS *Vandyck*. At a stop in Barbados, they picked up Leo Miller, returning from a collecting expedition in the Orinoco basin of Venezuela and British Guiana. Miller was under the impression that he had signed on to "a rather short and not too difficult trip up the Paraguay River and down the Tapajós, having as its prime object the study of the fauna and collection of zoological specimens."[14] Once aboard, however, he learned that a far more demanding trip was envisaged, and it worried him, for he could immediately see that Roosevelt was physically unfit.

Of the five itineraries Rondon suggested, the most ambitious was to descend the Rio da Dúvida, the River of Doubt, which he had come upon in 1909. Because of the difficult conditions he encountered during that mission, Rondon had been unable to explore the stream, but he had been yearning to return there. No one knew how long it was, nor the kind of terrain through which it flowed, much less where its waters discharged—hence its provisional name. Did it run northwest, into the Ji-Paraná, in which case its descent would be short and relatively easy? To the northeast, thus feeding into the Tapajós, which would link it to Roosevelt's original itinerary? Could it possibly turn back toward the south and flow into the Paraguay, which would also involve little element of risk? Or did its course take it almost straight north, into the mighty Madeira, as Rondon suspected? There was only one way to know: navigate and map the river from its source to its mouth.

Roosevelt arrived in Rio de Janeiro on October 21 to a surprisingly warm reception, given the opposition to his "Big Stick" diplomacy in Latin America. After making his way through an enthusiastic throng downtown, he paid a courtesy call on President Hermes da Fonseca, who spoke glowingly of his former subaltern and his leadership skills when conversation turned to Roosevelt's voyage into the interior. Then it was on to the Foreign Ministry for a cordial meeting with Müller to plan the final details of the expedition.

Roosevelt later wrote that Müller was "not only an efficient public servant but a man of wide cultivation, with a quality about him that reminded me of John Hay,"[15] his own secretary of state. Rondon would not arrive in Rio until November 11, long after Roosevelt's departure, so Müller carefully laid out each of Rondon's alternatives to Roosevelt. The expedition could follow the route Father Zahm had originally planned down the Tapajós in central Brazil to its junction with the Amazon, he explained. But, he went on, there was also the possibility of descending Rondon's unexplored river, which, Müller hinted, could even be baptized the Roosevelt if it proved sufficiently grand and challenging. If, on the other hand, it was merely a minor tributary of the Ji-Paraná, then Rondon had a backup plan in mind: another unexplored stream in the same area called the Rio Ananás, which was believed to flow into the Tapajós.

Roosevelt promptly chose the itinerary that, in the understated bureaucratic language of Rondon's assessment, "offered the greatest number of unforeseen difficulties":[16] descent of the River of Doubt. He "eagerly and gladly" did so, he later explained, because "I felt that with such help" as Müller was offering, "the trip could be made of much scientific value, and that a substantial addition could be made to geographical knowledge."[17] Not familiar with Roosevelt's no pain, no gain psychology, Müller may have been surprised, for he then offered an honorable escape hatch. "Now, we will be delighted to have you do it, but of course you must understand we cannot tell you anything of what will happen," he said, "and there may be some surprises not necessarily pleasant." But Roosevelt had decided.

With this perhaps impulsive choice, the entire nature and objective of the undertaking changed. Father Zahm had suggested—and Cherrie and Miller were expecting—an expedition whose primary purpose was, in Roosevelt's own words, "biological reconnaissance":[18] as many animal specimens as possible would be gathered along an established route known for the richness of its wildlife. Rondon, in contrast, was proposing an expedition whose main motive was exploration in its purest, most challenging form. Certainly there would also be opportunities along the way to acquire samples of new species of birds, mammals, insects, and fish for the museums in New York and Rio. But the principal focus would now be cartography, not collecting, with the work to be carried out in terrain utterly unknown to either science or geography. That elevated risk-to-reward calculus thrilled Roosevelt.

Müller, of course, knew Rondon well enough to have complete faith in his former classmate's ability to safely shepherd Roosevelt and his party through the most hazardous terrain. But when Roosevelt reported the drastically revised itinerary to the rest of his traveling party later that day, reaction was mixed. Kermit judged it to be a "slightly more hazardous plan," Zahm concurred, and, at least according to Roosevelt, Cherrie and Miller were "more eager than the others" because "they both believe they may get collections for the museum which will be really worthwhile."[19]

But Fiala, having acquired nearly five tons of equipment and supplies, expressed some very practical reservations. How was all of that baggage going to be transported across hundreds of miles of trackless wilderness? What if the River of Doubt turned out to be riddled with rapids? And Edith Roosevelt, who was the most realistic about the former president's health, was especially apprehensive. "Thank heaven Kermit is going," she wrote to her youngest daughter, Ethel, "for though I don't think he is well, at least he is young and strong & Father Zahm already has constant falls by the wayside."[20]

Back in New York both Chapman and Osborn were even more

shocked and alarmed when they learned of the change of plans. Osborn immediately sent a telegram to Roosevelt saying that he "would never consent" to Roosevelt "going to this region under the American Museum flag" and "would not even assume part of the responsibility for what might happen in case" any of the Americans "did not return alive."[21] Chapman was less blunt, but later wrote that he fully realized that "in all South America there is not a more difficult or dangerous journey"[22] than the one Roosevelt had chosen. Neither man's concerns could have been allayed when Roosevelt responded, in typically flippant and fatalistic fashion, that "I have already lived and enjoyed as much of life as any nine other men I know. I have had my full share, and if it is necessary for me to leave my bones in South America, I am quite ready to do so."[23]

So the River of Doubt it would be. Roosevelt and most of his party were scheduled to board an ocean liner that would steam its way from Rio to Montevideo, the capital of Uruguay. After a lecture there, he would cross the Rio de la Plata to Buenos Aires, where he would begin an Argentine tour of speaking engagements, hunting excursions, visits to elegant *estancias* in the pampas, a train trip across the Andes to Chile, where he had more speeches to deliver, then a return to Argentina on horseback and finally on to Paraguay, where he would board the vessel that would deliver him to Rondon. All told, the non-Brazilian legs of his journey were scheduled to last about six weeks.

Though this itinerary gave Rondon additional time to finalize the details of the expedition, he still had to hurry to his ultimate destination. He departed from Rio on November 28, took an overnight train from São Paulo, pausing briefly to check the situation of the recently pacified Kaingang. Disembarking in Mato Grosso, he then galloped his way across his native state on horseback, sometimes riding all night across the plains, until he reached Brazil's border with Paraguay, at the junction of the Apa and Paraguay Rivers, where a vessel requisitioned by the Brazilian government, the *Nyoac*, arrived on December 11. Rondon was now as prepared as he could hope to be, and ready to receive Roosevelt. But one unspoken question now loomed: Would Roosevelt and his party be ready for the Amazon?

XII

Dismissals, Resignations, and Two Colonels

ROOSEVELT AND RONDON finally met around noon on December 12 at the Brazil-Paraguay border. Rondon was wearing a perfectly creased, formal high-collared white dress uniform in anticipation of the first encounter, as he watched the *Adolfo Riquelme*, a Paraguayan military vessel, approaching. He later reflected on the oddness of that moment. Here he was, a humble product of the Brazilian interior, "a man who in the wilderness frequented the courts of the Bororo, the Paresi and the Nhambiquara"[1] and subsisted on the roughest of fare, suddenly thrust into a complex political situation. Now he had to "submit to the ceremonies typical of European diplomacy" and play host to the first American president ever to visit Brazil. Once again, his two worlds—the rugged frontier where he had grown up and the sophisticated upper echelons of power in which he now operated—were converging.

In the end, there was no reason for concern; the introductory ceremonies went off without a hitch. Rondon officially welcomed Roosevelt back to Brazil, introduced his subalterns, and informed his "illustrious guest" that they were completely at his service. "I found myself perfectly at ease," he wrote, in a passage that also revealed his sense of cultural hierarchies. "When we greet each other Bororo-style, we are ready for the strong odor of naked bodies, stained with dye. In contrast, when we trade niceties in the language of Molière, we are imperceptibly led to gestures and words of the most refined elegance."[2]

Once the protocols and pleasantries were over and practical considerations resolved, a formal lunch was served aboard the *Nyoac*, a small steamship owned by the state-controlled Lloyd Brasileiro Navigation Company. Rondon automatically conferred on Roosevelt the soldierly title of "Colonel," which the former Rough Rider treasured. Roosevelt responded in kind, and for the next five months the two men would invariably address each other by the military rank they shared, a sign of mutual respect.

The language issue was trickier. Kermit had always shown a talent for languages, and had acquired excellent Portuguese since coming to Brazil. So he could serve as an interpreter when the entire group was together or his father needed to talk to one of the porters or boatmen. But what about when Roosevelt and Rondon were alone? Rondon was far from confident in English, and Roosevelt spoke no Portuguese. But Rondon spoke and wrote a polished French, and Roosevelt's command of that language was adequate, if heavily accented and often, as he put it, "without tense or gender."[3] So French became the preferred vehicle for direct, unfiltered communications between the expedition's co-leaders; Rondon, Roosevelt, and Kermit would also trade volumes of French poetry and lighter fare, such as the "Arsène Lupin" novels.

Other equally delicate matters were left for later. Roosevelt's supplies and equipment were in crates labeled "Colonel Roosevelt's South American Expedition for the American Museum of Natural History." But when Roosevelt boarded the *Nyoac*, he noticed that the Brazilians' crates bore a different label: "Roosevelt-Rondon Scientific Expedition." This name gave the Brazilians equal standing with the Americans, and emphasized the serious technical work that Rondon hoped to accomplish. In the initial article of the series he wrote for *Scribner's Magazine*, Roosevelt stuck to his original terminology. But as he came to know Rondon and respect his acumen, he relented, and by January 1914, the undertaking had officially become known as the Roosevelt-Rondon Scientific Expedition.

The morning after their first meeting, Rondon and Roosevelt left the rest of the expedition party aboard the *Nyoac* and went hunting together. In the end, their foray became a bonding exercise, with the two commanders getting to know each other and discussing the expedition's itinerary. Rondon noted approvingly that Roosevelt had a calm, steady aim and did not like to waste bullets. Back on board, he was impressed when Roosevelt upbraided the *Nyoac's* Brazilian crewmen for killing a magnificent *biguatinga*—part of a flock of anhingas that Roosevelt had been observing with admiration as they rested along the riverbank—just for the sheer sport of it.

"For Mr. Roosevelt it was unforgivable to kill any animal without a purpose," Rondon noted. He soon realized that Roosevelt was a genuine naturalist, someone who "let no opportunity to acquire knowledge pass" and who "passionately devoured books,"[4] just like Rondon.

The admiration was mutual: "We are very much pleased with Col. Rondon," Roosevelt wrote to his wife in a Christmas Eve letter. "He is very hardy, and fitted for this kind of business by twenty-five years' experience, and is evidently agreeably surprised by our conduct; and he is most anxious to do all in his power for us. Everything possible is done for my comfort, in the little ways that mean so much to a man of my age on a rough trip."[5]

But the favored treatment of Roosevelt, and to some extent the other Americans, rankled a few of the Brazilian members of the expedition. None was more resentful, Rondon wrote, than Fernando Soledade, the expedition's chief physician, a public health specialist who had compiled a distinguished record combating yellow fever, malaria, and Chagas disease in Rio de Janeiro, exactly the type of tropical diseases the expedition was likely to encounter. From the start, though, he and Rondon clashed, with Rondon complaining that Soledade was insolent, arrogant, and undisciplined.

With the expedition barely underway and more than 1,100 miles from Rio, Rondon needed to find an immediate, high-quality alternative to Soledade, who was already starting to undermine morale. Fortunately, he had a backup plan in place due to his meticulous advance preparation. On arrival in Rio in November, Rondon had asked the army high command to designate a second physician to accompany the expedition, and even suggested a name: José Antônio Cajazeira, director of the military hospital in Corumbá. This turned out to be an extraordinarily fortuitous move, because "dear little Dr. Cajazeira,"[6] as Roosevelt came to affectionately call him, would emerge as the great unsung hero of the Roosevelt-Rondon Scientific Expedition.

Cajazeira had enlisted in the army only in 1909, at the age of forty, impelled by a deep interest in tropical diseases and their treatment. Before assignment to Corumbá in 1913, he did tours of duty on the lower Amazon and in Mato Grosso.[7] That was where Rondon came to know him and respect his professionalism.

By far the biggest challenge Rondon had to resolve in Corumbá, however, had to do with the expedition's finances. From the expedition's inception, he had been under unrelenting pressure to reduce traveling costs. In the formal letter appointing Rondon as head of the expedition and delineating his duties, Müller originally empowered Rondon to "take along the assistance he judges appropriate," a very broad mandate. But the foreign minister then crossed out the last word, writing instead that Rondon was authorized to take along only what was "indispensable"[8] to the undertaking, a change in orders that significantly reduced Rondon's discretionary powers.

In the same letter Müller also stipulated that "the Federal Government expects you will make every effort to provide Mr. Roosevelt with the necessary comfort and security during the itinerary." This apparently contradictory set of instructions had bedeviled Rondon for a month, and compounded his concerns once he arrived in Corumbá. Rondon had been sending daily messages to Müller, informing him of all relevant developments, and five days after greeting Roosevelt, he received a worrisome response. "I have received your telegrams, for which I thank you," his old friend began, before expressing his main point: "Insisting necessity shorten expedition in view current financial difficulties."[9] To raise funds for the expedition, Müller suggested that Rondon himself ask the state of Amazonas to help with funding, since it had accumulated significant tax revenues during the rubber boom.

This put Rondon in an impossible position. In order to reduce outlays, he had already declined the government's offer of bonus payments for him and his men, telling the Foreign Ministry that "I already receive wages as an Army officer and, therefore, will proceed on the expedition with that salary."[10] But the ministry had not been as obliging toward him, for Rondon reached Corumbá to find that some of the funding for expedition expenses had not arrived and indeed may not even have been authorized. As a result he had to purchase supplies, equipment, and pack animals on credit, using his own name as guarantor, and to draw from funds Congress had designated for the Telegraph Commission and the SPI. Indeed, it is no exaggeration to say that the Indigenous peoples of Brazil paid for some portion of Roosevelt's foray into the Amazon, since it took years for the federal government to reimburse Rondon for most of the money he advanced.

Rondon's troubles worsened when Botelho de Magalhães, the expedition's de facto quartermaster, described the equipment the Americans had brought from the United States. The Brazilian side had thirty-eight containers in all: "9 for campaign tents, one with the markers for the Roosevelt and Kermit rivers, and 28 with foodstuffs for the troops and with their respective baggage," he wrote. The much smaller American contingent, in contrast, had ninety-nine containers weighing some five tons, "almost all of them made up of foodstuffs." In a tiny gesture that spoke volumes, Botelho de Magalhães indicated his astonishment at this amount by appending an exclamation point between parentheses after that number: "(!)"[11]

As a result, more pack animals and more soldiers would have to be found to haul and guard provisions on the trail—which meant more expense. Caught between the contradictory demands of the Foreign Ministry's tightfistedness and the extravagance of the Americans, Rondon chose the option that would cause the least embarrassment: the expedition would proceed exactly as originally planned, with no stinting on necessities.

The Americans were eager to leave Corumbá, especially Cherrie and Miller, who had arrived while Roosevelt was in Argentina and had exhausted the possibilities for collecting. Roosevelt, too, was impatient to start the expedition, and did not want to be bogged down by the flood of invitations to social events. But Rondon was still hamstrung by logistical problems, and needed to wait until the high command in Rio approved Cajazeira's transfer. So the explorers paused for just over a week in Corumbá, resuming their travels only on Christmas Day 1913.

Once again aboard the *Nyoac*, they steamed into the Pantanal, Rondon's native region. Rondon regaled Roosevelt and the others with stories about his childhood and described the local flora and fauna. There were also frequent stops for hunting and collecting excursions and at ranches where local bosses plied them with lavish meals. On December 28, they were greeted by the governor of Mato Grosso, accompanied by a military brass band and assorted dignitaries, who had traveled south from Cuiabá. As the days passed, one stream gave way to another: the Paraguay, the São Lourenço, the Cuiabá.

"The pantanal, invaded as always this time of year by water, was an immense lake whose serene surface reflected the slender trunks of carandá and uacari palms thrusting upwards," Rondon wrote. "The life of that entire swollen region was now concentrated in charming refuges that had emerged from the enormous flood. And in the thickness of the forests wandered the famished jaguar, while from the branches grotesque howler monkeys leaped and flocks of jet-black cormorants landed, offering a sharp contrast to the snowy-white herons."[12]

For Rondon, this otherwise idyllic interlude was marred by the knowledge that he was again missing a significant family event back in Rio. Devotion to duty had kept him absent from the birth of all seven of his children; now, thanks to a force majeure named Roosevelt, he was unable to attend the wedding of Aracy, his twenty-one-year-old daughter. She was marrying Emmanuel Amarante, one of Rondon's favorite adjutants, who was therefore unavailable for the expedition. At lunch on December 27, the same day the couple was married in a Roman Catholic ceremony, the captain of the *Nyoac*, seconded by Roosevelt, offered a toast to the newlyweds.

On January 5, the voyagers and their vessel left the Pantanal behind and arrived in São Luís de Cáceres, the last sizable settlement that they would see until they reached Manaus, some 1,500 miles away. During the day they had already observed the terrain changing: small hills had begun to dot the landscape, and vegetation grew denser, though broken by small clearings with humble straw huts. Arrival in São Luís de Cáceres starkly marked the end of the expedition's easiest stage: upon disembarking, the garrison commander told Rondon that of the men he had requested for the next phase of the trip, three had drowned while exploring the Ji-Paraná River, and the fourth, Capt. Cândido Cardoso, a longtime stalwart of the Telegraph Commission, had succumbed to beriberi. But fortuitously Lt. João Salustiano Lyra, whom Rondon envisioned as his second in command in the absence of Amarante, had now joined the expedition.

From here on in, Rondon warned the Americans, there would be no more excursions "aboard small but comfortable ships, with good meals and pleasant nights in hammocks swinging from the aft, without mosquitos."[13] For the next few days, they would travel on *lanchas*, small and simple wooden craft whose only protection from the elements was a crude overhead canvas canopy. After that, he advised, the explorers would journey overland to the River of Doubt, for several hundred miles, on horseback, on mule, and on foot, mostly following the path of the telegraph line. When they took to the water again, at the end of that land journey, it would be in canoes, not in any kind of mechanized vessel. The greenhorns had been forewarned: when Rondon jokingly asked the *Nyoac*'s cook, whose skills had been much appreciated by Brazilians and Americans alike, if he wouldn't like to continue with them into the wilds, the cook just as lightheartedly replied, "Sir, I've done nothing to deserve that kind of punishment!"[14]

Two days later, the expedition set up camp for the first time, at a river landing known as Porto Campo, initiating a routine that would be invariably repeated over the next eight weeks. First, tents were erected, with those of Roosevelt and Rondon on wooden flooring at the center and the others arranged around them. In an open area in front of the leaders' tents, two tall wooden poles were installed, for flags to be flown. Since the expedition was technically a military undertaking, at least on the Brazilian side, Rondon insisted "even on the most difficult days"[15] that both the Brazilian and American banners be hoisted each morning and lowered at dusk, with a cornet sounding, and with all personnel present.

Rondon, always an early riser, began his day whenever possible with a predawn swim in whatever water was closest to camp. After reveille, when everyone was assembled, he would read the order of the day. Briefly summarizing the past days' activities, he would then announce future objectives and assign each man his duties. He did this habitually until the expedition ended, ignoring the element of repetition involved: like the flag-raising ceremony, reading the order of the day was a way of imposing structure, regularity, and stability in the midst of often chaotic situations.

In camp, all food was prepared by a Brazilian cook, with the Americans and the Brazilians eating together. Rondon's normal practice on previous expeditions was to ignore differences of status and rank at mealtime: the officers, enlisted men, and local caboclos usually ate side by side, or sitting together on a large oxhide thrown onto the ground. Early on, Kermit and Cherrie embraced the custom of having a whiskey together at day's end, but Rondon drank the tealike maté as his only concession to stimulants, and discouraged any other consumption of alcohol. After supper was eaten and darkness fell, the expedition's members gathered around a blazing fire to tell stories.

Already, Dr. Soledade's querulous relationship with the other members of the group, especially Rondon, was beginning to fester. Throughout the early stages of the expedition, Rondon was constantly shifting Brazilian military and civilian personnel from one work unit to another, carefully evaluating the chemistry among members of each team and each member's performance, all part of the process of selecting the best group possible for descending the River of Doubt. In an order of the day read after arriving at Tapirapoan in mid-January, Rondon announced that Cajazeira, rather than the more eminent Soledade, would accompany Roosevelt and Rondon on that journey; Soledade was instead assigned to a secondary group under the command of Botelho de Magalhães. It was a public humiliation, and Soledade was resentful, but Rondon would not relent.

Roosevelt, on the other hand, was proving to be a boon traveling companion, affable and uncomplaining, and quickly gained the affection of the Brazilians. He peppered his hosts with questions about every aspect of the local wildlife, much to their delight, and wanted to know everything about the Indigenous peoples the expedition would soon encounter: their cultures, religions, sports, family arrangements, and so on. He also developed a taste for *canja*, a rice-based soup most often consumed with bits of chicken in it, and requested it wherever he went.

Occasionally, though, Roosevelt would grow impatient at the expedition's slow pace or what he saw as the Brazilians' failure to share information. On January 20, for example, he pulled Botelho de Magalhães aside to complain of a sudden change in plans, knowing that Botelho de Magalhães, as Rondon's most trusted adjutant, would immediately transmit that objection to his chief. Roosevelt was willing, Botelho de Magalhães recorded in his diary, to do "whatever was most agreeable" for the Brazilians, but insisted "that there be total frankness with him and that he be forewarned about everything," especially any delays. Botelho de Magalhães chalked this up to Roosevelt's inexperience as an Amazon explorer, and politely told him so: "It was only today that it was possible to alert you, since in the wilderness not everything can be predicted,"[16] he said, according to his diary.

The Telegraph Commission maintained its headquarters at Tapirapoan, where the expedition paused for several days to resupply and regroup. Rondon and his men organized the pack animals for the long haul over the plateau, while Cherrie and Miller, with Kermit accompanying them, did more collecting. By now the naturalists had accumulated at least 1,000 bird specimens and 250 mammals, the majority of them unknown. At the next major stop, Utiarity, these were to be duly preserved, catalogued, and prepared for shipment back to New York. Frank Harper, Roosevelt's private secretary, had contracted malaria, and became the first American to leave the expedition; the specimens would return with him.

On January 23, the expedition ascended the plateau, pausing occasionally to catch a last glimpse of the northern edge of the Pantanal, before crossing the continental divide. All the rivers they had seen and traversed previously flowed south into the Paraguay and eventually the Rio Plata and the South Atlantic Ocean. But from now on, all water would flow north, toward the world's largest river, a body of water so immense that Brazilians called it "the river-sea." Five weeks after setting off, the explorers had finally entered the Amazon basin.

Though the expedition was gradually advancing toward its objective, Dr. Soledade's constant carping and belligerence were becoming intolerable. Increasingly irked, on January 24 Rondon dismissed him, and told the rest of the Brazilian contingent that anyone else unhappy with the deference being shown the American guests was welcome to join the doctor. Two specialists on the technical side, a botanist and a taxidermist, also chose to leave, as did Luiz Thomaz Reis, who was frustrated at Roosevelt's restrictions on his ability to photograph and film.

Rondon was irate at this embarrassing development, and blamed the disagreeable situation solely on Soledade, whom he accused of being the "author of the revolt" against the preferential treatment he was extending to Roosevelt in accordance with the orders received from the highest government levels in Rio. In a blistering confidential telegram sent to Lauro Müller he castigated Soledade, explaining to the foreign minister that he was writing "so that you can avoid greater unpleasantness" in case Soledade began spreading negative stories about the expedition and its leaders when he returned to the capital.

Soledade, Rondon told Müller, "has only made my diplomatic mission more difficult, leaving a very bad taste in everyone's mouth and finally rebelling against my provisions to implement Col. Roosevelt's desires, dragging some companions along with him" on the path to "disobedience and insubordination." Although the "incorrect conduct of this group," Rondon added, "filled all the members of the expedition with indignation, including Col. Roosevelt," he hastened to assure Müller that Roosevelt was not offended. "Col. Roosevelt fortunately has understood everything and continues this thorny expedition confident in the support of the government."[17] In fact, Roosevelt never mentioned the unpleasant incident in a best-selling account of the expedition published the next year—and neither did Rondon in his memoirs or in any of his many speeches or interviews about his travels with Roosevelt.

By now, it was also clear to all that Father Zahm was both a burden and a shirker. "Of our whole expedition, everyone works hard except good little Father Zahm," Roosevelt wrote to Edith. Kermit's verdict was harsher: Zahm, he observed in his diary, was simply "a very commonplace little fool."[18] The breaking point occurred during the slog from Tapirapoan to Utiarity: Zahm was having such difficulty riding his horse, and complaining so much about it, that Rondon ordered Dr. Cajazeira to ride with him in case a medical problem developed. So when a pair of trucks suddenly appeared, laden with supplies for the next staging point, it seemed typical that Zahm, rather than continue on his mount with the others, would cadge a ride on one of the trucks.

The original plan had been to send only Cherrie and Miller ahead to Utiarity in one of the trucks. That would allow the naturalists more time to collect and properly process specimens, a difficult task when they were constantly in motion. An Indian driver took them on, as the two Americans noted in their diaries, and proved quite skilled both at dealing with engine problems and in extracting the vehicle when it inevitably became mired in sand or mud.

But Father Zahm pressed for a seat for himself aboard another vehicle, and then seemed unhappy and ill at ease to have to sit with a Black driver. In a letter to Roosevelt after the expedition, he complained of being placed next to "an ignorant and careless negro" who demonstrated "his incompetence in many ways"[19] during the drive, which lasted three days instead of one, as Rondon had predicted. Zahm made his resentment clear about Rondon's supposedly deliberate slight, and he may well have been correct.

Then, when Rondon and Roosevelt arrived in Utiarity a few days later, the priest floated an idea as preposterous as it was insulting: going forward he wanted to be borne on a palanquin, a sedan chair that would be carried by four strong young Paresi men.

Roosevelt and the other Americans were acutely embarrassed by what they recognized as a racial slight to the expedition's co-leader. "You realize, of course, that you are offending the principles of my good friend Col. Rondon,"²⁰ Roosevelt said to the priest as Rondon looked on. But Zahm persisted. "Indians are meant to carry priests," he said to Roosevelt later, out of Rondon's earshot. "I have resorted to such transportation myself several times" in Peru, where, he said, Indians considered such a task "an honor worth disputing."²¹

As if this were not enough, Father Zahm was also making himself a pest among the Paresi, whose terrain the expedition had now entered. He boasted of the success of his efforts to proselytize the tribe's members, much to the amused derision of the other Americans, and vowed to energetically preach the gospel in "Nhambiquara land" as the expedition moved northwest. This, of course, came close to defying regulations of the Indian Protection Service. Policy on the matter was clear: Indigenous people were free to practice their own traditional faiths, or embrace another, whether Roman Catholicism or a Protestant denomination. But they could not be proselytized. Zahm was flouting this principle in Rondon's face, but Rondon said nothing, afraid to offend the visiting Americans and to be viewed as an ungenerous and intolerant host.

In the end, Roosevelt resolved the disagreeable situation, calling Zahm to his tent after the expedition set up camp on February 3. "Since you can't stand to ride any more, you will return to Tapirapoan immediately,"²² he bluntly told the priest, evading the real reason for his decision. Rondon described the exchange between the two Americans as one marked by "heated words."²³ Evidently fearing that Zahm might make a fuss on returning to Rio and talk to the press, or concoct an even more self-acquitting account of events once he reached the United States, Roosevelt also took the precaution of carefully drafting a written statement explaining his dismissal.

"Every member of the expedition has told me that in his opinion it is essential to the success and well being of the expedition that Father Zahm should . . . return to settled country,"²⁴ he wrote. A draft of the statement shows that Roosevelt originally wrote "Every American member of the expedition,"²⁵ but clearly there was strength in numbers, and so the Brazilians were also recruited: the final version had nine signatures, including Rondon's and the other Brazilian officers'.

"Dr. Zahm had gotten much on 'T.R.'s' nerves!"[26] Cherrie wrote in his journal. With the most difficult part of the mission still ahead, and the expedition's morale in jeopardy, both leaders had already found it necessary to act decisively to rid themselves of malcontents.

XIII

Boxes and Rain

ONCE FATHER ZAHM was banished, Fiala was in jeopardy. His situation, though, was more complicated: he was a hard worker who pulled his weight without complaint and an entertaining storyteller, which made him popular with the others. But he was not really needed. So after camp was made on February 4, Roosevelt summoned Fiala and delivered the bad news: he, too, was being cut from the group to descend the River of Doubt.

Roosevelt tried to soften the blow—and reward Fiala's constructive role—by suggesting that rather than return home immediately, in disgrace like Zahm, he join a secondary group Rondon was organizing to explore and map a pair of other rivers, both tributaries of the Tapajós, under the command of Lt. Alcides Lauriadó de Sant'Anna. If all went well, Roosevelt added, that team would reach Manaus in about three months, Fiala could await the arrival of the main party there, and then return to New York with the other Americans and share in some of the glory.

So "Fiala left us and started back toward Utiarity at 10 p.m.," Cherrie wrote in his diary. "I think his going had a saddening effect on all of us, and Fiala himself was almost in tears. Of the North Americans only four of our original party are left!"[1]

The conditions were about to become significantly more difficult, requiring an even greater level of teamwork and alertness. The Rondon Commission's improvised truck trail ended at Utiarity, which meant that all land travel from that point on would be by foot or on mules or oxen, through terrain that, as the explorers turned westward toward Nhambiquara territory, would eventually become densely forested and full of wild animals.

Rondon had carved out the overland route across the Mato Grosso highlands, and at a high cost. Along the route, simple wooden crosses—surrounded by small, rudimentary fences to keep foraging animals away from the makeshift graves—marked spots where members of earlier expeditions were interred, felled by dysentery or malaria, attacked by jaguars or caimans, struck by poison-tipped arrows, bitten by venomous snakes, or simply consumed by exhaustion.

The Mato Grosso highlands are also known as the Paresi plateau, and on the trail to Utiarity, beginning around Aldeia Queimada, Roosevelt had come into contact for the first time with members of that tribe. The telegraph stations Rondon built after his 1907 expedition soon became magnets for the Paresi, offering protection and sustenance. Rondon introduced Roosevelt to Paresi telegraph operators, and also to other salaried tribal members whose task it was to maintain the line or manage the ferry service Rondon had installed at key river crossings. Out on the plain, following the path of the telegraph line, clumps of Paresi men, on hunting forays and armed with spears or bows and arrows, crossed paths with the explorers, greeting Rondon and the other Brazilians affably. "The Paresi received me as a friend and chieftain, to be loved and obeyed,"[2] Rondon noted in his diary.

Before long, the explorers arrived at the first Paresi village, a place Rondon called Salto Belo, or "Beautiful Waterfall," a literal translation of its original Paresi name, Timalatiá. The cordial Paresi had set up camp for their visitors, with the Brazilian and American flags flapping in the breeze. Roosevelt was struck by the Paresi's gentleness, especially the affectionate way the men treated their wives and children. For his part, Rondon noted that this group of Paresi seemed "exceptionally happy and good-humored" and that "the children approached without fear, as if seeking caresses." This was exactly the sense of social harmony he wished to convey to the Americans, so he was greatly pleased. To cap things off, the next morning, breakfast was served at tables overlooking the waterfall: it was "impossible to imagine a more sumptuous dining room,"[3] Rondon wrote contentedly.

The next stop, just eight miles away, was Utiarity itself. About a half mile from the telegraph station was a large village, whose inhabitants included recent arrivals from other locales who sought to benefit from Brazilian civilization. The residents had received collective title to the land, and were now learning to raise cattle; there was also a school where the stationmaster's wife gave lessons in reading, writing, and arithmetic to the Paresi children, and even a rudimentary infirmary. Roosevelt must have been paying close attention, because *Through the Brazilian Wilderness* teems with colorful details about the daily life of the Paresi.

Rondon also showed Roosevelt Utiarity's natural wonders, the most important of which was the waterfall, which Rondon had camped nearby in 1907, cementing his role as the supreme leader of the Paresi. The drop here was twice that of Salto Belo, and water flowed into a deep gorge adorned on both sides by what Roosevelt described as "a towering growth of tropical forest." Roosevelt was impressed: despite overcast skies, he passed the better part of an afternoon just sitting and observing the cataract. "I doubt whether, excepting, of course, Niagara, there is a waterfall in North America which outranks this if both volume and beauty are considered," he wrote. "At all times, and under all lights, it was majestic and beautiful."[4]

Roosevelt also spent part of each day hunting, alone and armed only with a rifle. "Almost always," Rondon noted, Roosevelt "returned without any game whatsoever, because, being extremely near-sighted, he could not spot the animals from a distance, and so they had time to flee upon hearing the noise of his footsteps."[5]

On joint excursions away from the others—whether to hunt, observe nature, or discuss matters related to the expedition—Roosevelt and Rondon conversed animatedly. Roosevelt the naturalist was fascinated by the new animal species he was seeing, and peppered Rondon with inquiries. But sometimes their conversation, stimulated by Roosevelt's contacts with the Paresi and stories he had heard about the Nhambiquara, veered toward the very different policies toward Indigenous peoples pursued by Brazil and the United States. Roosevelt had been exposed to Positivism as an undergraduate at Harvard, and while unconvinced by Comte's philosophy, he was curious about Rondon's "Die if you must, but kill never" dictum, and its effect.

Rondon, in turn, wanted to know everything about the U.S. Bureau of Indian Affairs, and questioned Roosevelt incessantly. How did the reservation system work, and who determined a reservation's boundaries? What did Indian agents actually do, and how were they chosen and trained? What role did commissioners play in Washington? How were Indian children educated? What was the policy regarding the preservation of Indigenous languages and cultures? To what degree had Indians been assimilated into white society? Ever since the establishment of the SPI, the Brazilian embassy in Washington had been sending Rondon the U.S. government's *Bulletin of Indian Affairs*, but now he could question Roosevelt directly.

In office, Roosevelt had at best a mixed record on Indigenous issues. His youthful experience as a cowboy in the Dakotas resulted in a certain sympathy for the Indians' plight, and Indigenous advocacy groups initially had high hopes for his administration. "No man in the country has a fuller or more practical sympathy with the Indians than President Roosevelt, nor a better understanding of their needs and conditions,"[6] the Indian Rights Association declared shortly after he was sworn in. But his public declarations as president were inconsistent, as were his policies. Visiting Oklahoma Territory in 1905, he declared: "Give the red man the same chance as the white. This country is founded on a doctrine of giving each man a fair show to see what there is in him." But he also said that "the truth is, the Indians never had any real title to the soil," and argued in favor of "pulverizing" collective tribal identities, saying, "The time has arrived when we should definitely make up our minds to recognize the Indian as an individual and not as a member of a tribe."[7]

His views thus diverged markedly from Rondon's. But upon returning to the United States, Roosevelt seems to have slightly modulated some of his opinions. He pulled back from endorsement of the "pulverization" approach, and also explicitly recognized that there might be an alternative to the policy of violent extermination that successive American administrations had pursued.

Rondon clearly influenced this shift, as Roosevelt acknowledges in his later writings. He praised Rondon for transforming Indigenous groups "who previously had often been exploited and maltreated" into "loyal friends of the government" by his "just, kindly and understanding treatment."[8] Rondon's policy, he felt, consisted of an enhanced role for a benevolent and nonviolent state, and a reduced one for religious and charitable groups: "Indians must be treated with intelligent and sympathetic understanding, no less than with justice and firmness; and until they become citizens, absorbed into the general body politic, they must be the wards of the nation, and not of any private association, lay or clerical, no matter how well-meaning."[9] This, Roosevelt added, was "the exact view that is taken in the United States by the staunchest and wisest friends of the Indians," among whom he presumably included himself.

"It has been his mixture of firmness, good nature and good judgment that has enabled him to control these bold warlike savages, and even to reduce the warfare between them," Roosevelt admiringly wrote of Rondon after witnessing his pacifist approach to the Nhambiquara. "They were originally exceedingly hostile and suspicious, but the colonel's unwearied thoughtfulness and good temper, joined with his indomitable resolution, enabled him to avoid war and to secure their friendship and even their aid. He never killed one."[10]

At their next stop, the Juruena station, on February 8, Rondon and Roosevelt received a telegram informing them that Fiala's group, with young Lt. Sant'Anna in command, had left Utiarity the day before, but within hours had nearly come to a disastrous end. Two of the group's three dugout canoes, including the one in which Fiala was traveling, had been pulled into a turbulent whirlpool known as "the Devil's Rapids" and their contents spilled into the Papagaio River. The Brazilians on board fought their way to the riverbank, but both Fiala and the bulk of the party's supplies—which included animal specimens, photographs, canisters of film, guns, ammunition, and letters that were supposed to be sent from Manaus to New York or Rio de Janeiro—were swept downstream. About half the group's food and most of its equipment were lost, requiring a return to Utiarity to obtain replacements.

Fiala survived and, fortunately, no further mishaps occurred— except that every member of the secondary party contracted malaria as they made their way north toward the Tapajós River; they arrived in Santarém, where the Tapajós flows into the Amazon, on March 22. The high incidence of malaria among Sant'Anna's group seemed peculiar to Dr. Cajazeira when he later learned of it, and in his final report on the health of each of the expedition's participants, he placed responsibility for the problem squarely on the commander's shoulders. "A young, enthusiastic, organized and robust officer, he surely imagined that we were exaggerating the dangers emanating from malaria, as well as our praise for the benefits of quinine," Cajazeira wrote. "What is clear is that he abandoned the prophylaxis followed as far as Utiarity just as soon as he began to navigate the Papagaio."[11]

Meanwhile, the main expedition was beginning to suffer the consequences of its poor planning and execution. Perhaps the most fundamental issue was its inopportune timing. Rondon knew this unforgiving terrain and climate well, having been there in 1907 and on expeditions in 1908 and 1909 and again in 1912 and 1913. But in each instance, he had headed into the wilderness in June or July, to maximize his time in the field during the dry season. By the time the rainy season began around mid-November he would be wrapping up his activities for the year. The Roosevelt-Rondon Scientific Expedition, in contrast, was operating on an almost completely reversed calendar, to accommodate Roosevelt's schedule. Heading northward, it had crossed the Tropic of Capricorn on December 10, when more prudent explorers were heading home.

It is possible to travel in the Amazon basin during the rainy season; Rondon would never have agreed to the expedition with Roosevelt otherwise. But the bad weather so common during that period certainly increased the difficulty of the undertaking. Heading north, toward the equator, torrential downpours began to slow the expedition's progress, sap its morale, and make its participants more vulnerable to fatigue and disease. Rondon, however, was laconic— "a truly difficult stage for the expedition,"[12] he commented in his diary—but the Americans, unaccustomed to such conditions, were astonished and dismayed.

"Everything became moldy except what became rusty. It rained all that night; and daylight saw the downpour continuing with no prospect of cessation,"[13] Roosevelt lamented. Even when it wasn't raining, "there was so much humidity in the air that everything grew damp,"[14] he noted.

The incessant rains also exacerbated another problem: the Americans' excess equipment and supplies. For the mules and oxen, crossing the plateau was a trial even in the best of times, given the paucity of edible grasses for grazing. In the rainy season, however, they were constantly bogging down in the mud or slipping and sliding as they lost their balance on the slick rocks. The Americans' heavy crates made matters even worse for the pack animals.

Cherrie, the most experienced of the Americans, had worried about this problem from the very beginning. When he and Miller arrived in Corumbá in late November, two weeks before meeting the Brazilians, they were dismayed. "I have not written anything about the organization of our expedition, but now I am going to record my opinion that a greater lack of organization seems hardly possible!" Cherrie noted in his diary on November 25. "There is no head, no chief of the expedition." He considered Fiala "utterly incompetent for the work he has to do, without previous experience in the tropics & the almost insurmountable handicap of not having any knowledge of the language."[15]

Fiala had also presumed the expedition would obtain much of its nourishment from hunting and fishing. "For meat, the rubber hunter and explorer depends on his rifle and fish-hook,"[16] he explained. That might have been a safe assumption in parts of the Amazon already familiar to travelers, but it was a risky notion going into unknown territory like the River of Doubt, especially in the wettest months of the year. At the height of the rainy season, as the Americans had already seen in their brief excursion through the Pantanal, rivers rise to peak levels, dispersing fish that during the dry season normally congregate in smaller, isolated pools, where they are so hungry that they snap eagerly at almost any kind of bait, making them far easier to catch.

Nor was it going to be easy to shoot the game animals that are staples of the river dweller's diet: tapirs, peccaries, armadillos, deer, anteaters. As the waters rose and rivers spilled over their banks, animals living at ground level no longer foraged or sunned themselves near the river's edge, but fled to drier ground, far from the explorers' reach. The situation for birds, monkeys, and other inhabitants of the canopy was much the same. They, too, had gone deeper into the jungle. To hunt them would require more patience, a sharper eye than Roosevelt had, and perhaps even more ammunition. Obtaining even honey and hearts of palm, basic ingredients of the caboclos' diet, was going to entail greater effort once the main party began its descent of the River of Doubt.

The Brazilian custom was always to travel light, live as much as possible off the land, and not be burdened with superfluous items. Rondon's expeditions were always aware that until they reached unexplored territory they could easily purchase basics like rice and beans from peasant farmers; they also knew that cattle, fruit, and vegetables were being cultivated on farms and ranches springing up around telegraph stations. In addition, they often slaughtered their oxen for food as they progressed deeper into the wilderness and the weight of the supplies they were carrying diminished.

They had assumed, incorrectly, that the Americans would travel in just as lean a fashion, and now confronted a growing logistical problem: the expedition's pack animals were unable to tolerate the heavy loads they were carrying. Rondon sent a large team of muleteers ahead with the bulk of the supplies and equipment, but as the main party eventually caught up with the slow-moving supply team, it encountered boxes that had fallen off the backs of mules or oxcarts as well as the corpses of exhausted pack animals littering the trail.

The expedition had gradually been shedding equipment and supplies as it moved deeper into the wilderness, but now the time had come to jettison anything superfluous: men, pack animals, provisions, equipment. All but a pair of the water-resistant tents presented to Roosevelt by Lauro Müller, specially designed for Amazon conditions but heavy and cumbersome to transport, were now discarded: the four Americans would sleep in one of them, and Rondon, Lyra, and

Cajazeira would sleep in the other. One smaller, lighter tent was also spared, but was reserved for ailing expedition members to be quarantined or protected from the rain. The caboclos would have to string up their hammocks wherever they could, exposed to the elements.

Writing to the Royal Geographical Society's secretary, John Keltie, a year later, Roosevelt blamed the Brazilians for bringing excess equipment. "The Latin American mind puts a totally different emphasis on things from ours," he claimed. "Our companions cared immensely for what they regarded as splendor."[17] By this, Roosevelt explained, he meant not just the tents the Brazilian government had provided, which he thought "utterly unsuited for the work," but also "a most elaborate silver-mounted saddle and bridle"[18] the foreign minister had also given him.

Roosevelt claimed that he "had to exercise real tact, because it almost broke the heart of good Colonel Rondon"[19] to jettison the tents, but Rondon's journal tells a different story. With no particular love of luxury himself, as his record makes clear, Rondon was nonetheless under strict orders from Rio to provide Roosevelt as much comfort as possible, so he held on to the tents. When they were finally gone, Rondon actually expressed relief at being rid of them.

The difference in cultures also became apparent in disagreements over the types and quantities of food needed. Roosevelt was distressed by what he considered a grievously insufficient supply of bread and sugar, and after the expedition wrote how he and the other Americans, pitying the situation of the *camaradas*, as the caboclo paddlers and porters were called, had generously shared their own rations with them. In reality, this implicit chiding of Rondon reflected nothing more than Roosevelt's own lack of experience in the Amazon.

At that time, few residents of the Brazilian frontier would ever have tasted bread made from wheat flour. The staple of their diet was farinha, the coarse-ground flour made from cassava and consumed at nearly every meal. Bread made from wheat flour was a luxury whose consumption in Brazil a century ago was confined mainly to urban elites; it did not keep well in the hot and humid climate of the tropical wilderness.

Rondon knew that cassava, whether harvested in its original form as a tuber or processed into farinha, was durable, more resistant to heat, and easier to carry. Cassava was plentiful and easily found in the wilderness: anytime one of Rondon's expeditions exhausted its supply of it, he would just purchase a new stock from local peasants or trade for it with the Indigenous tribesmen he encountered. There was no reason for the expedition to haul sacks of wheat flour.

Similarly, Brazilian expeditions simply did not travel with stocks of refined, granulated white sugar, prone to absorb water and become moldy in the tropical climate. Instead, they consumed *rapadura*—unrefined whole cane sugar derived from the boiling and evaporation of sugar cane juice and formed into dark brown bricks for easier transport. Or honey could be purchased, bartered for, or even obtained by climbing trees with beehives—a skill many residents of the frontier had mastered. And finally, the sap of certain palm trees could be boiled down into a sweet syrup with a high-calorie sucrose content.

As the expedition pushed northward, leaving Paresi country behind, it entered the domain of the Nhambiquara. Although Rondon had made an initial peaceful contact with the tribe in 1912, his efforts were not yet complete, and he was wary of possible attacks. He had succeeded in allaying the suspicions of many individual Nhambiquara settlements—indeed, the headman of one village even came to Utiarity to pay his respects to Rondon and Roosevelt—but a handful remained either openly hostile or would flee en masse into the jungle the instant their sentinels detected intruders. War parties had occasionally attacked not only Rondon's surveying teams but also telegraph stations and river ferries manned by the commission's Paresi employees.

In February 1914, as he and Roosevelt crossed the Mato Grosso highlands, Rondon confronted a serious crisis. The Nhambiquara periodically replenished their female population by kidnapping Paresi women, and had recently raided a village where the expedition had halted. Paresi men hunting nearby, hearing the screams of their wives, daughters, and sisters, had rushed back to defend their womenfolk. They were accompanied by a civilian employee of the Telegraph Commission armed with a good rifle, who had been hunting with them and now shot and killed a member of the Nhambiquara raiding party, which immediately withdrew.

Roosevelt, a winner of the Nobel Peace Prize, was fascinated watching Rondon adjudicate the dispute. "The Paresis were, of course, in the right, but the colonel could not afford to have his men take sides in a tribal quarrel," Roosevelt wrote as Rondon, sitting on a hammock, conferred in "a very serious council" with Paresi elders, "an Indian child solemnly cuddling up to him, by the way." Additionally, Rondon had concluded that the commission employee "had really been urged on and aided by the Paresis"[20] in violation of the SPI edict to "kill never." So, the Paresi were not completely in the right.

Roosevelt provided no details about how the episode was resolved, but SPI records indicate that Rondon decided to arm the Paresi so that they could live without fear of Nhambiquara raids, and, just as importantly, continue their work for the Telegraph Commission. There was one caveat, however: the Paresi would be bound by the same strict rules that applied to other employees of the commission, which meant they could fire their weapons only into the air to warn off attackers and were not allowed to shoot with deadly intent. Remarkably, the Paresi seem to have kept their promise, for there are no reports of their armed tribesmen killing Nhambiquara. As for the Nhambiquara, Rondon agreed to pay reparations for the death of the raider, on condition that tribal leaders take steps to prevent rogue groups from launching attacks on Paresi villages or on Paresi working for the Telegraph Commission. This pledge, too, seems to have been honored.

The effectiveness of Rondon's diplomacy enabled the expedition to cross Nhambiquara territory without incident. In fact, as the explorers descended the plateau and neared the River of Doubt in mid-February, Rondon felt confident enough to allow Kermit to visit a Nhambiquara village alone: following the protocols of the jungle and Rondon's instructions, Kermit loudly announced his arrival and ceremoniously laid down his weapons outside the village's perimeter. He was received, his father reported, "with the utmost cordiality" and returned to camp with a group of men whom

Roosevelt described as "bold and friendly, good-natured—at least superficially—and very inquisitive."[21]

By the last week of February, the expedition had reached Três Buritis, where the Telegraph Commission operated a cattle ranch, and its members were finally able to relax comfortably for the first time in nearly two months. Rondon's uncle Miguel Evangelista managed the ranch and made a vivid impression on the Americans. Roosevelt describes him as being of "practically pure Indian blood . . . dressed in the ordinary costume of the Caboclo—hat, shirt, trousers, and no shoes or stockings."[22] Uncle Miguel boasted of having killed three jaguars in the past year, which Roosevelt found remarkable coming from "a hale old man of seventy, white-haired but as active and vigorous as ever; with a fine, kindly, intelligent face."[23]

Surrounded by lush forest and well-watered pastures, it was easy for the explorers to be lulled into a deceptive sense of security. There were comfortable beds to sleep in, and fresh milk and eggs at breakfast. Dinner was Roosevelt's beloved *canja* as an appetizer, followed by huge slabs of beef roasted on the spit; "we even had watermelon,"[24] Roosevelt noted, delighted. This was the last chance to enjoy such indulgences before embarking in canoes and having to subsist on tight rations, so both the Rondon-Roosevelt and the Botelho de Magalhães groups, which would be descending the Ji-Paraná River, made the most of the opportunity.

But on February 24, when the two parties reached the José Bonifácio station and began dividing up the food supplies they had transported all the way from Corumbá, they received an unpleasant shock. Breaking open some of the crates Fiala had assembled specifically for Roosevelt when the expedition was envisioned as a cruise down the Tapajós, they found that many of the items purchased were more suited to a gourmet feast than a jungle expedition. "We discovered here whole cases of olive oil, cases of mustard, malted milk, stuffed olives, prunes, applesauce, etc., etc. Even Rhine wine," Miller informed Chapman. All these were "nice enough in their place," the young naturalist continued, but "were simply dead weight on such a tremendous journey" into unexplored territory. "Most of his equipment was useless."[25]

This was unfortunate, even potentially disastrous, but there was no choice but to forge ahead. Rondon told Roosevelt that by his calculations they had fifty days' worth of rations, and could live off the land if it came to that. But Roosevelt worried that "we would have to reckon with starvation as a possibility" if something went wrong during the descent of the River of Doubt. "Anything might happen," he wrote. "We were about to go into the unknown, and no one could say what it held."[26]

XIV

Portage, Pole, and Paddle

THE MORNING OF Friday, February 27, 1914, dawned hot and bright, but without the torrential rains of the Mato Grosso plateau. After a breakfast of jerky, hardtack, and coffee, the last supplies were loaded onto the canoes and a final inspection conducted. Rondon and his officers checked the caulking of the dugouts for leaks, and tested the knots that held the equipment firm. They took special care to examine the canvas covers meant to protect the valuable bundles underneath from both water and the broiling sun, and ran through a checklist of scientific instruments and other vital items to make sure nothing would be left behind.

Back in November, before the expedition's itinerary was determined, Rondon had arranged for seven canoes, all of them wooden dugouts, to be brought to the headwaters of the River of Doubt. But he had not actually seen any of them until arriving there, and neither he nor Roosevelt, who had plenty of experience on the water as an outdoorsman in North America, had a favorable first impression of the vessels that were supposed to take them down the river. "One was small, one was cranky, and two were old, waterlogged, and leaky," Roosevelt wrote. "The other three were good."[1]

When loaded up, the canoes seemed even less secure, as they gently rocked and sloshed from one side to another. Their gunwales, or upper edges, sat uncomfortably close to the water, and would quickly take on water if the expedition encountered rapids, shoals, or even a very strong current. To improve buoyancy, the boatmen lashed bundles of spindly palm branches to the sides of the canoes.

"If our canoe journey was prosperous we would gradually lighten the loads by eating the provisions," Roosevelt observed. "If we met with accidents, such as losing men and canoes in the rapids, or losing men in encounters with Indians, or if we encountered overmuch fever and dysentery, the loads would lighten themselves."[2]

Rondon had carefully planned the order of the canoes. The smallest, and thus most maneuverable, of the dugouts should be first in line, and carry only three men: two of the most skilled paddlers and one of the expedition's principal members, who turned out to be Kermit. Rondon and Lyra would follow together in the next boat, a larger and sturdier canoe because it carried the surveying tools needed to map the river. Roosevelt, who for security reasons had Dr. Cajazeira constantly at his side, was assigned, along with Cherrie, to the last and largest of the canoes, a hefty twenty-five-footer weighing more than a ton, and given three paddlers.

Sandwiched between Rondon's and Roosevelt's canoes in this fluvial procession were a pair of motley jerry-rigged rafts. Rondon had been so dissatisfied with the condition of four of the canoes left for the explorers that he ordered them lashed together in pairs, rather than squander valuable time having the boatmen build new, waterworthy dugouts. They were loaded with cargo; four boatmen were assigned to each of the rafts.

To Brazilian eyes, there was nothing unusual about the sixteen camaradas, the "fellows" or "comrades" who would bear the burden of navigating, paddling, and performing most of the other physically demanding tasks during the descent of the River of Doubt. Like Rondon, almost all were caboclos—tough backwoodsmen who seemed to thrive on hardship. Rondon put Manoel Vicente da Paixão, a towering Black soldier, in charge of the group and gave him the rank of corporal, and detailed Antônio Paresi, a full-blooded Indian from the tribe of the same name, to steer Roosevelt's canoe. All the others were of mixed race: Indigenous, African, and Iberian in every possible permutation of those groups. Only the olive-skinned Julio de Lima, a native of Bahia and also one of the paddlers assigned to Roosevelt's canoe, as bowsman, seemed to be white.

The Americans, coming from a society that criminalized miscegenation, a practice widespread in Brazil, found much about the camaradas to be remarkable, as their diary entries made clear. The extraordinary range of physical types and skin tones, from Paixão's dark, almost purplish black to Rondon's tawny copper, of course drew their attention, but it wasn't just that. The Americans were amazed, too, by the uncomplaining durability of the men, most of whom wore just a raggedy pair of pants and went about without shoes or shirts, sleeping in randomly strung hammocks and working long hours with little food. And after nearly three months together, the Roosevelts and Cherrie had also learned to respect the caboclos' vast knowledge of the jungle, rivers, and wildlife.

The camaradas were "a strapping set," Roosevelt wrote. "They were expert river-men and men of the forest, skilled veterans in wilderness work. They were lithe as panthers and brawny as bears. They swam like water-dogs. They were equally at home with pole and paddle, with axe and machete." They "looked like pirates," he continued, "but most of them were hard-working, willing, and cheerful. . . . Good men around camp."[3] He came to be particularly fond of two of the boatmen assigned to his canoe: Antônio Paresi and Antônio Correa, whom Roosevelt described as "an intelligent, daredevil mulatto, probably with also a dash of Indian blood."[4]

Just after noon, they departed. Rondon looked to Roosevelt to give the signal to move off, and when it came, paddles dipped into the dark, swirling water. From a makeshift wooden bridge spanning the narrow stream, Miller and Botelho de Magalhães waved and shouted, "Good luck!"[5] As the seven canoes departed, Miller snapped a last few photographs, stopping only when the flotilla rounded the first bend in the river and silently disappeared behind the dense vegetation that crowded the riverbank.

It was a poignant moment. "For several minutes we stood upon the fragile structure that bridged the unexplored river and stared at the dark forest that shut our erstwhile leader and his Brazilian companions from view," Miller later wrote. "And then, filled with misgivings as to whether or not we should ever see them again, we turned our thoughts to the task before us."[6]

After the exhausting slog across the Mato Grosso plateau, what would prove to be the most arduous and dangerous phase of the expedition was at last underway: two months on water, which would push some members of the group to the brink of suicide and others into homicidal rage. The first day, however, passed tediously, without incident or challenge, as Rondon and Lyra began to map the upper reaches of the River of Doubt from where they had left off when they first stumbled across it in 1909. Such work would be quick and easy today. But a century ago, there was no such thing as GPS, and even aerial mapping existed only in its most primitive form. As a result, Rondon and his men did everything manually, by compass and solar observation, using a traditional method known as "fixed position" sighting. For this, two canoes were involved: the one in the lead position carried a spotter, whose job it was to locate places along the shore that could be easily observed from the other boat. The wider the clearing along the riverbank, the better, because that gave the surveyors more time to fix on the spotter's position and take readings.

When an appropriate location was found, the spotter's canoe halted. He would jump ashore, clear away brush with his machete, and then raise a red-and-white sighting pole. There he would stand, besieged by voracious insects and a blazing sun, or in drenching downpours, until those in the other canoe measured the angle and distance between their position and the sighting rod and entered the data in their notebooks. Then the spotter would hop back into his canoe, the boatmen would resume paddling, and the process would be repeated at the next stop.

Initially, the division of labor during the descent of the River of Doubt called for Rondon himself to be in the second canoe with Lyra, meticulously registering the actual measurements. Lyra used a state-of-the-art theodolite, a precision instrument that computes angles in both the horizontal and vertical planes, and Rondon had a compass and a barometer to gauge the river's altitude above sea level, which he expected to decline as the expedition descended the last stretch of highlands and advanced toward the river's mouth. The data from those readings was immediately entered, in Rondon's fine, elegant hand, into notebooks custom made in Rio de Janeiro. He and Lyra also sketched natural features that might be of interest or concern to future travelers.

Kermit had volunteered to be the spotter, so the most onerous duties fell to him. His exposed position in the lead canoe worried his father, for the expedition was entering a territory of uncontacted, possibly hostile Indian tribes, and in the event of an ambush, the lead canoe, with Kermit and his two Brazilian paddlers, João and Simplício, would likely be the first attacked. And making so many stops to calculate position soon grew exhausting: Rondon's field journal indicates that the expedition halted 114 times that first day, barely advancing seven miles.

The River of Doubt was a puzzling and unpredictable stream, twisting and turning in every direction, at times seeming to double back on itself. Rondon's logs from that first afternoon show that at one time or another the river's course flowed in the direction of each of the four cardinal points of the compass. The rainy season had caused the river to overflow its banks, and water had spread everywhere, at times making it seem like the expedition was navigating an immense lake rather than a river.

Rondon was pleased, though, at how the trip had begun. "We obtained an abundant supply of game and thus an appropriate ration for the overburdened camaradas," he wrote. "In addition to game birds, we retrieved honey; it was jubilation when we came across a milk tree, a giant of the forest called that because of the thick white liquid that oozed from any cut made in its bark and which the camaradas drank avidly."[7] On the water, "it was a delight to paddle slowly on the beautiful tropical river" and savor "the intense perfume of flowers" growing on tree trunks. At day's end, a welcoming campsite, already erected by the camaradas, awaited: "Tents set up, fire crackling, the promise of a good meal under the stars that dusted the sky."[8]

The next day was more of the same, with nearly one hundred stops to measure location and the expedition covering an additional twelve miles.⁹ A work routine was quickly shaping up, one that would underscore the often conflicting goals of the American and Brazilian members of the expedition, generating tensions that would persist throughout the River of Doubt exploration. Roosevelt wanted to get down the river as rapidly as possible, reach Manaus, and get home with equal dispatch. He was still very much a public man, with political aspirations, and during the five months he had been away from home, he had watched anxiously as the global situation deteriorated. Unable to voice his opinions from afar, he was impatient to leap back into the fray.

Roosevelt was naturally concerned about events in Europe and the danger of regional conflicts in the Balkans spreading and igniting a continental conflagration. But even more worrying was the possibility the United States might be dragged into Mexico's ongoing civil war, which had erupted in 1910. After Woodrow Wilson took office early in 1913, the violence of the Mexican Revolution had taken a more ominous direction: one president had been assassinated; his successor was trying to combat rebellions led by Pancho Villa, Emiliano Zapata, and others; and the United States had imposed an arms embargo. More and more it appeared Wilson would send in American troops to protect American property and citizens, and intervene in Mexico's internal politics. Roosevelt had been following these events as closely as he could, but now he was in a complete news blackout, thousands of miles from a major city, beyond the reach even of telegrams and newspapers, and contemplating a voyage of unknown duration. He wanted the trip to be as short as possible. (In fact, American troops would land in Veracruz on April 21, while Roosevelt was still in the jungle and out of the reach of communications.)

Kermit was equally impatient. Ever since Belle Willard had accepted his offer of marriage, he was obsessed with reuniting with her. His diary was filled with musings about her and dreams of their future together, and he carried her letters to him in a pouch around his neck so that they would not be lost. Lovesick, he wanted only to get to Spain or New York or wherever it was they were to be married, and make her his wife. Also on his mind was the fear that she might yet change her mind and he might still lose her to some other suitor: she was a very attractive match—pretty, intelligent, and from a prominent Virginia family.

Rondon, on the other hand, had waited nearly five years to return to the river he had discovered and named, its mystery lingering in his thoughts, and he intended to fully exploit this opportunity. That meant mapping the river's course as accurately as possible and collecting basic information about the geology, biology, and ethnology of the unexplored region. Roosevelt had been forewarned, both by the Foreign Ministry and by Rondon himself, that this would not be a safari but a bona fide scientific expedition, and Rondon expected every member to do his part.

Late in the afternoon of March 2 the expedition encountered its first big challenge. All of a sudden, the flow of the river began to accelerate, and then a dull rumble was heard off in the distance. Almost before they knew it, the explorers found themselves bouncing through a short series of rapids. Up ahead, they could see the water angrily foaming and heard its deafening roar. The paddlers quickly pulled off to the right bank, secured the canoes, and set up camp, and a scouting party hacked its way through the brush to reconnoiter.

What they discovered gave everyone pause. For half a mile, the river bounded downward through a series of boiling rapids, which were broken by a pair of waterfalls six feet high. Then it narrowed dramatically and surged through a jagged sandstone gorge, so constricted that Kermit was able to photograph Cherrie kneeling at one edge and almost touching the other side with the barrel of his shotgun. "It seemed extraordinary, almost impossible," Roosevelt wrote, "that so broad a river could in so short a space of time contract its dimensions to the width of the strangled channel through which it now poured its entire volume."[10]

They would have to portage around the waterfalls and rapids. First the camp had to be relocated to a point below the rapids, which Rondon named Navaíte Falls, after a subgroup of Nhambiquara who lived nearby. It took an entire day and required every able-bodied member of the expedition to tote food crates, tents, duffel bags, and scientific equipment to the new site. Rondon exempted from that task one ailing paddler and Kermit, who had developed so painful a case of boils on his thighs that he had to remain prostrate, but both of the expedition's commanders joined the others in transporting the gear.

Early the next morning, after waking to find an army of termites feasting on their clothes and supplies, Lyra and a work party of camaradas headed into the forest with axes and machetes and began to fell trees, dozens of them, and cut their trunks into rounded logs. They placed these rollers along a portage trail that evidently had long been used by local Indians, at intervals of about two feet, thereby creating a skidway along which they could drag the canoes. Meanwhile, another team heaved the empty dugouts from the river-bank up to the high ground, and positioned them to be pulled down the skidway, one by one.

This was backbreaking work, magnified in difficulty by the insects that swarmed, bit, and stung, drawn by the rivers of sweat dripping from the bodies of camaradas and officers alike. A pair of camaradas was stationed in front of each of the canoes, each man connected to it by a firm drag rope fastened around his torso. A third stood behind with a sturdy pole, which he used to push and guide the canoe in the desired direction as it clumsily slid down the bumpy, uneven log pathway. The process left much to be desired: several of the dugouts slammed into sandstone ledges just to the left of the skidway, and the one Roosevelt had been using actually split badly enough that its future viability was dubious. Still another made it all the way down the trail only to slip free of the ropes and sink to the bottom as it was being lowered back into the water at the new launch point; it was retrieved with strenuous effort by the exhausted camaradas.

The expedition finally resumed its journey at midday on March 5, and advanced eight miles that afternoon, prompting a cheerful mood around the campfire that night. At mid-afternoon the next day, though, signs of more rapids ahead were detected, and once again the lead canoe, followed quickly by the others, pulled over to the riverbank so that a scouting party could investigate on foot. Some four hundred yards downstream, they discovered, the river smashed into a line of giant boulders, impeding all passage. Rondon went on alone, following the river's twisting course on foot, and when he returned to the others, he had sobering news: the rapids continued for at least a mile, and included a pair of waterfalls, about one hundred yards apart. Another portage awaited, even longer and more difficult than the first.

This was to become a familiar and depressing pattern. The expedition struggled through one grueling portage after another, each time hoping it was the last. The river would broaden and calm, encouraging them for a while, only to turn turbulent soon and taper again. It was exhausting not only physically but above all mentally: since the expedition was in territory that had never been explored, they had no way of telling how long the maddening alternation of portage and paddle, portage and paddle would repeat itself. "We had no idea how much time the trip would take," Roosevelt would write once it was over. "We had entered a land of unknown possibilities."[11]

The enormous energy expended on these portages, which would continue almost until the end of the expedition, no doubt grated on the Americans, for they had argued for traveling in the lightweight canoes they had brought with them, with canvas stretched tightly over wooden frames, then treated with multiple layers of varnish and paint to make them durable and waterproof. Compared to the Brazilian dugouts, these were far more portable: they weighed only 160 pounds each, while the lightest of the dugouts weighed 900 pounds and the heaviest more than a ton.

Roosevelt deferred to Rondon, but when he returned home, he made his preference clear. "Unless the difficulties of transportation are insuperable, canvas-and-cement canoes, such as can be obtained from various firms in Canada and the United States, should by all means be taken," he wrote. "They are incomparably superior to the dugouts."[12] Since then, every explorer of note trying to retrace the course of the Roosevelt-Rondon Scientific Expedition, beginning with the Anglo-American George Dyott in the mid-1920s, has avoided cumbersome wooden dugouts and relied on lightweight canoes, either of canvas or fiberglass.[13]

On March 10, after negotiating yet another set of rapids, the expedition confronted new problems with the canoes. Passage through the shoals had proved so treacherous that the smaller of the two rafts was swamped and sank, and as the boatmen worked to retrieve it, one camarada was swept away and severely gashed his face on sharp rocks hidden below the water's surface before somehow reaching the shore. Tired and discouraged, especially after a heavy rain began to fall, the explorers decided to make camp early, and chose a spot on a high bank, taking care to haul all their provisions up the slippery slope to the site.

The deluge continued through the night, and when the first boatman arose the next morning, he discovered that the river had risen several inches while everyone slept, and so much water had seeped into one of the canoes that it had begun to sink. Unfortunately, it was moored to the largest and heaviest of the dugouts, the one in which Roosevelt had been traveling, and eventually it dragged the larger canoe down with it. Then the moorings broke, and the two vessels were swept away downriver. Both dugouts were destroyed, and Rondon was now forced to build a new one, big enough and long enough to accommodate those who had been displaced.

This was a significant setback. Food supplies were so tight that the expedition could not afford a long delay, so all six principals, not just Roosevelt and Rondon, gathered to assess the situation. They had been on the river now for nearly two weeks, but had traveled barely fifty miles; at that rate, given the many portages and pauses to map the river, they would run out of rations before they reached their destination, and be forced to subsist on whatever they might shoot or catch. "There were sufficient rations for the men to last about 35 days,"[14] Cherrie calculated, referring to the sixteen Brazilian camaradas, "while the rations that had been arranged for the officials," meaning the three American and three Brazilian principals, "would perhaps last 50 days."[15]

Rondon's response was to begin immediately to construct a canoe. He instructed four teams, of four camaradas each, to each cut a twenty-five-foot length of trunk from a large tree, and, amid a heavy rain, dispatched them in four different directions. Of the four trunks, Rondon chose a *tatajuba* tree, five feet in diameter, and ordered the boatmen to begin to hollow it out. A yellowish fine-grained hardwood, *tatajuba* is so strong and durable that Brazilian military engineers often used it in bridge construction in Rondon's time.

Working in shifts under Rondon's insistent supervision, the camaradas succeeded in transforming the bark-encased *tatajuba* log into a serviceable canoe in just four days, and by the morning of March 14, the explorers resumed their travels. Amid heavy rains, it took all twenty-two of them to haul the newly made dugout down the muddy slope to the river, but by midday they were on their way. Soon, though, they were again confronting one treacherous series of rapids after another, six in all. Impatient to make progress, worried about food supplies, they decided not to portage and to take their chances running the whitewater. They managed to advance ten miles in half a day, their best performance yet, but not without a close call: at one point the heavy new canoe, with Roosevelt in it, was sucked into a whirlpool and began to take on water so rapidly that Dr. Cajazeira and Cherrie jumped into the water to lighten the load and prevent the dugout from swamping. With great effort, the boatmen were able to right the craft, and no supplies or personnel were lost.

Roosevelt, fearing death by starvation, thought this a gamble worth taking. "Of the two hazards," he wrote, "we felt it necessary to risk running the rapids."[16] But the next day, the Ides of March, the expedition was struck by what he called a "grave misfortune."[17] As the first two canoes rounded a bend in the river early in the afternoon, the stream suddenly widened and whitened, dividing into two sets of roiling rapids separated by an island in the middle. Rondon, immediately sensing trouble, ordered his dugout to pull to the side, and called to Kermit's canoe to do the same. But Kermit either did not hear Rondon above the din or chose to ignore his shouted command. The lead canoe plunged forward, heading directly for the island.

Kermit and his two boatmen, João and Simplício, had progressed barely a dozen yards when their canoe seemed to be sucked into a powerful downdraft, which spun the craft around and propelled it directly into the fast-moving water, broadside. As they descended the rapids, they struggled with their paddles to force their dugout to face frontward, taking on water all the while. The canoe reached the end of the rapids still upright, and the camaradas strained with their paddles to guide it to the safety of the shore. They were nearly there when yet another whirlpool seized the canoe, hurling it back to midstream and overturning it.

Now all three men, tossed into the foaming water, were battling for their lives. João grabbed for the towline at the front of the canoe and started swimming for shore, hoping to save himself and the canoe, but could not maintain his hold on the rope. Simplício simply vanished beneath the water. But Kermit somehow managed to climb onto the keel of the overturned canoe and rode it, almost like a bull at a rodeo, through a second set of rapids before being thrown off. Desperate and exhausted, his waterlogged clothing weighing him down, he swam for shore, where he could only cling to a branch until he had recovered his breath.

Kermit was already back on land and walking back toward the others when Rondon and Lyra encountered him on the trail. "Well, you have had quite a splendid bath, eh?"[18] were Rondon's first words to the younger Roosevelt. There is no way to know if Rondon's tone was sarcastic, in reproach to what he perceived as Kermit's youthful heedlessness, or whether he was making a sympathetic joke, relieved that the son of his eminent guest had not perished. But where were João and Simplício? Kermit said that he thought they had both swum to the other bank of the river, and together, Kermit, Rondon and Lyra set out to find them.

João showed up not long after, having swum back across the river. But there was no sign of Simplício. In addition, the lead canoe was lost, either smashed to bits in the rapids or sunk to the bottom of the river, along with the supplies in it. Devastated, Kermit set out on his own to search for Simplício, accompanied only by his dog Trigueiro, who had also been tossed into the rapids and somehow made its way to safety. He walked downstream along the trail for several miles, but found only one paddle and a single food tin.

Simplício's death cast a pall over the remaining camaradas, who were easily influenced by what they took to be omens. A new dugout could be fashioned from a nearby tree, though that would require effort because several adzes, a special hatchet needed for that kind of construction, also went to the bottom during the accident. But now the expedition was not only down a man, it had also lost at least ten days of provisions, also irreplaceable.

In his diary, Kermit was extraordinarily guarded about his boatman's death, writing only that "Simplício was drowned."[19] For his part, Roosevelt portrayed the disaster in his book as simply an accident of fate, an example of man overwhelmed by the force of nature. But in the inquest Rondon quietly ordered, the surviving boatman told a more complicated story, one implicating Kermit. According to João, Kermit heard Rondon's command to stop, but decided to approach the island and see if it was possible to run the rapids to the right. He decided it was, and ordered the boatmen ahead. When they argued it was too dangerous, he merely repeated his order, and João and Simplício felt they had no choice but to obey the son of the expedition's co-commander. Simplício, the youngest of the explorers, thus paid the price for Kermit's reckless error of judgment.

With no body to bury, Rondon ordered that a simple memorial cross, reading, "Here perished the unfortunate Simplício,"[20] be erected the next morning at the edge of the rapids, just before the twenty-one surviving explorers resumed their journey. He also named the falls in Simplício's honor, and they appear as such on Brazilian maps even today.

In all of the many accounts of the Roosevelt-Rondon Scientific Expedition over the past century, Brazilian or American, Simplício has always been identified merely by his first name or, at best, as "poor Simplício." But in Rondon's own records, and in one of the early orders of the day he issued during the expedition, is Simplício's complete name, which deserves to be restored to history. He may have died anonymously, just another hapless caboclo, but he was born Antônio Simplício da Silva.[21]

XV

Passion

FTER THE CEREMONY to honor Simplício, another exhausting portage began, amid sheets of rain that further darkened the explorers' mood. While the camaradas felled trees for a new skidway, cleared brush, and once again hauled the remaining canoes out of the river, Rondon and his favorite dog, Lobo, headed down a jungle path to do reconnaissance and, with any luck, to shoot a game bird or a monkey for some meat in the pot later in the day.

Before long, about a half mile from camp, a peculiar howling began to echo through the forest—almost, but not exactly, like that of a spider monkey, the largest simian in the jungle and an excellent source of meat. Lobo instinctively bounded ahead to investigate as Rondon peered into the canopy for signs of monkeys, his rifle at the ready. Within seconds, though, he heard his dog yelping, first in surprise, then in pain. He advanced cautiously, thinking Lobo had been gored by a peccary or slashed by a jaguar, but then heard distinctly human sounds: "short exclamations, energetic and repeated in a kind of chorus with a certain cadence" that he had heard before only when Indigenous war parties were "ready to commence the attack."[1] He fired a single warning shot in the air, "overcoming my initial impulse to run and defend Lobo,"[2] then quickly hurried back to camp to warn the others.

Rondon's immediate concern was an ambush. He dispatched Cherrie to alert the camaradas upstream at the beginning of the skidway, asked Roosevelt to mount guard at the end of the portage, and with Antônio Paresi, Kermit, and Lyra accompanying him returned to the trail in search of Lobo. When they reached the dog, it was already dead, pierced by a pair of arrows whose design was unfamiliar to Rondon and his Paresi scout. Unlike Nhambiquara arrowheads, these had barbed bamboo tips, which could only mean that the expedition had entered the territory of some new, completely unknown tribe.

Before returning to the site of the ambush, Rondon had grabbed several ax heads and stuffed his pockets with colored beads, as presents for what he assumed was a small hunting party frightened by his approach. He buried Lobo next to a long pole with a basket full of animal entrails attached to it, which the Indians had brought along as bait, probably for fishing, but had hastily abandoned as they fled. Around the pole and Lobo's grave Rondon then arrayed his gifts, to signal to the Indigenous group—most likely members of the people known today as the Cinta-Larga, whose relations with the outside world have continued to be tense and even violent into the twenty-first century—that his intentions remained peaceful despite their killing of his dog.*

---

* In November 2006, Cinta-Larga leaders invited the author of this book to visit them on their reservation, a 10,425-square-mile area straddling both sides of the Roosevelt River and formally known as the Roosevelt Indigenous Area. Members of the tribe had killed diamond miners and gold prospectors who, despite repeated warnings to stay away, had invaded the territory the Brazilian government had demarcated for the Cinta-Larga, or "Broad Belt." The intruders were tied up and bludgeoned with wooden war clubs; as a result, the Cinta-Larga, whose name derives from their habit of wearing bark sashes around their waists while doing battle, were excoriated in the Brazilian press. There was a clamor for them to be arrested and tried for murder, and they wanted to tell their side of the story to a foreign reporter.

During two days of conversations in a settlement just a few feet from the west bank of the Roosevelt River, tribal leaders referred periodically to the Roosevelt-Rondon Expedition, providing details from oral histories passed on to them by their fathers and grandfathers, who had lived the events described. According to these accounts—which coincide with stories that Roosevelt's great-grandson Tweed Roosevelt, president of the board of trustees of the Theodore Roosevelt Association, says he heard when he descended the River of Doubt in 1992—the Cinta-Larga had been intently observing the explorers since they first entered the tribe's territory, and had been debating among themselves how to respond.

Rondon had been extremely lucky, and he knew it. Had he been in the lead, and not Lobo, he would have been struck by the ambushers' arrows, probably fatally, since the arrowheads were tinged with poison: "I thought, mournfully contemplating my dead companion, that perhaps he had given his life for mine."[3] But whatever relief he felt evaporated when he returned to camp and received more bad news about the portage. Four of the canoes were safely transferred downstream, but as the last, largest, and most recently built was being lowered back into the river, a rope broke, and it plunged into the water and was carried away, taking with it the various ropes and pulleys to which it was still attached.

Now the expedition faced a series of unpalatable choices. Before Lobo's death, they might have remained where they were to build a new canoe. But the danger of an Indian attack at the site, which Rondon quickly baptized Broken Canoe Rapids, now seemed too high.[4] Yet the explorers had only four canoes, simply not enough to carry twenty-one men and all their equipment. So that night, the six Brazilian and American leaders conferred and decided on a drastic course of action: the four canoes would be lashed together to form a pair of rafts, each with three paddlers and one principal aboard, and loaded with as much equipment as their frames could support. The remaining equipment would have to be discarded, and the remaining men would walk along the riverbank, attentive to any sign of an Indian presence, until a new campsite was reached.

Because the risk of ambush made it too dangerous to venture into the jungle and use existing paths there, the explorers had to hack their

---

One faction wanted to attack the intruders immediately, deeming their presence no different from that of rubber tappers who occasionally appeared in Cinta-Larga domains. But another group urged a wait-and-see approach, preferring to shadow the trespassers until their intentions were clearer. In the end, the more cautious policy prevailed, for two reasons, the Cinta-Larga leaders explained, speaking of events of nearly a century ago as if they had just taken place. First, their tracking party had observed the memorial service for Simplício and deduced that the outsiders were mourning their dead, and thus were likely peaceful and soon to be on their way. And second, the gifts Rondon left at Lobo's burial site were interpreted as he hoped: a sign that he not only held no grudges but also understood that the Cinta-Larga had reacted out of fright.

way through luxuriant growth along the riverbank—suffering cuts and scratches and being poked by sharp branches as they advanced. With no choice but to go on, the expedition, its load significantly diminished, continued its descent of the River of Doubt on foot, with Roosevelt and Dr. Cajazeira on the two rafts and the others moving single file. Two sets of rapids were successfully navigated in this fashion, though Roosevelt had a close call when a vicious cross-current threw his raft against some large boulders while his paddlers were trying to steer among seven small islands.

At the end of the rapids, Rondon and Kermit, reconnoitering together, encountered a deep river some seventy feet wide gushing into the River of Doubt from the west. This discovery was significant: enough was known about the Ji-Paraná River to be certain this tributary was not part of that river system. In the face of this new evidence, Lyra relinquished his theory that the River of Doubt flowed westward into the Ji-Paraná. Though there remained a slight possibility that the River of Doubt might still turn eastward and flow into the Tapajós, Rondon's original hypothesis was the most likely: that the stream would continue northward for hundreds of miles and eventually disgorge into the Rio Madeira. There would be no shortcuts to Manaus.

There were, however, two encouraging developments that day, which briefly lifted spirits. Kermit found several more food tins washed away when Simplício drowned, and brought them back to camp, which had been set up at the mouth of the new tributary. Lyra, the youngest Brazilian official, also provided a welcome addition to the food supplies; he returned from fishing with a pair of large *pacu*, a succulent whitefish with a sweet, mild flavor when grilled, much favored by Amazon caboclos. Roosevelt was almost as enthusiastic, writing of the pacu that "they were delicious eating."[5]

The next morning, hoping to improve morale, Rondon announced that the new river would be called the Rio Kermit, and he produced an obelisk with that name already engraved on it. Furthermore, he added, now that the River of Doubt had been established beyond doubt as a major tributary, it would be renamed, and henceforth be called the Rio Roosevelt, with an obelisk in Roosevelt's honor to be placed at the spot where it joined the Madeira system, somewhere ahead of them.

Some in the expedition hoped that such a moment might not be far off, or that at least the worst of the rapids was over and calm waters lay ahead. Antônio Paresi noted that pacu are not normally found around rapids, preferring still pools to turbulent waters, and many of the camaradas rejoiced. Cherrie also found optimistic signs in nature: some of the bird species that suddenly appeared, like turkey vultures, were known to be native to plains, not jungle, which suggested to him that open, flat terrain was ahead.

Later that day, at a bend where the river turned sharply eastward and widened, Rondon found what he considered an ideal place to build two smaller new canoes and halted the expedition. Roosevelt initially objected, worried that the Indians trailing the explorers might be tempted to attack. But Rondon explained that the existence of many *araputanga* trees, ideal for constructing dugouts, outweighed other factors. The wood is easy to carve, resistant to rot, and, above all, light in weight and more buoyant in water than the *tatajuba* wood chosen for the first replacement canoe. Once he knew that, Roosevelt acquiesced, though Rondon further reassured him by mounting a nightlong guard for the first time. Rondon himself awoke at 2 a.m. to make sure the lookouts hadn't fallen asleep.

Since the death of Lobo, the Cinta-Larga no longer bothered to keep their surveillance secret, and waged an unrelenting campaign of intimidation. Though still concealed in the jungle, they were very close, for the dogs were constantly agitated, barking at some nearby but unseen presence. As the explorers hewed to a narrow path along the riverbank, they could see for themselves in the mud fresh footprints that were not their own, and could hear rustling in the bush just beyond. "The footprints, the abandoned camps, and the voices of unseen people became uncanny," Cherrie wrote.[6]

One of the "abandoned camps" was in reality a fishing spot with three small, subtly camouflaged huts built on the edge of the river. When he saw it, Rondon followed his usual practice, pulling over to investigate and catalog the design and contents of the lean-tos, and leaving gifts as a token of friendship. In the case of the Cinta-Larga, though, the context of his actions was different, and somewhat risky. The Cinta-Larga might indeed welcome presents of axes, knives, and machetes. But their surveillance had surely revealed the expedition's many vulnerabilities. What if they decided to take advantage of that, attack, and seize all the expedition's tools?

Two days later, the replacement canoes were finished, but by then another discovery caused morale to plunge again. As the expedition's emergency rations were being loaded, Corporal Paixão informed Rondon that fifteen of seventy-five food boxes had somehow gone missing. Suspicions immediately fell on Julio de Lima, because he was the only member of the expedition who was not losing weight.

After three weeks on the River of Doubt, the other camaradas had Julio pegged as a malingerer and complainer. Back in Tapirapoan, Julio had begged to be included, "perhaps attracted by the doubled wage,"[7] touting his prowess as a woodsman. Instead, he had proved to be lazy and untrustworthy. None of the other camaradas wanted to be paired with him, even to search for food in the jungle: after gathering up nuts or cutting down palm trees to cull their hearts, he would lag behind and furtively gobble some of the harvest, rather than share it with the others back at camp.

Roosevelt shared this generalized opinion. Julio was "utterly worthless,"[8] he wrote. "Under the strain of toil, hardship, and danger his nature showed its true depths of selfishness, cowardice, and ferocity. He shirked all work. He shammed sickness. Nothing could make him do his share; and yet unlike his self-respecting fellows he was always shamelessly begging for favors,"[9] like asking Kermit to give him tobacco. Now evidence of a betrayal even more grievous than laziness was accumulating. "On such an expedition the theft of food comes next to murder as a crime," an indignant Roosevelt wrote, "and should by rights be punished as such."[10]

But deep in the jungle, hundreds of miles from the nearest settlement, there was little Rondon could do. "By the time we discovered his bad character, his cowardice and complete lack of aptitude to complement the continuous efforts of his comrades in travel, we were already so far down the river that it was impossible for us to rid ourselves of his presence,"[11] he lamented. He did not want to have Julio flogged in front of "our American guests," fearing they might regard such punishment as barbaric. In addition, Rondon had no proof of a crime yet, only a hunch. So he put the rations under guard, and ordered Paixão to keep Julio under scrutiny.

To make matters even worse, various health problems were beginning to emerge among the overtaxed boatmen. "We were crossing enemy territory, tormented by mosquitoes and ants," Rondon wrote. "The camaradas who didn't want to wear shoes had feet that were now so swollen that they could barely carry on. Dr. Cajazeira tried to relieve everyone's suffering and maintain in good condition the health of everyone in the expedition, but there were already two cases of fever."[12]

Rondon had been through this before, and always came through unharmed, driven by his devotion to duty: "Death and danger should never, no matter how much suffering they may inflict, interfere in the duties of expedition members,"[13] he wrote. But the Americans were increasingly preoccupied, and Cherrie privately gave voice to those concerns. "Our position is really a very serious one," he wrote in his diary on March 16. "Provisions are every day decreasing. It is impossible to go back. The journey ahead is undoubtedly a very long one." He concluded the day's entry on a somber, fatalistic note: "It is very doubtful if all our party ever reaches Manaos [sic]."[14]

Roosevelt had been particularly shaken by Kermit's own brush with death in the incident that killed Simplício, and feared that something similar might happen again. After the Indians killed Rondon's dog, his concern about Kermit intensified visibly. "Mr. Roosevelt acting very worried,"[15] Rondon wrote in his diary. Roosevelt approached Rondon on March 22, and challenged him on how the exploration work should be carried out going forward, and who should do it.

His arguments were both personal and philosophical. "Kermit was extremely lucky to escape alive from the accident in which Simplício perished," he told Rondon, according to the only surviving account of the conversation, from Rondon's diary. "I simply cannot tolerate seeing my son's life threatened at every turn by the presence of the Indians, threatened more so than any other member of the expedition, since he is in the lead canoe."[16] Then Roosevelt shifted gears, questioning Rondon's insistence on cartographic precision. "It's not worthwhile to continue with this process," he told Rondon. "We need to limit ourselves to a speedy mapping" and be satisfied "with determining the main points."

"For me, personally, that is not possible," Rondon responded, somewhat stiffly. "But I am ready to direct the crossing of the wilderness according to your desires, reducing to a minimum the time required for the expedition."[17]

Roosevelt tried another, more diplomatic tack, perhaps hoping to soothe Rondon's feelings. "Great men don't concern themselves with minor details," he said. But Rondon seemed to bristle at this. "I am neither a great man, nor is this a minor detail," he responded. "Mapping the river is indispensable, and without it the expedition, as far as I am concerned, will have been entirely pointless."[18] With that, Roosevelt seemed to back off somewhat. But he remained adamant on one point, and Rondon acquiesced: "Kermit will no longer go in front."

Rondon also agreed to abandon the fixed-position method of mapping, which would mean a reduction in the number of daily stops. Henceforth, Rondon promised Roosevelt, he would use a less precise method that involved calculating location from a pair of canoes, both in motion at the same velocity. But the question of how thoroughly to map the river would flare again soon, and continue throughout the remainder of the expedition as Rondon looked for ways to fulfill his cartographic mission while appearing to appease Roosevelt.

After three months in the wilderness, the former president had shed much of the extra weight he carried at the start of the expedition, and looked lean, fit, and tanned. "He did everything we did, and he did it well," Rondon wrote in his field diary when the expedition was still back in Utiarity. Roosevelt had "physical vigor, a capacity to resist fatigue, a good disposition no matter what the inconvenience," all of which combined to make him "a splendid traveling companion."[19]

But, in fact, the former president was suffering from hidden medical problems that worried Kermit and that were not yet evident to Rondon or to Dr. Cajazeira. They obviously knew of the 1912 assassination attempt and the bullet still lodged in Roosevelt's chest, which had been front-page news worldwide. But they did not realize the severity of an earlier incident: while President Roosevelt was campaigning in September 1902, a horse-drawn carriage carrying him through the streets of Pittsfield, Massachusetts, was struck by a streetcar.

A Secret Service agent was killed in the collision, but contemporaneous press accounts reported that Roosevelt escaped serious injury. The president was "badly shaken up, but suffered only a facial bruise," according to one report.[20] In reality, his left leg had been badly injured and caused him considerable pain, though he continued to campaign in the South and Midwest rather than seek medical care. As a result, an abscess formed, and surgery was eventually required. There were long-term consequences, too: as Roosevelt himself acknowledged in a letter to Kermit six years later, "the shock permanently damaged the bone, and if anything happens, there is always a chance of trouble that would be serious."[21]

By October 1913, Roosevelt's health issues were even more severe, as Kermit immediately recognized when he encountered his father in Bahia for the first time in two years. "He has never quite recovered from the accident," Kermit wrote to Belle. "One of his legs is still pretty bad and needs a lot of care."[22] In addition, Roosevelt, nearsighted since childhood, had become virtually blind in one eye, the result of an accident while boxing in the White House.

On March 27, after exactly a month on the river, Roosevelt suffered an innocuous leg injury that proved to be the first of a cascading series of medical troubles that would compromise his health for the remainder of the journey and soon threaten his life. Some of the camaradas were in the water, maneuvering a pair of dugouts through yet another set of very narrow rapids, when they lost their hold on the canoes, which rammed into rocks at the water's edge and began to sink. Responding to shouts for help, Roosevelt jumped into the water and, chest-deep in the turbulent stream, joined the men in "straining and lifting to their uttermost."[23] Momentarily losing his footing, he gashed a shin badly on one of the jagged rocks, and blood began to spurt from the wound.

At first, Roosevelt tried to play down the severity of the injury, which he attributed to "my own clumsiness."[24] Fearful of infection in a humid environment awash with parasites and bacteria, Cajazeira promptly dressed the wound with antiseptic and wrapped it in gauze, so initially all seemed well. But to Cherrie and Kermit, Roosevelt's mishap constituted a turning point in the expedition, and in fact the injury never healed properly. "From that time on, he was a very sick man,"[25] Cherrie wrote. Roosevelt stayed off his feet for a couple of days, then, accompanied by Cajazeira and Cherrie, walked slowly and laboriously to the new camp, pausing several times along the trail when the pain grew too intense. When Roosevelt arrived, Cherrie noted, "he lay flat down on the damp earth for some time before recovering."[26] Kermit knew what that meant: his father was not just gimpy, he was also experiencing a recurrence of his past coronary problems.

Not only did Roosevelt's wound become infected; soon it was evident that he was also enduring attacks of malaria. His temperature soared to 105 degrees, and he slipped into moments of delirium. While the others slept, Kermit, Cherrie, and Cajazeira took turns sitting with him, listening to his ramblings. One night just before dawn, Cherrie heard Roosevelt calling his name, and rushed to his side. Kermit was there already. "Boys, I realize that some of us are not going to finish this journey," he said, looking squarely at Cherrie. "I want you and Kermit to go on. You can get out. I will stop here."[27]

Cherrie was horrified. He realized immediately that Roosevelt was talking about suicide, and that it would be dangerous to leave him alone. "There wasn't a moment from that time forward," he said five years later, during a memorial service in Roosevelt's honor, "that either Kermit or myself didn't watch the Colonel, to prevent him from carrying out what he felt was a necessity," namely that "he must relieve the party of what he considered a burden."[28]

As Roosevelt's condition worsened, Dr. Cajazeira grew suspicious. Finally, he went to Rondon with his misgivings: Roosevelt, he concluded, was not taking the quinine that Cajazeira had prescribed.

In a report filed after the expedition ended, Cajazeira noted that whenever he saw that Roosevelt had failed to take quinine at a meal, or had taken too small a dose, he would question him. Invariably, Cajazeira wrote, "he told us on those occasions that he had already taken it."[29]

Cajazeira clearly doubted this, however. As he explained in his report, he, Rondon, Lyra, and Cherrie "all took our established doses and arrived in Manáos without the slightest elevation of temperature."[30] To the camaradas he administered half a gram daily, with a double dose every third or fourth day, requiring them to take their medicine as he watched and checked their names off his list. In that fashion, he was at least able to limit the severity of the chills and fevers that afflicted them. How odd, then, Cajazeira reflected, that of all those regularly being dosed with quinine, Roosevelt and Kermit had suffered the strongest recurrences of malaria.

Why would both Roosevelts want to avoid taking the only medicine then known to effectively combat malaria? Perhaps it was because of quinine's many side effects, among them heart palpitations; in fact, today, quinine use is not recommended for people suffering from arrhythmia, atrial fibrillation, or other cardiac disorders, like those troubling Roosevelt. Quinine is also known to occasionally cause hallucinations, particularly in men in late middle age. Kermit complained of such incidents, and some of Roosevelt's delusions also might have been caused by quinine. Other side effects include dizziness or vertigo, tinnitus, blurred vision, headaches, sweating, susceptibility to sunburn, itchiness, skin rashes, and generalized nausea. To many forced to take quinine, the cure may seem as bad as the disease.

Because of his suspicions, Cajazeira began injecting quinine every six hours directly into Roosevelt's ample belly. His temperature immediately dropped. But the former president's leg pain continued, the wound still swollen and red, and Cajazeira worried that gangrene might develop. If it became severe enough, he would be forced to amputate Roosevelt's leg. Roosevelt also was having early symptoms of dysentery. Weak and feverish, he showed no signs of regaining his characteristic dynamism.

As the expedition entered its second month on the River of Doubt, Roosevelt's deteriorating health was only one of many menacing difficulties. Depleted food supplies affected everyone: men were hungry, and their physical performance was diminishing—increasing the likelihood of accidents—as was their morale. Despite rationing, food supplies were being consumed at an alarming rate, and halting for just a few days to hunt fish and game would, in such circumstances, be risky if they failed to catch or shoot anything. Their supplies would have diminished further, time and energy would have been lost, and no further distance covered. They were caught in a vicious circle.

Even Rondon, ever stoic in difficult situations, appeared disheartened. Early on March 28, he and Kermit, accompanied by Lyra and Luiz Correa, a paddler, set out on foot from their camp at the base of the rapids to reconnoiter a daunting canyon that lay ahead. When they returned in mid-afternoon, filthy, drenched in rain and sweat, bruised and drained of energy by their exertions, the dazed and somber look on Rondon's face told Roosevelt and the others that he had unexpectedly bad news.

The problem was not just the canyon, already an enormous challenge: it was almost two miles long, and its flow of water was broken by a half-dozen cataracts, one of which was more than thirty feet high. Rondon saw no way to navigate through that gauntlet in the canoes, but also deemed it impossible to detour around the gorge with another portage. The canyon marked the start of an area of rocky, hilly terrain that extended for several miles, he explained, with nearly vertical slopes, too steep for a portage and cluttered with sharp rocks and boulders.

In Rondon's view, there was only one desperate solution: abandon all the canoes, reduce equipment yet again, hike to the end of the mountains, and build new canoes there. This was a proposition fraught with peril, perhaps even suicidal, as everyone understood. There was no telling how long it would take to cross the gorge or build replacement canoes once it was traversed—assuming it could be traversed at all—while the expedition would be consuming precious and perhaps irreplaceable food supplies. Such intense, time-consuming labor would only weaken the exhausted men further, and raise the risk of additional injury. Finally, there was also the continued danger of attack by Indians who still shadowed the expedition. "To all of us his report was practically a sentence of death,"[31] Cherrie wrote.

By now, Kermit, at twenty-four the youngest of the three Americans, and Lyra, his counterpart on the Brazilian side, had formed a solid friendship. Fearing disaster, Kermit, supported by Lyra, openly disagreed with Rondon. Both young men thought it possible to get at least some of the canoes through the canyon intact, and wanted to try. Kermit had acquired formidable rope-handling skills while working on engineering projects in São Paulo, and had already demonstrated his mastery at several crucial moments earlier in the expedition; that gave him credibility.

Roosevelt naturally supported his son. But so did Cajazeira and the camaradas, who worked closely with Kermit and liked him, despite Simplício's death, because he treated them with respect and bothered to learn their names. Rondon was overruled and gave in. But his spirits appeared lower than they had ever been; he seemed uncharacteristically passive in the face of adversity, and for the first time the others could read doubt on his face.

Before setting out, the expedition members once again jettisoned equipment not deemed essential—the fourth instance since early January that they pared down their gear, this time to the absolute minimum. All but one of the tents was discarded; going forward, all six principals would sleep under the same canvas. Whatever could not fit into the single duffel bag that each carried was discarded. For his part, Rondon, the assiduous reader, abandoned some surveying tools and retained a single book, Thomas à Kempis's *The Imitation of Christ*, while Roosevelt kept only the last volume of Gibbon's *Decline and Fall of the Roman Empire*.

In the end, Kermit and Lyra were proved right. It took nearly four days of arduous labor to get the canoes through the canyon and into a stretch of calmer water, but it was achieved without loss of life and with only the smallest of the six dugouts sacrificed. Throughout the process, Kermit, Lyra, and the rest of their team had to cleave to the ledge almost as modern-day rock climbers do, though moving laterally and without the benefit of bolts, aware that the slightest slip could be fatal. "Hard work; wet all day; half ration"³² was Kermit's laconic summary in his diary on the second day.

At the new campsite below the canyon, the misfortunes started up again. The explorers had been spared rain during their passage through the canyon, but now the torrential downpours resumed. That night, the canopy of the single remaining tent collapsed under the weight of the deluge, but the tent's six occupants were too spent to leave their cots and try to set it right. For the exhausted boatmen, conditions were even worse: sleeping out of doors in their hammocks, with only tree branches to shield them, they were drenched. No one slept, and the next morning, the dugouts were swamped with water and needed to be bailed out before travel could resume.

Barely an hour after setting out, the canoes pulled up short of another narrow canyon. Once again Rondon, Kermit, and Lyra went ahead to scout, and once again they found waterfalls and rapids as far as they could see, framed by the same familiar sheer stone cliffs. They estimated that a portage would take at least two days, maybe three, and Rondon decided to pitch camp just above the main set of rapids. That meant the camaradas would have to tote the remaining gear along the narrow stone outcroppings that projected from the cliffs and overlooked the river.

That night, Paixão, whose surname means "passion" in Portuguese, caught Julio de Lima stealing food from the ration tins. The brawny corporal punched the thief in the face and warned him that worse would befall him if he ever raided the provisions again. Julio, his nose bleeding, went whining to Kermit and Roosevelt. But he received no sympathy: Kermit told Julio that "he had gotten off uncommonly lightly."³³ The next day, Julio was involved in two more altercations: another paddler caught him gobbling the last of the beef jerky and told Paixão, who berated Julio and promised to report him to Rondon for punishment. And a few hours later, with the camaradas struggling to haul food and equipment to the canoes, Paixão noticed Julio straggling behind the other paddlers, carrying a much lighter load, and dressed him down again.

Arriving at the staging point, Paixão deposited the crates he was carrying, carefully angled his carbine against the accumulating cases, and headed back down the trail to fetch another load. Julio added a box to the pile and turned to go, grabbing Paixão's weapon as he departed.

A minute or two later, the sharp, unmistakable crack of a firearm echoed above the din of the rapids, and shortly after that, a handful of frantic camaradas, crates still in their arms, arrived at the clearing, shouting that Julio had shot Paixão. Urged on by the boatmen, Roosevelt, rifle in hand, and Cajazeira, armed with a revolver, headed back up the trail while Kermit went to find Rondon and Lyra, who were scouting up ahead. Roosevelt and Cajazeira found Paixão lying facedown in a pool of blood, with a bullet through his chest. The doctor knelt to examine him, and on turning him over noted the gunpowder residue indicating that Julio had fired point-blank, shooting Paixão through the heart. Dr. Cajazeira also saw an entry wound at the armpit, a sign that the unarmed Paixão had raised his arm to defend himself.

It was mid-morning on Friday, April 3, 1914. The explorers had been on the River of Doubt for five weeks and had advanced barely one hundred miles. They had consumed more than half their rations, with hundreds of miles remaining before they reached their destination. One of their commanders seemed suicidal, the other immobilized by despair, and the anxious paddlers were seeking reassurance from the officers that they would get out of the situation alive. The Roosevelt-Rondon Scientific Expedition had hit rock bottom.

XVI

Expedition in Peril

EVERYONE WAS IN danger now, for Julio was still armed, and
hiding nearby. Dr. Cajazeira saw Roosevelt squinting at the
surrounding vegetation and told him: "My eyes are better than
yours, Colonel. If he is in sight, I will point him out to you, as you
have the rifle."[1] If Julio was planning to kill others, his next likely
target would be Pedrinho, the boatman who had reported him for
stealing beef jerky. He was serving as sentry at the base camp; there
was relief when the news came back that Pedrinho was unharmed.

By now, Rondon and Lyra had returned. The Americans seemed
dazed by the shooting, but the two Brazilians reacted with conster-
nation and fury when they saw Paixão's body in the middle of the
trail: Kermit wrote in his diary that Rondon was "in a blind rage to
kill"[2] Julio. But Rondon soon recovered his equilibrium, and ordered
Antônio Correa and Antônio Paresi, his most capable scouts, to try
to pick up Julio's trail and apprehend him. Roosevelt had already sent
Kermit and Cherrie to guard the canoes, so Rondon ordered a pair of
the other camaradas, duly armed, to watch over provisions, and put
the others to work digging a proper grave for the esteemed Paixão.

As all of this was taking place, the expedition's co-commanders
conferred about how vigorously to pursue Julio and what to do with
him if he were caught. And it was at this moment, perhaps more than
any other in their five months of living and working together under
ceaseless stress, that their worldviews collided.

Rondon's account described Roosevelt as tense and agitated, exclaiming: "We've got to send someone after Julio, apprehend him and kill him!"[3]

Rondon the Positivist, however, believed it preferable to adhere to rules and regulations. That, after all, was the foundation of order and progress, the Positivist values espoused on the Brazilian flag, and he often had chastised himself whenever, as a younger man, his own behavior fell short of those ideals. His mission was to civilize, and part of that task was to implant rationality and the rule of law in the wilderness. Gently, he reminded Roosevelt that Brazil's legal code did not provide for capital punishment.

"What you are asking for is impossible in Brazil," he said. "Those who commit crimes are tried, not killed."[4] If Julio was apprehended, Rondon continued, the law required the expedition to transport him to Manaus and hand him over to the legal authorities for trial.

But Roosevelt persisted. He reminded Rondon that both food and medicine were running low. What was the point of taking a murderer all the way to Manaus? Julio would contribute nothing, and only consume valuable provisions. "He who kills another deserves to die," Roosevelt said. "That's the way it is in my country."

"It is pointless to try to find Julio," Rondon responded, trying to allay Roosevelt's concerns about wasting scarce supplies on a criminal by suggesting they not search for him at all. "Looking for a man who flees into the disorder of this jungle is a task much more difficult than finding a needle in a haystack." After a pause, he added: "But if that's what you desire, I'll do it." When Roosevelt said that was exactly what he wanted, Rondon wrote, "I ordered a squad to search for the killer."[5]

The debate between Rondon and Roosevelt seemingly became academic a few minutes later, when the two Antônios returned, excitedly holding Julio's carbine aloft. It had been recovered from a tangle of vines, where Julio appeared to have abandoned it in a panic, not wanting to lose time struggling to pry it free and risk being caught. That greatly reduced the risk that Julio might attempt to kill someone else, and also left the murderer defenseless against both Indians and predatory animals. Turning to Roosevelt, Rondon remarked: "Now he will be punished by the force of the circumstances in which he has placed himself."[6]

But it still remained necessary to give Paixão a dignified burial. As the camaradas he had so ably supervised lifted him by the legs and torso, Rondon and Roosevelt secured his head and shoulders, and together they gently carried the body to a hastily dug grave. Rondon thought highly of Paixão—he had commended the corporal's "altruism" in his diary, about the highest praise a Positivist can offer another person—and wanted to salute him with an appropriate farewell. A rough wooden cross already stood at the head of the grave, but Rondon ordered a salvo fired in his honor, and declared that both the rapids and the range of hills around them would now bear Paixão's name.

Just as after Simplício's drowning, the explorers, now down to nineteen weary and dejected men and four battered canoes, resignedly returned to work and resumed their portage. But the physical exertion and emotional stress accompanying the murder of Paixão had further weakened Roosevelt, who was feverish again and so short of breath that he could take only a few steps before having to pause. Rejecting suggestions that he be carried on a cot, he struggled to reach the campsite for the evening. "At 5:30 in the afternoon, Mr. Roosevelt arrived after great effort, worn out by the pathway, which rose sharply along the rocky mountainside," Rondon wrote. "Such brutal exercise was excessive for his state of health, and made him suffer horribly."[7]

Roosevelt was now a mere shadow of the proud and confident man who had impressed the Brazilians with his energy and physical force in the expedition's early stages. "There is in Mr. Roosevelt a large dose of self-regard," Rondon's aide de camp Botelho de Magalhães observed in his diary then. "There are many things he does because he sees them done by Col. Rondon; he doesn't want anyone to think that he is not capable of enduring the same work and privations as the others. In his own eyes, it doesn't matter that Rondon is a veteran of great campaigns in the wilderness over the past 25 years, while for him, Roosevelt, what he was doing was merely an episode, interwoven with his life as a politician and a man of government offices."[8]

Aware he could no longer keep up and worried about the fate of the others, especially his son, Roosevelt now for the first time broached to Rondon the same drastic solution he had earlier suggested to Kermit and Cherrie. "The expedition cannot delay," he told Rondon. "On the other hand, I can't go on. Move on and leave me!"[9]

The request was irrational, a sign that Roosevelt's deteriorating physical state was also affecting his mental acuity. If Rondon had initially insisted on taking the "criminal deserter" Julio all the way to Manaus, why would he abandon his co-commander in the wilderness? Rondon was above all a military man, with a rigid code of honor that never would have allowed him to abandon anyone, even if he had not received explicit instructions to escort Roosevelt safely to Manaus. Rondon finally responded: "Allow me to observe that this expedition bears the names of Roosevelt and Rondon. It is therefore not possible for us to separate."[10]

That night was probably the closest Roosevelt came to dying while under Rondon's supervision. As Kermit and Dr. Cajazeira took turns caring for him, he again slipped into delirium, and began to recite, over and over again, the opening lines of Coleridge's epic poem "Kubla Khan": "In Xanadu did Kubla Khan / a stately pleasure dome decree." Then he descended into gibberish, with occasional bursts of lucidity reflecting his concern for his companions: "I can't work now, so I don't need much food," Kermit would recall his father saying, oblivious to his son's presence. "But he and Cherrie have worked all day with those canoes, they must have part of mine."[11]

Fortunately, Roosevelt's fever broke just before dawn, and on the morning of April 5, Palm Sunday, it appeared the expedition was finally nearing the end of the long, narrow, and unrelentingly perilous canyon. Kermit, feverish himself, accompanied Rondon and Lyra on a hike downstream and concluded, as he wrote in his diary, "that after these rapids we're out of the hills."[12] They returned to camp just in time to hear Antônio Paresi excitedly announce that he had spotted spider monkeys in the canopy of some nearby trees. Kermit and Cherrie grabbed their guns and managed to shoot three of the animals for that night's dinner; Kermit captured a turtle, too, which went into the pot, providing a tasty soup. "The fresh meat we all craved gave us renewed strength and energy," Cherrie wrote, "and the fact that the mountains that had for so long hemmed us in seemed at last to be falling away from the river brought us new courage."[13]

The next day, Rondon and Lyra were taking measurements along a placid stretch of river when they were startled by a familiar voice calling to them from a patch of jungle on the other bank. It was Julio, clinging to an overhanging branch, imploring "Senhor Coronel" to halt and take him aboard. "It is impossible to stop the canoe now and interrupt our surveying,"[14] Rondon responded, cold indifference in his voice. But as he acknowledged in his diary, he had also decided it was more "convenient to wait for Mr. Roosevelt" before determining Julio's destiny. That opportunity came only when the explorers made camp seven miles downstream, where a large tributary flowed into the River of Doubt from the east. Julio had pleaded with each of the passing dugouts to rescue him, and received the same response: no one would acknowledge him.

Roosevelt's initial reaction had been quite different. As soon as he saw Julio hugging the bough, he grabbed his rifle, raised the weapon to eye level, pointed it in the murderer's direction, squinted through the sights, and aimed. He had his finger on the trigger, and as they looked on in alarm, it seemed to Cajazeira, seated at his side, and Antônio Correa, steering the canoe, that Roosevelt was about to shoot "at the disgusting, cursed figure of that unfortunate criminal." But suddenly, "he withdrew the weapon, raised an eyebrow and told the doctor," Botelho de Magalhães wrote years later, citing Cajazeira as his source, "that he did not want the vessel to tie up and take the murderer on board."[15] Both men attributed Roosevelt's change of attitude to "the warning from Rondon, who wanted to assure the law be carried out, and had prohibited any individual exercise of justice."[16]

When Rondon and Roosevelt were finally able to confer about Julio's reappearance, their positions were reversed: it was Rondon who now wanted to send men out to search for Julio, who had vanished back into the jungle, and Roosevelt who insisted they abandon him to his fate. The camaradas were exhausted, he argued, and many were also sick, their clothes in shreds. No one in the expedition knew how long it would be before they reached the Madeira, so why take risks looking for a murderous thief who would only add to the many burdens being endured by honest, hardworking men? "The expedition is in danger," Roosevelt warned.[17]

But Rondon would not budge: an effort to retrieve Julio must be made. "Absolutely not," Roosevelt replied. "I do not agree." Rondon wrote that when Kermit tried to express an opinion, his father turned to him and bellowed, "Shut up!" This offended Lyra, by now Kermit's closest comrade on the expedition; muttering under his breath, he protested to Rondon in Portuguese: "He must think he's still president."[18]

In the end, Rondon simply wore down Roosevelt, who was becoming sicker and more exhausted by the hour. "Alright, my dear colonel, carry out the law of your country,"[19] Roosevelt said listlessly. Rondon immediately ordered the two Antônios to set out in search of Julio again.

All three of the Americans believed that what Rondon really wanted was time to conduct a more thorough survey of the area, and map the coordinates of the new river they had just discovered. The Americans were undoubtedly right. The scouting party tried hard to find Julio: the two Antônios fired their rifles into the air to signal their location, built small fires to attract him, and called his name until they were hoarse. The expedition remained immobile for two days, while the scouts searched, and Rondon and Lyra indeed took readings to determine exactly where they were—more than two weeks had passed since Lyra was last able to measure the expedition's precise latitude—and map both rivers more accurately.

This left the Americans more exasperated than ever, and in their diaries they registered their doubts about Rondon's honesty, judgment, and ability to command. "Rondon vacillated about Julio with 100 lies," an indignant Kermit wrote.[20] The next morning, Cherrie, too, was still steaming: "This resolution on Col. Rondon's part is almost inexplicable in the face of facts regarding our own position," he wrote. "From our point of view, this delay and the trying to carry a prisoner places in jeporday [sic] the lives of every member of our party."[21]

The quarrel proved pointless, for the scouts had no better luck finding Julio than they had three days earlier. So they returned to the canoes, and soon faced two new portages—the first about four hundred yards; the second, one hundred yards. After walking along the riverbank with Cherrie during the longer one, Roosevelt "was completely tired at its end, and yet it was over level ground,"[22] the naturalist noted. Rondon ordered camp pitched and travel ended for the day.

The explorers seemed stuck in a phase in which every piece of good news was followed by something discouraging. After camp was made, Cherrie shot three howler monkeys, adding to the food stock, and Lyra was able to catch a pair of good-sized piranhas. But the next morning, turbulent whitewater rapids, half a mile long, required yet another tiring portage. The explorers advanced barely three miles that day, and at their campsite they noted they were once again surrounded by hills, a sure sign that even more rapids lay ahead.

Cherrie took an almost perverse delight in the situation: "This long series of rapids," he wrote, "has taken some of the cock-suredness out of Rondon, who during the unnecessary delay at the Rio Cardoso insisted there were no rapids ahead!"[23] But his ire soon extended to the Roosevelts, father and son, after Kermit realized that he had somehow left his dog behind at the last camp. A search party was sent back to find Trigueiro, and though they returned hours later with the happy canine, Cherrie thought the effort a waste of precious time. It was "a great mistake on Col. Roosevelt's and Kermit's part, when we are so anxious to get ahead,"[24] he wrote.

During the search for Trigueiro, Luiz Correa made an intriguing discovery. While fishing on the other side of the river, he noticed a spot where a thick vine had been cut with either a knife or an ax. As Cherrie noted, "it was in a place where the work could only have been done from a canoe,"[25] which suggested that perhaps some rubber tapper had recently made his way upstream and might be nearby.

This momentarily lifted the men's spirits, but the next day, Easter Sunday, the explorers spent eight hours hauling their equipment through another portage while the canoes ran the rapids; the paddlers lost control of one of the dugouts, which slammed into rocks.

It took three hours to retrieve that canoe and then more time for caulking to make it serviceable again. As they set up camp at the end of the run, they could again see hills ahead—"not a good augury,"[26] Cherrie wrote.

That night, Kermit observed that "for the first time in a month," rather than the sound of roaring water being always audible, "we're camped in silence." But as always, there were other problems. "Father not well," Kermit wrote. "Much worried."[27] The next day, Roosevelt was so debilitated that he had to travel flat on his back; he was shielded only by a large piece of canvas and what remained of a broad-brimmed straw hat that insects had mostly consumed. At two portages, he had to be assisted off the boat and up the slope by Kermit and Cherrie, who would later recall thinking that " 'he won't be with us tonight'; and I would say the same thing in the evening, 'he can't possibly live until morning.' "[28]

Relief came only on April 15. After advancing sixteen miles, itself a formidable achievement compared to previous days, Rondon, now in the lead canoe, spotted a crude sign nailed precariously to a tree along the bank of the river, with the initials "J. A." carved into it. This was the first unmistakable evidence of civilization since departing the headwaters of the River of Doubt nearly seven weeks earlier. Rondon and the other Brazilians knew the initialed board marked the limits of a rubber gatherer's claim, so a curing shed was certain to be nearby, and would probably be stocked with supplies.

Sure enough, less than an hour later the explorers saw a thatched hut in the middle of a planted clearing, guarded by three yelping dogs. Jubilant and relieved, they paddled rapidly to the shore and jumped out. In the hut they found sacks of cassava flour and rice, twin staples of the Brazilian wilderness, as well as an ample supply of yams. But the owner, one Joaquim Antônio, was not there, and Rondon, adhering to the jungle's code of honor, refused to allow his famished men to help themselves to the proprietor's provisions. Instead, he left a note listing the names of all the surviving members of the expedition and where they had come from.

Several miles downstream, the explorers finally encountered a human being. An old caboclo saw them coming; assuming they were an Indian war party, because no civilized people had ever been seen coming from that direction, he frantically began to paddle away. It was only when Rondon stood up, waved his helmet, and called out to him in Portuguese that the rubber tapper relaxed and allowed the four dugouts to come alongside. But the conversation he then had with Rondon did little to dispel the sense of astonishment the old man felt when he first glimpsed the explorers—emaciated, feverish, bearded, and clad in rags.

The rubber tapper was Raymundo José Marques, a wizened Black man originally from Maranhão, nearly 1,500 miles to the east. Rondon explained the purpose of the expedition, and introduced Roosevelt to Raymundo, who could scarcely believe his ears. "So he is really a president?" the caboclo asked "half-incredulously." Rondon clarified that Roosevelt was a former president of the United States, to which Raymundo replied, "Ah, but he who was once king always retains the right of majesty." Roosevelt, though prostrate on his cot, could only laugh with delight when that statement was translated for him.[29]

Raymundo, who lived alone, also had valuable geographic information. The stream the expedition was descending, he told Rondon, was locally called the Rio Castanho, or "Brown River," because of the water's dark, murky color and the presence of trees with dark brown wood and nuts. Farther downstream, he added, the river was known as the Aripuanã—a name already familiar to Rondon, who had passed the mouth of that stream many times as he descended the Madeira on his way to Manaus. So Rondon's original intuition had proved to be correct.

Though Raymundo had no food to share, he told Rondon that the explorers would soon be able to obtain provisions from other rubber tappers just downstream. To announce the expedition's arrival, Raymundo advised Rondon to fire three shots into the air as he approached any settlement, and also to blow into a horn that he provided to Rondon. But when, a few miles downstream, the explorers saw puffs of smoke coming from another thatch hut and followed Raymundo's counsel, a woman with a baby in her arms rushed outside, took one look at the explorers, screamed, and ran off into the jungle.

Reasoning that the woman would eventually return with her husband, Rondon ordered the paddlers to stop and make camp in the clearing around the hut. Roosevelt could not walk, so Kermit and Cherrie carried him to the hut and laid him on a cot. The cook already had a fire going when the couple, flanked by two neighbors armed with rifles, reappeared; once they realized that their unexpected guests, though ragged and haggard, were actually part of an official government party, the rubber gatherers were extremely cordial, generous, and helpful with both food and information. "It seems like a dream to be in a house again, and hear the voices of men and women, instead of being among those mountains and rapids,"[30] Antônio Correa remarked to Kermit that night.

The next morning, Cajazeira operated on Roosevelt's leg, out in the open—and without anesthetic, for Roosevelt had not mentioned that he kept a vial of morphine hidden in his belongings, if he needed to commit suicide. Cajazeira had decided it would be unwise to wait any longer: Roosevelt was unable to walk, and Cajazeira could see that the ruddy inflammation around the wound was growing worse. He worried that a cellulitis infection could spread to Roosevelt's lymph nodes and bloodstream, threatening the former president's life. So while the canoes were being packed, he sliced into the swollen tissue and watched it empty of pus. He then inserted a drainage tube into the incision. All the while Roosevelt lay there, stoically silent, and when Cajazeira had finished, Kermit and Cherrie helped the weakened patient into the dugout.

With the worst of the rapids and waterfalls behind them, the expedition's members hoped their progress would accelerate. But nature once again intervened: that day, the current grew sluggish, and the next day, the rainfall was so intense that in the afternoon the explorers had to take refuge in an abandoned hut. As a result, they advanced just over forty miles. Though this was significant progress, especially compared to their rate on the days they had confronted rapids, it was not enough to satisfy hungry, tired men who knew they had nearly seven hundred miles ahead of them before reaching the majestic Madeira.

But there were positive developments, too. For one thing, Roosevelt's health seemed to be improving. His temperature had gone down, Cajazeira gratefully noted, and so had the swelling around the abscess in his leg. "Father better,"[31] Kermit wrote in his diary. Also, the explorers were able to eat: Leo Miller had loaned Roosevelt $500 at the headwaters of the River of Doubt, so Kermit was able to cross the broadening river to a rubber tapper's hut and buy a chicken, bananas, lemons, and pineapples, a bounty he shared with the grateful camaradas.

The next morning, the expedition encountered another large tributary, entering the River of Doubt from the left, and while Rondon and Lyra took advantage of a cloudless sky to plot the expedition's coordinates, Kermit visited the local rubber tappers again. Though he obtained only five pounds of rice, he was told that about six hours downstream, near some rapids, "a certain Barbosa" lived in a comfortable manor house and would be able to supply food and shelter and possibly even new canoes.

Now, the good news started coming in earnest. When they arrived at Barbosa's and he saw the state they were in, he not only "gave us a duck and a chicken and some cassava and six pounds of rice, and would take no payment,"[32] Roosevelt wrote, but furnished them with badly needed new clothes. Their host was also willing to accept one of the expedition's smaller canoes in exchange for use of a large flat-bottomed boat, big enough to erect a tent to protect Roosevelt from the elements. Barbosa told them that while several sets of rapids lay ahead, some were easily navigable; and even at those that were not, the local caboclos had either dug canals around them or could be hired to pilot the expedition's dugouts through them.

From then on, Rondon relied on the expertise of the caboclos, observed their choices, entered the information in his notebooks for the use of future travelers, and continued his sketching and mapping of the river. His worries about Roosevelt's health, however, persisted, as Cajazeira continued to update him. As the physician feared, the infection had spread throughout Roosevelt's body, and he had developed an abscess on his right buttock so severe that he could not sit down. In addition, he had come down with stomach ailments that killed his appetite and left him listless. "He eats very little," Cherrie wrote. "He is so thin that his clothes hang like bags on him."[33]

Fortunately, the expedition was moving rapidly now, advancing thirty miles or more on the ever-more-frequent days there were no rapids. And even at the Infernão ("Big Hell") Rapids, there were pleasant surprises: first Rondon was able to trade two more of the dugouts for another wide-bottomed boat in excellent condition, and then, just below the falls, the explorers found a general store, the first they had seen in more than three months. Its shelves were mostly bare and dusty, but the store's owner allowed them to spend the night there, dry and in relative comfort. To their delight, Cherrie and Kermit were able to purchase a bottle of imported vermouth, and finally dared to toast the success of the expedition.

The next day, April 23, the explorers began encountering heavily laden batelões making their way upstream, carrying food and other vital supplies to remote settlements deep in the interior. The boat pilots all recognized Rondon, and greeted him respectfully. One after another, they passed on the news the entire expedition had been longing to hear, and which set the camaradas to wild cheering: Lt. Pyrineus de Souza and his men were waiting for them at the junction of the Castanho and the Aripuanã, only four days away.

But they also learned that one last set of rapids lay ahead. They worried about the time it would take to navigate them, but when they got to a settlement called Carapanã, they had another stroke of good luck. The rubber boss of the region maintained a warehouse and general store there, and was visiting when the explorers arrived; he had traveled from his headquarters downstream on one of the steamers he owned. He went by the name José Caripé, and when he was told this was the famous Roosevelt-Rondon expedition, he immediately offered his help.

The Americans were impressed by Caripé's energy and generosity: Roosevelt described him as a man "risen from the ranks," praised him as "a first-class waterman, cool, fearless, and brawny as a bull,"[34] and listened raptly to his tales of jungle adventures. Rondon, though, was wary. He knew the rubber business was by nature exploitative. And as director of the SPI, Rondon also was aware of two other things: that Caripé's business encroached on lands the two main Indian tribes in the area, the Mundurukú and the Parintintin, had occupied for generations, and that able-bodied young men from both tribes had been forced into his service as rubber tappers.

Rondon's most urgent task, however, was to get Roosevelt to Manaus as quickly as possible, so when Caripé volunteered to guide the expedition through the Carapanã rapids and trade one of his fine wooden boats for the last of the explorers' battered dugouts, Rondon accepted the offer. Thanks to Caripé, they were through the rapids in less than two days, and without loss of cargo or life; he continued with them downstream, and after one final portage, the Roosevelt-Rondon expedition at last encountered a placid river "as big as the Paraguay at Corumbá."35

Early the next afternoon, the expedition finally reached the confluence of the Castanho and the Aripuanã. From a distance the explorers could see the American and Brazilian flags flapping in the breeze at Pyrineus de Souza's camp, and as they approached, they were greeted by salvos of gunfire, to which they responded with volleys of their own. Pyrineus de Souza had been waiting for six weeks, uncertain whether Rondon and Roosevelt would be coming from the Castanho, from the uncharted reaches of the upper Aripuanã, or, as in 1909, would not turn up at all. So he was greatly relieved to see his commandant, and helped him carry Roosevelt up to the encampment's main tent. A bottle of champagne was then opened, and Pyrineus de Souza delivered a laudatory toast, in Portuguese and English.

The next morning, April 27, exactly two months after the camaradas first dipped their paddles into the headwaters of the River of Doubt, Rondon officially renamed the river in Roosevelt's honor. Then it was time to go: a government steamer, the *Cidade de Manáos*, was waiting for the members of the Roosevelt-Rondon expedition at São João, Caripé's main base four hours downstream. The vessel was anchored at the rubber boss's residence, where they spent the night, sleeping in real beds. The next afternoon, they were greeted by applause and cheers as they boarded the steamer. Lying on his cot, Roosevelt was carried to a private cabin, wearing one of Caripé's finest suits because all of his own clothes had been reduced to rags. Now Rondon could finally relax: in about thirty-six hours, they would be in Manaus.

In preparation for the steamer's arrival there, Rondon took steps meant to spare Roosevelt any embarrassment from disclosure of his weakened condition. First, he arranged with the vessel's captain to travel at reduced speed, so as to guarantee that the explorers arrived in Manaus well after midnight, when clamorous crowds and curious reporters would presumably be asleep. Additionally, during a stop to take on cargo, Rondon rushed ashore to send a telegram to the state governor, himself a former military officer and also a physician, asking that the vessel's arrival time not be publicized. Finally, he requested that an ambulance and a stretcher be waiting at the port, so Roosevelt could be transported immediately to a medical facility.

It was 2:30 in the morning on April 30, a Thursday, when the vessel carrying the weary survivors of the Roosevelt-Rondon expedition docked at the wharf in Manaus. Roosevelt had spent most of the voyage in his cabin, his mobility limited by the abscess and with his stomach still in turmoil. Rondon was peeved to see that his request for a low-key arrival had been ignored: instead, the governor, members of his cabinet, the local military commander, and various reporters were waiting for the expedition at the dock. The official delegation came aboard, toting buckets of iced champagne, and insisted on celebrating in Roosevelt's cramped and stifling quarters. Only after those pointless pleasantries was Cajazeira able to have Roosevelt—who "lay helpless,"[36] in Rondon's words—whisked into an ambulance and taken to the governor's palace to recuperate.

Almost immediately, Cajazeira operated again on Roosevelt, lancing the abscess and draining it. He also prescribed a heart medicine not available in the jungle and recommended that Roosevelt continue to take quinine until he was back in the United States. With Cajazeira at his side, Roosevelt remained in bed at the palace, where he was forced to endure another exhausting courtesy call, by other government officials who had not yet greeted him.

In the midst of the hoopla, Roosevelt somehow found the strength to write out brief telegrams to his wife and his closest political ally,

Henry Cabot Lodge, announcing that he and Kermit had survived. He also sent a longer message to Foreign Minister Lauro Müller back in Rio de Janeiro. "We have had a hard and somewhat dangerous but very successful trip," he began, going on to enumerate some of the perils of the journey, and also its major achievements. "My dear Sir, I thank you from my heart for the chance to take part in this great work of exploration,"[37] he concluded.

While the camaradas ate and drank their fill, Rondon was, like Roosevelt, busy with official duties. He sent his first written reports off to the capital, but his main interest was to hear evaluations from the leaders of the two teams that had split off from the main expedition. Sant'Anna, with Fiala in tow, had arrived in Manaus in late March—safe, though disappointed by the loss of Fiala's films and equipment. Fiala had intended to wait in Manaus for the others to arrive but, short of money, thought it better to return home. Botelho de Magalhães and Miller had much better luck: they mapped unknown sections of the Ji-Paraná or Machado Rivers and bagged dozens of specimens of mammals and birds before arriving in Manaus on April 10. In fact, Miller was still around and still collecting for the museum, using Manaus as a base to make forays up nearby rivers.

The next morning, May 2, Rondon wrote his final "order of the day." All of the many mishaps and life-threatening crises the explorers had endured were now reduced to bloodless bureaucratic prose, with one exception: under the heading "Criminal Deserter," Rondon, "for the knowledge of members of this Expedition and for public purposes," officially declared that "having murdered on the 3rd his superior officer," Manoel Julio de Lima "was absent without leave as of the 4th." Another section, called "Deletions," made the briefest mention of his victim: "Stricken from the rolls of members of the contingent on April 3, due to his demise, was Corporal Manoel Vicente da Paixão,"[38] who was posthumously promoted to sergeant.

Rondon also praised the most deserving. Leading the list of "Accolades" were Dr. Cajazeira, who had saved Roosevelt's life and probably that of several of the boatmen, and Botelho de Magalhães, who had done vital organizational work. Also "worthy of commendation for the manner in which they distinguished themselves in the exercise of their respective duties" were Pyrineus de Souza and Lyra, "it being only fair to emphasize the technical capacity and practical qualities of First Lieutenant João Salustiano Lyra."[39]

With that, the Roosevelt-Rondon Scientific Expedition was officially over. In the reports Rondon transmitted to the capital, his superiors would read that the River of Doubt, like the Castanho and the Aripuanã, "were all of them parts of a single great river, with a length of 1,409.174 km, advancing uniformly, without deflection," and that this river was "the largest tributary of the Madeira River, with its headwaters at 13° and its mouth at 5° South."[40] But no one except Rondon, Roosevelt, and the small, brave band of men who accompanied them would ever fully appreciate just how terrible a price was paid to obtain that knowledge.

XVII

"Shifts and Contrivances Available in Wild Countries"

AFTER TRAVELING FROM Manaus, Rondon and Roosevelt said goodbye in Belém, at the mouth of the Amazon, following one last round of sightseeing and official receptions. Roosevelt's ill-health was visible to all: Rondon later described him as "walking with difficulty" and praised him for "the beautiful speeches he delivered, in spite of the suffering it caused him to be on his feet."[1] Roosevelt also met with reporters, emphasizing the expedition's accomplishments: "We have put on the map a river nearly one thousand miles long," he said. "It is the biggest tributary of the biggest tributary of the most magnificent river in the world."[2]

On the morning of May 7, 1914, Rondon and the other Brazilians came onboard the steamship *Aidan*, to say goodbye to Roosevelt, Cherrie, and Miller; Kermit was there, too, but was taking a different ship to Lisbon, on his way to Madrid and Belle. Roosevelt began by shaking hands with every camarada, then giving each two gold sovereigns, and finally making a brief speech, which Kermit translated into Portuguese. "You are all heroes,"[3] he told them, adding, as Rondon would recall his words forty years later, that they were "a fine set, brave, patient, obedient and enduring."[4] Nor was Simplício forgotten: Roosevelt directed that his gold coins be sent to his mother.

It was a sentimental occasion, and with the officers of the Brazilian commission, Roosevelt was even more effusive. He had special reason to be grateful to Cajazeira, of course, and upon arrival in New York would praise the doctor's competence; in one letter he called him "the best of the Brazilians." And whatever disagreements had divided Roosevelt and Rondon during their trip now gave way to what Rondon described as a mutual affection "spontaneously born of the dangerous but beautiful deed that together we had just accomplished."[5]

Rondon never allowed himself any emotional display in official settings, but he recalled feeling so moved that he had to tell himself, "Don't show your feelings." For his part, Roosevelt was astonished to learn that Rondon intended to turn around and immediately steam back up the Amazon to Manaus, ascend the Madeira to its upper reaches, and then plunge into the jungle and resume work on the telegraph line. He urged Rondon to return to Rio de Janeiro, visit his family, and get some rest to "restore your vigor," but Rondon was having none of that. "I left my encampment to receive you, and now I'm going back," he told Roosevelt.[6]

Roosevelt concluded by inviting Rondon to visit him at his home in Sagamore Hill. Rondon smiled and, still using the formal "you," replied: "I'll be there when you are again elected President of the United States, to attend your swearing-in."[7] And on that hopeful note, five months of adventure, discovery, and hardship came to an end. Though they would occasionally write, Rondon and Roosevelt never saw each other again, nor would Rondon ever visit the United States.

Of the principal expedition members, Rondon would live the longest, surviving another forty-three years and eight months and participating in a dozen more missions. Roosevelt, by contrast, would be dead within five years. On the *Aidan*'s twelve-day voyage home, he regained about half the weight he had lost on the expedition, but on arrival in New York, reporters noted how haggard and shrunken he appeared. Though he was able to travel to Spain for Kermit's wedding, and then to England and France to address geographic societies there, his participation in the 1914 midterm election campaign was severely curtailed. In addition, any plans to run for president in 1916 were shelved, largely because his once-irrepressible energy was still sapped. There was much talk of him running in 1920 as either a Republican or Progressive, but he did not live that long, dying at Sagamore Hill on January 6, 1919, at the age of sixty.

The first of the others to perish, however, was a much younger man. On April 3, 1917, Lyra drowned while surveying the Sepotuba River. The Roosevelt-Rondon expedition had ascended part of the river on its way to Tapirapoan in January 1914, and Rondon asked Lyra to complete its mapping. According to a tribute published in the Telegraph Commission's internal journal in 1917, Lyra lost his footing while at work and was pulled under by rapids. He was thirty-eight years old, and his body was never recovered; he left behind a wife and three children.

After marrying Belle Willard in June 1914, Kermit returned to South America—but this time to Argentina. He spent the next couple of years in Buenos Aires, where he was an assistant manager of the National City Bank there. He served in both the British and American armies during World War I, and afterward embarked on a series of business ventures, mostly unsuccessful, and wrote books. Prone to depression and heavy drinking, he died on June 4, 1943, of a self-inflicted gunshot wound at Fort Richardson, Alaska, while serving in the U.S. military. His drinking buddy Cherrie would continue to explore Latin America and Asia, amassing a huge ornithological collection, and died on his Vermont farm in 1948.

Leo Miller left the American Museum of Natural History in 1919, became a businessman, writer of adventure novels, and lecturer, settling in Stamford, Connecticut, where he died in 1952. Father Zahm died in Munich in 1921 of bronchial pneumonia while on his way to the Middle East to write a book about archaeology in the Holy Land. And last, but certainly not least, Dr. Cajazeira went on to enjoy a distinguished career as a military doctor and medical researcher, serving as director of several hospitals and laboratories. On retiring from the army in 1937, he was praised for "his extraordinary intellectual ability"[8] and settled in Rio, where he became Rondon's neighbor and died in 1949.

Before heading back into the jungle, Rondon had one last piece of business to take care of. He had learned that the foreign manager of a rubber plantation on the Madeira was about to sail for Europe, never to return to Brazil, and was taking his manservant, a young Indian lad, with him. Knowing that nothing could be done once the vessel left Brazilian waters, Rondon got an injunction prohibiting the minor from leaving Brazil without the written permission of his parents, who were more than 1,500 miles away and could neither read nor write. Police seized the boy and handed him over to Rondon, who took him on board as he headed back upriver. When their vessel arrived at the boy's village, it was greeted by the entire population, dancing and singing songs of praise to the Pagmejera. After a raucous celebration, Rondon and his men made their way back to the Barão de Melgaço station—the same place Rondon had been when, twenty months earlier, Lauro Müller had first contacted him about the Roosevelt visit.

In the jungle, Rondon was largely shielded from the nasty dispute that erupted as soon as Roosevelt's ship crossed into the Northern Hemisphere. The announcement that he and Rondon had descended the entirety of a previously unknown one-thousand-mile-long Amazonian river was greeted with a mixture of skepticism, condescension, and undisguised derision. The claim was "perfectly ridiculous,"⁹ said Alexander Hamilton Rice, a well-known American explorer of the Amazon who argued that Roosevelt was only "doing it for effect, as an asset in his next political campaign." Sir Clements Markham, a former president of the Royal Geographical Society in London, was even more dismissive. "I feel somewhat incredulous as to Col. Roosevelt having actually discovered a new river nearly a thousand miles long," he said, describing the claim as "a very remarkable story" that "did not seem to fit with the known aspects of the country."¹⁰ In both instances Rondon, the expedition's real leader, was completely ignored.

The most virulent attacks, however, came from the English explorer and travel writer Arnold Henry Savage-Landor, who loathed Rondon. All but forgotten now, Savage-Landor was at the time perhaps the most renowned author of adventure stories in the English-speaking world, though serious explorers regarded his tales of derring-do and miraculous escapes from hostile tribesmen in exotic locales like Tibet and Abyssinia as improbable and heavily embroidered. One leading Tibetologist dismissed Savage-Landor's *In the Forbidden Land*, the 1898 book that made him famous, as "an extraordinary Münchhausen romance."

"Though long on heroics and short on verifiable facts, his tales caught precisely the pre-1914 mood of imperial euphoria," John Keay wrote in *Explorers Extraordinary*, published in 1985, six decades after Savage-Landor's death. "Through thick and thin . . . he could be counted on to uphold the dignity—to reinforce the prejudices—of his class and race. . . . The more outrageous Savage Landor's claims and the more unlovable his behavior, the more popular his books and the more elevated his reputation."[11]

Rondon and Savage-Landor had clashed before the Roosevelt-Rondon Scientific Expedition. The Englishman had arrived in Rio in January 1910, intent on trekking across South America, and he wanted the Brazilian government to supply him with pack animals, river vessels, and a military escort during the Amazon leg of his journey. Rondon had returned to Rio in February to recuperate from malaria, just as Savage-Landor was trying to organize his expedition, and Brazil's president, Nilo Peçanha, asked Rondon about the benefits—whether scientific or public relations—of supporting the request. Savage-Landor was also proposing to cross Indigenous territory, another factor requiring evaluation.

When the two men met, at the president's request, things did not go well. It quickly became obvious to Rondon that Savage-Landor was proposing nothing of value. His intended route had been well explored, and the assistance he was seeking would be costly, depleting resources better spent on Brazil's own efforts to open the region. So Rondon declined Savage-Landor's invitation to accompany him and advised his superiors not to grant the Englishman material support. All Savage-Landor was given was a letter of recommendation to local authorities, tantamount to a polite brush-off.

Savage-Landor did not take this rejection well, and it was obviously galling to him to have his fate decided by a little brown-skinned Brazilian exactly his own age. After his expedition, when the two-volume *Across Unknown South America* appeared in 1913, its one thousand pages teemed with racist aspersions on the character, physiognomy, and values of Brazilians. They were "indolent and sleepy," with an "inborn reluctance"[12] toward manual labor, he wrote, as well as stupid, dishonest, and ugly, and the worst examples of all these traits were found in the mixed-race peasantry: "As we went farther into the interior the vegetation grew more beautiful, the people more repulsive," he wrote. "They were a special breed of stranded outcasts."[13]

Across Unknown South America—the title was preposterous, since, as John Keay has noted, Savage-Landor's "'unknown South America' was unknown only to himself"—also contained direct attacks on both Rondon and the political views he espoused. Savage-Landor lamented the passing of slavery and also praised the Salesians, Rondon's perpetual antagonists, deeming them the only ones doing anything worthwhile in Mato Grosso. "What little good in the way of civilization had been done in that State had been done almost entirely by those monks," he maintained.[14] In contrast, he claimed, Rondon and his men "feared the Indians and the wild beasts."[15]

Still, as Savage-Landor saw it, the problems of Indigenous people in Brazil were vastly exaggerated, as were their numbers. "My journey across the widest and wildest part of Brazil," he wrote, convinced him that "perhaps a few hundreds would be a more correct estimate. Counting half-castes, second, third and fourth crosses, and Indians who have entirely adopted Portuguese ways, language and clothes, they may perhaps amount to several thousand—but that is all." And though lamenting the massacres of colonial times, he also argued that the policy the Brazilian republic was implementing, with Rondon in the lead, was equally misguided: "Now, on the contrary, the Brazilian Government goes perhaps too far the other way in its endeavor to protect the few Indians who still remain within the Republic."[16]

When Savage-Landor's book was published in 1913, Rondon was disgusted and, at the request of the government, immediately set about rebutting it in Brazilian newspapers and magazines. The national press fanned public sentiment against *Across Unknown South America*, and portrayed Rondon as a patriot defending Brazil's honor against Savage-Landor's many slanders. Based on his book's own internal evidence, Rondon maintained, Savage-Landor could not possibly have gone where he claimed to have gone. In addition, the book was riddled with elementary errors of biology, linguistics, and geography that further undermined its credibility: for example, the distance between the Juruena and Madeira Rivers was not "thousands of kilometers," as Savage-Landor had written,[17] but just under four hundred miles, or fewer than 650 kilometers. He was, therefore, an impostor. In fact, Rondon's and Roosevelt's shared disdain for the English adventurer had helped the two bond in the early stages of their expedition.[18]

Given these antecedents, the Roosevelt-Rondon Scientific Expedition's descent of the River of Doubt offered Savage-Landor another opportunity for revenge, one he did not waste. Ignoring Rondon's role altogether, as if he were not even worthy of mention, he went directly after Roosevelt, calling him a "charlatan"[19] and accusing him of having plagiarized *Across Unknown South America*. "It seems to me that he has only copied the principal incidents of my voyage," Savage-Landor said in an interview with the *New York World* as Roosevelt was still steaming home from the Amazon. "I see he even has had the very same sickness as I experienced, and, what is more extraordinary, in the very same leg I had trouble with. . . . I do not want to make any comment as to so-called scientific work of Col. Roosevelt, but as far as I am concerned, he makes me laugh very heartily."[20]

With Rondon back in the wilds, it fell to Roosevelt to defend the River of Doubt expedition. He tried, via the Telegraph Commission office in Rio, to keep Rondon informed, but with his Brazilian co-commander often beyond the reach of telegrams, it was difficult. So Roosevelt took the offensive himself, first on friendly turf in Washington, at an event on May 26 sponsored by the National Geographic Society, and then, in June, at various venues in Europe, where he had traveled for Kermit's wedding in Madrid on June 11.

The Washington event, witnessed by an audience of nearly four thousand people, including Supreme Court justices, members of Woodrow Wilson's cabinet, and leaders of Congress, set the tone, more scholarly than polemical, that Roosevelt would adhere to until the controversy ran its course. He had already excoriated Savage-

Landor before leaving New York, calling him "a pure fake, to whom no attention should be paid," so he was able in Washington to focus on science and geography. He began his speech by praising Rondon and the Telegraph Commission, saying that "all we did was to put the cap on the pyramid of which they had laid deep and broad the foundations."[21] He then talked about maps that had been placed on stage, tracing the expedition's route, and described the difficulties it had encountered.

The performance, amply covered by the American and foreign press, was enough to win over both the National Geographic Society and the American Geographical Society, which announced it would award the Roosevelt-Rondon expedition credit for having discovered a new river and traversing it from source to mouth. But detractors in Europe still had to be silenced, and there Rondon provided help: when Roosevelt arrived in Paris in mid-June, the influential republican daily *Le Matin*, with a circulation of more than a million, published a letter that Rondon, at Roosevelt's behest, had written in French. It not only eviscerated Savage-Landor, who was living in Paris at the time, but offered specific details of the Roosevelt-Rondon expedition's descent of the River of Doubt.

Rondon had already provided his 1913 point-by-point refutation of Savage-Landor to Roosevelt, who now cited it to counter the post-expedition counteroffensive against him. "It would be well if a geographical society of standing would investigate the formal and official charges made by Colonel Rondon, an officer and gentleman of the highest repute, against Mr. Savage Landor," Roosevelt urged. "Colonel Rondon, in an official report to the Brazilian Government, has written a scathing review of Mr. Landor. He states that Mr. Savage Landor did not perform, and did not even attempt to perform, the work he had contracted to do in exploration" and "did not keep his word or make any serious effort to fulfil his moral obligation"[22] as a serious explorer.

By the time Roosevelt reached London and addressed the Royal Geographical Society, at that time the global arbiter of all questions cartographic, the battle seemed won. On June 16 he gave a lecture at the RGS, and though Rice and several thousand others attended, neither Markham nor Savage-Landor was present. Markham, however, sent a note, which was read to the audience, in which he retracted his earlier criticisms, saying that Roosevelt had made "a very important addition to our geographic knowledge" and acknowledging that "he must have overcome great difficulties in making this discovery."[3] Savage-Landor, however, never issued any statement acknowledging his own error.

As in Washington, Roosevelt made a point of praising Rondon and the achievements of the Telegraph Commission, which the English chose to ignore. "The work done by the Brazilian explorers in the hitherto unknown interior of western Brazil," he said, is "a very extraordinary work which has not received proper recognition, either in my country or in yours, or in any country of Continental Europe." He finished to a standing ovation, and afterward even Rice seemed to shift position, grudgingly conceding that "it was a very good lecture." Once back in the United States, a jubilant Roosevelt wrote to Rondon, singling out Savage-Landor for mockery: "I think that I have definitely put a stop to all serious consideration of his claims as an explorer so far as competent observers and witnesses are concerned."[4]

Though Roosevelt returned home feeling personally vindicated, the Royal Geographical Society would continue to overlook and ostracize Rondon for the remainder of his life, and even beyond. By contrast, Rondon is at least present, albeit in a secondary role, in American press accounts of the expedition published as it was taking place and just after. He is said to have "accompanied Col. Roosevelt," when it was Roosevelt who accompanied him, or is described as "a member" of the Roosevelt party or as "Col. Roosevelt's native guide." Though Roosevelt himself repeatedly tried to set the record straight, people simply would not listen.

To the RGS, however, Rondon was simply invisible, perhaps because, as an eminent and accomplished explorer who was not white, he stood as a living, breathing rebuke to its racist doctrine of European supremacy. As not just a Brazilian but especially as a man of Indigenous origins, Rondon and his many accomplishments as a cartographer and scientist completely negated the intellectual foundations on which the society's preeminence was based.

Throughout the Victorian and Edwardian periods, two manuals were used as the main textbooks in an RGS training course for explorers: *The Art of Travel; or, Shifts and Contrivances Available in Wild Countries* and *Hints to Travellers, Scientific and General.* They were written and edited by Sir Francis Galton, the originator of the "science" of eugenics and for several years the general secretary of the RGS.

"It is established that some races are inferior to others in volume and complexity of brain, Australians and Africans being in this respect below Europeans,"[25] the latter work declares. Indian tribes fared no better: after serving as a British diplomat in Brazil, the explorer and RGS fellow Sir Richard Francis Burton concluded that Indigenous people shared with Africans a "quasi-gorillahood" and belonged to a "sub-species" of mankind. For its part, *The Art of Travel* includes a chapter called "Management of Savages." "Recollect that a savage cannot endure the steady labour that we Anglo-Saxons have been bred to support," Galton writes. "His nature is adapted to alternations of laziness and severe exertion."[26]

Among the graduates of the RGS explorers' course was Percy Fawcett, a former British Army officer who became Rondon's most persistent nemesis. Born in 1867, the son of an RGS fellow, Fawcett served in British India and North Africa before becoming obsessed with the Amazon and Brazil, convinced there was a forgotten El Dorado deep in the jungle. He devoted most of the rest of his life to trying to locate that lost city, which he called "Z," disappearing in northeastern Mato Grosso during an expedition in 1925.

"Fawcett was deeply influenced by such ideas" as those propagated by the RGS, David Grann writes in *The Lost City of Z*, his account of Fawcett's search for El Dorado. "His writings are rife with images of Indians as 'jolly children' and 'ape-like savages.'" He "believed for instance that the jungle contained 'savages of the most barbarous kind, ape-men who live in holes in the ground and come out only at night.'"[27]

Rondon and Fawcett first learned of each other in 1909. That was three years after the RGS had recommended Fawcett's appointment to a joint Brazilian-Bolivian commission charged with demarcating the border between the two countries. As part of a treaty signed in 1903, each side was to survey the 2,127-mile frontier; official border markers would be erected only when both countries agreed on their placement, in situ. Fawcett's job was to lead the Bolivian cartographic team, and he would spend four years there, on loan from the British Army.

Heading the Brazilian surveying team was Rondon's protégé, Manuel Rabelo. He was then a twenty-nine-year-old second lieutenant who had been handpicked by Rondon to carry out a topographic evaluation of the route for a telegraph line between Cuiabá and the Bolivian border. But when the leader of the Brazilian border-surveying team was struck down with malaria, Rondon agreed to lend Rabelo as a replacement. It was a tough assignment: Brazil's border with Bolivia is its longest with any country, and it crosses a variety of rugged terrains.

Fawcett did not have a high opinion of his counterparts. "The Brazilians were likable chaps," he wrote in a book published after his return to London, "but not at all anxious to expedite the work. . . . In fact, they looked on any activity with marked distaste. It was up to me to complete it, and I intended to do so without any avoidable delays."[28]

But Fawcett's haste and overconfidence led to typical beginner's mistakes. Leaving Corumbá for the Bolivian border in June 1909, Fawcett piled all his men, equipment, dogs, and pack animals onto a single boat, reasoning that, even though the vessel was overloaded, the trip was so short that nothing would happen. He was wrong: that same night, he awoke to find the vessel sinking. No one drowned, and the surveying equipment was saved, but many of the mules and oxen were lost, and time and money were wasted buying new supplies.

Much worse was yet to come. Before the border could be officially demarcated, the joint commission's exploration protocols required that if either team reached a border-marker site first, they would await the arrival of the other. In the specific case of the remote Rio Verde area, it was understood that Fawcett and the Bolivians would arrive first, and bring food and medicine with them for the Brazilians, who would be coming from deeper in the jungle.

Instead, Fawcett grew tired of waiting for the Brazilians, who were slowed by the difficulty of terrain they were surveying for the first time, and ordered most of his team to leave. But the smaller group assigned to stay behind soon became nervous about its own diminishing supplies, and also departed. They left nothing behind, not even the border marker or a note of explanation, so when Rabelo's group showed up, famished, exhausted, and ill, there was nothing for them. They wondered where Fawcett was, and worried that he had been attacked or killed by Indians.

By this time Fawcett had made his way back to Mato Grosso. When he reached a Brazilian base, the officer in charge asked him why Rabelo's team was not with him. Upon hearing the answer, the Brazilians immediately dispatched a search team to find Rabelo and the others. Had they not rescued them—fourteen men in all—Rabelo and his men might all have died. In fact, the survivors admitted, the situation was so dire for a while that they considered suicide, rather than be killed by Indians, be eaten by animals, or die of starvation.

"For the Brazilian authorities, including Rondon, Fawcett had left the Brazilian expedition empty handed so as to be able to conduct his private archeological investigations," one recent Brazilian analyst writes. "After combing the territory of Mato Grosso" and finding no trace of his Lost City of Z, "Fawcett and Fisher," his second in command, "boarded a boat on the São Luiz River and decided to return to La Paz," offering not a word of explanation, much less an apology, for what had happened.[29]

After Rondon and Roosevelt emerged from the jungle and announced their descent of the River of Doubt, Fawcett, like other RGS members, belittled their achievement. Unlike others in London who had never traveled in the Amazon, he did not dispute the veracity of the Rondon-Roosevelt claim. Instead he dismissed it as merely a good trip "for an elderly man" like Roosevelt, as he put it in a letter to John Scott Keltie, secretary of the RGS, and also claimed the explorers had been "royally escorted along the Mato Grosso telegraph line to the Rio Duvida."[30]

In another letter to Keltie, written a decade later, Fawcett still felt much the same, arguing that his own forays into the jungle should be awarded extra points for degree of difficulty, since Rondon and Roosevelt took what he considered the easy way out. "I do not wish to deprecate other exploration work in South America," he wrote shortly before embarking on his fatal 1925 expedition, "only to point out the vast difference between river journeys with their freedom from the great food problem, and forest journeys on foot—when one has to put up with circumstances and deliberately penetrate Indian sanctuaries."[31] This, of course, clearly mischaracterized the Roosevelt-Rondon Scientific Expedition, as well as the nature of Rondon's telegraph work in Mato Grosso, all of which required both riverine and terrestrial travel in grueling conditions and clearly involved penetration of "Indian sanctuaries."

In 1920, Fawcett undertook a second Amazon expedition, the first entirely on Brazilian soil. When Brazil's president-elect visited London in 1919, he met the royal family and called on Parliament. Fawcett managed to wangle a meeting, during which he explained his theory of the Lost City to the Brazilian leader, Epitácio Pessoa, and asked for official Brazilian support for the expedition, which he intended to undertake the next year. Pessoa listened carefully, but did not offer assistance of any kind.

Fawcett remained undiscouraged, however, and put a positive spin on the London meeting. So he decided to renew his effort, and in February 1920 turned up in the Brazilian capital, where he checked into an elegant hotel overlooking downtown. "Perhaps I should have more success, I thought, in Rio, where I could make contact with the minister concerned with affairs in the interior," he wrote.[32]

But Fawcett's timing once again was off: he arrived just as Carnival was getting underway, when government and business offices close, and had to cool his heels for several days, worrying about his depleting reserves, "never free from anxiety about what might happen if my efforts failed to raise funds for the expedition."[33] When the British ambassador to Brazil, Sir Ralph Paget, invited Fawcett to join him at the embassy residence, Fawcett jumped at the opportunity, and it was Paget who then prevailed on Pessoa to meet again with Fawcett.

From Rondon's point of view, here was another haughty Englishman sashaying into Rio and presuming that Brazilians were too backward, lazy, and ignorant to know what was going on in their own country. "It's a fact that Rondon disliked the idea of a foreigner's coming here to do what he said Brazilians can do for themselves,"[34] Gen. Francisco Jaguaribe de Matos, for five decades one of Rondon's closest collaborators, told Fawcett's son, Brian, when the latter visited Brazil in 1952 to investigate his father's disappearance. In fact, Brazilians had been exploring their own country for decades, even if the rest of the world did not acknowledge it.

But to Rondon's dismay, as the meeting got underway, Pessoa seemed initially to side with Fawcett. He appeared, at least to Rondon, fascinated by Fawcett's tales of great wealth just waiting to be uncovered. The president also explained that he had promised Paget that Brazil would help with "this valuable project," and he wanted to keep his word. As a deft negotiator, he thought he could discern a compromise and, after Rondon had expressed his doubts, offered it up: Fawcett would go into the Amazon as the leader of a joint Anglo-Brazilian expedition, accompanied by veterans of Rondon's own expeditions.

Then Fawcett overplayed his hand. "I intend to go alone,"[35] he stiffly informed the two Brazilians, torpedoing any possibility of obtaining official support. There are multiple explanations for this unwillingness to collaborate. One was clearly his racial and class prejudices: in the proposal he would later submit to the RGS seeking its support of his 1925 expedition, he expressed a preference for working with English "gentlemen," because they supposedly had a "greater power of endurance and enthusiasm for adventure" than Brazilians. Another was his distrust of Rondon, who he suspected was trying to sabotage him. And perhaps he did not want to share the glory of finding the Lost City.

In addition, Fawcett felt "that Rondon sacrificed too many lives by traveling in large parties,"[36] and that a small and mobile group was superior. He also maintained, citing his experience in Bolivia and Mato Grosso, that mules and oxen were useless in jungle areas. And he was convinced, with no supporting evidence other than his own intuition, that Indigenous peoples in the areas where he planned to travel would not feel threatened by a small group of white explorers and therefore would not be dangerous.

So the meeting ended with all three participants dissatisfied. As Rondon and Fawcett left the palace together, Rondon asked Fawcett about his exploration plans, but Fawcett, suspicious of Rondon's motives, was evasive about his itinerary and even his date of departure. Rondon reminded Fawcett that, if at all possible, it was best to avoid travel in the southern Amazon during the rainy season, and provided a few more practical tips. "Colonel, I wish you the best of luck," he said to Fawcett as they parted.

Rondon soon had another reason to be irritated with Fawcett. In August, Paget contacted him, asking for copies of maps of Mato Grosso and other areas that the Rondon Commission had drawn up. Rondon suspected that Paget was asking for the maps on Fawcett's behalf because the latter could not bring himself to request them. Fawcett had bragged that he was about to cross territory inhabited only by cannibalistic Indians: if he was indeed penetrating uncharted territory, why was he asking for maps he knew that Rondon had made of those same areas?

Once in Cuiabá, Fawcett hired porters for his expedition's first phase, some of whom claimed to have previously worked for the Rondon Commission and had knowledge of the region that Fawcett himself did not. Along with Fawcett and two other foreigners—an American and an Australian—they headed northeast on land, eschewing a more convenient river route. But as Rondon had predicted, they encountered difficulties almost from the start. In mid-December, they decided to turn back.

When Rondon heard of Fawcett's failure, he gloated openly. In mid-December, he even composed a press release mocking Fawcett and sent it over the telegraph lines to the country's main newspapers. The language was harsh, disdainful, and full of schadenfreude:

"The man who left intent on crossing the wilderness of the Xingu, without thinking of how he would feed himself . . . is back, thin and naturally humiliated at having been forced to beat a retreat . . . before even starting the hard part of the expedition,"

Rondon exulted. By contrast, "none of our explorers has ever turned back at the halfway point."[37]

This was not Rondon's finest moment: he showed an uncharacteristically petty and vindictive aspect of his personality that he seldom, if ever, exhibited in public or even in his diaries. News of Rondon's scornful words reached Fawcett by early January, and, his courage and competence questioned, he replied testily.

Rondon's criticisms were "based on mere suppositions," Fawcett wrote. "I do not know from which source the general received his information," for "the expedition did not have the same objective as the Rondon mission, which concerned itself with tracing the course of the Culuene River in canoes. My work was terrestrial and was completed in December. Having a single companion, I decided to return to Cuiabá to wait for the end of the rainy season before tackling the most important part of the expedition. . . . As regards the Fawcett Expedition, it has not been abandoned. . . . Work shall resume in March, not requiring any different methods, nor the services of a larger group to carry out what is proposed." Instead, Fawcett waited until August, and then wandered around Bahia for three months before giving up and going home.

As engineers and scientists, Rondon and his men, many of whom were, like their commander, Positivists, had little use for Fawcett's speculations, which they regarded as superstitious claptrap. Ramiro Noronha, a future general who in 1920 was the captain mapping the Culuene River, was one of several Rondon Commission veterans who crossed paths with Fawcett and came away thinking his theory was simply too bizarre to even consider.

Fawcett carried around a strange statue of a human figure, made of either jade or basalt, with inscriptions on its chest and feet, which he claimed had mystical powers. "Col. Fawcett confided to me that that statue was the key to all his plans, and the password to be able to enter the hidden city, which was guarded by ferocious Indians," Noronha would later recall. "Showing that statue, he would exercise an irresistible power over the natives."[38]

As Rondon and his men knew from their own travels in the area, there were no Indians of that description at the locations Fawcett

indicated. The Englishman continuously spoke of a tribe of troglo-
dytes he called the Morcego, and while the story may have provided
appealing copy to British tabloids, the Rondon team knew it was hog-
wash. When Brian Fawcett later visited Brazil, Jaguaribe de Matos
told him flat out that "there are no such people as the Morcegos."[39]

The irony, of course, is that even after Fawcett vanished on his
1925 expedition, he remained a nuisance. In the decades that followed, reporters and the Brazilian government often requested
that Rondon evaluate theories about Fawcett's fate, no matter how
far-fetched. Fawcett wasn't the only missing explorer Rondon was
asked about, but the mystery of his disappearance would periodically
plague Rondon until the end of his life.

— PART IV —

*Rondon, newly promoted to two-star general,
mid-1920s, around the time of the Catanduvas
campaign against rebels in southern Brazil.*
(MINISTÉRIO DA GUERRA)

XVIII

"Is He a General Yet?"

AFTER AN ABSENCE of nine months, Rondon returned to the telegraph line in May 1914 to find that the project had fallen far behind schedule. Yet the date set for completion, January 1, 1915, remained unaltered and implacable, as did the pressure on Rondon. He had never missed a deadline, sometimes delivering projects well ahead of schedule. Now he felt compelled to live up to his own exacting standards by meeting the government-imposed deadline.

By May 16, Rondon, ascending the Madeira on his way back to the Barão de Melgaço telegraph station, had passed the mouth of the former Rio Aripuanã, now officially baptized the Roosevelt. While en route, he paused to meet with leaders of two tribes, the Parintintin and the Arikeme; because their territory lay directly in the path of the route intended for the telegraph line, Rondon wanted to ensure their support, and was lavish with gifts. At every stop, he was also encircled by rubber tappers desperate for a new line of work now that the rubber bonanza had collapsed. He hired many of them, knowing that the January 1 deadline required as large a workforce as he could muster.

Mixing Indian-conciliation and telegraph-construction endeavors had always been typical of Rondon, but it became even more urgent now. Descending the Ji-Paraná with Botelho de Magalhães in March 1914, Leo Miller was astonished to see that along the river-bank Rondon "had erected a number of small bamboo and palm-leaf sheds various distances apart, near some of the more recently used trails that led from the water into the dark jungle." Rondon's officers, he added, were accustomed "to stop at each of these stations and place beads, knives and trinkets on the benches as a peace-offering to the Indians," who "themselves had left a number of tokens of friendship in return,"[1] including beautifully adorned arrows, parcels of Brazil nuts and corn, feather headdresses, and pottery. Above some sheds the Rondon Commission had even placed posters with images of uniformed Brazilian soldiers, their weapons deposited on the ground as a sign of friendship, embracing and fraternizing with unarmed Indians. In this way Rondon communicated his peaceful intentions to societies that had no form of writing.

It was a necessary measure, because as the commission pushed northward and approached the Madeira, it increasingly encountered tribes who had been abused by rubber tappers and other adventurers. As a result of these interactions, their identities and cultures, indeed their entire way of life as Indigenous peoples, were rapidly disintegrating. This presented Rondon and the SPI with a challenge quite different from that posed by groups like the Nhambiquara, who traditionally kept their distance from civilization. In the case of tribes such as the Arikeme and the Taquatep, the damage was already done; now the challenge was to preserve what remained.

Rondon's solution was to group remnants of such tribes ravaged by disease, alcohol, and slave labor together in settlements around telegraph stations, irrespective of their linguistic or cultural differences or whether they previously had been allies or enemies. In the words of Botelho de Magalhães, Rondon created "a type of new Babel for jungle-dwellers"[2] with schools, clinics, and "rudimentary workshops" at which tribal peoples learned useful skills. He also "distributed work tools and clothing to the Indians" and established "agricultural colonies." Those who flocked to these centers may have had to sacrifice some of the specific characteristics of their tribes, but they were able to preserve a larger identity as Indigenous people. It was a desperate, last-ditch strategy, and one for which Rondon would later be criticized.

The Telegraph Commission finished its work before Christmas, and on January 1, 1915, the new line was inaugurated. The main trunk ran for 930 miles, the last half of which was jungle previously thought to be impassable, but there were also three branch lines that had required another 478 miles of construction. All told, Rondon and his men had built more than 1,400 miles of telegraph line in under eight years. In addition, the commission erected thirty-two stations, spaced no more than 50 miles apart, thereby, according to the army's official statement, "enabling the normalization of traffic on the accompanying road."[3] That artery was the basis for today's vital BR-364 highway, and the telegraph stations have evolved into cities and towns, some with populations of one hundred thousand or more.

Rondon felt no particular urgency to return to Rio de Janeiro, for his family was no longer there. Though he seems not to have disclosed this to Roosevelt, he and Chiquita had decided that their only son, Benjamin, who aspired to an engineering career, should receive a college-level French technical education and that the girls too would benefit from instruction in that language. So Chiquita and the children sailed for Europe as the Roosevelt-Rondon Scientific Expedition was ending, and, when World War I broke out a few months later, they were essentially stranded in France for the duration, except for an interlude in London when it seemed Paris might fall to the Germans. Though Rondon remained constantly in touch with his family through telegrams and letters, he would not see them again until October 1917, a lapse of four years.

Rondon was already a national hero even before he and Roosevelt plunged into the jungle, but the success of their Scientific Expedition—and the resulting international acclaim—elevated his status even more. To Brazilians, he was now a kind of living icon, whose toughness and persistence embodied the same pioneering spirit that had compelled his Iberian ancestors to penetrate Brazil's uncharted interior two centuries earlier. Henceforth, the national press would routinely describe Rondon as "the modern trailblazer," "the subjugator of the wilderness," "the great civilizer," "the giant of the wilderness," and other similarly mythic terms. "Everything in Rondon's work stirs me," the popular writer Alcides Maia declared in October 1915. "Rondon is an energy in the heart, Rondon is an apostle."[4]

Maia's euphoric words were written after he attended a lecture Rondon delivered that month about the expedition with Roosevelt. During the five years since Rondon last addressed a large public gathering, there had been important advances in communications technology, which he duly incorporated into his presentation. Now, instead of speaking to the audience with maps as his only visual aid, he was able to project lantern slides of color-tinted photographs, which Reis had taken in the field, and even some of the films the commission had made on its expeditions. This pioneering multimedia approach enhanced both the educational and entertainment value of Rondon's lectures; audiences and the press marveled at what they saw.

The use of film was especially innovative, perhaps unprecedented. In *Hero: The Life and Legend of Lawrence of Arabia*, Michael Korda credits the English World War I hero T. E. Lawrence and the American broadcaster Lowell Thomas as the first to integrate moving pictures into spoken lectures. But Thomas's lecture-film tour of the United States and Great Britain took place only after the war ended, commencing early in 1919. That was nearly three and a half years after Rondon delivered his lectures accompanied by moving pictures and still photographs. But the Lawrence and Thomas shows were seen by tens of thousands of people in major world centers such as New York and London, whereas Rondon's lectures were witnessed only by residents of Rio de Janeiro and São Paulo, drawing scant international attention.

Within Brazil, though, Rondon's mythical status made him a coveted political property, courted by each of the political groupings that dominated the First Republic. These cannot really be called parties, since they had only regional followings and were dominated by local political bosses with parochial interests. There were efforts, ultimately unsuccessful, to establish parties that were truly national and ideologically based, and two of them, one liberal, the other conservative, made overtures to Rondon. In addition, over the next decade Rondon was besieged with offers of ministerial posts, seats in the Senate or Chamber of Deputies, and the governorship of Mato Grosso.

His name even popped up occasionally in speculation about future presidents: three of the republic's first eight heads of state were military officers, and two of them had also served as governor of Mato Grosso. To all these propositions, though, Rondon always demurred, remaining loyal to the Positivists' absolute ban on involvement in partisan politics.

This may have been a laudable moral posture, but it was politically shortsighted, and ultimately hampered Rondon's ability to achieve his policy objectives. A term in the Senate, for example, lasted nine years, and would have given him a powerful platform to advocate for Indian rights and ensure that the Indian Protection Service continued to receive adequate funding. Instead, he had to go to Congress every year and lobby for money for the SPI and the Telegraph Commission. Undoubtedly Rondon could have accomplished much more had he been able to put aside his aversion to party politics and negotiate as an equal with those in power. And had he become governor, he would have had power over the police and the state government's budget, which in turn would have allowed him to challenge existing oligarchies and deploy the state police to prevent land grabs harmful to the Indigenous peoples he had promised to protect.

Rondon was first approached about the governorship of Mato Grosso almost as soon as the expedition with Roosevelt ended. The sitting governor, Joaquim Augusto da Costa Marques, who had invited the Roosevelt-Rondon contingent to join him on one of his rural estates for a hunting trip early in the expedition, was the first to serve a complete four-year term in Mato Grosso since the establishment of the republic, but he did not want to test his luck a second time. So Brazil's new president, Wenceslau Braz, sounded out Rondon about the term scheduled to begin August 15, 1915. Rondon was an attractive candidate because he did not belong to any of the state's warring political factions; considered to be above such things, he was acceptable to all. His birthplace near the center of the state also helped: Mato Grosso's two main political blocs still consisted of sugarcane growers and rubber bosses in the north, and cattle ranchers and maté growers in the south; Rondon had dealt with both groups without permanently alienating either.

The offer clearly tempted Rondon, for Botelho de Magalhães would later recall a night in which the two of them talked "for four hours without interruption, from 7 p.m. to 11, at the end of which, after long and erudite expositions, he concluded that he was obliged to reject the designation being offered." As always the reason was ostensibly religious: "The same motives that since 1889 have determined that I not aspire to a position of command in national politics prevail today, even more intensely," Rondon decided.[5]

When the job came up again, Rondon was once more approached and again declined to run. Given the chaotic condition of politics in the state, this was perhaps understandable. Seeking a consensus candidate who could avert such turmoil, however, local notables turned to Francisco de Aquino Correia, the thirty-two-year-old auxiliary bishop of Cuiabá, who had helped mediate several political disputes. This was the same Salesian priest who ran the Bororo schools that Rondon so disliked when he visited them in 1911, and Rondon soon issued a public statement advising the prelate not to accept the offer.

Rondon's opposition to Correia's candidacy put him at odds with virtually all of the state's political elite, especially after he sent telegrams to the national press criticizing the candidacy as antirepublican. On November 26, 1917, he wrote: "The new candidate, though one of Mato Grosso's most illustrious sons, is a priest without the slightest training in public administration, and is, even more alarmingly, a member of a foreign religious order whose program consists of administering Church assets and whose main political principle is to subordinate the destiny of society to its own vital interests."[6]

Sure enough, Correia won handily, and on taking office in January 1918 promptly adopted policies that strengthened and expanded the Church's position, just as Rondon had feared. These included the state government extending financial support to Salesian missionary activities and educational programs that Rondon had long opposed. So by rejecting the governorship, Rondon had brought about an outcome exactly the opposite of what he wanted, one inimical to his interests and those of the SPI. His position so exasperated his local opponents that when the bicentennial of Cuiabá's founding was commemorated in 1919, Rondon, the state's most illustrious citizen, initially was not invited to the celebrations; he was included only after Correia personally intervened.

Having closed the door on any kind of personal political ambition, Rondon therefore remained eternally a supplicant. This had been made painfully clear during and after the Roosevelt-Rondon expedition. When Rondon arrived back in Manaus on April 30, 1914, among the messages that awaited him was a telegram "regarding issuance of a credit" for "unforeseen expenses" for the just-completed expedition. The telegram bluntly stated that "it is absolutely impossible to fulfill your request."[7] In other words, Rondon was stuck with a bill equivalent to more than a quarter of the amount the government had authorized for the expedition.

Arriving in Rio in April 1915 for the first time in eighteen months, he immediately set about trying to retrieve from the Foreign Ministry the money he had been forced to advance in order to pay the extra costs of the Roosevelt expedition. This would prove to be no easy task: the ministry's archives for the remainder of the decade are full of letters and telegrams from the Rondon Commission's office in the capital imploring, beseeching, cajoling, and pleading to be reimbursed—and the Foreign Ministry bureaucracy offering one dubious excuse after another for failing to do so.

Only in 1919, after five years of constant prodding, were the last outstanding bills from the expedition and the publication of its scientific papers finally paid—and that required the direct intercession of the new foreign minister, Domício da Gama, who had been the Brazilian ambassador in Washington when Father Zahm first approached the embassy about a Roosevelt expedition. Da Gama thus owed a debt of personal gratitude to Rondon for cementing Roosevelt's favorable opinion of Brazil—and for the much-desired access to Roosevelt that expedition planning had allowed him as ambassador.

Rondon's most urgent task throughout the period 1915–19, however, was grappling with his commission's increasingly uncertain future. With a telegraph line now installed as far as the Madeira River, the next phase of construction, as envisioned in the original mandate a decade earlier, was supposed to be north into the heart of the state of Amazonas. There the line would split, one branch going northeast to Manaus, the economic hub and port at the junction of two giant rivers, and the other heading northwest toward Tabatinga, a small but vital military outpost on Brazil's border with Colombia and Peru.

In Europe and North America, however, wireless radiotelegraphy was already replacing the conventional telegraph, calling into question the commission's usefulness. Initially, these radiotelegraphs were primitive devices that could transmit only dots and dashes, not the human voice. But with World War I raging, just as Rondon's line to the Madeira River was inaugurated, even human speech was starting to be transmitted over short distances.

The future was clear: the land-based telegraph was obsolete, and radiotelegraphy would become the dominant form of communications across the globe. Indeed, it was an especially attractive technology for a vast country like Brazil, with its rugged terrain and severe budget constraints. To continue building a telegraph line across the Amazon, with all the expenditure of money and lives that implied, would be foolish and wasteful; Braz and his cabinet, including his military ministers, were already complaining about the high cost of maintaining the lines that Rondon had just put into operation.

As an early adopter of new technologies, Rondon knew that the land lines to which he had devoted twenty-five years of his career were now doomed. There was no way he could win a battle on those terms. But he continued to fight to save the commission from extinction, citing reasons related not to the telegraph line itself but to the commission's many other duties, and by doing so he gave it another fifteen years of life.

In its original charter, approved by Congress in 1907, the commission was charged both with building a telegraph line to the Madeira and also with mapping the territory being opened. That was what took Rondon and Roosevelt to the River of Doubt, and what led other teams to find and explore the headwaters of major rivers like the Xingu, the Tapajós, and the Araguaia. The commission also was given a scientific mission, and Rondon's expeditions always included specialists in botany, geology, zoology, astronomy, and ethnology, who had discovered species and produced reports that had practical applications and also raised Brazil's profile in the global scientific community.

Rondon feared, too, that closing down the Telegraph Commission would endanger the SPI, which he referred to as "the beloved child of the Commission."[8] Many of his most trusted aides flitted back and forth between the two agencies, and to some extent the entities commingled funds and duties, even sharing office space in Rio. As Rondon saw it, any blow to the Telegraph Commission would affect the Indian Protection Service, too.

Rondon proved to be as canny a tactician in the ensuing bureaucratic battles as he was in the wilderness. The locale might now be the hearing rooms of Congress, the cafés lining the Avenida Central in downtown Rio, or dinner parties in the elegant mansions of Botafogo and Santa Teresa, but he knew how to win over adversaries and make alliances there, too. He contacted governors of interior states that would be adversely affected by withdrawal of federal support from the commission, and they in turn pressured their congressional delegations. He met with the leaders of learned scientific and geographic societies, as well as with his many friends at the National Museum, and convinced them to write letters and give press interviews supporting the commission's valuable technical and scientific work.

Rondon himself also assiduously worked the press in the capital, stressing the practical benefits of the commission's discoveries in the Amazon: deposits of gold and diamonds, significant new reserves of iron ore, gypsum for use in cement and fertilizers, and manganese for use in industrial alloys. The list of precious minerals the commission and its scientists had uncovered during their years of combing the wilderness was endless, exciting the avarice of urbanites who still harbored visions of Brazil as El Dorado.

Throughout this period, Rondon was essentially fighting on two fronts, for the finances of the SPI were also becoming precarious. For the first three years of its existence, the agency had been adequately if not amply funded: between 1910 and 1913, the share of the budget devoted to "Indian assistance" nearly doubled. But once Braz was sworn in late in 1914, funds were mercilessly slashed: in 1915 the SPI's operational budget was less than 14 percent of what it had been just two years earlier. Funding for the SPI would remain pinched during the remainder of the Braz presidency.[9]

In response, Rondon did everything possible to make the line and its stations self-sufficient, hoping to reduce their drain on his limited budget. He considered no detail too small. Whenever possible, he selected members of local Indigenous groups who had distinguished themselves in the schools attached to the stations, had them trained in Morse code, and installed them as telegraphers, with their salaries paid out of transmission fees.

On his lengthy boat journeys from the capital to the Amazon, Rondon sometimes stopped in coastal cities to visit botanical gardens and local horticultural experts. There he would gather seeds, saplings, and cuttings of fruit trees, vegetables, and medicinal plants and transport them up the Amazon and the Madeira to the commission's regional office. From there, they were sent to stations along the telegraph line and planted in gardens, orchards, and fields. Growth and yields were closely monitored, with stationmasters keeping detailed logs and the commission's botanists, after field visits, reporting to Rondon which crops reaped the most promising results. These would then be cultivated in nurseries, and shared with stations all up and down the telegraph line.

In some instances, Rondon sought improved varieties of wild trees and plants he had first encountered in the jungle. For example, while exploring the far northwestern reaches of Mato Grosso, in today's Rondônia, he and his men came across wild cacao trees in the rainforest; he acquired commercial varieties and had them planted at telegraph posts. The commission's scientists also concluded that coffee, then grown almost exclusively at the higher altitudes of the states of São Paulo and Minas Gerais, might flourish on the Mato Grosso plateau. Both judgments proved correct: a century later, Rondônia, despite its relatively small size, is Brazil's third-largest producer of cacao and the fifth-largest of coffee. This is a direct result of Rondon's foresight and efforts as a kind of modern-day Johnny Appleseed of the Amazon; similar production centers exist, too, in Mato Grosso, Amazonas, and Pará. He saw the economic

Cândido Rondon at the headwaters of the River of Doubt on February 27, 1914, shortly before he and Theodore Roosevelt began their descent of that previously unexplored tributary, which proved to be nearly 1,000 miles long. Note the palm stems Rondon ordered be lashed to the sides of the canoes to improve buoyancy. (LEO MILLER— AMERICAN MUSEUM OF NATURAL HISTORY)

The earliest known photograph of Cândido Mariano Evangelista da Silva, as he was known until 1890, taken shortly after his arrival in Rio de Janeiro in 1881. He was sixteen years old and had just enlisted in the Brazilian Army. (ACERVO DO MUSEU DO ÍNDIO/FUNAI—BRASIL)

The Brazilian Army military academy at Praia Vermelha in Rio de Janeiro, in 1888, when Rondon was a cadet there. One of his classmates said that, at first glance, the building's grim appearance made him wonder whether he was entering "a convent or a prison." Sugarloaf Mountain, which Rondon climbed for sport in his free time, is at the rear left. (EDUARDO BEZERRA)

Rondon and his family, around 1902. From left to right are his son, Benjamin; his daughter Heloísa Aracy; his wife, Francisca, nicknamed Chiquita (seated); Rondon, an Army major at the time; and his daughter Clotilde Teresa. (ACERVO DO MUSEU DO ÍNDIO/FUNAI—BRASIL)

Rondon em expediente

Rondon in the field, dealing with paperwork, around 1905, during the construction of the telegraph line across the Pantanal. (ACERVO DO MUSEU DO ÍNDIO/FUNAI—BRASIL)

Terena Indians raising a telegraph post. Rondon's mother, Claudina, was partially of Terena descent, and Rondon himself would write some of the first linguistic and anthropological works about the tribe. (ACERVO DO MUSEU DO ÍNDIO/FUNAI—BRASIL)

A group of Bororo Indians—Rondon's allies and distant kin. As a token of his gratitude for their assistance in building the Pantanal line, he often gave especially helpful village chiefs military uniforms, which they wore proudly. (ACERVO DO MUSEU DO ÍNDIO/FUNAI—BRASIL)

Constructing the Mato Grosso–Amazonas telegraph line through the jungle, around 1910. When he encountered it in 1914, Theodore Roosevelt would call the project "a cyclopean achievement" as impressive as the Panama Canal. To protect the line, trees were cleared for twenty yards in either direction from poles. (ACERVO DO MUSEU DO ÍNDIO/FUNAI—BRASIL)

Members of the Rondon Commission stringing telegraph wire across a river in northwestern Mato Grosso (today's Rondônia) in 1911. (ACERVO DO MUSEU DO ÍNDIO/FUNAI—BRASIL)

Rondon alongside presents that he and his men left in the jungle for uncontacted tribes, meant as a gesture of friendship. Sometimes the gifts were accompanied by posters showing Brazilian soldiers embracing Indigenous people. (ACERVO DO MUSEU DO ÍNDIO/FUNAI—BRASIL)

Rondon holding a clay pot, left in the jungle by an Indigenous community he was seeking to contact, meant as a reciprocal token of friendship. To this day, Rondon remains the single largest donor of objects and artifacts to Brazil's National Museum. (ACERVO DO MUSEU DO ÍNDIO/FUNAI—BRASIL)

Members of the Paresi tribe, close allies of Rondon's, receiving training as telegraph operators at the Vilhena telegraph station, 1911. (ACERVO DO MUSEU DO ÍNDIO/FUNAI—BRASIL)

The Utiarity telegraph station, around 1910. (ACERVO DO MUSEU DO ÍNDIO/FUNAI—BRASIL)

Rondon and Roosevelt at Tapirapoan, where the Rondon Commission maintained its field headquarters, in January 1914. (GEORGE CHERRIE—AMERICAN MUSEUM OF NATURAL HISTORY)

Rondon and Roosevelt, right, on a break from their long slog through the jungle during their five-month expedition. (KERMIT ROOSEVELT—THE LIBRARY OF CONGRESS)

The principal members of the Roosevelt-Rondon Scientific Expedition during a meal break on the Mato Grosso plateau, January 1914. From left to right: Father John Augustine Zahm (seated in chair); Rondon (seated in chair); naturalists George Cherrie and Leo Miller; Kermit Roosevelt (seated on oxhide, left); Father Zahm's butler, Jacob Sigg; Amilcar Armando Botelho de Magalhães, the expedition's de facto quartermaster; Dr. Antonio Cajazeira; João Salustiano Lyra, Rondon's second-in-command; Theodore Roosevelt; and provisioner Anthony Fiala (seated at right on oxhide, with spoon). (ACERVO DO MUSEU DO ÍNDIO/FUNAI—BRASIL)

Hauling canoes uphill during a portage on the River of Doubt, March 1914. "Life became just one portage after another," Theodore Roosevelt wrote. (KERMIT ROOSEVELT—THE LIBRARY OF CONGRESS)

698

Rondon presiding over a Positivist funeral for Caio Espindola, a Rondon Commission engineer who drowned in the Jamari River, around 1915. (ACERVO DO MUSEU DO ÍNDIO/ FUNAI—BRASIL)

Rondon, at last a general, visiting his birthplace in Mimoso, Mato Grosso, on the shore of Lake Xocororé, in 1921. (ACERVO DO MUSEU DO ÍNDIO/ FUNAI—BRASIL)

Rondon and his general staff during the campaign against rebels in Paraná, early 1925. Though most of his aides prefer heavy winter coats, Rondon is dressed only in his regular uniform. (LUIZ THOMAZ REIS—ACERVO DO MUSEU DO ÍNDIO/FUNAI—BRASIL)

Rondon at the National Museum, mid-1920s. To the right of Rondon are Edgard Roquette-Pinto, a Rondon protégé and director of the museum, in white coat, and Alípio de Miranda Ribeiro, a herpetologist and ichthyologist who accompanied Rondon on several of his expeditions. Standing to the left of Rondon is Heloísa Alberto Torres, another of his protégés, who, with Rondon's support, would go on to become the first woman to lead a major Latin American museum. (MUSEU NACIONAL/UFRJ)

Rondon and Chiquita with some of their children and grandchildren, in the mid-1920s. In all, they had seven children and more than twenty grandchildren. (ACERVO DO MUSEU DO ÍNDIO/FUNAI—BRASIL)

Rondon and Chiquita in their later years. "When the arduous quest ended and I could at last withdraw to my hearth, it was already getting very late," he wrote in a memoir. (ACERVO DO MUSEU DO ÍNDIO/FUNAI—BRASIL)

Rondon and his men, a mixture of soldiers, Indians, and caboclos, at the summit of Mount Roraima, where the borders of Brazil, Venezuela, and British Guiana converged, on October 29, 1927. (MUSEU DO EXÉRCITO E FORTE DE COPACABANA)

Rondon and his men atop the Pedra do Cucuí, where Brazil's Amazonas state abuts the borders of Colombia and Venezuela. Other than Rondon, nearly none of the men, caboclos all, are wearing shoes. (MUSEU DO EXÉRCITO E FORTE DE COPACABANA)

Rondon showing his ticking watch to the chief of a settlement of the Wayana people, whose territory straddled both sides of Brazil's border with Dutch and French Guiana, in 1928. Rondon was pleasantly surprised to learn that the chief spoke some French, so the two conversed in that language. (ACERVO DO MUSEU DO ÍNDIO/FUNAI—BRASIL)

Rondon consulting leaders of a Tiriyó Indigenous village, seeking information about possible trails to and through the Tumucumaque Mountains; note the field diary in his left hand. Today, the Tumucumaque region, on Brazil's border with Suriname and French Guiana, constitutes part of the world's largest tropical national park, and the Tiriyó, thanks to Rondon's efforts, are among its residents and most zealous guardians. (ACERVO DO MUSEU DO ÍNDIO/FUNAI—BRASIL)

In the last of his three border inspection expeditions, in 1930, Rondon returned to his home state of Mato Grosso to verify conditions along the border with Bolivia. In an area where "life was lawless," he confided to his diary, he found himself thrust into "the role of defender of the Indians and the oppressed in general." (MUSEU DO EXÉRCITO E FORTE DE COPACABANA)

Rondon and his men at an aquatic border marker in Uberava Bay, at one of the most remote and hard-to-reach points along the 2,127-mile-long Brazil-Bolivia frontier, June 1930. (BENJAMIN RONDON—ACERVO DO MUSEU DO ÍNDIO/FUNAI—BRASIL)

Rondon on his ninetieth birthday (May 5, 1955) in his newly conceded uniform of Marshal of the Brazilian Army. A few months later, a territory the size of Great Britain would be given the name Rondônia, in his honor. (MUSEU DO EXÉRCITO E FORTE DE COPACABANA)

The old telegrapher, nearly blind, but with his skills still intact. (ACERVO DO MUSEU DO ÍNDIO/FUNAI—BRASIL)

potential in areas written off as inhospitable wilderness, and took the first steps to develop them.

But of all Rondon's ingenious gambits in his increasingly frantic efforts to generate the income needed for the SPI to continue its mission, none was more unusual than sending Luiz Thomaz Reis, the Rondon Commission's chief photographer and cinematographer, to the United States early in 1918 to sell the rights for films shot during the commission's various expeditions. Reis knew no one in the American movie business, and neither did Rondon, but they planned to ask Theodore Roosevelt to intercede on their behalf and make the necessary introductions.

After a series of delays, Reis and Roosevelt finally met on April 6, at the Harvard Club in New York City. Once they had seated themselves in commodious armchairs, Roosevelt "didn't give me a chance to speak," Reis wrote, but "started by saying he was immensely pleased to see me there, and that he would be particularly gratified to hear news of Colonel Rondon."[10]

"So how is Rondon doing?" Roosevelt asked. "Is he a general yet?" On hearing Reis's reply, he responded cheerily: "Oh, well, it won't be long now." The conversation eventually turned to the film scheme, with Roosevelt agreeing to help the Brazilians. "Monsieur Reis, I am happy to be of use in whatever way I can to Colonel Rondon," the cinematographer quoted Roosevelt as saying in a report he later filed to Rondon, "and it seems to me that I can do everything possible in that sense."[11]

Reis had already edited Rondon-approved highlights of footage from the commission's expeditions into a series of six short films that he called *Wilderness*. Their plan, Reis explained to Roosevelt, was to assemble the leading American film companies, the press, and other luminaries for a New York screening that would generate public interest in the movies and lead to showings of *Wilderness* in theaters across the United States. Reis wanted to invite not just representatives of the three main newsreel companies and Educational Film Incorporated but also executives from the main commercial film studios. He asked Roosevelt to throw his prestige behind the project.

Roosevelt agreed. "I share your opinion on this subject of such interest to my friend Colonel Rondon," he told Reis, "and will take immediate steps to do what you ask of me."[12] He proposed that the prestigious American Geographical Society be brought in as sponsor of the screening, and promised Reis that two officials from the society would help him organize the event. The former president was as good as his word: within a week, Reis was summoned to the society's headquarters in Manhattan for a meeting with its director, the scientist Isaiah Bowman, who had become deeply interested in the Indigenous peoples of South America while doing fieldwork in Peru. Bowman said that Carnegie Hall had been reserved for the evening of May 15, and that the society would pay for its rental; Reis, in turn, would be responsible for advertising, hiring an orchestra, and preparing title cards in English.

Roosevelt solved the last problem by authorizing Reis to excerpt passages from his book *Through the Brazilian Wilderness* as title cards, and also agreed to host the event. He took the Carnegie Hall stage promptly at 8:30 on the night of May 15, flanked by Bowman and Domício da Gama, still Brazil's ambassador to the United States. Before the screening began, Roosevelt, standing between Brazilian and American flags as he waited for the anthems of both countries to be played, delivered introductory remarks in which he reviewed the main aspects of the expedition and offered context for the film that the audience—2,800 strong and dressed mostly in formal evening wear—was about to see.

Once again, as in 1914, Roosevelt lavished praise on Rondon, whom he described as "an extraordinary soldier" and "intrepid companion . . . without whom it would not have been possible to make our journey. In our country, when a man becomes celebrated for some superior quality or some deed of merit, he is given a seat in Congress. So what place can we offer to a man like Colonel Rondon?" A solution, he continued, was to award Rondon the American Geographical Society's Livingstone Medal, "for scientific achievement in the field of Geography,"[13] which had been conferred on Roosevelt just the year before. Together, as the audience applauded, he and Bowman gave the medallion to da Gama on Rondon's behalf.

Reis was observing all of this from the projection booth, where his main concerns were first that no technical mishaps occur and second that there be a strong turnout from the movie studios, distributors, and theater chains. "Everything went perfectly well"[14] with the projection, he informed Rondon in his report, but it was only the next morning when he learned that the president of the powerful Loews theater chain and the chiefs of the leading studios had indeed attended: Metro, Paramount, Fox, National, Interocean, Goldwyn, and World. Several of them were interested in acquiring rights to *Wilderness*, and Reis immediately began negotiations with Louis B. Mayer and Richard Rowland of the Metro Pictures Corporation, which later became MGM.

Mayer and Rowland quickly made what Reis deemed an attractive offer: Metro and the Rondon Commission would evenly split the gross from exhibitions of *Wilderness* in theaters across the United States, with the Brazilians receiving $5,000 as an initial advance against future earnings. Rondon of course had the final say on the deal, so on May 26 Reis sent a telegram asking for his approval. A new and lucrative source of funding for the SPI, one that did not require Rondon to go hat in hand to the Brazilian Congress begging for support, seemed to have materialized, and both Rondon and Reis were elated.

Almost immediately, however, a major problem cropped up. *Wilderness* had to be approved by the film censorship board in New York City before it could be exhibited publicly, and while the censors found educational value in the film and agreed that it was suitable for exhibition in an academic setting, "they placed restrictions on public viewings, asking that scenes be cut in which completely naked Indians appear in the foreground,"[15] Reis informed Rondon.

This proved to be a deal-breaker as far as Metro was concerned: if film censors in New York, the most liberal city in the country, had difficulty accepting the innocent, Edenic nakedness of the Nhambiquara and the Paresi, what would happen when *Wilderness* was examined by the dozens of even more rigorous film censorship boards in more conservative places?

In the end, the best Reis could manage was a week's worth of showings at the Strand Theatre in Manhattan in June 1918, which, to his satisfaction, consistently drew a full house. But the version of the films shown was bowdlerized at the theater's insistence, and with that, Reis, discouraged, gave up: he returned to Rio early in August, after expenditures of nearly $2,500, with a paltry $325 in profits from the week of Manhattan screenings.[16]

Rondon's audacious plan to fortify the finances of the SPI with film revenues thus failed, a victim of American prudery. But he took away several important lessons from the experience, which served him well in years to come. First and foremost, the success of the Carnegie Hall event reinforced his conviction, instilled during his 1915 lectures in Rio, that film was a powerful medium, to be harnessed to build popular support for his policy objectives. He originally thought of film as an ethnographic tool, primarily of interest to specialists in that field, but gradually came to realize that movies also offered a way to build a mass constituency that regarded Indigenous peoples in a favorable light. Additionally, he now recognized the importance of having complete control, artistic as well as financial, of the product, so that when he returned to filmmaking in the 1920s, he made sure to deal directly with Brazilian theaters and distributors, cutting out the middleman—the international film studios that by then had also gained a foothold in Brazil.

Early in 1919, a few months after Reis's return from New York, Rondon embarked on another mapping expedition, this time to the far northwest corner of Mato Grosso. Unbeknownst to Rondon, it would be the last exploration he carried out under the auspices of the Telegraph Commission. Chiquita and all seven children were finally back in Brazil; Benjamin had finished his engineering course in France, earned a degree, and at the age of twenty-four was now, his father judged, ready for the rigors of a prolonged foray into the wilderness. With Reis occupied at commission headquarters back in Rio, there were slots on the expedition roster for both a photographer and a cinematographer, and so Benjamin, eager to spend time with his father after so long a separation, signed on as a "volunteer photographer."

Rondon does not seem to have spared his son any of the expedition's hardships. Once again, he and his men plunged into completely uncharted territory and lived as best they could off the land—or as he put it, "taking from the forest and the river the resources we needed to obtain due to deficiencies in transport"[17] from the rear. The insect infestations were so severe and widespread that Rondon was able to clock the phases of the day by them: in daylight, the tiny stingless bees were most troublesome, entering "through the ears, the nostrils, the mouth and entangling themselves in the hair."[18] At dusk came the diminutive Amazon black fly, which enjoyed feeding on human blood and tended to swarm around vulnerable, thin-skinned areas like the nape of the neck, the ears, or the ankles. With darkness came the much larger mosquito, also a blood feeder, making its way under mosquito netting.

Ominous new challenges appeared: near what is now Ariquemes, the entire expedition contracted the Spanish flu that raged globally in the aftermath of World War I. The Arikeme tribe and other Indigenous groups in the region were severely affected, but somehow, every member of the expedition, even though "weakened by the privations we were suffering,"[19] managed to survive, and by mid-June, the explorers arrived in the optimistically named Porto Renascença, or Port Rebirth, a dusty outpost some 250 miles from Porto Velho.

Benjamin survived the rigors of the 1919 expedition with distinction. From that point on, until Rondon's last expedition in 1930, he would accompany his father on official missions, mostly when Reis was not available, but sometimes in addition to him. However, there was to be a long interval before the next outing of father and son, for, as the result of a telegram received in Porto Renascença, Rondon's career was about to take a radical turn.

XIX

Jack of All Trades

ON JUNE 13, 1919, at the age of fifty-four, Cândido Rondon was finally promoted to brigadier general, just as Theodore Roosevelt had predicted the year before. Sectors of the Brazilian press and public had been clamoring for that promotion for "the Tamer of the Wilderness" ever since Rondon and Roosevelt emerged from the Amazon jungle five years earlier, but the War Ministry, which along with the president had final say over such matters, had been noticeably less eager to act. By contrast, some of Rondon's less prominent classmates, like his close friend Tasso Fragoso, had already achieved that rank.

The Brazilian Army had emerged from World War I deeply divided, and Rondon had become a symbol of those rifts. Some disagreements were ideological, others involved clashes over military doctrine, and still others simply reflected long-standing personal rivalries. Perhaps the best explanation of the situation came from Manuel Liberato Bittencourt, a writer and future general who in 1919 was a major teaching at the military academy. In an essay titled "Regarding the Promotion of General Rondon," published at midyear, he had this to say:

"At the heart of the army are two movements openly opposed to each other," he began. "The partisans of the first group . . . believe the pacifier of native tribes to be a leader of importance, rendering to the country services and organization of great value and merit.

The adherents of the opposing group . . . see this great Brazilian as an ordinary public servant, whose efforts would be perfectly compensated with a slight increase in salary. Some want him to be a one or even two-star general, respected and beloved for his virtues and accomplishments, commanding large units, in a position of true eminence and luster. Others, more demanding or less reflective, want him out of the army altogether, ignored and forgotten."[1]

The fundamental problem, as Bittencourt saw it, was that Rondon's achievements as explorer, cartographer, and peacemaker "are not directly connected to the army's combat activities." But, he added, because Brazil had been at peace since 1870, "an officer's service record must necessarily be judged by the projects he has completed in this period." And who more than Rondon had excelled in creating the physical infrastructure needed for combat, should that occur? In addition, "he and he alone has achieved the greatest of all scientific and social tasks of which we have knowledge in our times." In that broader context, Bittencourt argued, Rondon's promotion to general, "already overdue," was "minimal reward for maximum efforts."[2]

With Rondon's new rank came new responsibilities, some of which thrust him directly into the cauldron of military politics. Over the next five years, for example, he would serve on the army's Promotions Committee and also be called to preside over several courts-martial. Both of these areas would become controversial as the fissures within the army widened, especially after the Lieutenants' Revolt in July 1922.

In addition, the new president, Epitácio Pessoa, and Rondon were both born in May 1865 in provinces far from the center of power, and Pessoa soon came to trust Rondon's judgment on issues both military and civilian. As a result, Rondon found himself pressed into duty time and time again from 1919 to 1922 as a sort of Mister Fix-It for the Pessoa administration. Almost always, these new duties took Rondon away from what he loved best—exploring the wilderness—into bureaucratic offices where he had to exercise diplomatic and political skills.

Rondon's principal portfolio, assigned to him in September 1919, was director of engineering for the army. He accepted the post on

one condition: that he be allowed to continue to oversee the Telegraph Commission and the Indian Protection Service, the latter of
which would now be nominally under the command of one of his
adjutants. Pessoa agreed to this unorthodox arrangement because he
had ambitious plans to improve Brazil's infrastructure and wanted
Rondon to lead that process. But Rondon paid a personal price for
this: until stepping down as chief of engineering in January 1925, he
would continuously be overburdened.

In his new post, Rondon was required to work closely with the
recently appointed minister of war, João Pandiá Calógeras, a civilian
descended from Greek and French immigrants. In the thirty years
since the birth of the republic, no civilian had ever held the post
until Calógeras, and, as it turned out, no civilian would again until
1999. So Calógeras faced major tests, as Rondon recognized: the
commander of troops in the capital "did not hide his disapproval,"
Rondon wrote, while other "generals and ranking officers did not
favorably regard this innovation," which in their view "re-established
the political customs of the Monarchy."[3]

Born in Rio de Janeiro in 1870, Calógeras had trained as an engineer, like Rondon, and as a young man worked in the field as a geol-
ogist, mapping unexplored areas and cataloging possible mineral
riches. He later served in Congress for a dozen years as a representative of a mining region, also becoming Brazil's representative
to various Pan-American conferences and a member of its delegation to the Treaty of Versailles negotiations. He and Rondon were
first acquainted in 1914, when Calógeras was supervising the SPI
as minister of agriculture; two years later he became minister of
finance, controlling the budget for both the SPI and the Telegraph
Commission.

Despite some earlier friction over funding for the SPI and the
Telegraph Commission, Calógeras specifically requested that Rondon be put in charge of the engineering department. Later, he also
named him as liaison to the French military mission that arrived in
Brazil in 1920. Rondon in turn developed a very favorable opinion of
Calógeras, whom he viewed as "highly industrious" and possessing
"a privileged intelligence."[4]

Having returned to Brazil from Versailles aware of how military power translated into political clout, Calógeras embarked on a transformation of the Brazilian Armed Forces, so as to reshape them into a twentieth-century fighting force: on land, on sea, and in the air. "No one respects or seeks alliances with the weak,"[5] he wrote. Much of this modernization involved changes in doctrine, training, and organization. But it also required extensive construction of new arsenals, fortifications, barracks, and hospitals, and strengthening coastal and border artillery. In addition, a strong domestic defense industry capable of manufacturing arms and other war matériel was needed, and it was in these essential areas that Calógeras came to rely principally on Rondon.

This proposed overhaul was uniformly endorsed by all sectors of the armed forces. But the same could not be said of other strategic and doctrinal issues that had emerged in the wake of World War I, in which Rondon also became involved. When war broke out in 1914, Brazil had declared itself neutral. But that policy became difficult to maintain after May 1916, when German submarines began sinking Brazilian merchant ships en route to European ports. On April 11, 1917, Brazil broke off diplomatic relations with Germany over the sinking a few days earlier of a Brazilian steamship. Just before, on April 7, the United States, Brazil's closest hemispheric ally, had declared war on the Central powers.

With that, Brazil began a shift toward open alignment with the Western powers. Over the next six months, German submarines struck Brazilian-flag vessels three more times, and on October 26, 1917, following an attack in which the captain of one vessel was taken prisoner, Brazil formally entered the conflict. Swept by war fever, Brazil developed ambitious plans to become an active combatant. The army was to be quadrupled in size, to fifty-four thousand men, and early in 1918, the incoming government commissioned Calógeras to draw up a secret report with specific recommendations on deployments.

As matters turned out, the war ended before the Calógeras Plan could be implemented. Brazil's most active role in the war turned out to be naval, with a fleet of dreadnoughts, cruisers, and destroyers patrolling the South Atlantic under British command. But even that limited involvement was enough to signal glaring weaknesses in the structure and effectiveness of the Brazilian military. The army, for example, soon discovered that incorporating forty thousand new soldiers exhausted nearly all its resources. In addition, the war had shown Brazil's dependence on foreign-made armaments and munitions; purchases bought and paid for were arbitrarily canceled or seized by foreign powers. The need for a national arms industry was obvious.

By 1919, then, the military high command, of which Rondon was now a part, found itself grappling with basic questions about the future role and identity of the armed forces. Additionally, the war had introduced not just new combat technologies, like tanks and airplanes, but new military doctrines as well, some of which conflicted with others. Hard choices would have to be made.

Two main factions dominated this postwar debate. The first looked to Germany for inspiration, and hoped to restructure the Brazilian Army on a Prussian model, as Argentina and Chile were already doing. Before World War I, nearly three dozen Brazilian officers had spent two years in Germany as observers there, and when they returned, they recommended a thirteen-point program that included obligatory military service and military instruction in public schools. They also succeeded in having the bulk of the German Army's combat arms regulations adopted.

The other group wanted a French military model. Their hand was considerably strengthened by the German capitulation to France and its allies in November 1918, and a preliminary agreement was signed soon after and formalized in September 1919. As a Positivist and a Francophile, Rondon naturally preferred the idea of studying and adapting a French model, and quickly emerged as one of the principal spokesmen for that position.

Once the decision was made to invite a French mission, Rondon was appointed the liaison between the Brazilian Army general staff and the newly arrived foreign advisers. It was an assignment he was pleased to take on, even if it took time away from his other duties and his family, but it made him even more resented among the pro-German group. By now, these officers were being called "the Young

Turks," a nickname they cultivated because it referred specifically to Kemal Atatürk and the idealistic, strongly nationalistic military group around him—who had also trained with the Germans and were now trying to forge a modern secular state out of the ruins of the Ottoman Empire.

The pro-German faction wanted to instill a more martial spirit not just in the armed forces but throughout Brazilian society. They saw Rondon's focus throughout his career on nation building and peaceful reconciliation with Indigenous peoples as both a drain on the military budget and a diversion of the army from its central mission, that of preparing for and fighting wars. But the Francophile position Rondon advocated was supported by Calógeras, and, as far as the Young Turks were concerned, Rondon's close collaboration with the new civilian war minister constituted yet one more black mark against him.

The newly arrived members of the French mission enthusiastically welcomed Rondon's appointment as liaison; their commander, Gen. Maurice Gamelin, forged a particularly close relationship with him. In 1921, Gamelin admiringly described Rondon to a French magazine as an "energetic personality, open and sympathetic in appearance," combining "the supple intelligence so common among men of his race with a fierce and tenacious will."[6] The Rondon Commission "is a vast but coordinated undertaking," Gamelin also explained. "One feels the passion of a leader who has been able to impose on his collaborators, and communicate to them through his work ethic, his faith in the success of the enterprise and his unshakable confidence in the future of his native land."[7]

Rondon had always socialized with the French-speaking community in Brazil, but the years 1917–24 were a period in which his contacts were especially intimate. In addition to his ties to Gamelin, he became good friends with the French ambassador to Brazil, the poet and playwright Paul Claudel; with Claudel's personal secretary, the young composer Darius Milhaud, who was given access to Roquette-Pinto's field recordings; and with the embassy's chargé d'affaires, the diplomat and writer Henri Hoppenot. Claudel was a fervent Catholic, but that did not interfere in his relationship with Rondon, whom he saw as a saintly presence. "Rondon, this strong soul who penetrates the wilderness with the sublime mission of aiding the savages, is the Brazilian personality who most impressed me," Claudel would later say. "Pure, upright, and without blood on his hands, he conveys the impression of a figure from the Gospels."[8]

Rondon's command of the French language led to yet another mission in 1920, when he unexpectedly found himself assigned to chaperone King Albert I of Belgium on a four-week state visit. No sitting head of state had ever visited Brazil, and the government hoped that making a good impression on the Belgian sovereign would encourage other kings, prime ministers, and presidents to make the long voyage from Europe. On the way over from Antwerp aboard a Brazilian battleship, the king read Roosevelt's *Through the Brazilian Wilderness*, and asked that Rondon be added to the official royal party.

For Rondon, though, the timing could hardly have been worse. Beatriz, the fourth of his six daughters, had recently been diagnosed with the tuberculosis that would eventually kill her at a young age, and Rondon and Chiquita had taken her to a sanatorium and spa up in the mountains above Rio. He tried to beg off the assignment with Albert, citing those personal reasons and claiming not to know the proper protocol required for royalty. But what the king and the president wanted, they would get. So Rondon took the train down to Rio, leaving Chiquita alone with Beatriz.

And when Pessoa was preparing to leave office two years later, he again pressed Rondon into special service, but this time with an unwelcome outcome: in October 1922, he asked Rondon to head a commission to investigate the causes of a catastrophic drought in northeastern Brazil. Severe dry spells had regularly afflicted the region since colonial times, but a period of prolonged aridity began in 1919, the same year Pessoa took office, and had fueled an exodus from the rural Northeast to large southern cities like São Paulo and Rio, where food and jobs were available. Not only that, 1922 was the centennial of Brazilian independence, and a massive migration of refugees only cast a pall over the official celebrations, calling into doubt the central government's ability to provide basic services to the Brazilian people.

Pessoa was particularly sensitive to all this, and to the heartrending stories of famine and death that filled the pages of newspapers and magazines. The first northeasterner to be elected president of Brazil, he felt a special sense of obligation to address his home region's most enduring social problem. Accordingly, he created the Special Fund for the Irrigation of Arable Land in 1920 and set aside 2 percent of national tax receipts for that purpose. By 1922, more than two hundred reservoirs had been constructed throughout the Northeast to store water. Though that should have alleviated much of the drought's impact, the suffering and relocations continued. The national press was portraying the president's efforts as an enormous boondoggle. To investigate why the misery continued, and to counter the accusations of inefficiency and fraud at the Federal Inspectorate of Works Against Drought, Pessoa turned to Rondon.

On October 25, Rondon and the other two commission members—Ildefonso Simões Lopes, minister of agriculture, industry and commerce; and Paulo Moraes Barros, a physician and former congressional deputy—departed for the Northeast by boat, accompanied by Rondon's aide de camp, Botelho de Magalhães. They first visited Recife, capital of Pernambuco, the state most severely affected by drought, and then traveled overland to Paraíba, the president's home state.

As his diaries indicate, Rondon, thinking like an engineer, initially believed the drought to be a climatic problem whose solution was almost entirely technical: a question of improving agricultural methods, reducing erosion, eliminating inefficient forms of irrigation, enhancing analysis of meteorological patterns, and so forth. But he soon realized that the policies and actions of the Brazilian state, not nature, were the principal cause of the unending calamity.

The region's underlying problem, Rondon quickly realized, was a political system that concentrated power and wealth in very few hands. Local bosses, known either as colonels or *caciques*, or "chiefs," selfishly wielded authority for their own benefit. This problem had existed since independence—as Rondon knew from his own experience—but it had intensified over time and was especially entrenched in the Northeast. In a region where water was scarce, unlike Rondon's birthplace, access to the precious liquid meant everything. And the local bosses controlled the water supply.

Over the next month, Rondon and his team met with mayors, engineers, members of Congress, agronomists, governors, and civic, religious, and business leaders. They also talked with peasant families trying to eke out a living from the parched land, in many cases exploited by the same dignitaries who greeted the commission when it arrived in town. On their way back to Rio, the three commission members drafted their official report, which reflected the political and economic views Rondon had confided to his diary during the investigation.

Unusually for his time, Rondon also emphasized the long-term consequences of deforestation, and its linkage to drought. He had already noticed this phenomenon in parts of the Amazon where ranchers and colonists from the south had discarded traditional Indian methods of cultivation and crop rotation. In the Northeast, where European habitation had a much longer history, the problem was even more pronounced: "It is human agency that has taken on the strange role of maker of deserts," he wrote. When rain arrives, he noted, it "passes swiftly over the denuded tablelands whose intense solar irradiation alters the saturation point, diminishing the probability of rain."[9]

Nevertheless, Rondon added, "the past can be corrected" by working with, not against, nature. "Clearly the creation and conservation of forests constitute basic measures, no matter what your point of view, to modify the causes of irregular rainfall," he argued. "For reforestation to intervene positively as a climatic factor in the interior of the Northeast, it is indispensable that it be extended to the vast area of little rain and that it be done collaboratively, involving the largest number of states possible."[10]

None of this was what Pessoa had expected to hear, prompting the outgoing president to disavow the very report he had commissioned. After leaving office, he wrote a rebuttal to Rondon, which was distributed to the national press and published. This prompted a second document from Rondon in 1923, refuting the former president's arguments point by point. To Pessoa's most fundamental complaint, that the commission's outlook, analysis, and predictions were unduly pessimistic, Rondon offered a response as blunt as it was succinct: "My conscience mandates that I say what I perceive, because in the future, when reality confirms the facts foreseen by science, I do not want to be lumped together with the optimists of today."[11]

This two-month interlude turned out to be the only time in his long career that Rondon dealt directly with the problems of the Northeast. But short as it was, the experience produced one lasting side effect: Rondon became a good friend of both Ildefonso Simões Lopes and his son, the agronomist Luís Simões Lopes—a relationship that would, throughout the 1930s and into the first half of the 1940s, prove essential to his ability to survive in increasingly brutal and authoritarian politics.

Indeed, by the time of the 1922 election, signs of the coming unraveling of the constitutional order were already visible, making it harder for Rondon to remain neutral. In the past, he had often been away from the capital for months at a time on expeditions during the quadrennial presidential campaigns. But in the run-up to the vote of March 1, 1922, Rondon quite unwillingly was drawn into its most controversial aspects. Ultimately, with considerable agility and some stretching of the truth, he maneuvered through it, but generated much ill will against him.

The 1922 presidential election was perhaps the most contentious in the young republic's history, pitting Arthur Bernardes, governor of the state of Minas Gerais, against a former president and boss of Rondon's, Nilo Peçanha. On October 9, 1921, a Rio daily published a letter, on official stationery of the Minas Gerais state government and purportedly written by Bernardes, attacking the integrity of the Brazilian military and its leaders in language both insulting and mocking. But perhaps most explosive of all was the suggestion that a corrupt and "venal" officer corps was easily bought off by its attachment to "embroidery and insignias."[12]

Was the letter real, or simply a crude fabrication? The response depended on which candidate a newspaper or voter supported. It was therefore decided that a commission led by a nonpartisan public figure above all possible suspicion, dispassionate and levelheaded, should investigate the letter's origins. So on October 21, Rondon received a letter from Bernardes's campaign manager, appealing to his "honor and conscience" as a patriot and formally requesting that he accept the assignment.[13]

Rondon, however, wanted nothing to do with a mission so potentially explosive, and wrote back two days later to "decline the honor," saying, "I am in the habit of irrevocably distancing myself from all subjects and issues that exist and thrive solely on the strength of electoral processes related to democratic politics."[14]

This was true, but it was not the only reason Rondon rejected the clamor to resolve what had metastasized into a national crisis. "This was a serious matter that threatened to subvert order and undermine the foundations of the Republic," he wrote years later. "I was not keen to assume responsibility for a verdict of which I was not sure."[15] In fact, the commission that was eventually established, led by a navy admiral, erroneously concluded in a report that Bernardes had written the letters, as did handwriting experts hired by the military. Ultimately, two forgers came forward after the election, admitting they had fabricated the letters in hopes of selling them to the opposition. So Rondon was right to have been cautious and skeptical.

Privately, Rondon admitted his preference for his old friend Peçanha and worried about Bernardes's reputation for governing in an autocratic style, which he feared would undermine the republic.[16] Events over the next four years—including imposition of a state of siege and curtailment of civil liberties—would prove him right. Many officers shared Rondon's view, and when Bernardes narrowly won an election marred by fraud, they attempted to draw Rondon into the maelstrom of presidential politics.

Though Bernardes was elected in March 1922, he was scheduled to be sworn in only on November 15, the anniversary of the founding of the republic, and that eight-month interval gave his many enemies plenty of time to conspire. As Rondon would later recall it, he was on a mission to inspect new barracks in Rio Grande do Sul, eating dinner at a hotel in Porto Alegre on the night of March 29, when the maître d' advised him that an officer had just arrived from Rio and needed to speak with him. When he stepped into the lobby, he was surprised to see Capt. Manuel Rabelo, "my co-expeditionary, my friend, my coreligionist,"[17] nervously waiting for him.

Rabelo, it turned out, had been dispatched by a group of dissident officers in the capital trying to organize a coup to prevent Bernardes from taking office; they wanted Rondon to lead them. "The Army cannot go on enduring the affronts contained in Bernardes' letter without reacting," is how Rondon remembered Rabelo expressing the officers' discontent. "It is impossible that he become President of the Republic after so deeply wounding our professional pride and honor. There is a huge movement being prepared, and you have been chosen to command it."[18]

Rondon wrote three decades later that he was appalled at the suggestion, and rebuked his younger comrade. "Have you forgotten that we are Positivists and that as such we cannot take part in any subversive movement?" he replied. "Haven't we been taught that the most retrograde government is preferable to the most progressive revolution? Reflect, my friend, while you still have time."[19]

Rabelo apparently withdrew at that point, in Rondon's words "defeated though not convinced,"[20] but the matter did not end there. Two days later, Rondon was at the docks in Porto Alegre, about to embark for the town of Rio Grande to inspect naval fortifications on the water border with Uruguay, when an emissary of the state government tapped him on the shoulder. The governor of Rio Grande do Sul, one of the country's most important states, Antônio Borges de Medeiros, wished to see him as soon as possible. Borges de Medeiros was also a Positivist, who, with the exception of one five-year period, governed from 1898 to 1928. So of course Rondon immediately acceded to the request.

When he arrived at the governor's office, he found Borges de Medeiros seated at a long table with members of his cabinet and a group of other men, including Rabelo. The purpose of the meeting soon became clear: Borges de Medeiros floated the idea of creating a nonpartisan panel to review the recent vote and asked Rondon if he would be willing to serve as chairman of such a tribunal.

This plan, which Rondon's own preferred candidate had endorsed, offered at least a slight cloak of institutionality, though it was clearly

282 • INTO THE AMAZON

meant to achieve the same result as a coup: deny Bernardes the presidency, through a vote recount rather than a military rebellion. But Rondon's reaction to the new plan appears to have been identical. Once again he refused to be drawn in, citing Positivist beliefs. "Your Excellency knows, since we are both inspired by the same doctrine, that we are not permitted to take part in subversive movements,"[21] is how he would remember his response.

Borges de Medeiros, a lawyer by training, persisted, trying to draw legal distinctions between his plan and a coup, but, Rondon wrote, "I remained inflexible," arguing that it was the prerogative of Congress to certify election results. "And a solution via arms?" the governor asked, to which Rondon said he replied: "There is no cause for that! As for me, I know that I will never take part in any movement meant to resolve a political problem through arms." With this, Borges de Medeiros threw up his hands and, addressing the others seated at the table, said, "Well, gentlemen, as you can see, this is a revolution without a chief."[22]

But on July 5, a group of junior officers, most of them lieutenants, nonetheless attempted to overthrow the government and prevent Bernardes from taking office. The uprising began at Fort Copacabana in Rio but did not spread to other garrisons, and after a day of combat, most of the rebels desisted. When a final cluster of insurgents emerged from the fort and began to walk down Avenida Atlântica, they were shot dead by troops loyal to the government.

Once word of Rondon's refusal to lead an insurrection got out, especially after the failed Fort Copacabana Lieutenants' Revolt, he paid a high price politically. Both camps were now irritated with him: Bernardes's followers because he had declined the request to investigate the origin of the controversial letter, and his own allies in Peçanha's camp because he refused to countenance a coup d'état. Among some of his fellow officers, especially young ones who argued that he had failed the army as an institution, resentment ran especially high.

Rondon's unyielding stance had important consequences, particularly for his relationship with the Bernardes administration, but the short-term impact was most marked among his erstwhile allies. In anti-Bernardes newspapers, he was portrayed as a traitor to the cause and a coward. To his diary, Rondon would even complain that sectors of the press were "twisting and poisoning my gestures and attitudes."

Sympathetic members of Congress tried to come to Rondon's aid, passing a resolution in July that praised him for the "faithful dedication and unsurpassable loyalty with which he placed himself at the side of the constituted authorities in defense of the legal order, the Constitution, the Republic and the honor of the Brazilian nation."[23] A month later, Calógeras did something similar, issuing a statement that Rondon, "maintaining himself continuously at my side, assured me always of his straightforward and loyal dedications, his indefatigability in the carrying out of any mission entrusted to him."[24]

But when those documents were inserted into the army's official daily bulletin, they "incited the revolutionaries even further against me,"[25] Rondon ruefully noted. Barely three years after being promoted to general, Rondon had gone from national hero to a controversial figure, idolized by many, despised by others. Worse was still to come.

XX

Catanduvas

B Y THE MIDDLE of the 1920s, Rondon stood out as a military anomaly. Though he himself had been struck by arrows, he had never fired a shot in anger, much less killed anyone. He had shown unimaginable valor in the face of peril and privation, but had never fought in a war. His life's work was to build, not to destroy. His unconventional military career fascinated Brazil's press. Reporters covering him emphasized the paradox he embodied in epithets such as "the Warrior for Peace" and "the Pacifist General."

That would all end in mid-1924. On July 5, the second anniversary of the Lieutenants' Uprising in Rio de Janeiro, a new rebellion erupted, this time in São Paulo, the nation's economic center. The nominal leader was a retired general, but as in 1922, the real force behind the insurrection was a group of young mid-level officers, among them Miguel Costa, Juarez Távora, and Eduardo Gomes. Numbering more than one thousand fighters, including civilian sympathizers, the rebels sought the overthrow of President Arthur Bernardes, an end to corruption, and a battery of reforms ranging from greater support for public education to secret ballots for all elections.

Skirmishes with loyalist troops continued throughout July all over the state of São Paulo. To regain control, Bernardes ordered the state capital bombarded by both artillery and aircraft, which continued on an almost daily basis, affecting residential areas as well as military targets: more than five hundred people died, an estimated four thousand were wounded, and 1,800 buildings were leveled. On July 28, the rebels withdrew; heading northwest, they attacked a garrison in Mato Grosso early in August, but were decisively defeated, losing hundreds of fighters. In retreat again, they fled southward to the deep interior of the state of Paraná, where they intended to establish a new base and link up with allies they hoped would be coming from Brazil's two southernmost states, Rio Grande do Sul and Santa Catarina. It was at this point, in September, that Bernardes, anticipating a protracted struggle, ordered the creation of a large federal task force to suppress the rebellion and chose Rondon to command it.

Bernardes knew that in 1922 Rondon had rejected the urgings of younger officers to lead a military coup and install himself as president, and was aware of Rondon's criticisms of the Lieutenants' Uprisings. At a moment when Bernardes could not be sure of the army's loyalty—from the chiefs of staff down to the lowliest recruit—it reassured him to think he could count on Rondon, whose reputation for rectitude and courage, the president believed, might help sway an officer corps that seemed to be wavering in its allegiance.

Beyond that, Rondon also had recent field experience in the region. In 1922, Gen. Maurice Gamelin, director of the French Army training mission in Brazil, had wanted to observe the Brazilian Army in war maneuvers, and the locale chosen was the interior of Paraná. As liaison to the French mission, Rondon had accompanied Gamelin and helped oversee all aspects of the exercises, notable because land, water, and air units of the Brazilian military operated together for the first time. All told, more than eight thousand men, including a detachment from a fledgling air force under army command, participated. Rondon was thus the only general in the Brazilian Army who not only knew the terrain of battle personally, he already had command experience there.

Nonetheless, Rondon found the request that he lead the troops quelling the rebellion to be profoundly disturbing, and it provoked an immediate crisis of conscience. At one point Rondon even contemplated resigning from the army rather than accept the command. First of all, as a Positivist, Rondon embraced pacifism. He was also a nationalist, and while he might have had fewer reservations about commanding a unit defending Brazil against a foreign invasion, in this case he was being asked to fight fellow Brazilians, some of them friends or colleagues whom he respected; a few had even served capably under him on the Telegraph Commission. And finally, he knew from his own experience that many of the lieutenants' complaints, especially those about the government's corruption, were solidly grounded.

Rondon was in his office at the commission's headquarters on the afternoon of September 24, 1924, when a telephone call alerted him that an emissary from the Ministry of War was on his way with a message summoning him to a meeting the next morning with the minister and the chiefs of staff, at which he would formally be offered command of the loyalist troops. That night, as his younger children slept, Rondon and Chiquita discussed the situation until long past midnight, trying to decide what he should do; they were joined for a time by Teixeira Mendes, head of the Positivist Church.

"To go into combat against brothers!" Rondon would write later, recalling his conflicted emotions that long, sleepless night. "What a painful set of circumstances for someone who, like me, had spent his entire life enveloped by the dream of deserving the title of peacemaker."[1] But as a Positivist, Rondon also believed that Comte was right when he said that even "the most retrograde government is preferable to the most progressive Revolution."[2] For proof, he needed only to look at France in the 1790s, as Comte had described in his writings, or at Soviet Russia at that very moment. Two contradictory sets of obligations tugged at his conscience, and he could imagine no easy way to reconcile them. If he could not accept the mission to defend the constituted government, then "I saw no other alternative than to take off the uniform"[3] that had given his life meaning and purpose for so long.

Ultimately, Rondon devised an elaborate and rather self-serving rationale, based on Positivist principles, for obeying the president's wishes: "I would go to defend the legally-constituted Government in order to save my native country from revolutionary chaos, but I would go as a peacemaker, making every effort possible to call our brothers back to us."⁴

If he had to use violence, it would be as a last resort, after every other tactic was exhausted, and even then, designed to minimize fatalities. If Rondon allowed someone else to take command, he reasoned, the danger of a national conflagration would increase. Already, "the territory from Rio de Janeiro southward to Rio Grande do Sul was a single battlefield," he wrote. "The political crisis confronting Brazil was tremendous; either the Republic established order or all would be chaos and demoralization."⁵

A week later, Rondon was in Ponta Grossa, a road, railway, and river junction in the interior of Paraná that he had chosen as his headquarters. Knowing how much the president owed him, he made sure to obtain something significant for the cause that mattered most to him: the Indian Protection Service. When Bernardes took office in 1922, Rondon had requested a substantial increase in support from the federal government. The president, however, had delayed any decision on the matter. So, after arriving in Ponta Grossa, Rondon sent a telegram renewing his appeal for the money. There was never an explicit quid pro quo, but Bernardes promptly discovered a way to come up with the funds Rondon had asked for two years earlier. In fact, the SPI "enjoyed its greatest expansion during President Bernardes' administration."⁶

Simultaneously, Rondon managed to extract another concession. In 1917, over his objections, Congress had passed a law that allowed states to close Indigenous reservations on public lands and settle their inhabitants elsewhere. This was a boon to corrupt local politicians, who seized fertile land parcels and moved Indians to smaller, inferior, and more remote locations. In Paraná, the SPI had challenged this practice, arguing that two sites with Kaingang settlements were exempt from the new law because both had been privately held—one by the Roman Catholic Church, the other by a philanthropic nobleman—before the state government seized them. The dispute had been dragging on for years, but Bernardes now resolved it in favor of the SPI, and the Kaingang were allowed to remain where they were.

Before leaving Rio, Rondon was able to choose some of his adjutants; others were forced upon him by the chiefs of staff at their initial meeting on September 25. This in part reflected the rather top-heavy composition of the Brazilian Armed Forces at the time. The officer corps consisted of nearly five thousand men—more than six hundred of them generals, colonels, or majors—a relatively large number for an army whose ranks included about thirty-five thousand soldiers. Of these more than half were raw recruits with little or no military training. In total Rondon would have more than eight thousand fighting men at his disposal—meaning that he now controlled nearly one-quarter of the entire Brazilian Army.

Several of the mid-level officers Rondon commanded during the nine months he fought the rebels, and whose careers he energetically promoted, went on to play important roles in modern Brazilian history. He felt a special warmth for Capt. Eurico Gaspar Dutra, a fellow officer from Mato Grosso. Dutra, forty-one years old in 1924, was on a respectable though not brilliant career trajectory, but because of Rondon's favorable performance evaluations, he began ascending the ranks. By 1936, Dutra was war minister, and a decade later he was elected president. By then Rondon was eighty and had retired, but he and Dutra were neighbors in Copacabana, and Rondon often began his day by walking to Dutra's apartment, where the two men would discuss affairs of state while eating breakfast and drinking maté together.

In the first weeks after Rondon's arrival in Ponta Grossa, he discovered that in spite of the numerical superiority he enjoyed, suppressing the rebellion would not be easy. "One of the greatest obstacles faced by the legal troops is the great difficulty of transport, there being no railroads nor roads reaching the greater part of the region where this guerrilla warfare is in progress," an American military attaché, Capt. Hugh Barclay, wrote in a report to Washington. "The transport of supplies by pack train is difficult and expensive, and the revolters were known to be receiving supplies across the river,"[7] from Paraguay.

As for the government's own troops, the high command had already warned Rondon of the "deficiency and irregularity" of their training. A confidential assessment by the American military attaché was even blunter: though soldiers faced "danger and death with a creditable degree of coolness and calmness," there seemed to be "no recognition of constituted authority by the troops," who were also "easily persuaded to take part in uprisings, following their immediate commander without knowing why."[8] Indeed, on the night of October 28, a twenty-six-year-old army captain named Luís Carlos Prestes, in charge of a construction brigade building a railroad in the west of Rio Grande do Sul but disgusted by the corruption, joined the rebels and took three hundred men with him. Numerous civilians soon joined him, and by late December, Prestes began leading a column of about eight hundred combatants on a monthlong trek north to the rebel stronghold.

Luís Carlos Prestes is remembered today as the longtime leader of the Brazilian Communist Party, and as such is still revered by some of the Brazilian Left. But in 1924, he was just another idealistic soldier in the armed forces. A military academy graduate, he was a brilliant student like Rondon, earning an engineering degree. Also like Rondon, who had been a classmate of Prestes's father, he had the ability to inspire and lead his men because of his own courage, astuteness, and personal integrity.

The rebels' main fighting force, some six hundred men under the command of Miguel Costa, a former officer of the São Paulo mounted police, had been dug in for several months around the town of Catanduvas, awaiting reinforcements, and was preparing for a long siege. Rondon hoped to intimidate the insurrectionists into surrender. "It was necessary to make them feel that we were very strong, and that our strategic plan was irresistible," Rondon wrote, explaining his thinking. "That way I would be able to make peaceful overtures without running the risk that they would be interpreted as a sign of weakness."[9]

Rondon set about quelling the rebellion with the same strategy he used to placate a hostile tribe, like the Nhambiquara or the nearby Kaingang. He went from battalion to battalion, regiment to regiment, preaching to his troops a gospel of limited warfare. Though he was not advocating the same policy of absolute nonviolence he applied

290 • INTO THE AMAZON
290 • INTO THE AMAZON

in the Amazon, his focus was on maximum restraint and minimum bloodshed. "I spoke to all of them with the intent," he wrote, "of never distancing ourselves from the objective of reducing to a minimum, if not eliminating, the consequences of a fraternal struggle."[10]

In the Amazon, Rondon had sometimes, in addition to offering gifts to Indigenous tribes, left behind colorful posters, pinned to trees and depicting unarmed Brazilian Army soldiers in friendly poses. Now he adapted that same technique to the Paraná rebels, combining it with a technique the military now calls "psyops." His force included a small air detachment, which he mobilized to deluge the rebels with flyers offering a peaceful way out of the conflict.

"It will be in vain if you continue with the resistance you plan to mount against us," he wrote. "Save your sacrifice for the defense of other ideals that dignify and elevate you. We are well aware that you were deceived, and that is why we will be sympathetic when you lay down your arms. Don't believe in the false promises of your leaders—the fatherland cannot be content without peace. Abandon this ignoble struggle: not only will you have a guarantee of life, but you will be treated like brothers."[11] The handbill was signed simply "General Rondon."

Some insurrectionists did surrender to his troops and join the government side, or abandoned the struggle altogether and fled. Their numbers, though, were not large enough to be decisive—many could not read—and early in 1925 Rondon ordered that a siege begin.

Catanduvas was a small and relatively new settlement. Founded as a telegraph station in the far southwestern corner of the state, near Iguaçu Falls, it had originally been surrounded by pinewoods, which had been razed to allow for cultivation. German, Italian, Polish, and Ukrainian immigrants had settled there, farming on the mostly open savanna. These "new Brazilians," recently arrived from poor, oppressed, or war-torn corners of Europe, presented both a challenge and an opportunity to Rondon. Some of the newcomers could barely speak Portuguese, and most had not yet taken sides in what they viewed as a complicated political quarrel that had little to do with them. More than anything else, they wanted just to be left alone and allowed to prosper: if Rondon and his troops were seen as outsiders, so were the rebels who opposed him. The immigrant settlers were skeptical of both sides and loyal to neither.

But Rondon also knew that he had to tread carefully with the region's native-born population, which included mixed-race peasants and some descendants of freed slaves. Only a decade earlier, Paraná and its southern neighbor, Santa Catarina, had been immersed in a bloody conflict known as the "Contestado War," in which an estimated ten thousand people were killed, wounded, or disappeared. What began as a border dispute between the two states erupted in 1912 into an uprising with strong overtones of class warfare. And as at Canudos in the late 1890s, there was also a strong strain of millenarian religious sentiment: many of the rebels were followers of a monk they believed to be a saint, and the main rebel force took the name Blessed Army of St. Sebastian. The war formally ended in 1916, but as late as 1921 peasants without formal titles to land they had long tilled were still fighting with land surveyors working for private land-colonization companies that coveted their fertile tracts.

So, late in 1924 and early in 1925, before the worst fighting got underway, Rondon undertook an effort to win over—or at least ensure the favorable neutrality of—the local populace. He and his officers visited many of the small towns that dotted the plains and rolling hills, where they met with municipal officials and religious, ethnic, and business leaders. At each gathering, they explained the government's aims and promised not to harm civilians.

Throughout the Paraná campaign, Rondon could at no time assume that his troops would remain loyal. For that reason, police regiments from faraway states were brought in to supplement army units, drawn mostly from the south: "I avoided deploying Army officers on certain missions because I was certain that many of them sympathized with the revolutionary cause," Rondon wrote, and "did not want to throw one part of the army against the other."[12] In one incident during the shelling of Catanduvas, Rondon noticed an artillery officer who was visibly reluctant to fire his battery. Rather than rebuke or discipline him, Rondon simply said, "You look to me like you can't perform your duties because of illness, so I am going to send you to the hospital."[13] And on at least two occasions, Rondon escaped attempts to capture or assassinate him only because of last-minute changes in his schedule.

Once Rondon took the offensive early in 1925, he did so cautiously. He sent troops northwest toward Porto Mendes, on the Paraná River, to cut off the rebels' supply lines from the rear and prevent reinforcements from that direction. This was necessary because Prestes's force by then, early in February, was approaching the zone of conflict. In fact, Prestes's eight hundred men, only five hundred of whom had weapons and even fewer had ammunition, made four attempts to break through the circle but were easily repulsed.[14]

For the most part, however, Rondon avoided infantry engagements of any kind, preferring to let the overwhelming might of his artillery do the bulk of the work. For weeks on end, cannons, howitzers, and mortars battered Catanduvas, until the town was reduced to rubble; then his guns bombarded it some more. "Unfortunately, our artillery inflicted enormous damage on Catanduvas,"[15] Rondon wrote. But the rebel force remained hunkered down in the trenches it had earlier dug, absorbing one blow after another, refusing to retreat or surrender.

In general, Rondon did his best to apply the doctrine taught by the French military mission, which advocated cornering an adversary in a disadvantageous geographic setting and then slowly suffocating him until he surrendered. He was aided in his task by disagreements among the rebel leaders about both strategy and tactics. The senior rebel commander, thinking of the long stalemates of World War I, was convinced that the only route to victory was through trench warfare, and ordered his men to settle in for a conflict that would be largely stationary.

Costa reluctantly accepted that decision, but Prestes did not. He wanted to fight a mobile war, including attacks on Rondon's flank. "War in Brazil, no matter what the terrain, is a war of movement," he wrote to them. "A fixed-position war is one that most works to the advantage of the government, which has munitions plants, presses to mint money and plenty of illiterates to throw against our machine-guns."[16]

The arrival of the Southern Hemisphere winter, in March, also worked to Rondon's benefit. Most of the combatants on both sides were from northern Brazil and not accustomed to the cold and rain of a southern winter. The government troops were better equipped: Reis's photographs from the campaign show not only Rondon and his general staff fitted with comfortable greatcoats, warm hats, thick leather boots, and snug gloves, but also some soldiers in the field similarly dressed. The rebels, by contrast, had no protection from the weather, and thus were vulnerable to pneumonia and other illnesses that weakened them physically and sapped their morale; as the rebel command acknowledged, "officers and many soldiers are semi-naked and shoeless."[17] In the trenches, conditions were especially bad: scabies, dysentery, and chiggers raged there, and combatants received only a single meal a day.

Catanduvas fell on the night of March 29, 1925, after one of Rondon's officers sent a note to the rebels, informing them that the government's troops were two hundred yards away and would attack at dawn unless the insurgents capitulated. Exhausted and discouraged, soaking wet and skeletal, several hundred rebels emerged from the trenches, their hands in the air. A memorable photograph taken by Reis the next day shows a column of the defeated, stretching to the horizon, marching single file across a vast and empty plain, Rondon's soldiers guarding them. Other insurgents refused to surrender, though, and fled westward under cover of darkness, hoping to connect with the Prestes detachment. "The doubt now was no longer if the conditions for victory existed, but whether it was even possible to survive,"[18] a biographer of Prestes later wrote.

The two rebel columns finally linked up in the early days of April: Prestes and Costa met for the first time on April 3, and began to work out a joint strategy. In Foz do Iguaçu, at the triple border with Argentina and Paraguay, they conferred with forty other senior officers on April 12, including Juarez Távora, to take stock of their grim situation: Costa now commanded about 1,400 men, and Prestes had perhaps half that number. Even worse, fewer than one man in ten were adequately armed, and with the wide and powerful Paraná River behind them, it seemed there was no way to escape. Rondon's troops, on the other hand, not only enjoyed a numerical superiority of more than four to one, they were also feeling confident after their victory at Catanduvas. As Rondon put it, he had his adversaries "corked up in a bottle,"[19] and their end appeared near.

After the defeat at Catanduvas, though, Prestes's emphasis on mobility gained more acceptance, and this time his views prevailed. "First of all, let's try to get out of here,"[20] he told his fellow rebels at the Foz do Iguaçu meeting, according to an account he wrote years later. Clearly unsuited to the guerrilla tactics Prestes proposed, those responsible for the debacle in the trenches were now pushed aside, and Costa assumed command of a reorganized "First Revolutionary Division," composed of two brigades based on the geographic origins of the fighters: Juarez Távora was named chief of the northern brigade and Prestes leader of the southern.

In the end, though, Prestes, in his new role as chief strategist for the rebels, decided that the best way for the rebels to counter Rondon's boast was simply to "break the bottom of the bottle."[21] He sent a decoy unit in a feint toward Iguaçu Falls, which led Rondon and his staff to believe that the insurgents intended to cross the Paraná River below the falls, into Argentine territory. Instead, the main force headed in the opposite direction, marching stealthily north to Porto Mendes, opposite Paraguay, where they arrived, exhausted, on April 27, 1925.

There, over the next three days, the rebels managed to safely transfer nearly two thousand men and some five hundred horses and mules—plus all of their artillery, machine guns, and supplies— to the other side of the Paraná River, some 1,200 feet wide at that point. At their disposal they had only a canoe, one barge, a single motorized launch they had constructed themselves, and a small steamboat they had boarded and commandeered from the Paraguayan government. It was an impressive evacuation, one that caught the Paraguayans completely by surprise, for they had no troops of their own in the region, and the feat immediately lifted the insurgents' morale.

Rondon's troops arrived in Porto Mendes barely twenty-four hours after the operation concluded, but by then the rebels had wisely destroyed or incapacitated the vessels they used to cross into Paraguay. With "hot pursuit" thus ruled out, Rondon's forces were thwarted; Costa, Prestes, and Távora had been able to make a clean getaway.

What followed was a feat of endurance and daring that Brazilians even today compare to Mao Zedong's Long March. The Prestes Column, as it came to be known, crossed through eastern Paraguay, then reentered Brazil on May 2, 1925. For two years, the rebels meandered through the vast interior, across plains, jungle, and the northeastern desert. All told, the Prestes Column traversed more than fifteen thousand miles of difficult terrain, battling federal army troops, state police, and private gunmen working for landowners as it tried, unsuccessfully, to recruit peasant support in poverty-stricken rural areas. The campaign sputtered out only in 1927, when Prestes and his men finally gave up and crossed into Bolivia.

Rondon's leadership of the Paraná campaign met with mixed reviews. The federal government was chagrined to have declared the rebellion smashed, only to see it immediately pop up again. But it was pleased to have transferred the problem from a prosperous southern state deep into the interior wilderness, far from the main urban centers, and was certain the insurrection would peter out there, like so many others. That assessment was shared by foreign embassies: "As a movement threatening the peace of Brazil and the stability of its government, this revolt ceased to be of importance long ago," Barclay informed Washington, "and its present status is simply that of a few scattered groups of outlaws preying on the surrounding settlements."[22]

Officially, Rondon, who had already been promoted to two-star general in December 1924, was deemed to have "admirably" fulfilled his mission and was praised for his "brilliant intelligence, culture, initiative, thoughtfulness, magnanimity and tenacity" in a special citation the War Ministry issued in August 1925, after he returned to Rio. General Gamelin also continued to bolster Rondon's reputation: asked by reporters who he would want to see in command of the Brazilian Army in the event of war, he replied "Rondon, without a doubt."[23]

In retrospect, Rondon took great pride in his achievement of the pacifist political goals set before the campaign, which he continued to believe were more important than any military victory. "I felt pleased by the conviction that the shedding of much blood and tears had been avoided," he wrote. "I had served my fatherland by bringing peace, by putting an end to a struggle that threatened to degenerate into a catastrophic onslaught in the wilderness, with the hatred between brothers growing ever more fierce."[24] He took particular pride in having marched vanquished rebels through the countryside, rather than on the main highways that ran through towns. "I wanted to spare them all the humiliations of defeat,"[25] he wrote, while at the same time, truth be told, also avoiding opportunities for both displays of popular sympathy for the rebels and even for his own garrisons to take vengeance on the enemy.

But Rondon paid a high personal price for his decision to accept the command. On March 28, just as the siege of Catanduvas was concluding and its survivors beginning their flight toward Foz do Iguaçu, he received a telegram from Chiquita, telling him that Beatriz, the fourth of their six daughters, had died of tuberculosis. His adjutants would remember him crumpling the message in his hands, bursting into tears, and retiring to his tent. "She may be dead, but not to me,"[26] he was overheard to say. His absence from Rio meant he was unable to console his wife, and he was strangely reserved in the telegram he sent her acknowledging their loss: he spoke of his own sadness, but also urged Chiquita to maintain her composure and instructed her to make sure Beatriz was buried according to Positivist rites.

In his own diary that evening he struggled to control his feelings, invoking, as he always did in moments of crisis, his Positivist faith. "I will not profane your beloved image, allowing a cortège of discouraging, selfish emotions to emerge around it,"[27] he wrote of Beatriz, going on to characterize her "objective existence," as Positivists call a person's lifetime, as "a source of altruistic emotions" that he would seek to emulate. But he was also clearly wrestling with a burden of guilt, stemming from his decision to once again place duty to country above family: "Instead of cursing myself and losing myself in useless and unjust recriminations," he wrote, "I will make every effort to rise to the occasion." That was the only way, he concluded, to transform "a heart full of pain, the most bitter pain," into continued service to his divine trinity of "Family, Country and Humanity."[28]

In the long term, the Paraná campaign had negative political consequences for Rondon. He had promised humane treatment to all rebels who surrendered, and took pains to treat them compassionately as they were marched down to the coast for loading onto ships that would take them north. But that gentle treatment ceased the instant the prisoners were out of his jurisdiction. Instead, many were sent directly to disease-ridden penal camps deep in the Amazon. There is no indication in Brazilian Army records that Rondon knew in advance of this betrayal, which President Bernardes had ordered. But there is also no documentary evidence to suggest that he protested once he learned of it upon returning to Rio in June 1925.

The leaders of the Lieutenants' Movement never forgave Rondon for what they considered his failure to keep his word, and from then on they would always harbor enormous personal animosity toward him, especially Juarez Távora and Miguel Costa. Prestes was less inclined to hold a grudge, several times describing Rondon as a capable adversary, but over the years, his partisans on the Left, from Brazilian Communist Party leaders to sympathizers in academia and the press, were far less generous. For them, Rondon became the personification of everything they despised about the First Republic. Five years later, the many enemies Rondon had accumulated would have the opportunity to exact their revenge—but before that happened, he still had vital missions to fulfill for the government he continued to serve.

XXI

Back in the Field

BY THE TIME a new president was sworn in late in 1926, Rondon had turned sixty-one, and was a two-star general with few opportunities for advancement left. He had always lacked the temperament for a desk job at the high command in Rio de Janeiro and there was really no place for him to go within the uppermost echelons of the military bureaucracy: his friend Fragoso was staying on as army chief of staff, and the new minister of war was one of Rondon's former adjutants.

For his part, what Rondon wanted most of all, especially after devoting the second half of 1925 and most of 1926 to routine and often tedious duties, was simply to return to the field and accomplish one last great feat to cap his extraordinary career as an explorer. Not only that, he wanted his only son, Benjamin, now an accomplished engineer and photographer, to accompany him.

Fortunately for Rondon, the armed forces and the Foreign Ministry had no objection to his desire to plunge back into the wilderness, and had even prepared a project for him. Brazil was entering a new stage of development, consolidating its control of the Amazon and other outlying areas; a vital part of that process was to precisely delineate Brazil's borders with its neighbors. There were ten of them in all, and Brazil's frontier with them twisted and turned for nearly ten thousand miles, from French Guiana in the north to Uruguay in the far south.

Since the Amazon basin, Rondon's native environment, accounted for roughly two-thirds of the country's land borders, he was the logical choice for the job. His tasks would be multiple and varied: part cartographic, part engineering, part strategic, part scientific, part political. Not only would he have to take measurements to actually demarcate the border, he would also have to inspect military fortifications and troop deployments along the frontier, recommend ways to strengthen and modernize them, and suggest locations where climate and topography were appropriate for new settlements to "Brazilianize" the border. And he would have to do all this, as usual, on a shoestring budget.

Rondon was thrilled by the idea, even though his survey would have to be completed and all reports filed by the conclusion of the presidential term late in 1930. "I was brimming with enthusiasm,"[1] he wrote, at the idea of reuniting his old exploration team for another trek across Amazonia's rugged terrain; his longtime associate Luiz Thomaz Reis was among those who immediately agreed to join him. In addition, he would be able to inspect SPI posts in the far north and meet with Indigenous groups there.

The government ordered Rondon to start at the extreme northern border, by first delineating Brazil's boundary with the last three European colonies on the continent: British Guiana, Dutch Guiana, and French Guiana. Establishing precise boundaries there would be important in any potential confrontation with the three major European powers, all victorious combatants in World War I and all more formidable militarily than Brazil's Spanish-speaking neighbors in the south.

British Guiana was deemed especially problematic. In the mid-nineteenth century, English antislavery campaigners were furious that Brazilians were crossing into British territory to enslave Indians and carry them off to work on rubber plantations or at gold mines, so they began pressing their government to demarcate the border. Even after slavery ended in 1888, Brazilian miners, hunters, and farmers continued to ignore the frontier, which led the British colonial authorities to send constables to the remote upper Essequibo River.

In 1901, Brazil and the United Kingdom signed a treaty sub-mitting the border issue to an arbitrator, King Victor Emmanuel III of Italy, who in 1904 awarded Brazil about four thousand square miles of territory that the British had always claimed. That eased tensions, but by the late 1920s, the border still had not been formally demarcated. The authorities in Rio de Janeiro were finally forced into action by reports of British subjects—mostly Black Guyanese traders, trappers, and loggers, but also white Englishmen—crossing into Brazilian territory without authorization. Rondon shared these concerns: in his diaries he calls the Dutch and especially the French "friendly neighbors," but never once applies that term to the British.

By the time Rondon reached Belém, at the mouth of the Amazon River, it was almost the end of June 1927. There he divided his force into eight different units, taking personal charge of the group working in the most politically sensitive areas. Because of his meager budget, supplies and equipment were minimal, which forced him to improvise. River travel would be nowhere near as comfortable as on the Madeira or the Paraguay: the best that Rondon could procure as a command vessel was the *Cassiporé*, a humble *gaiola*, a small craft, originally powered by steam, that is crudely constructed and requires passengers to sleep in hammocks rather than private cabins.

More planning than usual was required, since this part of the Amazon basin was less familiar to them than Mato Grosso or Amazonas. Rondon did not really know the main northern tributaries of the Amazon in Pará—a state larger than Germany, Italy, and France combined—or the towns and people along those rivers. Different plants and animals lived here, different Indigenous groups with unfamiliar customs and languages occupied the interior, different wind and water currents prevailed, and, since Rondon and his men would be working north of the equator, even the night sky would be filled with different stars, or the same stars in different positions.

Thanks to new technologies, though, this expedition would be less dangerous than the ones Rondon had undertaken several decades earlier. Now, he traveled with a radio, which allowed Rondon and his men to keep in touch with their families and supplied news of the outside world. Being able to transmit an expedition's coordinates to headquarters via radio also reduced the likelihood of disappearing forever in the jungle. And even if an expedition lost its bearings or ran out of food, there was now a way to get supplies to its members: in 1924 and 1925, the American Alexander Hamilton Rice had shown that aviation could be a useful tool in exploring the Amazon basin, employing biplanes for aerial photography as he navigated a pair of rivers just north of the equator. Rondon quickly adopted these innovations, including the use of shortwave radio for mapping.

Rondon also embraced radiotelegraphy and shortwave as a way to increase productivity. "With the radio station we carried with us and installed at our campsites, I was receiving and sending dispatches from Rio, Belém and Óbidos," he exulted. "I was thus able to attend to administration of the Telegraph Commission, the Indian Protection Service and the Border Inspectorate."[2] So at the end of a long day confronting the elements—or early in the morning, as others slept—Rondon typically found himself addressing bureaucratic and budgetary headaches.

The far north was then the most remote, inaccessible, and neglected area in all of Brazil. The border existed there mostly as a series of abstract points on a map; no one other than the nomadic tribes that roamed the region had actually been there, and cartographers had merely drawn lines to reflect political, rather than geographic, realities on the ground. Here rivers flowed in the "wrong" direction, away from the border, not toward it. It was as if Rondon now would have to ascend, rather than descend, the River of Doubt.

The expedition's first stop was Macapá, today a city of a half million and capital of a state that borders French Guiana. At the time of Rondon's visit, though, it was a muddy outpost in a somnolent backwater. Bisected by the equator, Macapá and its eighteenth-century fortress sit on a plateau above the northern channel of the Amazon River. Historically, that had given the location strategic value. With automobiles and trucks now starting to make their way into the Amazon, Rondon wanted a team, led by a cousin, Lt. Joaquim Rondon, to ascertain whether it would be possible to build a highway from Macapá north to the border with French Guiana.

Back aboard the *Cassiporé*, Rondon skirted the shoreline until arriving at the mouth of the Oiapoque River, the northernmost point on the Brazilian coast, where he was dismayed by the neglect he saw. Granted, this was some of the most unwelcoming terrain on earth: both British- and Dutch-chartered companies had tried to colonize the area in the seventeenth century, and went broke doing so. The Brazilian authorities had sent a small and ill-equipped military detachment to the area for the first time in 1907 and established a customs collection post nine years later, but there were few signs of Brazilian sovereignty, or effective fortifications. This would be repeated during all three of Rondon's border-inspection expeditions: examining dilapidated cannons in one location, he noted ruefully in his diary, he found that the date of manufacture stamped on them was 1681.

Whether from discretion or embarrassment, Rondon was always extremely circumspect about the next stage of his journey. Leaving the *Cassiporé* behind at the mouth of the river, he and a pair of his officers paddled up the Oiapoque in a canoe, with French Guiana on their right and Brazil on their left, to Clevelândia do Norte. Officially, Clevelândia, named for American president Grover Cleveland, who had mediated South American border disputes in Brazil's favor, was an "agricultural nucleus," founded in 1919 as a permanent civilian presence. But it had become a brutal penal colony, warehousing opponents the government considered especially dangerous.

By 1924, Clevelândia's population included anarchists, members of the newly formed Brazilian Communist Party, dissident officers who had participated in the Lieutenants' Uprisings, labor union activists, and also common criminals, mostly beggars, thieves, and pimps. A year later, its population would swell further with the arrival of hundreds of the rebels who had surrendered to Rondon at Catanduvas. The prisoners lived in wooden barracks they constructed themselves under the harsh equatorial sun, with each category of prisoner grouped together and assigned its own quarters. Food was scarce, especially after a new commandant arrived and cut rations, and disease was rampant and often fatal. By 1927, more than half of the 946 prisoners who had arrived in 1924 and 1925 were dead, many from malaria, tuberculosis, or beriberi; an epidemic of dysentery in 1926 took an especially heavy toll, killing more than 300 prisoners.

As the crow flies, Clevelândia was barely one hundred miles from France's notorious prison on Devil's Island, and escape was nearly as difficult. Only a small military garrison was deployed at Clevelândia, because prisoners had nowhere to go. The Oiapoque River, almost a mile wide, had caimans and strong currents, and the colony was surrounded on its other three sides by dense jungle, with the nearest civilian settlement more than twelve miles away. Occasionally, local fishermen paddled by in their canoes, but they all knew that if they picked up prisoners trying to conceal themselves in the brush on the bank of the river, they risked being incarcerated too.

In contrast to most jails in the south of Brazil, at Clevelândia prisoners had to work to earn their keep. What provided the penal colony's economic sustenance was the fragrant rosewood tree, whose oil is an essential ingredient in perfumes and therefore enormously lucrative as an export. Convicts first had to fell the trees, which can grow to be one hundred feet high and seven feet in diameter, then chop them into logs a yard long and haul them to a distillery on the prison grounds. There, they made the logs into chips and fed them into a steam distiller. The oil that resulted from this process was the equivalent of about 1 percent of the weight of each tree and thus was easily transferred to the port of Belém or smuggled across the river and on to Cayenne, capital of French Guiana. In both cities, this precious oil was auctioned off to buyers representing the leading French fashion houses and then shipped to Paris for transformation into costly scents worn by some of the world's richest and most elegant women.

We do not know what Rondon thought of what he saw at Clevelândia, whose main administrative building he used as his headquarters for nearly a month, or what he wrote when he eventually filed his report to the authorities in Rio. In fact, we don't know if he said anything at all about the forced labor and other abuses he had to have seen. If he did, any record of it seems to have vanished from the archives of both the Brazilian Army and the Ministry of Agriculture, which was nominally in charge of the "agricultural nucleus" at Clevelândia.

In his memoirs, dictated nearly thirty years after his border-inspection expedition, Rondon again passed up an opportunity to denounce the harsh conditions imposed on the prisoners. Instead, he described his visit as ordinary and the settlement as innocuous, even pleasant. After determining the geographic coordinates of what he euphemistically calls "the Clevelândia Colony" and placing a border marker there, he wrote, "I visited all of the lots of the Colony," including the rosewood-distilling operation, "and after a dinner offered to the officials and members of the Clevelândia Agricultural Center Commission in return for the kindnesses we had received, we departed for Amazonas."[3]

On the way to Manaus, Rondon had hoped to stop somewhere near Óbidos, seven hundred miles up the Amazon from Belém, and explore the Tumucumaque mountain range, forming Brazil's border with Dutch Guiana (today the independent republic of Suriname). But an advance scouting team brought him bad news: this was such a rugged and inaccessible area that no land route from the south, not even an Indian trail, existed. In addition, funds were starting to run low, and Rondon already had other commitments. "Our resources would not permit us to organize a reconnaissance expedition," he wrote regretfully. "So we're leaving that inspection for another opportunity."[4] Thus, it was on to Manaus, where he boarded a vessel heading up the Rio Negro to its junction with the Rio Branco. But the Tumucumaque remained very much on his mind.

Entering the Rio Branco, he was bombarded with discouraging news. Floods had destroyed the crops of local settlers, sending them fleeing and making it impossible to acquire foodstuffs in the amounts Rondon needed. Farther on, he was told that a backup plan he had devised, to approach the Tumucumaque range overland from the west, would not work. "Such was the cacophony of information that I decided instead to draw up plans to reach the frontier only at its most important points,"[5] he wrote dejectedly, once again reluctantly postponing his plans to explore the formidable Tumucumaque.

But as part of his survey of the northern border, Rondon also intended to climb Mount Roraima—where the northernmost fragment of Brazil's border converged with British Guiana and

Venezuela—and this now became his main focus. This ascent was necessary for cartographic purposes, but it also posed the kind of challenge Rondon had always relished, dating to his days climbing Sugarloaf Mountain as a cadet. Though not Brazil's highest peak, Mount Roraima is unusually difficult to scale because it belongs to a class of mountains known as tepuis. Found only in the Guiana Highlands of South America, tepuis are imposing tabletop peaks—*tepui* means "house of the gods" in the language of the Pemon people who inhabit the area—jutting from the tropical savanna and forest around them, with sheer sandstone sides and flat summits, often pitted with caves and sinkholes up to one thousand feet deep. Waterfalls cascade from the tops, from which one can enjoy commanding views of the clouds that congregate below the summit.[6]

Of the more than 150 tepuis dotting the Guiana Highlands, which separate the Amazon basin from the Orinoco River basin to the north, Mount Roraima stands the tallest, at 9,219 feet. As such, it occupies a prominent place in the cosmology of the Indigenous peoples of the region. The Pemon and other tribes in the area believed Mount Roraima to be the stump of a gigantic tree whose branches once accommodated all the fruits and vegetables in the world. But when the shape-shifting trickster Macunaíma, a recurring figure in Brazilian folklore, cut down the tree and it crashed to the ground, a terrible deluge resulted, creating the network of rivers that make up the Amazon and Orinoco basins.

Rondon's Roraima expedition happened to coincide with another, sponsored by the American Museum of Natural History and jointly led by the zoologist and botanist George H. H. Tate and the mammalogist T. D. Carter. They were initially not aware that Rondon was also in the area, but learned of his presence when they reached Limão, a market settlement on the Rio Branco, and tried without success to hire Indian porters and guides there. "Although Limão had become almost a Mecca and hundreds of Indians swung their hammocks wherever they could find room, I was unable to persuade any to leave with me for Roraima," no matter how much money he offered, Tate wrote in an account published in *National Geographic* in 1930. "They wanted first to see the general," he explained. "From far

and near the Indians gathered—men, women, and children—ready
to do his slightest bidding."[7]

Worried that his expedition might collapse before it even had
a chance to begin, Tate rode on horseback for two days until he
reached Rondon's base camp at São Marcos, not knowing what kind
of reception he would get. He need not have worried: "I found him
courteous and attentive," Tate reported, "also, widely read, authoritative, and in manner the ideal of a soldier and a gentleman."[8] For his
part, Rondon was favorably disposed toward the Americans: on the
expedition with Roosevelt, he had come to respect the professionalism of both George Cherrie and Leo Miller, also naturalists from
the American Museum of Natural History. Before long, the two
expedition leaders agreed to join forces. Tate was grateful for this,
very much aware that Rondon was doing him a great favor by lending his immense prestige to the Americans' undertaking: "Among
the tribes themselves his name is reverenced," Tate wrote, and "his
person is held to be almost a god."[9]

Compared to Rondon's previous experiences, the first phase of
his travels with Tate and Carter was tranquil, even comfortable.
Knowing he was going to be traveling across savanna, Rondon
assembled a large herd of cattle to keep the expedition fed. The combined group was a very large and hungry one, with more than three
hundred Indigenous porters to accommodate all the Americans'
supplies, plus assorted cartographers, scientists, and soldiers. "Progress was very slow with such a concourse of people," Tate reported,
but no one really minded: Rondon had the time he needed to map
the uncharted region, and Tate and Carter were delighted to find
so many unfamiliar plant and animal specimens as the expedition
"crossed hot arid grasslands studded in parts with countless pagoda-
shaped ant hills or relieved here and there by green swamps and
palm-fringed brooks."[10]

After three days, the Rondon-Tate expedition switched to a trail
that took them into a region of gently rising hills and enormous
granite boulders, where they reduced the size of their party by shedding most of the porters. The explorers now followed the Miang
River through dense, humid forests and then suddenly emerged to a

view of the Serra Pacaraíma, which marks the border between Brazil and Venezuela. Energized, they made camp and then needed only one more day to make their way into the heart of the range, where for the first time they saw their objective, a mere forty miles away, framed by another massive tepui just to the northwest, called Kukunam. "Although mist and cloud wreathed their tops, their sheer sides towered starkly against the afternoon sky," Tate wrote. "The twin giants, Kukunam and Roraima, loomed before us serene and majestic. Flat-topped and of almost equal height, they towered above us."[11]

But when the joint expedition commenced its ascent of Mount Roraima, it encountered problems almost immediately. "There was an interruption of the ledge, because the narrow passageway had slipped down to a cliff below," Rondon wrote. "Since it was not possible to launch a bridge over the chasm, the Indians rigged a descent to a point where the ledge had settled. An Indian secured a very long rope ladder to the trunk of a tree, and all of us, including the dogs, made our way down and then up again, secured by ropes."[12]

At the summit, Rondon's real scientific and cartographic work began. He, his men, and the Americans made camp next to a giant boulder that had attached to it a bronze plaque left by English visitors a decade earlier, inscribed "God Save the King." The area was teeming with animal and plant species that existed nowhere else on earth. Because each tepui is isolated from others and also from the jungle and savanna below, it constitutes a distinct environment, in which unique species evolved. In addition, there are microclimates at various altitudes: the weather at the summit is cool and rainy, with temperatures that sink into the forties at night, while the mountain's base is hot and humid.

The top of Mount Roraima is a plateau occupying fourteen square miles, an extraordinarily large area, so there was much flora and fauna for Rondon and his team to discover and classify. As Rondon surveyed, he determined that just 5 percent of the summit is actually in Brazilian territory. Because the soil was poor in nutrients, carnivorous flora like the pitcher plant had carved out a niche for itself, as had unusual species of orchids and bromeliads, Rondon's team found. Numerous species of frogs and toads also flourished, and the sandstone surface of the summit harbored previously unknown varieties of moss and heather.

Unfortunately, though, Rondon himself was forced to descend earlier than he planned, and left the Americans behind with some of his scouts. A group of Wapixana Indians from just south of the mountain had accompanied Rondon's expedition, eager to see for themselves a natural cathedral sacred in their cosmology. They were suitably impressed, Rondon wrote, but "the cold increasingly tormented the Indians, who were already feeling ill at being unable to sleep out in the open" because of temperatures colder than they could ever have imagined at ground level. "We had to accelerate our return for that reason."[13] It was an unusual show of deference on Rondon's part, but consistent with his philosophy of treating Indigenous peoples with respect.

Before leaving, though, Rondon did two things that were typical of him. First, he organized a flag-raising ceremony, in this case hoisting not just the Brazilian banner, with its Positivist motto, but also the standards of Venezuela and Great Britain, as all the expedition's members, Indians included, shouted, "Viva o Brasil!" This patriotic exercise was both filmed and photographed for subsequent distribution to newspapers, magazines, and movie theaters around the country. Then, with the cameras still rolling, Rondon had his men chisel into the rock, right next to the bronze plaque the British had left, an inscription that read: "General Rondon—Viva o Brasil."

Climbing Mount Roraima was the highlight of the first phase of Rondon's complex border mission, but he still had much work to do. After a six-month interlude, spent first inspecting the Cuiabá-Madeira telegraph line and then in Rio writing reports and drawing up maps, he arrived back in Manaus in August 1928 to begin the second border-inspection expedition: an arduous ascent of the Cuminá River in hopes of finally being able to explore the Tumucumaque range and survey the remainder of the border with Dutch Guiana. As in 1927, Benjamin was with him, and a pair of other civilians, both longtime friends, also joined the expedition. One was the novelist Gastão Cruls, son of Rondon's old chief at the astronomical observatory in Rio. The other was the botanist Alberto José Sampaio, remembered in Brazil today chiefly for two closely related efforts: his early and passionate embrace of the conservationist cause, expressed in large part through his strong and effective advocacy of a system of national parks.

Rondon and Sampaio had known each other since 1905, when Sampaio, then twenty-four, interrupted his medical studies for lack of funds and qualified through a civil service exam to work at the National Museum. Early on, he wrote a comprehensive study of the flora of Mato Grosso, dedicated to the botanists of the Rondon Commission, in which he sought, in Sampaio's own words, to "gather information from all of the work undertaken by domestic and foreign researchers in that state, thus enabling the mapping of all known components of the local flora."[14]

This naturally caught Rondon's attention and sparked a friendship between the two men despite their sixteen-year age difference. In 1912, helped by Rondon's endorsement, Sampaio became chief of the botany division at the National Museum; shortly before the Tumucumaque expedition he published *The Forestry Problem in Brazil*, perhaps the first systematic examination of a subject that would become increasingly important as the twentieth century wore on.[15]

The Tumucumaque expedition would strengthen the bonds between Rondon and Sampaio, and over the next two decades, until Sampaio's death in 1946, they would work together to advance the conservationist cause in Brazil, which both regarded as closely linked to the fate of Native peoples. Rondon saw Indigenous groups as natural stewards of the forest—a common enough idea today, but radical in the 1920s—and the maintenance of a healthy ecosystem as essential to the well-being of their societies and cultures. As a plant scientist, Sampaio approached the issue from a different angle, but recognized the importance of enlisting collaborators, and saw Indigenous people, with their reverence for the natural world, as innate allies.

In this effort they were joined by another botanist who had a long history with Rondon, Frederico Carlos Hoehne. Born on a farm to a German immigrant couple, Hoehne also had gravitated to the National Museum, which assigned him to several of Rondon's expeditions during the first two decades of the century. The orchids his parents grew in their hothouse had fascinated him as a child, and Hoehne wrote extensively on that subject for both the National Museum and the Rondon Commission; eventually, he became director of the São Paulo Institute of Botany and founded the country's first environmental group.

The Cuminá River was not quite the River of Doubt, but it presented stiff challenges even in 1928 for any expedition traveling by canoe, especially one with novices like Sampaio and Cruls aboard. Three decades earlier, Henri and Marie Coudreau, a French husband-and-wife team, had surveyed the lower reaches of the stream at great personal cost, illustrating the difficulties Rondon could expect to face. Henri died of malaria while traveling with his wife in November 1899 on the nearby Trombetas River, into which the Cuminá flows, and so she proceeded alone, accompanied only by six oarsmen, finishing her work in 1906; she eventually published four books and several valuable monographs, all of which Rondon read before embarking.

As was his custom, Rondon also relied on local Indigenous peoples for information and assistance, and received the usual warm response when he did so. The most important group in the region was the Pianocotó, whom Cruls described as physically stronger than tribes dwelling in the lowlands and in appearance "fairer than Englishmen."[16] They were excellent hunters and, like Rondon, doted on their dogs. Their skills, knowledge of the terrain, and willingness to assist Rondon as guides and oarsmen once again made it possible for the expedition to live off the land. All told, there were now fifty-eight men, divided among ten canoes, several of which were loaded with equipment and supplies.

Like the River of Doubt, the Cuminá was dotted with waterfalls, large boulders, and other "encumbrances that occurred in an uninterrupted series." This complicated navigation, but the Cuminá also had fine beaches of white sand that made ideal campsites; and edible wildlife like fish, turtles, and tapirs were plentiful. Nevertheless, as a precaution, Rondon sent a junior officer back to Óbidos to obtain more provisions, "since our delay would be greater than initially supposed"[17] due to the natural obstacles. There was no point, he concluded, in repeating the privations endured during the descent of the River of Doubt, if it could be avoided.

Illness, however, was inevitable: several expedition members were quickly struck by malaria and had to be evacuated back to Óbidos; after a couple of weeks, Cruls began coughing up blood and was bedridden for several days. On October 26, the expedition crossed the equator heading northward—with no ceremony to mark the occasion, much to Cruls's disappointment. Even without using their instruments, the explorers could tell now that the altitude was rising, as the intense heat of the savanna abated and the risk of malaria fell: Rondon estimated a drop of ten degrees on the thermometer for every thousand feet of increased altitude.

Outsiders rarely were able to witness Rondon's first interaction with an uncontacted tribal group, but Cruls had that opportunity this time. On November 10, 1928, the expedition came upon a settlement squeezed between a hill and the riverbank; Rondon steered his canoe toward the riverbank, ordering the others to remain behind on the water, out of sight, and walked into the village unarmed, with only his son Benjamin accompanying him. "No one could be seen," he noted, but there were many signs that the residents had just fled out of fear: ample supplies of food in baskets, a fire still going, even bows and arrows hung next to hammocks.

Rondon left everything intact, and had Benjamin return to their canoe to bring gifts, which were then distributed next to the hammocks, along with a large machete left at the entrance to the lodge house. "We were certain that they were observing and appreciating our movements in their front yard," Rondon wrote, and sure enough, just as the expedition was pulling away in their canoes, cries broke out from the bush. "It was the Indians, reciprocating our gesture of friendship," Rondon continued. "Carrying bananas and cassava pancakes, they came down to the port to show that they welcomed our affectionate attention."[18] So Rondon disembarked once more, only to have the Indians retreat again to the bush.

Rondon had learned a few words of Pianocotó from his scouts for just such an occasion, and now he employed them: "Aquiché anaoro uiá," or "You can see that I am your friend." With that, four Indians cautiously appeared on the path, three men and an older woman. "The remaining Indians, probably out of fear, had retreated to their lodge house, but once again the General and Benjamin appeared, and this time finally caught a glimpse of them," wrote Cruls, whom Rondon had asked to bring even more gifts from the canoe, and who thus witnessed the encounter. "All of them were left visibly nervous by our presence."[19]

"They trembled upon speaking with us," Rondon wrote. "We embraced them, inviting them to come close to our canoes to get a better look at our cargo."[20] With that, the ice was broken: the Indians accompanied Rondon to the port, and even petted his dogs, which were unlike any they had ever seen. He gave each of them a machete, a knife, and a piece of red cloth, while Cruls gave them bracelets made of beads and shells, and other members of the expedition presented them with scissors and mirrors. When it came time for the expedition to depart, the Indians asked Rondon when he might return, and he told them "in three moons."[21]

Rondon's own Pianocotó scouts told him the expedition was now at the limit of the tribe's domain and that, so far as they knew, the land ahead was completely uninhabited. Rondon was delighted to think that "we would now traverse totally unknown stretches of territory."[22] By the time the expedition reached the headwaters of the Cuminá in late November, however, Sampaio was ill, and so Rondon asked Cruls to remain with the botanist at the base camp and help process specimens already collected. Rondon and a small contingent decided to continue into the mountains, which Rondon likened to a "pronounced geographic hernia"[23] rising out of the savanna, with Pianocotó guides. Every few days, Rondon would send someone back to camp with new specimens and data that Sampaio and Cruls would then catalog and preserve for eventual delivery to the National Museum. When enough material was accumulated, Cruls and Sampaio, accompanied by a small team of paddlers and scouts, began their return to Óbidos.

Christmas came and went with the rest of the expedition still exploring the Tumucumaque range, and so did New Year's Day of

1929. The weather was delightful, cool and dry, but a few days later Rondon decided it was time to head back: he was disappointed to discover that the Pianocotó were right, that "this area was utterly devoid of Indians."²⁴ But he was pleased with the scientific and geographic findings he had made. All that remained was to install a final border marker at the highest point the expedition had reached—which happened to be a continental divide, with some rivers flowing south into the Amazon and others flowing north into the Orinoco basin or the Atlantic—and erect the flags of Brazil and the Netherlands.

Alongside, Rondon buried a bottle with a letter he had written for any future explorers, Dutch or Brazilian, and signed along with Benjamin. It began with a precise cartographic description of the locale as proof of "effective possession of the frontier"²⁵ and concluded with a hearty and patriotic "Long live the Brazilian Republic!" Ever the Positivist, Rondon gave the date in the letter first in accordance with the Positivist calendar—the tenth of Moses, 141—and then by the conventional calendar: January 10, 1929. A month later, after stops along the way to do ethnographic work at three Pianocotó villages and to cement the peaceful relationship with the settlement contacted on the way upriver, he and his men were back in Óbidos.

Cruls turned his experience into a best-selling travelogue in diary form called *The Amazon as I Saw It*, which portrayed Rondon as a figure of great stamina and with a remarkable capacity for leadership. "As always, the one who surged to the front of the group, erect, gallant, firm, was the general," Cruls wrote one afternoon as a Rondon-led scouting party returned from a mission. "The energy of this man is incredible, his spirit fearless and his strength inexhaustible."²⁶ Finding that Rondon washed his own clothes in whatever stream was available, Cruls and Sampaio, out of embarrassment, immediately stopped expecting porters to handle that task for them and also began doing their own laundry.

As for the data Rondon gathered in the Tumucumaque, it enabled Sampaio to prepare the first comprehensive scientific studies of that uninhabited eco-region, which in turn provided the foundation for a decades-long campaign to declare the area a "protected corridor." That effort came to fruition only in 2002, but the Tumucumaque

Mountains National Park, which at 14,980 square miles covers an area larger than Belgium, is today not only Brazil's biggest national park but also the largest tropical-forest national park in the world, as well as the central piece in what is formally known as the Amapá Biodiversity Corridor. Many of the park's protected animal species, principally fish and aquatic birds but also including brilliantly colored hummingbirds, harpy eagles, and large feline carnivores and primates, cannot be found anywhere else in the world; its plant life is similarly varied and exuberant. And all of the effort to protect, preserve, and catalog the region's wildlife began with Rondon's persistence in fulfilling his mission, finding a way into a place that no one, not even Native peoples living nearby, had ever braved.

XXII

"I Think It Advisable the General Not Continue His Journey"

THE YEAR 1930 was one of the most consequential in the history of modern Brazil, and also in Rondon's life. In both cases, the events of that year constitute a clear demarcation point, with a sharply defined before and a drastically different after. Had Rondon been a less important actor in national life, he might have remained immune to such vicissitudes. But just as November 15, 1889, and the birth of the republic marked the conclusion of the first phase of his life, the upheavals of 1930 would signify the end of another.

Forced to remain in the capital until the end of September 1929, attending to paperwork while waiting for funding for his third border-inspection expedition, Rondon returned to the Amazon via a route that was unusual for him. With Benjamin and Luiz Thomaz Reis as companions, he traveled to Cuiabá by automobile, then drove east along the telegraph line he had erected under Gomes Carneiro's command nearly forty years earlier: at Registro do Araguaia, the line's original terminus, he was gripped with nostalgia when he realized that the telegraph station where they were overnighting "functioned in the same house that Gomes Carneiro had dedicated on April 30, 1891."[1] He remembered the original date because it fell on his twenty-sixth birthday; now he was sixty-four.

Next, Rondon and his companions descended the Araguaia by boat, pausing at Bananal Island to inspect SPI posts there. At Marabá, just downstream from the confluence of the Araguaia and

Tocantins Rivers, they made another stop, to check on fortifications and investigate reports that local Indians were being forced to work on the Brazil nut plantations that formed the backbone of the local economy. "It was always the same painful story for the Indians," Rondon wearily observed, "plundered of their belongings, dishonored in front of their families, their homes profaned by adventurers sometimes called rubber tappers, other times known as miners, but always people who invaded native land in order to conquer it by force of arms."[2]

From Marabá it was a straight shot to Belém, where Rondon boarded a larger vessel and headed up the Amazon. When he reached Santarém and the Tapajós River, he disembarked, boarded a motorboat, and headed south to Fordlândia, where Henry Ford a year earlier had opened a plantation to supply rubber to his automobile manufacturing plants in Detroit. Because of press reports suggesting that Ford was creating an American enclave on Brazilian soil, the federal government had ordered Rondon to determine whether or not Ford was "conserving the indispensable Brazilian character of these population centers."[3]

Rondon liked what he saw: "I concluded, expressing my personal opinion, that the great American industrialist had founded there on the Tapajós a school to train workers, with a social organization that could serve as a model for counterparts established throughout our national territory."[4] But the workers obviously disagreed. Within a year of his inspection, they revolted against management, complaining about having to eat an American diet instead of the beans, rice, and cassava to which they were accustomed; of being forced to live in American-style housing; and of being required to wear identification badges. To quell the uprising, Brazilian Army troops were dispatched, and changes in the menu at the town cafeteria were negotiated.

By now the new year—one in which a new president was scheduled to be elected—had arrived, and after filing his report on Fordlândia from Manaus, Rondon resumed his route upstream, which is when intrigue in the historical record begins: as his mission drew him nearer to Brazil's far western border with Peru, Rondon increasingly heard alarming stories about the persistence of slavery on rubber plantations in that country. There were even accounts of Peruvian raids across the border into Brazil to capture Brazilian Indians for that purpose, which enraged him.

Rondon had assumed that the slavery question had been mitigated two decades earlier, as a result of the efforts of Sir Roger Casement and other antislavery campaigners whom he had supported, conspired with, and supplied with information. So he was disturbed to learn of a resurgence of the practice, and determined to investigate it himself. Casement, Irish by birth, was knighted by the British government for his work in the Amazon, then later convicted of treason and executed in 1916 for his role in a plot to obtain German support for a rebellion against British rule in Ireland. And by 1930, with much of the world plunged into the Depression, international interest in the situation in the Putumayo region, named for the tributary of the Amazon that forms the border between Peru and Colombia, had shifted to problems much closer to home. Rondon was on his own, with few allies for this cause.

He decided to shed his uniform, go undercover, and visit Iquitos, still the center of Peru's rubber industry and all its illicit practices. His superiors back in Rio de Janeiro, however, fearing damage to cordial relations with a neighbor and no doubt realizing how difficult it would be for Rondon to appear incognito anywhere in the Amazon, refused to authorize his plan. Rondon then quietly defied them: dressed in civilian clothes, he continued upriver from Manaus to Iquitos, with a brief stopover in Tabatinga, on Brazil's border with Colombia and Peru. It is possible, of course, that he actually was on a government, rather than a personal, mission, and that the authorities in Rio simply wanted deniability in case of trouble with the Peruvians. But Rondon remained silent on the matter, even years later in his memoirs, and since information in government records is also lacking, there is no way to be certain.

Arriving in Iquitos, Rondon was, predictably, soon recognized, and subjected to several days of ceremonies and official fetes—all of it intended, he thought, to keep him in the city and away from his objective. Eventually, though, he was able to make his way into the Putumayo jungle. There he gathered intelligence about who was engaged in human trafficking and who benefited from it, and also intervened to rescue Brazilians, both Indians and mixed-race peasants, from servitude. Rondon never wrote about these activities, but an English explorer happened to witness an encounter between Rondon, unarmed and out of uniform, and the swaggering, heavily armed German overseer of a rubber plantation. He described the man retreating from Rondon "like a dog" after the two of them had a "quiet private conversation."⁵ With no legal authority to back him up, Rondon had prevailed through sheer force of personality.

On returning to Manaus, Rondon boarded another vessel and headed up the Purus River for Acre, bordering both Peru and Bolivia, where he intended to resume his inspection mission. This was a delicate task: twenty-seven years after signing the Treaty of Petrópolis, which conceded Acre to Brazil in return for £2 million and construction of the Madeira-Mamoré Railway, many Bolivians now felt they had been shortchanged. The railway was finished in 1912, just before the collapse of South America's monopoly on rubber production, and by 1930 it was obsolete. With an economy devastated by the worldwide depression that sharply cut exports of industrial metals like tin, its principal export, Bolivia was also being swept by a wave of irredentism; this resulted two years later in the outbreak of the Chaco War with Paraguay over control of an oil-rich area. Everywhere he turned, Rondon encountered destitute Bolivian prospectors, rubber tappers, and subsistence farmers who had crossed over into Brazil in hopes of improving their fortunes. But he could not expel them, for fear of exacerbating an already tense situation, nor did he have the financial means to ease their woes.

Already troubled by what he had seen along the Peruvian border, Rondon began to doubt the wisdom of his decades of efforts to open the Amazon. At his next stop, Porto Velho, he visited the grave of his son-in-law and loyal aide Emmanuel Amarante, who had died the year before during a typhus epidemic that also had killed several hundred Indians under his charge. Putting aside his aversion to religious ceremonies, Rondon attended a memorial mass in Amarante's honor. "My tears were such that I could only utter a few words of fond nostalgia," Rondon wrote. He was haunted by the thought that

Amarante "could have been saved from the typhus that killed him if he had only been willing to leave his post."⁶ But Rondon had instilled in his son-in-law a sense of duty so intense that the younger officer felt compelled to remain, and now Rondon's eldest daughter, Heloisa Aracy, was a widow, with five children to raise on her own.

Continuing south and east after leaving Porto Velho, following the border with Bolivia, Rondon encountered many of the same problems that earlier troubled him, with similar causes: the inability of the Brazilian state to exercise effective sovereignty over the most distant corners of its domain, and the toxic combination of corruption and indifference of public administration in areas it actually did control. Here Rondon was back in familiar territory, where he and his men had demarcated the frontier not even a quarter century before. But he soon discovered that many of the border markers the Rondon Commission originally installed had been destroyed by criminal gangs operating in both countries, who wanted to confuse the two governments as to where the authority of one ended and the other began.

Even more distressing, he was again assailed with stories of Brazilian Indians being kidnapped and taken across the border, wherever it might lie, and forced to work as slaves. "My presence had the effect of a bomb detonating in those distant locales, where life was lawless,"⁷ he wrote, but there were also strict limits on remedial actions he could take. This was demonstrated when leaders of the Palmela tribe came to him, imploring him to rescue their compatriots who were being held on plantations in Bolivia owned by German and Italian interests.

A basic problem blocked Rondon's way: the diminishing numbers of remaining Palmela lived on both sides of an ill-defined border, and often lacked papers from either country. In one instance, "I was able to act and repatriate them" only because the nationality of the small group was easily determined. But in other cases, "I was unfortunately unable to act because the establishments where they were being held were in Bolivian territory,"⁸ and those particular Palmela could not provide proof of Brazilian citizenship. This gnawed at Rondon, as did the subsequent tragic history of the

Palmela: their numbers continued to decline rapidly, and in 1956 the Brazilian government formally declared them extinct as a tribe.[9]

As Rondon headed south, he continued to encounter one discouraging situation after another. Traveling along the trail of the telegraph line, he was welcomed by the tribes he had contacted in the first decade of the century. Their leaders wanted to celebrate his return with feasts in his honor, but they also had a litany of complaints they hoped the Pagmejera, the Chief of Chiefs, could resolve, many of them stemming from official neglect. Foremost of these was the continuous encroachment of Brazilian ranchers, loggers, miners, and rubber tappers on Indigenous lands, and the inability— or unwillingness—of local police to respond to complaints the SPI filed on behalf of tribal peoples.

In addition, Rondon could see that the telegraph line itself was falling into disrepair and that the stations he had built were functioning precariously, if at all. Longtime employees, Indigenous and *civilizados*, whom he had persuaded to man the posts, people he considered friends, confided to him their fears that they were being abandoned, and asked him to intercede. In some cases, they had not been paid in years and, lacking money to return home, were forced to subsist on the crops they planted and the animals they tended. Where Indigenous schools were attached to the station, books and other basic supplies, like chalk and paper, were in short supply or falling to pieces. Everywhere he turned, it seemed, everything was in disarray.

As his journey progressed, Rondon increasingly felt pressured from all sides. The border-inspection missions of 1927–29 had been carried out in remote and sparsely inhabited corners of Brazil. But as he moved south into more densely populated areas, his role as the emissary of a central government that had largely ignored its border residents exposed him to their urgent needs and the deficiencies of the republic. Officially, his task, he said, was purely a technical one, that of "verifying the border and conducting a census." But he also found himself thrust into "playing the role of defender of the Indians and the oppressed in general, and of the interests of their communities."[10] It was an exhausting task, and one for which he did not have adequate resources. And so, for instance, when he somehow wangled a sum to build a road linking a small town to the outside world, it seemed a major victory, worth recording in his diary.

South of Corumbá, after leaving behind the Paraguay River and the boats that plied it, he crossed into Paraná, traveling by automobile, sometimes driving the car himself, reveling in the pleasure of motoring across the vast, open prairie. Road conditions, though, were dreadful, which distressed Rondon from both a military and a practical point of view: in a typical expression of his thrifty nature, he complained to his diary of constant breakdowns that not only slowed his progress and would surely hamper an army in any future military campaign but also "really irritated me because they required, in addition, a pointless expense."[11]

Rondon's route took him back into the region around Catanduvas, where he discovered that the situation had deteriorated since 1925. The central government had done little to help rebuild settlements damaged during the campaign against the rebels, and former fighters were now terrorizing the western half of both Paraná and Santa Catarina. As he traveled from one small settlement to another, Rondon was sobered too by visits he insisted on making to small local cemeteries, where combatants from the 1925 conflict were buried. Much blood had been shed on both sides, and for what? he wondered.

"The revolutionary wave seemed now to want to rise even higher," Rondon wrote, reflecting on what he found during his tour of the countryside. "We now came across populations in panic"[12] at the thought of another insurgency, but also resentful of the central government's lack of support.

Prestes, after two years of wandering on a fifteen-thousand-mile circular path around the Brazilian backlands, eventually took refuge in Argentina, where he read Marx and Lenin and edged closer to Communism. By 1930, he was complaining of being "a general without soldiers,"[13] and in a series of manifestos called for a new uprising against the central government. Rondon was concerned about this as he traveled through the southern borderlands. He had not relished his experience on the battlefield in 1925, fighting other Brazilians, and dreaded the possibility of new strife.

But as Rondon continued his work on the frontier, back in the capital the complex web of bargains, compromises, and unwritten understandings that had held the republic together for decades was now disintegrating. A presidential election held on March 1, 1930, marred by widespread vote fraud on both sides, immediately exacerbated a nascent political crisis. The presidency had long alternated between the country's two most powerful states, São Paulo and Minas Gerais, but the outgoing president, Washington Luís, a São Paulo native, decided to end that practice and hand the office off to the governor of his home state, who was declared the winner of the vote.

The governor of Minas Gerais, a great-grandson of Rondon's hero José Bonifácio and a cousin of Rondon's main ally in Congress, was unwilling to accept this breach. A year earlier he had offered not to press a claim for the presidency so long as the office went to a neutral third party: Getúlio Vargas, governor of Rio Grande do Sul. After that proposal was rejected and the vote held, he and Vargas began to conspire with leaders of the Lieutenants' Movement to prevent São Paulo's candidate from taking office on November 15.

Months of maneuvering followed, punctuated by outbursts of violence. Even before the vote, the congressional deputy Ildefonso Simões Lopes, a Vargas supporter whom Rondon had befriended during their service together on the drought commission in 1922, pulled a gun and shot dead a deputy from the rival side during a debate on the floor of Congress. In another incident, police from the two southernmost states, whose governors supported different candidates, skirmished on their common border. Then, on July 26, the governor of a state in the northeast, a Vargas ally, was assassinated; blame was immediately placed on the federal government, even though it was eventually determined that a personal dispute had motivated the killing. An uprising intended to put Vargas in power now seemed inevitable.

On October 3, the conspirators launched an attack on army headquarters in Porto Alegre, capital of Vargas's home state, which quickly fell into their hands. At dawn the next morning, army troops in the Northeast, encouraged by leaders of the Lieutenants' Movement, revolted too. In the south, Vargas's supporters began a march north toward São Paulo. In the Northeast, the rebel forces headed south, hoping to take control of Bahia, the largest state in the region. With some eighty thousand combatants soon in the field, Brazil appeared headed for a conflagration.

Rondon had been observing all this from afar, kept abreast of events by occasional newspaper reports or radio broadcasts but mostly relying on telegrams his office sent from Rio. Despite close ties to the Minas Gerais group, he sought to remain neutral as the dispute worsened: he had served all thirteen of Brazil's presidents, and had friends in both camps. But his enemies were concentrated in only one: throughout the decade, Rondon had antagonized the Lieutenants' Movement, which commanded both the manpower and the firepower the conspirators needed to seize control. That group viewed him not just as unreliable but as their nemesis, personally and politically.

The uprising caught Rondon in transit, on his way to Porto Alegre by train. His plan, after a brief pause in the state capital, was to inspect Brazil's southernmost border with Uruguay. At 1:30 a.m. on October 4, when his train halted at a rail junction called Marcelino Ramos, Rondon was fast asleep in his cabin when he was awakened by a racket in the corridor. It turned out to be a rebel contingent that, on the orders of Miguel Costa, one of the leaders of the insurrection, was looking for Rondon, in order to detain him until receiving orders from Vargas. Five years after Rondon's troops defeated him at Catanduvas, forcing him on a long march across Brazil with Prestes and then into exile in Argentina, Costa was exacting his revenge.

Miguel Costa himself arrested Rondon. "I hadn't even realized where I was when the group of soldiers came in," Rondon would explain in an interview a month later. "A tall, light-skinned man at the head of the group addressed me: 'I think it advisable the general not continue his journey.' Really, I didn't grasp the meaning of the warning, and so there came another: 'To avoid greater complications, Your Excellency should stop here.' But I still didn't get what was going on, so the unknown man had to spell out why it was undesirable that I continue my travels," and introduced himself. "That's when I realized the reality of the situation, and extended my hand to Gen. Miguel Costa."[14]

Rondon was ordered off the train. He refused, telling Costa he preferred to wait for Vargas's verdict right where he was. A standoff ensued: Rondon was accustomed to giving orders and having them obeyed, and his polite but steely demeanor seemed to intimidate his captors, some of whom were openly apologetic. Under guard, Rondon also heard one of the rebels comment to another: "He is really quite dark-skinned, but when he was arrested, he turned white." (The reporter interviewing Rondon noted in his article that "the general laughed with great gusto when he mentioned this."[15])

What happened next is unclear. Vargas sent one of his main political operatives, lieutenant governor and future foreign minister João Neves da Fontoura, to meet with Rondon. Confronting delays "because the rail lines were terribly obstructed by trains" due to "the huge mass of troops that were in transit to the front," Neves da Fontoura went straight to Rondon's train car after disembarking at the station, and soon realized that "a very tall guy with a bright red kerchief around his neck" was in charge. When Costa confirmed that Rondon was inside, Vargas's emissary entered and registered that "there, truly, sat the glorious explorer, with a calm and natural air about him, surrounded by some officers." Rondon quickly explained that "he had come to our state in fulfillment of an entirely apolitical mission." Neves da Fontoura would write later in his memoirs that he tried to intervene on Rondon's behalf, telling the soldiers, "Nobody can arrest Gen. Rondon in Rio Grande do Sul. He's an old friend of our people and one of the best Brazilians there is."[16]

Those flattering words notwithstanding, Rondon remained under arrest. Neves da Fontoura wrote years later that he intervened so that "steps be taken to assure that no violence be committed against Rondon."[17] But as a trophy and bargaining chip, "the glorious explorer" was too valuable to be released: that same day, as part of an effort to discourage resistance and undermine morale, Vargas sent a telegram to the central government declaring that "the entire garrison has made common cause with the people, here and in the interior" and that the regional military commander "along with his entire staff are prisoners, as are Generals Medeiros and Rondon."[18]

To gain the prisoner's cooperation, Rondon was now told—whether by Fontoura or someone else is not clear—that Vargas was still in Porto Alegre and would see him there. Vargas had asked a group of judges to bring Rondon to the governor's palace, so the entire party departed, Rondon in tow, in a caravan of automobiles. But on arriving in Porto Alegre, Rondon discovered that he was not, after all, going to see Vargas. Instead, he was told that he was being placed under house arrest at the Grande Hotel—the same place where, in 1922, Manuel Rabelo, speaking on behalf of young military coup plotters, had offered Rondon the presidency.

For Rondon, learning that he was to be confined to a five-star hotel was especially irksome. It clashed with the ascetic streak in his character: he had never been one to seek luxury or special privileges, and now those were being imposed on him. He expressed a preference to be held aboard the navy vessel where the regional military commander and other political prisoners were being held. But the word that came back from Osvaldo Aranha, who as Vargas's interior and justice secretary oversaw the police and the state militia, was "no." The ship was already crammed full of prisoners, Aranha claimed, and could not accommodate even one more.

When Rondon was escorted to the hotel and assigned a room, he learned that Aranha and his wife were staying on the same floor. This was by design. Aranha, an eloquent lawyer, politician, and diplomat, hoped to exploit that proximity and his notable verbal skills to convince Rondon to come over to the Vargas camp. Aranha had much to recommend him to Rondon: he came from a military family, had supported the Positivist Borges de Medeiros's long reign as governor, and had fought the Costa-Prestes forces in Rio Grande do Sul while Rondon was leading the campaign against them next door, in Paraná and Santa Catarina.

Over the next quarter century, Rondon and Aranha would frequently cross paths, sometimes on opposite sides of a political or foreign policy fight, at other times as allies, but always cordially. During his public career, Aranha would serve as Brazil's justice minister, finance minister, foreign minister, and agriculture minister, ambassador to Washington, and ambassador to the United Nations, where in 1947 he was chosen president of the very first General Assembly. But over the course of several days in the Grande Hotel, his wife at his side to echo and amplify his arguments, he made no headway in his efforts to persuade Rondon to defect.

"He employed every means to convince me that I should not oppose the movement" Vargas was leading, Rondon would recall. The republic that Rondon had served so loyally over the years, Aranha argued, was now so decrepit and corrupt that it had lost all legitimacy and popular support. Under Vargas, he predicted, Brazil was going to experience a glorious process of renewal in every area, from the economy to politics. It was Rondon's patriotic duty to contribute his experience and knowledge to this revival.[19]

Rondon was unmoved. "As a Positivist," he told Aranha, "I could not agree to turning to a revolution as a means of resolving political problems. Brazil's problem was a moral one, and for that reason, only a moral solution would be admissible." Exactly what Rondon meant by this is not clear, but we can guess: as a follower of Comte, he could only accept political and social transformations that were organic and nonviolent. The "Revolution of 1930," as it came to be called, was neither. It was being imposed from above and being birthed in bloodshed.

Having played the Positivist card to dodge endorsing a position he wished to avoid, as he had done so many times before, Rondon now had Mrs. Aranha play it back at him. "It's precisely due to the fact that you are a Positivist, general, that we want your collaboration," she said. "We need you to make things clear for us."[20] But flattery did not work either.

Though he was allowed to send telegrams and letters to his wife and children and also to attend Sunday services at the Positivist Chapel in Porto Alegre, Rondon would remain in confinement for the remainder of October, as Brazil's political situation grew more confused and turbulent, and into mid-November. Forces loyal to Vargas initially controlled only pockets in the far south and the Northeast, and armed confrontations in contested areas resulted in the deaths of hundreds of people. Then, on October 24, just twenty-two days before he was scheduled to leave office, Washington Luís was deposed in a military coup and replaced by a Provisional Military Junta with three members, one of whom was Rondon's old friend Tasso Fragoso. Barely a week later, on November 3, 1930, the junta handed power over to Vargas, who quickly had the president and other leading figures of what is now called the First Republic arrested and sent into exile.

Isolated in detention, the flow of information to him strictly controlled, and without access to the usual military gossip, Rondon often misread the rapidly changing political situation developing outside. He seemed initially encouraged by Fragoso's assumption of power and by the installation of another of his old friends and classmates as governor in São Paulo, apparently not realizing both were mere stopgap appointments. And he also seemed not to comprehend that a revolution truly was underway, with no possible return to the old order. "The dictatorial situation created should last for only the absolutely necessary period, even if that enters the presidential term beginning November 15,"[21] he wrote in his diary on October 27.

The circumstances of Rondon's departure from the Brazilian Army seem complicated, messy even: Did he jump or was he pushed? Rondon himself may have contributed to this ambiguity, not wanting to admit, in order to preserve his dignity, that he was in essence cashiered; better to make it seem he left of his own volition. Thus, in the memoirs he dictated at the very end of his life, a quarter century after the events he was recounting, he described himself as profoundly insulted by the new regime's treatment of him and added that "upon assuming the leadership of the Provisional Government, Dr. Getúlio Vargas received my request for retirement."[22]

Particularly offensive—and potentially damaging to Rondon's image—were the comments of Juarez Távora. After escaping from prison in 1927, Távora went underground, and when the uprising in favor of Vargas came, though he was only thirty-two years old, he emerged as the commander of rebel troops in the Northeast, his native region. That earned him the nickname "Viceroy of the North" and made him a powerful figure in the new regime taking shape. It also gave him the chance to settle old scores, and he immediately took advantage of his newly elevated status.

In an interview with a Rio daily published on November 7, 1930, an article that was immediately picked up and republished across Brazil and which Rondon was allowed to read while still in detention, Távora renewed his old attacks on Rondon and the Rondon Commission, and added some startling new accusations. Rondon, he charged, had for decades "squandered the public's coffers, distributing telegraph lines throughout the brutish wilderness for the Indians, who used them as toys." Furthermore, he insinuated, Rondon and his men had personally profited from a lack of official oversight of their activities. "In any civilized and decently-policed country, this general would be in jail,"[23] Távora proclaimed.

Távora also made a point of noting that when Rondon was arrested, an Indian boy was in his company. This, in the context of those times, was clearly intended as an exercise in character assassination, the unspoken implication being that Rondon was a homosexual and a pedophile. But for forty years, Rondon and other members of his commissions had always followed a policy of providing medical assistance to Indigenous peoples—preferably in their own villages, but transporting them to the nearest hospital when necessary. It didn't matter whether the sick person was man or woman, young or old, boy or girl; that privilege was available to all. Everyone in the armed forces knew of this practice, Távora included, and it had been praised in various military publications as an example of the army's civic mission. But Távora put a sinister spin on a laudable humanitarian policy in an effort to besmirch Rondon's reputation.

After more than four decades on duty, Rondon felt both aggrieved and infuriated to read that he was being accused of corruption. His field diaries and other documents now on file at the army archives in Rio show him to be a scrupulous and detailed record keeper, with even the smallest of expenses—including the tips he gave to the obliging staff at the hotel where he was detained—dutifully recorded. A quarter of a century later, when Rondon dictated his memoirs, Juarez Távora's accusations still stung: "I felt offended," he wrote, citing the "long years of service to the Fatherland, totally unmindful of myself, and, what is more, with the sacrifices of my family."[24]

In November 1930, the entries Rondon made in his diaries reveal an even more pronounced sense of bitterness and resentment. "No general or official surrounding the revolutionary chiefs at this moment of delirium and revolutionary lunacy"[25] was willing to come to his defense, he lamented. "I shouldn't cooperate with a government" like the one that was taking shape, he added a couple of days later, as cabinet appointments were being announced. "I need to defend myself, to launch a vehement protest against this audacious distortion of truth and justice."[26]

Thus Rondon's immediate response was to seek vindication through official channels. He wrote to the new minister of war requesting that a court formally examine the financial records of the Rondon Commission, the Indian Protection Service, and the Border Inspectorate, and then rule whether any irregularities had occurred. But the ministry turned down that entreaty: the best that Rondon could obtain was a lukewarm statement that, given the political context of that moment, can be read in two very different ways, as either an endorsement or a veiled condemnation echoing Juarez Távora's attack. "Everyone is aware of your services,"[27] Rondon was told.

So Rondon felt betrayed by the institution that had nurtured him for so long. His departure from the army also seems to have been handled in a graceless and irregular fashion, as if to inflict maximum humiliation. In his diary, Rondon says he sent a telegram resigning his commission one hour after Vargas was sworn in, but no formal letter of resignation is on file at the Army Historical Archives in Rio de Janeiro; the only relevant document in the Rondon folders is a brief letter, two sentences long and dated November 6, 1930, Vargas's third full day in power, ordering that Rondon be removed from active duty. The document is just a blank sheet of paper, with no letterhead of any kind, but both Vargas and the new war minister signed it, and its brevity and chilly tone indicate that Rondon, after being forced to wait for a response for two days, was being deliberately cast into the political wilderness, with not even a cursory expression of thanks for all he had done for the nation.

At the time, Rondon was, along with Fragoso, the second-most-senior officer in the army, and therefore, in keeping with the principle of seniority, entitled to a post close to the heart of power. Fragoso, of course, had already made his accommodation with the new political alignment. But Vargas, aware of Rondon's opposition to the overthrow of the existing order and by now surely also aware of Aranha's failed efforts to get him to change camps, wanted Rondon out of the way; not even his friendship with Fragoso and close ties to others in the Vargas camp could save him. It thus seems more accurate to endorse the historian Frank McCann's phrase and say that Rondon was "purged," both because of ideological differences with the new regime and because Vargas wanted to put loyalists in key positions without formally violating the principle of seniority.

In total, nine two-star generals were expelled, including two of Rondon's friends who were classmates at the academy and fellow Positivists. An even larger group of brigadier generals and colonels was also dismissed, thereby giving Vargas and his minister of war latitude to remake the military high command. Though some friends were later restored to active duty, no such second chance was forthcoming for Rondon. After forty-eight years, eleven months, and eleven days of service, his splendid military career was over.

"I withdraw from a service to which I have applied myself for 40 years with constant dedication and zeal for public service, always with the greatness of Brazil and the renown of the Republic in mind," he wrote in his final diary entry as a soldier. "I take home with me the imperishable satisfaction of a duty fulfilled."[28]

— PART V —

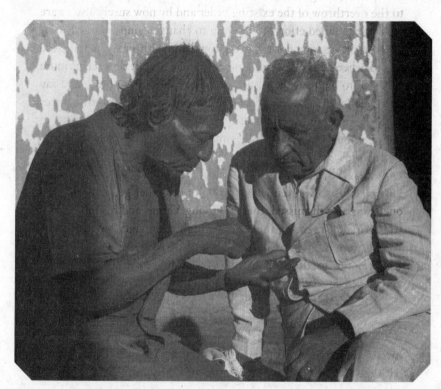

*Rondon, nearing eighty and retired from the Brazilian Army, with, at left,
Cadete, his closest Bororo friend, in Mato Grosso in 1944.*
(ACERVO DO MUSEU DO ÍNDIO/FUNAI—BRASIL)

XXIII

In the Wilderness

THE ABRUPT TRANSITION to civilian status was devastating for Rondon, especially as it was accompanied by deliberately inflicted humiliations, one after another. As a soldier, he may have spent year after year deep in the jungle, thousands of miles from the capital and its comforts, but he was always engaged in missions central to the construction of the Brazilian republic and had access to those in authority when he needed it. Now, at sixty-five, he suddenly found himself living in Rio de Janeiro, at the locus of national power, but cast out into the political wilderness, with few means to defend himself from an onslaught that seemed to come from all sides.

Released from detention on November 14 after thirty-seven days of confinement, Rondon arrived in Rio on November 21, and the next day was summoned by Vargas to the provisional government's headquarters. In his first meeting with the new "provisional" chief of state, Rondon reiterated requests that the minister of war had already summarily rejected, and each was again denied. First, feeling that his honesty and honor had been tainted, Rondon wanted the army to convene a formal court-martial, as was theoretically his right under the military code of justice then in place, to decide whether there was any substance to Távora's accusation, and then deliver a public verdict. Vargas's negative response was couched in flowery language that could be read two very different ways: "No [panel] whatsoever will be constituted," he told Rondon, "because the highest tribunal, that of the nation's public opinion, has already judged you, general."[1]

Since seizing power, Vargas himself had made no effort to defend Rondon's reputation. The new chief of state did send a telegram praising Rondon for his service to the nation, and in their first meeting "listed, with the greatest praise, all my services,"[2] Rondon wrote. But those were private communications, designed perhaps to assuage Rondon's wounded amour propre, and were not made public or even leaked to the press. Nor was any other kind of public statement attesting to Rondon's honesty and patriotism or refuting Távora's intemperate accusations.

In addition, Rondon assumed that since he was now a civilian, his military duties had ended, and promised the president to turn over the data compiled during the three border-inspection and mapping expeditions to whomever the military high command chose as his successor. But Vargas again said no, insisting, Rondon wrote, that "the reports had to be written by me." Rondon might not be a soldier anymore, but "the Fatherland hasn't discharged you yet,"[3] Vargas told him. After ordering Rondon jailed for more than a month, this was yet another way for the new chief of state to remind the heroic "Trailblazer of the Wilderness" that his destiny was not in his own hands, that Rondon's fortunes, like those of 33.5 million other Brazilians, were now under Vargas's control.

The next set of blows came when Rondon met with the government's director of telegraphs on November 25. Ordinarily, he would have conferred directly with the minister of transport and public works—but that post was being held temporarily by none other than Távora. Thus, it was the head of the telegraph department who told Rondon that the government had decided to eliminate the commission he had led for nearly a quarter century, and that management of the lines themselves was to be turned over to a new body, with new leadership. Furthermore, as of January 1, 1931, no more money would be spent on maintaining the lines, because the government had determined that its limited resources would be better spent elsewhere.

Rondon was shocked and distressed, though he should not have been surprised. "In that fashion, the Revolution decreed the extinction of a service that had cost the Nation a great deal of money and required the sacrifice of many lives, as well as the health of all of those who had thrown themselves into the task," he wrote with bitterness years later, after Vargas was dead.

Before long, a similar fate would befall the Indian Protection Service, the institution most important to Rondon. On November 26, the revolutionary government merged the existing Ministry of Industry and Commerce with a newly created Ministry of Labor. This was an early indication of the focus that would characterize Vargas's fifteen years as Brazil's dictator, during which time he became known as "the father of the poor." By putting "Labor" first in the combined ministry's name, Vargas was making a symbolic statement in favor of the urban working class, an increasingly important constituency in Brazilian society during his tenure.

For the Indigenous cause, however, this new arrangement immediately proved damaging. Quite aware of the new government's antipathy toward him, Rondon had already stepped away from any public role in the SPI, as had Botelho de Magalhães, who, fatally tainted by his association with Rondon, would soon be assigned to a remote border post. The SPI's new director was a very capable military man and veteran Indian expert, Lt. Col. Vicente Vasconcellos, who had been on several expeditions with Rondon as a junior officer and also advocated a policy of nonviolence. But he had nowhere near the same clout or negotiating skills as Rondon.

So when the SPI was folded into the new Ministry of Labor, Industry and Commerce, Vasconcellos could not prevent it. As part of the Agriculture Ministry, where it had resided since its founding in 1910, the SPI had always enjoyed some autonomy, in large part because of Rondon's prestige. But within the new ministry, Vasconcellos would later complain, it was reduced to "constituting a simple Section of the Directorate of Settlements" in the labor department of the new ministry, a significant downgrade.

This relocation to a new ministry pointed to the government's intention, sooner or later, to begin a settlement program for surplus labor, from the urban as well as the rural poor, that would be national in scope and inevitably encroach on designated Indigenous areas. And secondly, it suggested that the Vargas regime regarded the Indian population primarily as a source of labor to be integrated into the workforce, not as peoples deserving of special status. Looking back in 1939, Vasconcellos wrote that this initial step was tantamount to "extinguishing" the SPI.[4]

The budget cuts began in 1931, and they were crippling. Vasconcellos would later say that the SPI "constantly, and under all pretexts," tried to convince the new authorities of "the necessity of caring for the Indians" and "requesting the indispensable resources"[5] to do so. But with coffee exports severely affected by the worldwide depression, the new government's finances were constrained, and it had already made clear that its priorities lay elsewhere. So the SPI was forced to make cutbacks so drastic that even routine maintenance of its posts in tribal areas had to be suspended. "As regards the past, our Service has only nostalgia," Vasconcellos remarked ruefully, "and as regards the future, great hopes."[6] The present, however, was one of frustration, one disappointment after another.

The impact of this new attitude was immediate, and obvious to travelers venturing deep into the interior. Joseph Audrin, for example, was a French-born Dominican friar and senior cleric for his order in the diocese of Conceição do Araguaia, just a bit downriver from the point where three Amazonian states meet. His area of responsibility included Bananal Island, the world's largest freshwater island, more than twice the size of Puerto Rico, home to the Carajá tribe, with a flourishing SPI post that Rondon had inspected late in 1929 and at which Audrin often stopped while on pastoral missions.

Visiting the Bananal station in August 1930, Audrin wrote a year later to SPI headquarters in Rio, he could not help but be "impressed by the prosperity of the Post. There was a large nucleus of Carajá Indians who were well-dressed, well-fed, already engrossed in productive work under the direction of employees of the Service." In addition, there was a school that both the Carajá and the SPI employees and their children attended, as well as "a large number of buildings, trim and neat," and well-tended fields, along with processing mills for the crops they produced, like cassava and sugarcane.

But when Audrin passed through again, early in September 1931, everything was in disarray. "I saw a very different spectacle," one that allowed him to "verify the more than precarious situation of the colony," he continued. "Such was my disappointment, my sadness, I heard so many complaints from the Carajá that I cannot help but communicate all of this to someone who can understand."

"Such a transformation is inadmissible," Audrin concluded. "The Government born of the Revolution should not disdain and interrupt an effort that was one of the most effective initiatives of the regime that has fallen. It can monitor and correct, but it cannot destroy."[7]

But it was not only Bananal that was affected. Along Rondon's telegraph lines in Mato Grosso, the situation soon became even more dire, for the Vargas regime was as a matter of policy neglecting both the stations and the Indians who had flocked to them. When the French anthropologist Claude Lévi-Strauss traveled along the route in 1935 as part of the journey that would inspire his classic study *Tristes tropiques*, he could not help but notice the state of desolation and abandonment that prevailed in the region. This was true both for whites who had remained behind after the line was built, expecting to be joined by subsequent waves of settlers, and the no-less-credulous Indians who had flocked to these "poles of attraction."

"Anyone living on the Rondon line might well believe he was living on the moon," Lévi-Strauss wrote. "The unfortunate inhabitants . . . stranded there, cut off from all contact with the civilized world . . . developed different forms of madness so as to adapt to their solitary existence in tiny stations, each consisting of a few straw huts and separated from each other by distances of 80 to 100 kilometers, which can only be covered on foot."[8]

The stations were, of course, meant to serve a dual purpose, functioning as both telegraph posts and SPI bases. But in the absence of the promised and initially provided support and services, some Indian groups began to drift back to the jungle, Lévi-Strauss noted. Others, however, found themselves unable to resume their former way of life: now dependent on government support, they had already begun to lose essential wilderness skills. Both outcomes were an unraveling of Rondon's carefully established methodology.

The government's disdainful, deliberately demeaning treatment left Rondon dejected and depressed. For forty years, ever since leaving the military academy, he had always kept a diary, filled with scientific observations, accounts of his adventures, and reflections on subjects ranging from the books he was reading to expressions of his yearnings for Chiquita. But now, for the first time, he went completely silent: "True happiness consists of precisely carrying out one's duty," he wrote in his last entry of the year, in mid-December. More than a month went by before he picked up his pen, and then shortly after, he went quiet again. It was not until March 1931 that he resumed writing in his journal on a daily basis, though the entries were curt.

Stripped of the day-to-day responsibilities of command, Rondon turned to scientific pursuits, which provided some solace. He was still welcome at the National Museum, where Roquette-Pinto had been appointed director in 1926. At home, he began work on the manuscript that would eventually yield his three-volume work *The Indians of Brazil*—published only in 1946, after Vargas's ouster—and also continued his linguistic studies of Indigenous languages, compiling grammars and dictionaries that were also published in the late 1940s. His diaries show him socializing, with accounts of lunches with old friends and outings with Chiquita.

Rondon was also able to deepen his involvement in the cause of "nature protection," a forerunner to today's global environmental movement. Concepts such as conservation, preservation, and ecologism were used interchangeably during this early phase, but certain values were held in common by all who worried about the future of Brazil's vast landscapes and natural resources. These included imposing limits, if not an absolute halt, on deforestation, as well as strengthening the country's toothless Federal Forest Service, organized in 1925, but chronically underfunded, and pushing for federal legislation to regulate the commercial exploitation of forests, rivers, and wildlife.

Rondon's embrace of this cause was as much intuitive and emotional as intellectual. From his earliest years he had been enthralled by natural wonders. His field notebooks and diaries were filled with keen observations and drawings of animal and plant life. He admired the reverence of Indigenous peoples for the physical world, and wished to preserve it for them. And on the rare occasions he was moved to write poetry, it was almost always to rhapsodize about some aspect of nature, as in "Invocation," a recollection of his childhood home in Mimoso that begins: "Incomparable Garden of Nature, framed by green hillsides, adorned with towering palms and dense ranges of marsh plants, surrounded by voluminous bays flowing into the Ibitiraí River."[10]

Aware that his association with any reform movement would be harmful, Rondon was careful not to take a public role in such efforts. But he was in regular contact with the two most prominent advocates of the "nature protection" movement: Alberto José Sampaio and Frederico Carlos Hoehne, botanists who had accompanied him on expeditions. With the increasingly authoritarian Vargas government planning to draft a new constitution to replace the original republican charter of 1891, Rondon advised his former subordinates where they might find allies within the government and pointed them toward sympathetic voices in the press, all the while remaining in the background as the Constitutional Assembly began its deliberations in November 1933.

Both Sampaio and Hoehne had thrown themselves into this battle and organized new entities with two related objectives in mind: to pressure the government and to educate and engage the public. Hoehne's group, centered in São Paulo, was called Society of Friends of the Brazilian Forest, while Sampaio's, founded in 1931 and based in Rio, took an even more quixotic name: Society of Friends of the Trees. They were joined by colleagues and Rondon Commission alumni from the National Museum in Rio, including Roquette-Pinto.

The new constitution, promulgated in June 1934, did indeed include articles that imposed on the federal and state governments the duty to protect "natural beauties" and "monuments of historic or artistic value,"[11] but their implementation was left vague. Shortly before, in April, the "First Brazilian Conference on Nature Protection" had been held in Rio, drawing scientific, civic, horticultural, religious, feminist, and other groups, each intent on pressuring the Vargas regime to implement the promises already known to be contained in the new draft charter. Rondon attended the weeklong conference, whose chairman was Sampaio, reminding delegates not to forget Indigenous peoples and the role they could play in protecting Brazil's rich natural patrimony.

Rondon's lack of influence in the early years of the Vargas dictatorship, however, crippled his ability to achieve the goal he regarded as most important. During the assembly that drew up the 1891 constitution, the Positivist bloc proposed creating independent Indigenous homelands within Brazil, but that idea was ridiculed and rejected. By 1934, Rondon's objective was far more modest: working through intermediaries, he sought an explicit statement of official protection of Indians and their lands.

On one level, he succeeded, because the new constitution, for the first time in Brazilian history, formally guaranteed Indian rights. Specifically, Article 129 promised that "Native ownership of land they permanently occupy will be respected, it being prohibited, however, to divest said lands." But Rondon was wary of this formulation: he knew from decades in the field that many tribes were nomadic, and thus would not be eligible to have the territory in which they roamed protected in any form. Furthermore, Article 5 specifically called for "incorporation of jungle-dwellers into the national community," which seemed to open the door to all kinds of abuse.

Almost simultaneously with the proclamation of the new constitution, Rondon's official ostracism suddenly ended. He was given an important diplomatic mission, much to his surprise and initial suspicion. He did not trust Vargas, whose real intentions he found hard to gauge, and he was also being asked to take on a daunting responsibility in a field that seemed, at least on the surface, outside his area of expertise. In addition, if he failed, the result most likely would be war.

Rondon was being asked to resolve a border dispute in the western Amazon between two of Brazil's neighbors. In 1932, Peru and

Colombia had briefly fought over the so-called Leticia Trapezoid, a long finger of territory adjacent to Brazil that gave Colombia access to the Amazon River and, by extension, the South Atlantic, which it had coveted since independence a century earlier. The town of Leticia, with excellent port facilities, had actually been founded by Peruvian settlers in 1867, but was awarded to Colombia in a 1922 treaty that proved widely unpopular in Peru, provoking riots so severe that the Congress there dared to ratify the accord only in 1928.

Four years later, on September 1, 1932, some three hundred armed civilians from Peru seized Leticia; when Colombia responded by ordering 1,500 troops to the town, two Peruvian Army regiments were dispatched, and seized both Leticia and Tarapacá, another settlement in the disputed area. Colombian troops resisted, there was skirmishing in the streets with military and civilian casualties, Peruvian planes bombed the town and Colombian vessels at the port, and both countries ordered their Pacific fleets to begin the journey north to the Panama Canal, after which they were to proceed across the Caribbean to the mouth of the Amazon and finally upriver through Brazilian territory to the zone of conflict. To make matters worse, Ecuador, which had unresolved border disputes of its own with both Colombia and Peru, was threatening to deploy its troops, since in return for receiving Leticia, Colombia had relinquished to Peru land in the Amazon that Ecuador also claimed.

Looming in the background was the threat of American involvement: the original 1922 treaty was brokered by American secretary of state Charles Evans Hughes, and Washington wanted it fully enforced. Peru was convinced—as were Ecuador and even Brazil—that Washington had been exceedingly generous with Colombia as a form of indirect compensation to that country for the American seizure of Panama, originally a province of Colombia, two decades earlier. Then, when Colombia bought a dozen war planes and hired American pilots to fly them—pilots who just happened to be U.S. Marine Corps reservists—and a Peruvian warship was denied access to repair facilities in the Panama Canal, the United States seemed to be taking sides even while trying to avoid intervening openly in the region.

For Brazil, historically averse to armed conflict, this was a situation fraught with peril. Its westernmost frontier on the Amazon River abutted Leticia, and it maintained friendly relations with both hostile parties and also with Ecuador and the United States, ties it wanted to preserve. This was one of the most inaccessible sections of Brazil's land borders: the sole official presence along it was a small military garrison at Tabatinga, hard to supply or protect and separated from Leticia only by a small obelisk demarcating the frontier. If the conflict were to spill over into Brazil, as seemed possible, the Vargas government would have great difficulty defending Brazilian territory and would be pilloried in the national press.

In addition, the few Brazilian residents of the area, known as the Three Frontiers, were already complaining loudly to newspapers back in the capital, as trade with both Colombia and Peru plummeted. So when the League of Nations negotiated a cease-fire on May 24, 1933, and dispatched an international peacekeeping force— the first in its history sent to the Americas—to take control of the contested territory, the Vargas regime had little choice but to acquiesce to the league's request that Brazil mediate the dispute.

It was in every way a prickly situation, and it soon became clear that Vargas expected Rondon to resolve the standoff. The Brazilian Foreign Ministry had given the president a list of potential mediators, and Vargas later claimed that as soon as he saw Rondon's name, he said to himself, "He's the one!" Rondon protested that he was not a diplomat, but Vargas came back with a reply designed to appeal to Rondon's patriotic instincts while also acknowledging the depth of the mutual suspicion that existed between the two men.

"Pardon me, Your Excellency, but I can't accept this undertaking," Rondon would later, in his memoirs, recall telling Vargas at the start of their conversation. "With the Indians, I was in my element, because I dedicated my life to them and their problems, concluding that this was the best way for me to serve the fatherland. I only accept those assignments that I am certain I can efficiently carry out, and this one, from the beginning, is destined for resounding failure." Another factor, one that Rondon did not mention to Vargas but that he disclosed in his memoirs, was his reluctance to take on the assignment due to "being a friend of Washington Luis," whom Vargas had so recently overthrown and sent into exile, and for fear of "being branded a camp-follower."[12]

The president, used to getting his way, was not pleased: Rondon describes him as stiffening, rising to his feet, and becoming quite solemn upon hearing Rondon's initial refusal. But Vargas was always an astute judge of character and never above appealing to an individual's vanity, before invoking threats. After unsuccessfully trying several other gambits, which Rondon efficiently parried, he resorted to the final opening provided by Rondon's protests, and promptly maneuvered right through it.

"Well, General, this is precisely about serving the fatherland," Vargas responded after Rondon again expressed his doubts about the mission. "You're not serving me or my government. It is the nation that demands that you accept."[13] With that, Rondon was effectively cornered, and could only choose the lesser of two unpalatable options: either accede to Vargas's entreaty or betray the patriotic values he had embraced as a military cadet fifty years before.

Rondon left Rio on June 16, 1934. He had been away from the Amazon for four years, the longest absence from his native region since graduation from the military academy in 1890. After flying directly to Manaus, he reunited with Joaquim Tanajura, the doctor on the grueling 1909 expedition, and enlisted him as both the secretary-general of the newly formed border-dispute commission and its attending physician. Also joining the Brazilian permanent staff was Lt. Joaquim Rondon, who was not only kin to Rondon but had also explored and mapped the Putumayo River east of Brazil's border with Colombia, where it changes name and becomes known as the Içá.

As Rondon spelled out their mission to his two aides, the complexity of the challenge became clear. Colombia and Peru had signed a "protocol of friendship and cooperation" in Rio just weeks before, in which they promised to "continue, through normal diplomatic means, to seek a just, enduring and satisfactory resolution to all pending problems," including demilitarization of the contested zone. To supervise and monitor this process, the accord called for creation of a tripartite mixed commission whose president would be a Brazilian—namely, Rondon.

That was an even more difficult task than it appeared, Rondon explained. For while the protocol ordered him to "assure the execution"[14] of its terms over a four-year period, it gave him precious little authority. He had no troops or police under his command, and the League of Nations peacekeeping force had been withdrawn when Brazil assumed responsibility. The Rio Protocol explicitly stated that the mixed commission "does not have police powers, administrative functions or judicial competency,"[15] and within its area of operation, existing local civilian and military forces "will exercise their authority to the fullest." In other words, Rondon would have to operate almost entirely on the basis of moral suasion and personal prestige. It would require the same negotiating skills he had employed with Indigenous groups.

From Manaus, Rondon and his aides journeyed up the Amazon to the Three Frontiers. Once there, they had to establish an office for the commission and decent housing for themselves. This proved a difficult task. Despite its status as "capital" of the Colombian Amazon, Leticia had barely two hundred inhabitants, about half of whom considered themselves Peruvians and were loyal to Lima rather than Bogotá. Most residents lived in wooden shacks built on stilts along the riverbank and many suffered from diseases like malaria, dysentery, and hookworm. Bogotá was 675 miles away, separated from its precarious Amazon outpost by several hundred miles of impassable jungle and the peaks and valleys of the Andes Mountains. That meant that mail, basic foodstuffs, medicine, and other essential supplies were exorbitantly expensive and reached Leticia only irregularly.

In spite of all of this, Rondon made his headquarters in Leticia rather than look for housing on the Brazilian side, at the military base in Tabatinga. This allowed Rondon to become privy to all of the local doings and gossip—political, military, and commercial— that were included in the reports sent back to the Foreign Ministry in Rio. That inside information allowed him to intervene immediately, as proved necessary anytime hostilities between Peruvians and Colombians erupted at the port or in town and threatened to escalate.

In the end, the only adequate location for a headquarters that Rondon could find was at a hacienda just outside the town limits. He lived there for a time, with Tanajura and Joaquim, but at the end of 1934 asked the three governments for permission to have a simple house of wood planks built as his residence. It was in this austere, even monastic, setting, with little more than a photograph of Chiquita, a radio, and stacks of books, newspapers, and magazines as decoration, that Rondon lived for nearly four years, trying to prevent another outbreak of war and fashion a lasting peace, "never absenting myself from my post for even a single day" during the duration of the commission's work.[16]

Beyond his diplomatic duties, Rondon had little to occupy him other than the fiestas the two delegations regularly celebrated. Chiquita twice joined him for long stays in Leticia—first in 1935 for ten months and then again in 1937—so he was able at times to have a normal home life in his spartan surroundings. But he nonetheless ended up paying a high personal price for his stubborn attention to duty.

"I began to feel something abnormal was happening with my eyes and, supposing it to be cataracts, I awaited my return to Rio to consult an oculist" in 1938, he wrote in his memoirs. "But by then it was already too late, glaucoma had rendered one of my eyes useless and reduced the other to one-quarter of normal vision, which gradually began declining even further."[17] Eventually, Rondon would become legally blind, and would spend much of the last decade of his life almost entirely sightless.

In his free time, Rondon acquainted himself with the Indigenous peoples of the Three Frontiers. There were several different groups, among them the Huitoto, whose population had been devastated by decades of slave raids and impressment by rubber-plantation owners, and the Inga, Quechua-speaking descendants of the Inca. But Rondon drew especially close to the Ticuna and the Tucano, peoples whose traditional territory straddles the Brazil-Colombia border. His formal agenda may have been filled with meetings and dress-uniform diplomatic receptions on national holidays, but his diary indicates how much he relished the time spent talking with chiefs and shamans of the two groups, who regularly came to visit him in Leticia. That these tribal leaders also happened to be excellent sources of intelligence about everything happening in the region, including troop movements, was, in Rondon's view, a bonus: these informal encounters gave him real pleasure, and lightened his official burdens.

Whether for reasons related to the border dispute or because of continued reports of slave labor in the Amazon, Rondon also very much wanted to inspect the upper Putumayo River, which forms the border between Colombia and both Peru and Ecuador. He had been monitoring such activities even before reading Casement's 1910 account of abuses there; now he again had an opportunity to assess the situation himself, under official auspices. Neither Colombia nor Peru, however, particularly wanted him to do that, initially requesting that the Brazilian staff "clarify the motive of our visit" and demanding over and over again that he supply "information they already knew" about an itinerary. So many bureaucratic obstacles were placed in Rondon's way that in the end "I was forced to speak energetically"[18]—his diplomatic way of saying that he lost his temper.

In August 1936, the commission finally departed. Much to Rondon's amusement, the voyage was a rustic one, bringing back memories of his old days of adventure and demonstrating that, in contrast to his citified companions, he was still in top physical form at the age of seventy-one. "It would have been an agreeable voyage but for the lack of firewood, for which we had to stop many times to retrieve from the riverbank," he wrote. "We also were constantly jumping off to hunt and cut grass for the cattle we had on board with us."[19] Passing through Leticia just before the Putumayo voyage, the Swedish explorer, photographer, and human rights campaigner Rolf Blomberg met Rondon and described him as "a vigorous personality and humane character" who struck Indians and Europeans alike as "a colorful mix of soldier and apostle."[20]

What Rondon saw on his new journey up the Putumayo left him aghast. The global economy was still mired in the Great Depression: as a result, automobile sales everywhere had plummeted, together with the demand for rubber. Once-prosperous plantations were in "ruins," he found, due either to the collapse of markets or to the earlier fighting between Peru and Colombia. And the workers were in a pitiable state. "I was able to verify the sad situation of the Indians, abandoned by the authorities and exploited by the businessmen and rubber-tappers, who enslaved them."[21]

In places where small, independent plantations once operated, Rondon found that enslaved Indian workers had simply been left to their fate. This was a significant problem, he concluded, because after so many years of forced servitude, the Indigenous groups had lost not only their cultural identity and health but also skills that had allowed them to live self-sufficiently in the jungle. Peru did not have any kind of government Indian service, Rondon noted ruefully, and Colombia had essentially outsourced responsibility for Indigenous affairs to Franciscan friars from the Roman Catholic Church. So he ordered Dr. Tanajura to provide as much medical care as possible to ill and hungry Indians living in the depopulated zone.

Initially skeptical of the Franciscans' presence, Rondon came to see them, albeit reluctantly, as a force for good. On a philosophical level, loyal as always to the teaching of Comte, he continued to oppose any fusion of functions between church and state. But during his years in Leticia, Rondon visited several Franciscan-run schools and missions on Colombian soil, and expressed approval of their methods of instruction and catechism, which he saw as more gentle and tolerant than those of his Salesian adversaries. Rondon's experience in Colombia, combined with reports from Brazil of Catholic orders trying to mitigate the collapse of the SPI, slightly improved his view of religious missionaries.

By September 7, 1936, Brazil's Independence Day, Rondon was on his way back to Leticia and was able to reflect on his own mission as his boat chugged its way downriver. As he observed the tortuous zigzag course of the river, it seemed to him a metaphor for both his own situation and the larger "bilateral struggle." He was descending "the river that is central to the question, as sinuous as the path on which the diplomacy of the two countries had for so long exhausted itself," he wrote, and full of "twists and turns, bends and switchbacks, of advances and retreats," through "truly parallel tracks along which two vessels some distance from each other, though following the same course, offer the curious spectacle of heading in opposite directions."[22]

Early in 1937, Rondon had to fend off efforts to drag him back into Brazilian politics, a reminder of the messy presidential transition fifteen years prior. The 1934 constitution had granted Getúlio Vargas a four-year mandate as president, but he could not succeed himself. Wishing to remain in power, and with just a year remaining in his term, he was seeking ways to circumvent this term limit. One possibility was to have his party run a pliant yes-man on its ticket, allowing Vargas to continue wielding power indirectly after an election victory ensured by systematic ballot-stuffing. He hoped to appoint a seven-member electoral tribunal to supervise and certify such a vote, and wanted Rondon as a member, perhaps even its chairman.

Rondon regarded this prospect with dread and alarm. He was loath to sacrifice his reputation for rectitude in the service of a caudillo he deeply distrusted. In fact, his aversion to Vargas and his autocratic style of rule was so widely known that in April 1937 a coalition of opposition forces approached him about running for president in 1938 against Vargas or his handpicked candidate.

But that idea also held little appeal for Rondon. "I was never ambitious" as regards politics or wealth, he explained. "I began my career, after concluding my military engineering courses, by declining the offer of a large sum of money to survey the vast holdings of a rich landowner, because I had already promised to accompany Gomes Carneiro into the wilderness." His reservations about accepting elected or appointive offices were "widely-known facts," he added. "I therefore considered it a joke" either to run as a candidate or to sit at the head of an electoral tribunal. Both were courses of action that "do not mesh with my ideals." In the end, the issue proved moot because Vargas decided to forgo any kind of election and simply hold on to power. Rondon's reservations, once again, were justified.[23]

In sending Rondon to Leticia, Vargas probably had a variety of motives, one of which, in all likelihood, was simply to park him in a kind of prestigious exile where he could engage in no mischief. If so, Vargas was successful, for Rondon was out of sight and out of mind for almost exactly four years, unable to protect the institutions that he had created and that Vargas was eviscerating. But Rondon was successful, too: he fulfilled his diplomatic mission, preventing Colombian and Peruvian tempers from flaring and thereby averting another outbreak of armed conflict. This was no easy task, for within three years, Peru would again go to war over a disputed border, this time with Ecuador. But by then, Rondon had returned home to Rio de Janeiro, and was sparring once again with Vargas.

XXIV

Old Rondon versus the "New State"

FTER A LEISURELY journey down the Amazon and along Brazil's Atlantic coast, his diplomatic service finally over, Rondon arrived in Rio de Janeiro on August 4, 1938, to a hero's welcome. Osvaldo Aranha, who had sought in vain to convince him to support Vargas in 1930, was now foreign minister, and made the homecoming another instrument to try to win Rondon over. A Carnival-like reception was organized at the dock. Then came a downtown parade, a ceremony, and a lavishly laudatory speech at the Foreign Ministry, where Rondon was awarded a medal, the Great Cross of the Order of Military Merit.

Amid the multitude greeting Rondon were members of his family. One of his granddaughters, the future nun Maria Cecilia Rondon Amarante, was ten years old at the time, but eighty years later she would vividly recall details of an event suddenly marred by an unknown man's words behind her: "What, he's colored?!?!" the stranger blurted out, astonished, on seeing Rondon descend the gangplank. "Yes, and what of it?" Maria Cecilia replied indignantly. She would have said more, she recalled, but her mother, Clotilde, silenced her, and the festivities continued.[1]

"The extraordinary homages rendered yesterday to General Rondon are more than deserved, since they are due to his exceptional qualities," one columnist wrote, in an account that typified the floridly enthusiastic tone of press coverage the next day. "This rustic wanderer in a patriotic cause, a traveler with ideals, a trail-blazer by destiny, devoted to his task, a pioneer by temperament, indefatigable in pursuit of his duty, stoic by profession, a soldier for peace, guardian of frontiers that he himself helped demarcate and of a wilderness that he himself helped unveil as part of the most noble of conquests, the holiest of victories, this Rondon is a national glory who combines the highest military and civilian virtues."²

Such effusive praise signaled the high public esteem Rondon continued to enjoy despite his political problems and four years away from the capital. Brazil itself, however, had changed drastically during his absence, and not for the better. In November 1935, Communists and dissident military officers led by his old adversary Prestes had attempted to overthrow Vargas, and were crushed. Using the uprising as justification to expand his own power, Vargas gradually established a quasi-Fascist tropical police state: in November 1937 he decreed the Estado Novo, or "New State," shutting down Congress, declaring a state of emergency, disbanding all political parties, outlawing strikes, creating a permanent political police, appointing interventors to replace governors and mayors, and unleashing the persecution of political dissenters on both the left and the right. Angered by what they saw as Vargas's betrayal of a tacit alliance, the Integralists, Brazil's homegrown Fascist movement, then twice attempted—on March 11 and May 11, 1938—to seize power, including with an attack on the presidential residence meant to assassinate Vargas. Those involved in the Integralist uprisings were either executed, imprisoned, or forced into exile, further adding to a somber and anxious political atmosphere that Rondon could not fail to register once he returned home.

Rondon was now seventy-three, but still fit and clearly wanting to continue to play a role in public life despite his worsening eyesight. As always, he was most interested in the fortunes of the SPI, which had been gutted in his absence and allowed to become a den of incompetence and corruption. But he proceeded with caution in the climate of repression and fear, especially because of his own complicated relationship with Vargas. The president, fortified by another new constitution, promulgated in 1937, giving him extraordinary and arbitrary powers, returned Rondon's distrust. Rondon had seen friends who had supported the overthrow of the republic in 1930 fall into disgrace as Vargas consolidated his hold on the country, and had also observed others, more opportunistic, rise to powerful positions through flattery, deceit, and betrayal of friends and principles.

Luckily, though, Rondon had a handful of sympathizers sprinkled throughout the upper echelons of the New State. Among them was his former protégé from Mato Grosso, Eurico Gaspar Dutra, who had distinguished himself during the quelling of the Communist uprising in 1935, had been promoted to general, and was now minister of war. But Rondon's chief protector and ally was a civilian with an innocuous-sounding but influential post deep within the bureaucracy: Luís Simões Lopes, director of the newly created Public Service Administrative Department, known by the acronym DASP. Only thirty-five, Simões Lopes was the son of Rondon's colleague on the commission investigating the drought in the Northeast in 1922; he had accompanied his father, serving as his secretary, and admired Rondon's intelligence and rectitude. His current position gave him enormous sway over appointments to government jobs, the budget, and access to Vargas himself.

From the start, DASP was "an extremely powerful organ," perhaps even "all-powerful," Simões Lopes would later write. "Operating alongside the president, it sought to give him counsel, so as to enable him not only to reform, renew and transform the old administrative machinery, but also to make decisions about the many thousands of documents, projects and studies that came into his hands for deliberation."[3] Especially important was DASP's control of the government's purse strings, he added: "He who controls the federal government's budget ends up dominating the administration, in various aspects. The budget is simply a translation into numbers of a plan for governing."[4] Simões Lopes, considered by some to be the second-most-powerful man in Brazil, trusted Rondon, and was often willing to run interference for him, repeatedly refuting Vargas's misgivings about him.

And despite the legacy of mutual suspicion between Vargas and Rondon, the corporatist New State and its ideologues now regarded the old explorer as a valuable trophy, if only for purposes of propaganda and promotion of the emerging racial doctrine of the "new tropical man." With Vargas's ascension to power, Brazil had finally begun to turn away from a policy of "whitening" its population through European immigration and instead expressed pride in the miscegenation that had been a feature since colonial times. No longer a source of shame, it was transformed into a symbol of national self-esteem, and Rondon was the ideal poster boy.

Rondon was thus often prominently featured in newsreels and written about in newspapers and magazines, all of which the Vargas regime heavily censored in order to exclude ideas that clashed with official positions. As a younger man, Rondon—whether through his own work or via the writings of his acolytes—had always fought against the prevailing scientific racism of the time, which prevented him from receiving the global recognition he deserved. Now the trajectory of his own life, as manifested in both his racial background and his many achievements, had become one of the foundations of a new doctrine, meant to turn scientific racism on its head and argue for the superiority of mixed-race individuals.

Perhaps the best example of how the New State employed Rondon's name and image for its own purposes came in connection with its "March to the West," which was announced with great fanfare in 1938 and quickly became one of the Vargas dictatorship's most important objectives. Overtly modeled on the United States' expansion to the Pacific following the American Civil War, the "Marcha para o Oeste" was intended to fill Brazil's "empty" spaces and shift population growth away from the Atlantic coast, reducing social inequalities while sparking an acceleration of the economy. Only through this great patriotic crusade, Vargas argued, could Brazil truly find its national identity and destiny—what he grandly called "the true sentiment of Brazilianness."[5]

Parts of this program coincided with positions Rondon had long advocated. To implement the March to the West, the New State created new government agencies to aid the drive to open the interior: a National Council of Cartography, the Brazilian Institute of Geography and Statistics, a National Highway Construction Department.

But, as always, it was the status of the Indian Protection Service and overall well-being of Indigenous peoples that preoccupied Rondon. After he was arrested, the shrunken SPI had been passed from one ministry to another, losing authority and funding with each transfer. By the time he returned to Rio, it was part of the War Ministry, subordinate to the Border Inspectorate. When Rondon was expelled from the army at the end of 1930, the SPI supervised scores of posts in every region of the country, but most had been neglected and many were now abandoned. Fearful for the fate of the Indians, Rondon was determined to revive the agency, and was willing to accommodate Vargas to do so.

There is no documentary evidence that Rondon and Vargas formally negotiated an understanding, and they avoided the subject in memoirs and other books written by their subordinates. But the sequence of events throughout 1938 and especially 1939 is highly suggestive, and Rondon's public declarations are striking in their tone. His first objective was to liberate the SPI from the inattention it was suffering under military control and return it to its original home, the Ministry of Agriculture. This was achieved on November 3, 1939, after Rondon lobbied Minister of War Dutra. In a decree authorizing the move, Vargas argued that a change was necessary to the success of his March to the West: "The problem of protecting the Indians is intimately linked to the question of colonization, since one is dealing, from a material point of view, with orienting and encouraging indigenous peoples to cultivate the soil, in order that they become useful to the country and able to collaborate with civilized populations."[6]

On November 19, a speech Rondon had delivered four days earlier to mark the fiftieth anniversary of the overthrow of the monarchy was published in leading newspapers in the capital. In his remarks, Rondon favorably compared Vargas to Benjamin Constant, using Positivist arguments to do so. He condemned the concept of a republic as "a negative organization, metaphysical and democratic," and praised the Vargas dictatorship as progressing toward the ideal regime his philosophical guides Constant and Comte sought: "a responsible government, alien to rhetoric, theological and philosophical fictions, the absurd majority process; and to political deals and the resultant exploitation of the productive base of the nation, the proletarian masses."[7]

This was nonsense, pure and simple, and Rondon, given his knowledge of the inner workings of the Vargas dictatorship, had to have known it. Vargas's rule was built on a series of fictions, and he maintained his power through dealmaking and, when that failed, intimidation. But Vargas must have liked what he heard, because three days later, he decreed the creation of a new government agency, to be called the National Council for the Protection of the Indian, and put Rondon in charge. The SPI would continue to exist, but it would now have a more limited function. The job of the new CNPI, as it came to be known, was to determine overall policy toward Indigenous peoples, while the SPI would be confined primarily to executing those guidelines. After nearly a decade of marginalization, Rondon was once again able to implement, this time from within the New State, "an indigenous policy that could maintain the social cohesiveness of the race and assure the happiness of the Indian."[8]

In his memoirs, Rondon equivocated about the process that brought him back into government. "I was not consulted about the appointment, about which I only became aware when it was published" in the official gazette, he claimed. "I acquiesced to this honorable designation and with the idea of continuing in active service, despite my advanced years."[9] In reality, he was playing a complicated, multilevel political game, and would continue to do so for the duration of the New State. Though Rondon was now formally an official of the Vargas regime, he had an agenda of his own, and would quietly pursue it even when it clashed with the president's. In some instances over the next six years, he would also actively conspire from within to weaken Vargas's hold on power or frustrate his objectives. But of course Vargas was engaged in the same kind of game with him, for, as Machiavelli wrote, "the Prince must strive to hold close his allies, but it is of more importance to hold close his enemies."[10]

One result of Rondon's gradual rapprochement with the Vargas regime—and his friendship with the young director of DASP—was a sudden infusion of money into the moribund SPI. In the early

1950s, the young anthropologist Darcy Ribeiro, the last of a long line of Rondon protégés, analyzed forty years of SPI budgets, and his findings are illuminating. Between its founding in 1910 and the end of the First Republic in 1930, the agency's budget had more than tripled in real terms, thanks largely to Rondon's efforts. In 1931, however, the SPI suffered cuts of 60 percent, and further reductions followed, so that by 1937 its budget was only a quarter of what it had been in 1930. But immediately upon Rondon's return from Colombia and the creation of the CNPI, funding began to rise again; by the end of the 1940s, the budget was as robust as it had been at its peak two decades earlier.[11]

"The preservation of the SPI and the rehabilitation of Gen. Rondon's political prestige from 1938 onward . . . began to change the panorama for Brazil's indigenous peoples," the anthropologist Mércio Pereira Gomes, author of *The Indian in History*, explains. "In the last years of the Vargas dictatorship, amidst the March to the West program, and through the early 1950s, the SPI renewed itself, opened itself to new cadres, especially anthropologists, and began the process of demarcating indigenous lands by using anthropological criteria, thereby confronting political diktats with greater boldness. As a result, the delineation of indigenous lands now took into account the cultural modes of indigenous peoples, their areas of economic production, including the territory they roamed for hunting and fishing, and thus indigenous landholdings came to be of a size much greater than they had been in the 1920s and 1930s."[12]

The long, awkward courtship between Rondon and the New State culminated in August 1940 in a carefully choreographed trip in which Vargas, following an itinerary Rondon helped plan, flew initially to Goiânia, for the inauguration of the first of what were meant to be several planned cities built under the aegis of the March to the West. From there, it was just a short hop to Bananal. That island is inhabited by several Indigenous peoples, some of whom were still hostile to outsiders in 1940, but at Rondon's suggestion, Vargas decided to visit a village of the Carajá tribe, which had first come in contact with Europeans in the mid-seventeenth century and in the early years of the nineteenth century fought a war that forced Portuguese troops to withdraw.

By the time of the New State, the number of Carajá had been greatly reduced by disease, and they were officially classified as "pacified," with an SPI post on the island to attend to them. The Posto Redenção, opened in 1928 and visited by Rondon later that same year, quickly attracted members of both the Carajá and Javaé tribes with offers of medical care, education, and agricultural extension courses. But "the protection of the republican government was interrupted in 1931," as Rondon put it in the deliberately dry and neutral tone he adopted so as not to offend Vargas and his coterie, when the post became "extinct due to lack of funds."[13] What really happened was this: at Távora's order, the post had simply been shut down, and the Indigenous people who had settled around it were left to fend for themselves. But Indians remained near the site, hoping that Rondon's men would return, as they did late in 1939. This was, therefore, a perfect opportunity for Vargas to see what the SPI had already achieved—and how much more could be accomplished if only the agency could obtain greater official support.

Vargas's visit to Bananal marked the first time that any Brazilian president had ever visited an Indigenous area, and the dictator was determined to maximize its impact. His handlers envisioned the trip as an evocation of one of Rondon's own expeditions, though of course it was nothing of the sort. With newsreel cameras rolling and still photographers clicking away, Vargas, the self-styled "Father of the Poor," distributed knives, machetes, and other implements to the Carajá, and was photographed cuddling a Carajá infant. So that Vargas could claim the limelight, Rondon was deliberately left behind, to his displeasure: when Vargas landed at his first stop, there was a telegram from Rondon that began, "Surprised [by] Your Excellency's departure [for] this new capital," and concluded, "As president of the CNPI, I accompany you in spirit."[14]

When Vargas arrived on Bananal Island, the Carajá, armed with bows and arrows but on their best behavior, greeted him with loud horns and ritual chants; the Javaé were also there, having walked from their nearby village in uniforms the SPI had distributed to them some years earlier. Together, the groups sang the Brazilian national anthem (always an important rite in any event in which Rondon had a hand), performed traditional dances, offered a display of wrestling, and crowned Vargas with a ceremonial headdress. The highlight of the encounter was a ceremony in which a Carajá chief presented Vargas with a clay pipe full of tobacco. Advised in advance by Rondon, the leader of the New State took pains to respect Carajá tradition: facing eastward, he took several deep puffs and blew them toward the birthplace of the sun, which the Carajá "revered as the benefactor of nature and everything that lives."[15]

Rondon had an ulterior motive in subjecting Vargas to all of this: as he wrote, he hoped that Vargas would "draw the proper conclusion and appreciate the mentality of the Indian."[16] Indeed, his curiosity duly piqued, Vargas would, upon returning to the capital, pepper Rondon with questions about the island's inhabitants. He was especially interested in the unacculturated Xavante, who had a reputation for being "fierce." This derived mainly from the fact that in the eighteenth century they had resisted the explorers from São Paulo who sought to enslave them, then fled Mato Grosso and pushed deeper into the hinterland until they reached Bananal, where their relations with other tribal peoples were often unfriendly. As the president's plane lifted off to return to Rio de Janeiro, it flew westward over the Rio das Mortes, or River of Death, where a pair of nearby still-uncontacted Xavante villages were pointed out to the president.

Adept at playing off rivals against each other, Vargas had brought along as part of his official delegation on the Bananal trip a French Salesian priest named Hipólito Chavelon, who had worked as a missionary on the island since 1935. Politically astute, the Salesians had already proclaimed that "making the Xavante Indians friends and good Brazilians"[17] and "opening this new and vast zone to agriculture, cattle-raising,"[18] and mining were their main goals, and they wanted government help. But those objectives clashed with Rondon's, whose anticlerical sentiments were still strong. So Vargas opted for a Solomonic approach: though he soon reopened various SPI posts, as Rondon wished, within weeks he also authorized the Ministry of Education and Health to resume subsidies to the Salesians, and a year later the interventor of Mato Grosso gifted the religious order a land grant and a ten-year tax exemption that applied to Chavelon's Xavante mission project.

As part of his larger effort to consolidate power, Vargas had long sought a rapprochement with the Roman Catholic Church. To the immense displeasure of dedicated republicans and the dwindling number of Positivists like Rondon, the new constitution Vargas rammed through in 1934 restored some of the privileges that the original republican constitution of 1891 had stripped from the Church in areas like education, marriage, and even state subsidies. With the advent of the New State and the 1937 charter, Vargas accelerated this approximation.

One result, thanks to the efforts of Foreign Minister Aranha, a devout Catholic, was negotiation of an accord between the Vargas regime and the Holy See, completed in 1941 and modeled on similar Vatican agreements with Nazi Germany and Fascist Italy, which also harnessed clerical anti-Communism for Vargas's own purposes. A draft of the proposed treaty was circulated among government agencies that might be affected, and when Rondon read the document, he was furious and determined to torpedo it. Not only would the treaty grant religious orders active in Brazil a complete tax exemption and rights to purchase land in border regions, it also would thrust its missionaries directly into aspects of Indigenous policy that for thirty years had been the exclusive responsibility of the SPI. To Rondon, this was simply unacceptable.

Rondon and his allies quietly launched a two-pronged attack on the draft treaty. Inside the government, SPI documents show, Rondon personally lobbied other officials, including the powerful gatekeeper Simões Lopes, to undermine support for the proposed agreement. Externally, the SPI helped sponsor a massive public relations campaign opposing the accord on patriotic grounds—which made it more difficult for Vargas's censors to keep the debate out of the press and off the radio. Thanks to Rondon and his friends, Vargas had to shelve the proposal, and only in 2007 did the Brazilian government and the Holy See agree to a de facto concordat.

From his perch at the CNPI, Rondon also sought to thwart

360 · INTO THE AMAZON

aspects of the March to the West that troubled him, influenced by three decades of bitter experience. If in 1910 Rondon had advocated the gradual, voluntary integration of Indigenous peoples into Brazilian society, by 1940 he harbored profound doubts about such an approach. So much negative evidence had accumulated that it was impossible for him to maintain his original view, optimistically based on Positivist beliefs. Indeed, the SPI's archives were full of reports documenting this failure: massive seizures of Indian land, massacres, epidemics of disease that ravaged entire tribes, the unwillingness of the army and police to enforce laws favoring the Indian, the SPI's own impotence in carrying out its mission.

Increasingly, Rondon believed that Indigenous peoples should simply be left alone, and that the task of the SPI should be limited to protecting tribal groups from incursions by so-called *civilizados* so that Indians could continue their traditional way of life. As for the "catechism" that had also been one of the agency's main objectives during the First Republic, Rondon now felt that its focus should shift to educating white and Black Brazilians about Indians and their cultures, rather than indoctrinating Indigenous peoples to integrate them into national life.

In November 1943, however, Rondon suffered a blow to his authority when Vargas, still ruling by decree, ordered the creation of yet another government body that would have a voice in Indian policy, the Central Brazil Foundation. True to Vargas's corporatist instincts, the new entity was given powers to supersede the authority of state governors, all in the name of speeding up the March to the West. In theory Rondon might have welcomed this federal intervention, because he was constantly wrangling with state leaders trying to seize Indigenous lands for themselves or their followers. But other features of the new foundation's charter deeply alarmed him and fellow advocates of the Indian cause.

In the name of self-sufficiency during wartime, for example, the foundation was empowered to accept private donations as well as to operate businesses of its own and regulate commerce in the area under its domain. In addition, profits from its businesses were to be distributed among its administrative personnel, with only the foundation itself authorized to audit the books of its subsidiary companies. This was clearly a step back in history, to the days of mercantilist ventures like the Hudson's Bay Company or the Dutch East India Company.

Even more alarming, the president of the Central Brazil Foundation was also Coordinator of Economic Mobilization and president of the Council for Immigration and Colonization. Reporting directly to Vargas, João Alberto Lins de Barros was a kind of economic superminister, in charge of wartime rationing, price controls, and distribution of raw materials; leading companies, squeezed by austerity measures, soon realized that it was wise to make "patriotic donations" to the Central Brazil Foundation. Those payments were widely viewed as bribes, but for as long as the scheme remained in place, Rondon would be outflanked.

These tensions grew once the Central Brazil Foundation began building roads and landing strips and opening up the interior for settlement, even in areas previously designated as Indian land. The most important of these efforts was the Roncador-Xingu Expedition, named for the mountain range and river basin that were its principal targets. In command was Col. Flaviano Vanique, who had no real qualifications for the job other than an absolute loyalty to Vargas; his previous posting had been as head of the presidential guard. Not surprisingly, Vanique's main interest was not working for the well-being of tribal groups already living in the Xingu, whom he saw as an obstacle to development, but opening the region to settlement by colonists from the coast.

Providentially, though, Rondon had three informants deep inside the expedition: Orlando, Cláudio, and Leonardo Villas-Bôas. The Villas-Bôas brothers are today revered as Rondon's spiritual successors in championing the Indian cause, but in 1943 they were still very young, quite inexperienced, and completely unknown: Orlando was twenty-nine, Cláudio twenty-six, and Leonardo only twenty-four. Born in the interior of the state of São Paulo into what their friend and contemporary Darcy Ribeiro characterized as a "petit-bourgeois family" of lawyers and coffee farmers and thus seemingly "condemned to a mediocre bureaucratic life,"[19] they were initially inspired by the life of adventure and public service that Rondon exemplified, familiar to them from newspapers, magazines, and newsreels. This never changed: even as an old man nearing ninety years of age, Orlando Villas-Bôas, the last surviving brother, in reviewing his career would say, "The most impressive figure I've ever known during this long trajectory was Rondon."[20]

And so, when the Roncador-Xingu Expedition was being organized in mid-1943, three of the Villas-Bôas brothers—a fourth, Álvaro, would eventually join them—decided to enlist. But Vanique wanted only illiterate backwoodsmen, so the brothers, pretending to be uneducated peasants, hired on as laborers. Eventually, after months of backbreaking work opening a landing strip and building a rudimentary hostel, their ruse was discovered, and they were immediately promoted to administrative positions—Orlando as chief clerk of the main base, Cláudio as supervisor of personnel, and Leonardo in charge of the supply warehouse.

All the while, though, the brothers were secretly informing Rondon of abuses of Indigenous peoples that the expedition encountered and, in some cases, encouraged. The expedition's initial mission had been to scout unoccupied regions suitable for colonization, but at the very first outpost it discovered that the area was not in fact uninhabited, that Xavante lived on the other side of the river. The brothers were even more disgusted to learn that rubber tappers were giving tribal groups arsenic-laced cassava flour and decided to act. "We had the good fortune to kindle Rondon's attention, and he acted in defense"[21] of the affected peoples, Orlando would later explain. As a result of Rondon's denunciations to the press, "the expedition then changed its objectives. Instead of focusing on opening population centers in the direction of Manaus, it began to set up aviation safety signaling posts" for flights on their way from Rio to Miami, which until then had to follow a coastal route, adding up to six hours of flight time.[22]

As Orlando Villas-Bôas would later recall, another such letter to Rondon led directly to a shake-up in the expedition's command structure. The brothers learned that a detachment of the trigger-happy Goiás state police was being sent to "clear the path for the expedition,"²³ that is, rid it of Indians. "I wrote a letter to Rondon," Orlando Villas-Bôas explained decades later, and Rondon alerted Barros that a massacre was in the making. Rondon even showed the letter to the minister, who flew immediately to the front line to castigate the officer in charge. "If I were you," he said, "I'd grab the Villas-Bôas brothers and put them in the vanguard of the expedition."²⁴

The Villas-Bôas brothers devoutly believed in Rondon's non-violent philosophy, and under their direction the Roncador-Xingu Expedition's scouting team tried to put those methods into effect. It was a difficult challenge: Rondon's army troops had been subject to military discipline, but the men the Villas-Bôas brothers led were mostly miners, former rubber tappers, and refugees from the coast whom Orlando referred to as "the criminals of the Center-West." These needed persuading, so "every night, we put the workers around the campfire and talked with them. We shoved into their heads the idea that we were intruders on Indian lands. We talked a lot about Rondon with them. We talked about that old custom of Rondon's, 'Die if you must, but kill never.' But then a backwoodsman said 'This is very pretty, but what I think is 'kill if you must, but never die!' But the fact is that we initiated contact with the Kalapalos, and things went very well."²⁵

Rondon, approaching eighty and with his eyesight nearly gone, was no longer up to the rigors of extended exploration of the hinterlands. But from his position back in Rio as director of the CNPI, he provided the bureaucratic support and protection the young brothers needed, and lobbied intensively for them to receive adequate funding. After years of work in the wilderness, his was now exclusively an inside game, and would remain so for the remainder of his life. But his efforts were essential to the success of his protégés, who henceforth would increasingly serve as his eyes and ears in the field.

"We followed three themes," Orlando Villas-Bôas would explain during a long television interview in 1987, "which were perfectly in harmony with Rondon himself. In other words, first of all that there is no place for the Indian in today's Brazilian society, and secondly that the Indian can only survive within his own culture, and third, that since our civilization offers nothing positive to the Indian, let's at least respect his family."[26]

At the same time this struggle over the direction of Indian policy was taking place, Rondon was also openly diverging from the government's official position on other issues. Throughout the 1930s, and increasingly after the establishment of the New State in 1937, he had been distressed by Vargas's deepening flirtation with Fascism and the Axis powers. When World War II broke out, and especially after the fall of France in June 1940, that uneasiness only increased. And after the Japanese attacked Pearl Harbor, it turned to alarm. It was bad enough to see his beloved France suffering under Nazi occupation following the humiliating defeat of its forces—under the command of his old friend Gen. Maurice Gamelin—but the prospect of an Axis victory that would extinguish freedom across the world was intolerable.

Given the limits on public activity and expression under Vargas, a Brazilian response to that challenge was hard to organize and fraught with risk. But in September 1942, Rondon was one of the founders of a new organization called the Society of Friends of America. Gen. Manuel Rabelo, a former member of Rondon's old Telegraph Commission team and still a close friend, was chosen as president of the group, which announced a platform to support the Allies and defeat the Axis and its sympathizers, both at home and abroad; Rondon became a member of the group's board of directors. On November 6, the government granted the permit that allowed the SAA, as it was known in Portuguese, to function legally, and Rabelo, Rondon, and their associates plunged into the political battle.

High on the list of the group's aims was to force the Vargas regime to send troops to fight with the Allies in Europe. Brazil had finally declared war on Nazi Germany, Italy, and Japan a month before the SAA was formed, but the Vargas government, still infested with supporters of the Axis, showed little inclination to get involved in the conflict. From its office in downtown Rio, the SAA also organized conferences on the issues at stake in the war, and tried to combat Axis propaganda through news releases and essays it sent to Brazilian newspapers, magazines, and radio stations. In addition, the SAA held donation drives whose proceeds were, according to its charter, destined either for "the acquisition of war materiel" or for the residents of "Cities and Nations when they are liberated by the Allied Armies."[27]

But like Rondon himself, the SAA was playing a double game: it also had a domestic agenda, which it had to disguise, intended to speed the redemocratization of Brazil. How could it oppose totalitarianism and support "democratic ideals" abroad without taking the same stance at home? Vargas's political police suspected this, and kept the organization and its leaders under constant surveillance. But there was not much they could do, at least not in the beginning. The SAA had powerful allies—the American ambassador to Brazil attended the group's initial meeting—and besides, both Rabelo, then serving as vice president of the Supreme Military Tribunal, and Rondon were distinguished military officers whose patriotism could not be questioned.

Other founders also had distinguished records of public service, and were either inspired by Rondon and Rabelo's example or persuaded to join after one or the other met personally with them. Some were fellow Positivists or protégés of Rondon, or other long-time military colleagues, like Fragoso, who had ridden with Rondon more than fifty years before, on the night the emperor was overthrown. In 1930 he led the coup that brought Vargas to power and later served as army chief of staff, but now he shared Rondon's alarm at the direction the regime had taken. On the civilian side, the president of the Banco do Brasil signed on, as did a varied group of former cabinet ministers, governors, and intellectuals. Two people especially close to Rondon were also listed as founders: his wife, Chiquita, and a young cousin, Francisco Xavier Rondon. Overall, as a court noted when the government eventually challenged the group's legality and sought to shut it down, the SAA directorate was a distinguished group of "patriots with immense services rendered to Brazil."[28]

In part thanks to the SAA's credibility, the effectiveness of its lobbying within the government, and its ability to mobilize public opinion on behalf of the Allies, Brazil on July 31, 1943, announced it would send an expeditionary force of twenty-five thousand men to fight in Italy; those troops eventually took part in battles at Monte Castello and the Po Valley. Within Brazil, this was considered quite unusual, in view of the country's history of deftly avoiding entanglements in foreign conflicts: an old saying had it that "Brazil will go to war when a snake can smoke a pipe." (Naturally the flag the Brazilian Expeditionary Force carried into battle showed a snake smoking a pipe.)

But once aligned with the Allies, Brazil aided the war effort in other, even more substantial ways. With the Allies' access to rubber supplies cut by the Japanese invasion of Southeast Asia, Brazil revived its moribund rubber industry in return for millions of dollars in loans, credits, and equipment. Brazil's biggest strategic contribution, however, was to allow the United States to build air bases in the northeastern city of Natal, the closest point in the Western Hemisphere to Africa. Because planes of that era had limited range and bad weather made a northern route from Canada across Greenland inoperative part of the year, thousands of American soldiers and tons of equipment made the 1,844-mile journey over to Freetown, Sierra Leone, and then on to Europe or Asia after flying down from Miami in transport planes. By late 1943, Natal had the busiest air base in the world, designated by the U.S. War Department as "one of the four most strategic points in the world,"[29] along with Suez, Gibraltar, and the Bosporus.

Having succeeded internationally, the SAA now shifted its focus to the domestic front. This proved to be more problematic because it directly affected the dictatorship and its long-term plans for a "controlled opening" that would allow Vargas to retain power under a less repressive structure. Thanks to its intense lobbying efforts on the war issue, the SAA had established links with entities like the left-wing National Student Union, an influential political force always critical of the status quo, with liberal sectors of the press, and with other opposition groups; members of the outlawed Brazilian Communist Party also joined. "Let us all march together, struggling for liberty" and opposing "tyranny, oppression, deceit," Rabelo urged during a 1943 speech in São Paulo that was part of a tour to organize SAA chapters all over Brazil.

In March 1943, the SAA issued a manifesto, with Rondon among its signatories, denouncing the surveillance to which members were subjected and protesting the government's Department of Press and Propaganda's new prohibition on any mention of the SAA or Rabelo in newspapers, magazines, or on the radio. When the army colonel in charge of the capital police stepped down early in 1944 to take command of an army unit bound for Italy, a new Federal Department of Public Security was created and control of it given to a Vargas loyalist notorious for ordering police in São Paulo to shoot student demonstrators. With that, the double game in which Rabelo and Rondon and the others were engaged—opposing the government while simultaneously serving in it—became harder to play.

The breaking point came not long after, in August 1944. Rabelo and Rondon had sounded out Aranha, still the sitting foreign minister, about becoming the SAA's vice president, and he had agreed. But on August 11, the day before Aranha and the rest of a new directorate were to be sworn in, police raided an SAA-sponsored luncheon. Rondon was not present, and so was not arrested, and neither was Aranha. But about a dozen lesser-known participants were; the organization's records were also seized and its formal banning announced. Proclaiming himself the victim of "a police Pearl Harbor,"[30] Aranha immediately resigned as foreign minister; it would take several months for a court to overturn the police action, but the SAA, as part of a broad coalition of civic groups, continued to press for democratization. At the end of October 1945, Vargas finally was driven from power, following a military uprising.

When the struggle to succeed Vargas began, Rondon faced a new predicament. Both main candidates in the election of a new president, held on December 2, were military men whom Rondon knew well. Each, though, had associations that troubled him. Prominent supporters of Gen. Eduardo Gomes, who had participated in the original Lieutenants' Uprising at Fort Copacabana in 1922, included Rondon's old adversaries Juarez Távora and Luís Carlos Prestes, returned from exile and still the leader of the Brazilian Communist Party. On the other hand, Gen. Eurico Gaspar Dutra, though a Mato Grosso native like Rondon and one of his former adjutants, had loyally served Vargas as minister of war, opposed Brazilian entry into World War II, and was instrumental in the closing of the SAA.

In the end, Rondon opted to support Dutra, the more conservative of the candidates, who triumphed handily in the hastily organized vote and took office in January 1946. Almost immediately, Rondon's decision yielded benefits, in the form of a shift in the government's attitude toward Indigenous peoples. Vargas's former bodyguard was still in charge of the Roncador-Xingu Expedition, but when his wife committed suicide and he returned to Rio, the new president, at Rondon's urging, decided to replace him and put the Villas-Bôas brothers jointly in command.

This was an encouraging sign. Albeit bruised, Rondon had survived fifteen years of Getúlio Vargas and outlived the New State. Occasionally he may have sacrificed some of his personal integrity to achieve his larger goals. But now, at the age of eighty and with a new cohort of young, energetic allies to supplement the dwindling band of comrades who had accompanied him into the wilderness a half century before, a fresh beginning under democratic rule seemed to beckon, and he was determined to exploit whatever time remained to him. But like much that preceded them, the last dozen years of Rondon's life would be full of obstacles and unexpected defeats as well as hard-won victories.

XXV

The Gandhi of Brazil

I N HIS FINAL years, Rondon grudgingly adjusted to the role of elder statesman. His mind was still sharp, and he remained intensively engaged with government policy. But his body betrayed and immobilized him, curtailing his ability to verify for himself the information from official reports and the press, which now had to be read to him since he could no longer scrutinize long, small-print texts on his own. As a consequence, he increasingly had to act through his younger proxies and rely on their judgment.

His beliefs and values also seemed more and more antiquated. In Dutra he had a friendly presence in the presidential palace for the first time in fifteen years, someone with whom he regularly shared breakfast and who authorized record outlays for the SPI. But that did not mean the president always acted in accord with Rondon's wishes. In part because of Rondon's efforts during the first three decades of the century, Brazil's interior was now open to penetration, and both large businesses and small peasant farmers were flocking there, pushing aside Indigenous peoples and ignoring the legal guarantees meant to defend them. Try as Rondon and his allies might, they were unable to get additional rights and protections inserted into the new constitution promulgated during Dutra's first year in office: the document's language concerning Indians was virtually identical to that of the Vargas-era charters.

In reality, Rondon's explorations had unleashed economic and social forces that he could not—and Dutra would not—contain. Meanwhile, he clung to his Positivist beliefs for consolation, still convinced that events would eventually take a turn in the direction that he desired and which Comte had predicted. But the causes that inspired his entry into public life—abolitionism and republicanism— were irrelevant now, distant historical memories overtaken by more immediate concerns. Brazil had moved into a different historical phase. Rondon had not.

On the rare occasions Rondon traveled outside the capital now, it was for reasons more personal or nostalgic than professional. In 1947 and 1948, for instance, he devoted a great deal of effort to establishing a pair of rural schools around Mimoso, his birthplace, to honor his mother and the father he never knew. At Rondon's direction, the first, named the Santa Claudina Rural School and opened in October 1948, was erected just yards from the spot where the mud-and-straw hut in which he was born had once stood. (The school continues to function to this day, with a small memorial at its entrance to his parents, "both deceased in this place," meant as an expression of "the eternal devotion of their only child, Cândido Mariano.")

As he aged, Rondon also became more assertive about his own Indigenous identity. In one memorable incident in the late 1940s, he was meeting with reporters to discuss the SPI's efforts to establish peaceful contact with the Xavante, and in response to one question began his answer with the phrase "If I were white . . ." Before he could continue, one of the journalists interrupted him, apparently surprised. "So you are saying you're not white?" he asked.

Rondon replied that no, he was not white, and "in the face of this declaration," the reporter "asked for a clarification, claiming it was essential. And abruptly he asked: 'Are you Bororo?'" According to press accounts, which appeared under headlines like "General Rondon Declares That He Is Not White," Rondon "answered that he is a Bororo and that the Bororos refer to whites as 'braides,' which is to say strangers, outsiders or foreigners."[1]

In fact, Rondon's remaining Bororo friends treated him as one of their own. His oldest comrade from the tribe had adopted the Portuguese name Cadete, chosen after Rondon gave him a military uniform as a token of thanks for his work on the Pantanal telegraph line in 1900–1903, and he sometimes stayed with Rondon when he came to the capital on tribal business. Repeatedly, he advised the Pagmejera to retire to Mato Grosso and settle among the Bororo. "Come to us to die," he once urged Rondon. "The Bororo know how to mourn their dead."[2]

But Cadete ended up dying first, and when Rondon was unable to travel to the São Lourenço River region for burial ceremonies in his friend's honor, he sent Darcy Ribeiro as his emissary, along with a letter of introduction and a recorded funeral oration in Bororo. "Look at this man," Rondon began. "He is Darcy. He is there in my place. I am old, I can no longer bear the long journey from Rio de Janeiro. Look closely at him. His eyes are my eyes, looking at everything so that he can tell me about it. His ears are my ears. They hear everything that you say, which will be repeated to me. Pay attention to his mouth. Everything he says, it is I, Rondon, who is speaking to the Bororo." That endorsement allowed Ribeiro, he would later write, "a total openness to participate and document the most elaborate funeral ceremonies that exist . . . as if I were myself a Bororo returning to the village, to participate in all the rituals as an eminence comparable to Rondon."[3]

The 1940s ended with a loss that was even more shattering and close to home. Chiquita had always said that she hoped Rondon would die first, because she could not bear to imagine the sorrow he would feel having to live on without her. Rondon, being seven years older than his wife, expected that outcome, too. But on November 2, 1949, in the fifty-eighth year of their marriage, Chiquita died of a massive heart attack. "The blow was instantaneous, no one expected it," Rondon wrote. "She died in my arms," he continued, "without being able to say a single word to her Cândido."[4]

Later that month, still bereft, Rondon sent a letter to an old friend in Cuiabá, a former Rondon Commission telegraphist who oversaw his business affairs there. "I write to you today still under the weight of the emotion that shook my soul on the Day of the Dead, when I lost my pristine Wife and Companion during every moment of my life," he informed the friend with a trembling hand in a letter dated

November 27. "I have become completely incapable of any act not related to my pain and my turbulent and infinite emotions."[5]

Chiquita's passing left Rondon not just emotionally devastated, but deeply regretful, too. As a young couple, they had anticipated that his would be a life of service to the nation, with long periods apart; the vision of a quiet life together once he completed his mission helped make the separations bearable for both of them. But "when the arduous quest ended and I could at last withdraw to my hearth, it was already getting very late," he reflected after her funeral at the Positivist Church. "We were able to spend only a few years together in the sublime fulfillment of our eternal dream of love."[6]

The growing limitations imposed by Rondon's near blindness compounded his melancholy. "My books too sit pointlessly on their shelves, awaiting me and the delicious evenings I so often looked forward to with such anticipation," he wrote, "the two of us under the same lamp, she sewing or embroidering, me reading out loud, both of us offering our comments. . . . I leaf through those books now, or, rather, grope at them, useless because my wife is gone and I can no longer read them."[7]

Minutes from CNPI meetings indicate that Rondon missed several sessions immediately following Chiquita's death, so intense was his grief. But as a new decade began, he gradually resumed his professional activities. Two initiatives, both related to Indigenous matters, now consumed him: the Museum of the Indian and the Xingu National Park. Although Rondon never characterized either project as his last hurrah, the young anthropologists and explorers around him knew better, and acted accordingly. These included the Villas-Bôas brothers; their friend Noel Nutels, a Ukrainian-born Jewish doctor who accompanied them on the Roncador-Xingu Expedition; and the anthropologists Eduardo Galvão and Darcy Ribeiro.

Of this group of talented and dedicated young officials committed to Rondon's philosophy of nonviolence, the one closest to Rondon in his final years was Darcy Ribeiro. Born in Minas Gerais, Ribeiro earned an anthropology degree in 1946 and immediately signed on with the SPI, working among tribes in the Amazon and Pantanal. Rondon had interviewed and hired Ribeiro, who soon became devoted to the old man; Rondon returned that affection. Ribeiro sent a constant stream of reports, letters, and telegrams from the field, often about problems his mentor could resolve from the capital, and sought out Rondon's company when he was in Rio. By 1950, Ribeiro had risen within the SPI hierarchy to become the director of the agency's educational service and Rondon's most trusted aide.

"The Communist Party didn't want me because it thought me too agitated, and the Brazilian Army didn't want me because its doctors thought I was too much of a runt to be an officer,"[8] Ribeiro would explain later, near the end of a distinguished career as a cabinet minister, presidential chief of staff, university president, writer, and senator. But "I got along well with Rondon, and spent ten years with the Indians."[9] Even after that, he would remain Rondon's closest collaborator, until the older man's death.

The first of Rondon's two objectives, creation of the Museum of the Indian in Rio de Janeiro, was more easily achieved because it threatened no entrenched economic or political interests. Rondon envisioned the museum as a permanent extension of his efforts over the years, through media as diverse as his lectures, pamphlets, and the films the Rondon Commission had made, to inculcate Brazilians with a correct image of their fellow citizens living in the wilderness. Ribeiro shared Rondon's vision: the museum was, he would write, "set up to eradicate the idea that Indians are violent and bloody, savage and brutal, wicked and crafty—all stereotypes that the Brazilian population holds of them."[10]

The division of labor between the two men was as follows: Rondon used his enormous prestige to lobby for a site and for funding for the museum while Ribeiro focused on the content of the exhibits that were planned, in consultation with Rondon. The government did not object, for it saw that the museum could enhance Brazil's image globally. This turned out to be an accurate assessment, for as Ribeiro noted, the project was "hailed internationally as the first museum exclusively focused on eliminating prejudice."[11] Generations of Brazilian schoolchildren have now visited the museum, which also has a splendid collection of documents and artifacts.

Establishing a national park in the Xingu, though, was immensely more complicated. The idea seems to have emerged one night around a campfire during the Roncador-Xingu Expedition in a conversation among the Villas-Bôas brothers and Nutels. When they presented the concept to Rondon the next time they were in the capital, he immediately embraced it. To him, it seemed an ideal way to combine two of his main policy interests: protecting Indigenous peoples and safeguarding the environment. In fact, under Rondon's conception of the project, the Indigenous inhabitants of the region, perhaps supplemented by other tribes who might be willing to settle there, would formally become stewards of the environment.

But the Xingu was a vast and enormously alluring river basin, promising vast wealth once jungle and savanna could be transformed into ranches and plantations, its rivers dammed, roads and highways built, colonists transported, and settlements founded. What's more, in the presidential election held in October 1950, Getúlio Vargas had been returned to power for a five-year term, this time by popular vote. In all likelihood that meant Rondon and his allies would once again have to contend with some kind of developmentalist, March to the West–style push into the region. And, as with anything else involving Vargas, caution, intrigue, and political jockeying would surely be required.

After consulting with his young collaborators, early in 1952 Rondon presented Vargas with a proposal drawn up by Ribeiro to establish a national park in the Xingu. Rather than be timid, Rondon boldly requested that seventy-eight thousand square miles—an area slightly larger than Nebraska and which would include all the tributaries of the Xingu—be set aside for that purpose. He knew this was an overly ambitious goal, but thought it better to begin large and have to go smaller. He also had an ally within the Vargas administration: vice president João Café Filho, who was sympathetic to the Indigenous cause. Elected separately from Vargas, who regarded him as a dangerous leftist, Café Filho never enjoyed the president's confidence. But by law, he retained his seat in Congress, and he lobbied his fellow legislators to support Rondon's proposal.

Nine years would elapse before the Xingu National Park was created: by that time Rondon had died and Jânio Quadros was president of Brazil. He authorized an area of 17,800 square miles, less than a quarter of what Rondon had requested, and that was later reduced to just over 10,000 square miles, an area about the size of Massachusetts. Nevertheless, Rondon's sponsorship of the Xingu National Park was crucial: Quadros, a former geography teacher, came to the presidency after serving as mayor and then governor of São Paulo, but he was born in Mato Grosso and grew up fascinated by Rondon and his exploits. Once in politics, he sought to have his picture taken with Rondon as much as possible, and regarded the decree creating the Xingu National Park as an homage to his childhood hero.

Throughout the early 1950s, though, Vargas had opposed the decree. But in August 1954, embroiled in scandal, he committed suicide, bringing to an end nearly a quarter century of sparring with Rondon—and ushering in a new era in Brazilian politics. As part of that makeover, legislation unimaginable during the Vargas regime was soon introduced in Congress to promote Rondon to marshal of the Brazilian Army.

This long-overdue gesture reflected two complementary intentions. One was to honor Rondon's decades of dedicated service to the Brazilian nation one last time before his death—a sentiment that also encouraged Congress on February 12, 1956, over Rondon's vigorous objections, to formally give the name Rondônia to what had been known as the Territory of Guaporé, comprising terrain that Rondon had explored during the first two decades of the century.

The promotion was also an implicit apology to Rondon for the shabby treatment—arrest, confinement, expulsion from the army, opportunistic and slanderous attacks on his person and policies, persecution of his adjutants—to which he had been subjected during Vargas's seizure of power in 1930. This belated honor, however, meant that some bureaucratic maneuvering had to be undertaken, beginning with Rondon's official restoration to the ranks early in 1955. That was followed in rapid succession by congressional authorization of his promotion and the formal approval of Rondon's admirer Café Filho, who had become president after Vargas's suicide.

Finally, on May 5, 1955, Rondon's ninetieth birthday, Congress convened in a special joint session to honor him. Newsreels show

Rondon, leaning on a cane and with a pair of escorts to prevent him from falling, hobbling to the podium to receive the commendation. Because he was unable to read the speech he had written with input from Darcy Ribeiro, it was delivered instead by the president of the Senate.

In his remarks, Rondon, describing himself as an "unassuming old man," thanked by name his "worthy companions, dead or alive," from the Rondon Commission, but reserved his highest accolades for "the invaluable cooperation of our Indians," without whose help "I could not have accomplished anything," singling out the Nhambiquara and the Bororo for praise. "The Indian, honorable senators and deputies, is our brother," he wrote. "Wandering through the forest, he leads the most primitive life, and is worthy of our sympathy and our assistance. Stout-hearted, he only takes arms in self-defense. The problem is one of education and protection."[12]

This was vintage Rondon, as was the patriotic peroration and plea for pacifism that followed. "As my life draws to a close at a time when world events are generating an atmosphere of confusion and skepticism, I am confident that a promising future awaits Brazil," he concluded. "Speaking with the authority of a man who has never been entangled in politics, I can assure you that differences of opinion are human and even understandable, but they should never be allowed to exceed the boundaries of common sense. Brazil must stay united, so that her example may light the way for other peoples striving for peace."[13]

Rondon's remarks that day have the tone of a valedictory, but a year later, increasingly infirm and retired from public life, he found himself drawn into one final campaign—this one conducted both on his behalf and for the benefit of the Indigenous peoples he had long championed. Aware that this was probably their last chance, in 1956 a group of Brazilian and international notables lobbied for Rondon to be awarded the Nobel Peace Prize. Rondon was initially skeptical, but acquiesced because he thought it might draw international attention to the plight of Native peoples in the Americas.

Since the 1920s, Rondon had been mentioned as a candidate for the prize. The initial impulse, curiously enough, came from Albert Einstein, who in 1921 won the Nobel for physics and had just begun to enjoy global recognition. Concluding a tour of South America in 1925, Einstein spent a week in Rio before returning to Europe in mid-May. Though he never met Rondon, who at the time was trying to quell the rebellion in the south, Einstein's diary of the visit records numerous mentions of Rondon, in terms that were always laudatory and demonstrated the powerful impression that Rondon's pacifism made on him.

The first mention came on May 6, when Einstein visited Brazil's president and various cabinet members, who responded to his questions about policy toward Indigenous peoples by citing Rondon's motto, "Die if you must, but kill never." On a visit to the National Museum the next day, Edgar Roquette-Pinto and other scientists there explained that many of their most important specimens and artifacts had been gathered by Rondon on his Amazon expeditions. Intrigued, Einstein asked for more information at a reception following a speech that evening to the Brazilian Academy of Sciences, and learned of Rondon's work in areas as diverse as astronomy and ethnology, botany and zoology. Einstein also requested to be shown films of Rondon in action in the field, including footage of him with the Paresi, Nhambiquara, and Bororo.

Rondon's unwavering pacifism led Einstein on May 22, on the boat back to Europe, to write to the Nobel Committee in Oslo, nominating him for the 1925 Peace Prize, which at that juncture had been given only to Europeans and North Americans—and had not been awarded at all in 1923 and 1924. "I take the liberty to draw your attention to the activities of General Rondon in Rio de Janeiro, since during my visit to Brazil I have gained the impression that this man is highly deserving of receiving the Nobel Peace Prize," the letter begins. "His work consists of adjusting Indian tribes to the civilized world without the use of weapons or coercion. . . . He is a philanthropist and leader of the first order."[14]

Despite Einstein's support, Rondon did not win the prize that year. Instead, in a Eurocentric decision typical of the times, it was awarded to Austen Chamberlain, the British foreign secretary, and Charles Dawes, the American vice president. The next year, the prize went to European diplomats.

In 1953, his name surfaced again, and as in 1925, a former Nobel Prize winner took the initiative. Emily Greene Balch, an American pacifist and feminist and longtime leader of the Women's International League for Peace and Freedom, had shared the prize in 1946, for advocating for the humane treatment of prisoners of war and stateless people. But her awareness of Rondon dated to 1911, when she attended the First Universal Races Congress in London and learned of his nonviolent approach to relations with Indigenous peoples.

In the nominating letter she sent to the Nobel Committee, Balch wrote that "while General Rondon has a military title, his life's work has been dedicated to the service of peace, which he has served on several different levels—political, social and ethical." She noted his role in averting a war between Peru and Colombia, "the efforts of the League of Nations having failed," but concentrated principally on his activities among Amazon tribes, directing special praise to the "Die if you must, but kill never" approach that had successfully implemented peaceful first contact with dozens of Indigenous groups and saved them from extermination.

"Using every possibility of appeasement and gift-giving," Rondon "founded a policy and framed a school of followers that meant a new day in the relations between whites and Indians," Balch continued. His years of work in the Brazilian hinterland had greatly reduced "a bitter and cruel struggle" between the two races and banished what seemed, until he appeared, to be "as real a threat to peace as a formal war between organized governments."[15]

Balch concluded her nominating letter with an appeal to what today would be called diversity. "The choice of General Rondon for the 1953 Nobel Prize would be a novel and interesting choice," she suggested, and would "illustrate the policy of the Committee of giving a broad basis to its awards, both as to geographic distribution and variety of types of service dedicated to the cause of peace."[16] In the end, though, it was to no avail. The prize that year did indeed go to a general—but he was an American: George C. Marshall, originator of the Marshall Plan for the reconstruction of Europe following World War II and a former secretary of state and defense.

In 1956, though, Rondon's Brazilian supporters, correctly suspecting that he did not have much longer to live, decided to organize one last attempt of their own. To kick off the drive, the new president of Brazil, Juscelino Kubitschek, visited Rondon at his apartment on November 1 and, with reporters, photographers, and television cameras present and a domestic audience very much in mind, articulated Brazil's debt to its great explorer and humanist. "All honors are insufficient to pay proper tribute to you, Marshal," the new president said, employing the formal "you" used in Portuguese to deferentially address one's elders, betters, or any other admired figure. "The more I travel in the interior of Brazil, the more I appreciate your admirable work. You deserve much more, Marshal."[17]

But Kubitschek also had a more immediate motive in mind. He was about to undertake an epic project that was both long desired and long delayed: the construction of a new capital for Brazil in the country's interior savanna. The nation's political elite, quite willing to continue enjoying Rio's sybaritic comforts, was opposed, and Kubitschek wanted the endorsement of the great "Tamer of the Wilderness" as a counterweight—much like Getúlio Vargas when he sought Rondon's support in order to legitimize his March to the West.

Kubitschek's position was one Rondon had promoted in lectures and other public declarations dating back to as early as 1910, and the entire trajectory of his career, as well as his upbringing as a man of the frontier, pointed in the same direction. So he was delighted to give his blessing to the construction of Brasília, especially since it was to be accompanied by the building of new highways and the paving of existing dirt roads that would for the first time link the coast and new capital to far-flung outposts like Cuiabá, Belém, and even Porto Velho.

At the president's behest, the Brazilian Foreign Ministry joined seven Brazilian institutions and the Explorers' Club of New York to lead the final Nobel effort on Rondon's behalf. To support him, they rounded up a more-than-respectable list of international luminaries and institutions. At Columbia University, for instance, the international law expert and diplomat Adolf A. Berle, a former U.S. ambassador to Brazil who knew and admired Rondon, signed on, as did Charles Wagley, perhaps the leading anthropological expert on Indigenous issues and the Amazon, and the sociologist Frank Tannenbaum. In Latin America, the Inter-American Institute in Mexico endorsed Rondon, as did intellectuals around the region; officials of the International Red Cross also advocated for him, albeit in an individual capacity.

The thirty-two-page supporting document submitted early in 1957, though, was a work of absolute ineptitude, and scuttled whatever chance Rondon had of winning the prize. It started off well enough, recalling Einstein's recommendation thirty years earlier. But instead of emphasizing Rondon's credentials as a humanitarian and pacifist, it veered off into subjects unrelated to the prize's declared purpose of honoring the person who "shall have done the most or the best work for fraternity between nations" or "for the abolition or reduction of standing armies."[18] Instead, it embarked on a long, dry, and irrelevant recitation, complete with longitudes and latitudes, of Rondon's achievements as explorer and cartographer. The all-important phrase "Die if you must, but kill never" was never mentioned, and the work of the SPI was confined to a single paragraph buried deep in the text. In addition, no mention was made of Rondon's own Indigenous ancestry.

When the 1957 prize winner was announced in October, it was Lester Pearson, Canada's foreign minister and future prime minister, "for his role in trying to end the Suez conflict and solve the Middle East question." Rondon died four months later, and Nobel rules prohibit awarding the prize posthumously; no Latin American would win until 1980, when the Argentine human rights advocate Adolfo Pérez Esquivel was honored for his nonviolent efforts to "fight the military junta that was ruling his country." And it was not until 1992, the five hundredth anniversary of Columbus's arrival in the Americas, that an Indigenous person won the peace prize. That year, Rigoberta Menchú of Guatemala was honored for "work for social justice and ethno-cultural reconciliation based on respect for the rights of indigenous peoples"[19]—exactly what Rondon had been doing for decades before Menchú was even born.

As part of the publicity effort accompanying the unsuccessful Nobel campaign, Rondon agreed to what turned out to be his last interview. It was published on May 5, 1957, Rondon's ninety-second birthday, and in a book the reporter, Edilberto Coutinho, wrote years later that Rondon's health was "relatively good" when they met. "Though he seems not to remember with precision some facts of recent Brazilian national life," Coutinho observed, "he relives the experience of the jungle with surprising clarity, citing names and dates, recounting episodes rich in details, referring to comrades, bringing to life images of people, things and animals."[20]

Rondon was by then living in an apartment overlooking the sea at the far end of Copacabana. From his window, Fort Copacabana, which he had inaugurated while director of engineering for the army, was visible, as was the long, gentle curve of the beach just across the street. When the weather was hot, which was nearly always, the windows were opened to let the sea breeze enter, since the aged general had no use for novelties like air-conditioning. When Coutinho entered Rondon's apartment, the marshal was "resting in an indigenous hammock hung up on the terrace."[21] Mementos of Rondon's years in the jungle adorned the walls, and there were songbirds in cages chattering away, as well as a pair of yapping Pekingese dogs.

After the Nobel Peace Prize winner was announced, Rondon's health took a turn for the worse, and by January, the end was near. Bedridden, he drifted in and out of consciousness, and Maria de Molina, his caretaker and the second youngest of his daughters, began urging his friends to come say their farewells. His surviving children and their children also paid visits, including a grandson who was a Roman Catholic priest. Some press accounts reported, excitedly but incorrectly, that Rondon was experiencing a deathbed conversion to Roman Catholicism. By some accounts, the grandson wanted to administer last rites, but, according to others, Botelho de Magalhães and Rondon's other Positivist friends intervened to prevent it.

Also among those summoned to the Copacabana apartment was

Darcy Ribeiro, who was with Rondon when he died and left a written record of that moment. It was the morning of January 19, 1958, a typically steamy midsummer day in Rio. It was also Auguste Comte's birthday, and Rondon proved faithful to the Positivist creed until his last breath. "Rondon died with his hands in mine," Ribeiro recalled, "reciting, with his voice quivering, phrases from the Positivist catechism: 'The living are led by the dead / Love as a principle, order as a foundation, progress as an objective.'"[22] Rondon's long journey was finally over.

XXVI

Battle over a Legacy

THE MANEUVERING TO control and shape Rondon's public image and political legacy began within hours of his passing, at the elaborate funeral ceremonies held on January 20, 1958, under the aegis of the army and the government. Throughout the day, Rondon's family, friends, and colleagues—joined by political figures, diplomats, the military high command, and other dignitaries—gathered somberly at the Military Club downtown, where his body lay in state. President Juscelino Kubitschek, who had already decreed three days of national mourning, was among those who came to pay his respects, lingering for several minutes at the open casket.

"Marshal Rondon is a symbol of the pioneers who built Brazil," Kubitschek said. "His name can be found in the consciousness of Brazilians and on the map of the nation, where Rondônia immortalizes him. Explorer of the wilderness, caring friend of the Indian, soldier who held in his heart the mission of national integrity, he sacrificed the best of his life and the light of his eyes for that distant and humble Brazil, in which he sought for culture to peacefully replace primitive savagery. Rondon's dream is a legacy to posterity, his work a glory of the Brazilian people, and his biography a gift to humanity."[1]

The pallbearers standing vigil around the casket and during its subsequent transmission to an army vehicle were all generals and marshals, with former president Dutra at the head. But following a religious service at the Positivist Church on Rua Benjamin Constant and the twenty-one-gun salute from a nearby hill that greeted the casket's arrival at São João Batista Cemetery, the ceremonies took on a different coloration. As one eulogy after another was delivered in front of Rondon's tomb—engraved with the Positivist slogan "Love as a principle, order as foundation and progress as objective"—civilian voices now dominated.

The Villas-Bôas brothers were there, as was a member of the Kalapalo tribe whom Rondon had encouraged to come to Rio de Janeiro to be educated. "All of us regard Marshal Rondon as a Tupã," or deity, he said. "He is for us truly a father."[2] But of the homages offered, perhaps the most stirring was that delivered by Rondon's young disciple Darcy Ribeiro. "In front of Rondon's body, I wish to speak of Rondon as he was when alive, of the legacy and struggle and ideals he now bequeaths to us," he began. Rondon, he continued, was "the most profound, most coherent, most energetic and most generous personality ever to emerge from the Brazilian people," worthy of praise for "his fidelity to unchanging ideals" and his "zeal and combativeness" during a "long and arduous lifetime of work." It was important, Ribeiro added, in remarks printed over the next few days in various newspapers and eventually in a book, not to let those ideals wane, citing what he called "Rondon's four principles."[3]

Naturally, "Die if you must, but kill never" led the list. It was followed by what Ribeiro called "respect for indigenous tribes as independent peoples"; then "guaranteeing to Indians the possession of the lands they inhabit and which are necessary to their survival" as independent peoples; and finally, "assuring to Indians the direct protection of the state." These principles, he added, apply to all of humankind, not just Brazil, and indeed are "the most lofty formulation of the rights of the 60 million indigenous people scattered around the world."

Returning to the Brazilian situation, Ribeiro complained that the "lack of understanding and support from the authorities" which Rondon had battled incessantly was directly responsible for the disappearance of more than eighty tribes since the founding of the Indian Protection Service nearly a half century earlier. "If a butchery of that dimension was possible while Rondon, the great hero of our people and the paladin of the indigenous cause, was still alive," he asked, "what will happen now, his vigilance extinguished, his energy exhausted, his voice stilled?"

Perhaps, he suggested, turning to address Rondon's coffin directly, if "a thousand of us gathered under the sponsorship of your name" and continued "your work," those abuses could be halted, or at least slowed. He concluded by positioning Rondon as the "Marshal of Peace, Marshal of Humanism, Protector of the Indians."[4]

The next day, newspapers across the country published a poem, called "The All-Encompassing Mourning of the Indians," that the national laureate, Carlos Drummond de Andrade, had composed in Rondon's honor. Written in the voice of an Indian in lamentation, the poem's core consists of these lines: "You were calm, diminutive, determined / Your gestures paralyzed fear / Your voice consoled us, it was brotherly / Protected under your arms, we saw / The chief's headdress covering your brow and the sun singeing your face / But you wanted only our loyalty. / You were one of our own, returning to his origins / and you carried in your hands the talking wire / extending it into the deepest secrets of the jungle."[5]

Brazil's other great poet, Manuel Bandeira, turned to prose to express his appreciation. Rondon, he wrote, was destined to go down in history as "one of the purest glories of Brazil. Even if he had not carried out the scientific and social projects he achieved . . . there was in Rondon the presence of the most noble of human virtues—courage, probity, selflessness—that by themselves would justify the homages we see being paid to him at this moment when we are losing him."

But that was not all: writing just two years after an attempted military coup meant to block the inauguration of Kubitschek, ensured in the end only by a countercoup also led by the military, Bandeira praised Rondon as the exemplary soldier, respectful of political institutions. "Although a military man, he was not one of these soldier types who usurp the prestige of the Army to carry out shows of strength to advance their personal ambitions, nor one of these generals who can repeat as their own the words that Shakespeare put in the mouth of Richard III: 'Our strong arms be our conscience, swords our law,'" Bandeira wrote. "He knew how to awaken the energies and self-sacrifice of those who served under him in the wilderness, heroic men, soldiers who are almost unknown but who played a part in the genuinely epic adventures that were Rondon's expeditions."[6]

In the first years following Rondon's death, this humanist vision of his complicated legacy would predominate, thanks in large part to Ribeiro's efforts. Just thirty-five when Rondon died, Ribeiro became an increasingly important figure in Brazilian intellectual and political life, moving into positions of authority that gave him the opportunity to propagate and attempt to implement his conception of Rondon and Rondon's values. Along with the jurist and educator Anisio Teixeira, for example, he founded the University of Brasília in 1960, where he worked to ensure that its anthropology, sociology, and ethnology departments reflected the philosophy of Rondon and his disciples, such as Roquette-Pinto.[7]

That same year, Ribeiro drew up the final draft of the statute that in 1961 created the Xingu Indigenous Park. By repeatedly invoking Rondon's name, philosophy, and field reports, Ribeiro and his allies were able to get the Brazilian government to carve out more than ten thousand square miles in northeastern Mato Grosso—an area the size of Massachusetts—as a refuge for nearly a dozen Indigenous peoples. Not by coincidence, the reserve's boundaries consisted largely of rivers the Rondon Commission had first surveyed decades earlier, such as the Culuene, Ronuro, and Tanguro.

But then, on March 31, 1964, came the right-wing coup that introduced twenty-one years of repressive military dictatorship. Rondon's former army colleagues—and enemies, too, for Juarez Távora became the new government's minister of transport, just as he had been under Vargas more than three decades earlier—were now in charge, and their vision of Brazil and of Rondon could scarcely have been more different from that of Ribeiro, who was the deposed president's chief of staff and soon went into exile in Uruguay. They immediately set out to eradicate the image that had been constructed since 1958 and remake Rondon in their own likeness.

In place of the humanist, pacifist, and military intellectual, the new government offered a version of Rondon that stressed his nationalist credentials: love of country, decades of self-sacrifice for the greater good of the nation, a vision of its greatness, and an embrace of a kind of manifest destiny. Other martial qualities, such as his physical courage and his iron discipline, were also highlighted, with his espousal of Positivism and pacifism relegated to footnotes. In a deeply divided society desperately in need of anchors and icons around which it could rally, Rondon was transformed into a symbol of *brasilidade*, a kind of high-minded but amorphous "Brazilianness."

The centennial of Rondon's birth, in 1965, was thus marked by official tributes that painted him in this narrowly nationalistic light. Here and there, a few tributes managed to escape official management and emphasize Rondon's humanist side: at one university he was hailed as "the Indian who civilized the whites."[8] But for the most part, the official remembrances adhered to the new government's edict: all such events should, in addition to "reaffirming his love for the Indian," also highlight "his work for the integration and defense of our borders."[9]

A year later, at a seminar titled "Education and National Security," held in Rio and sponsored by the general staff of the Brazilian Army, a university professor named Wilson Choeri warned the high command that the Communist Party was making more inroads than ever among Brazilian youth, thanks to its opposition to "the Revolution," the term the military used to denominate its 1964 coup. As an antidote, he proposed a state-sponsored program to win university students over to the government's side by sending them deep into the interior and immersing them in "'a bath of Brazil,' to feel, smell and taste Brazilian reality."[10]

That suggestion held enormous appeal for the military, which already tended to regard university students as an undisciplined and subversive rabble in need of haircuts and a good cuffing. "The military was convinced that the young people of those times, now today's leaders, should get to know remote Brazil, sharing experiences with our brothers born there, living there and buried there," Gen. Ivan de Mendonça Bastos wrote forty years later. "Young people needed to hear other accents, taste other flavors, see other landscapes and, above all, join hands with other young people."[11]

The new program was quickly baptized the "Rondon Project," and to further emphasize its hypothetical connection with Rondon, the first participants, recruited from universities in and around Rio de Janeiro, were sent to Rondônia. There, the Fifth Battalion of Army Engineers, Rondon's old unit, was working on a pair of projects seen as continuations of his mission. The first was to construct a highway from Cuiabá to Porto Velho along the path of Rondon's long-abandoned telegraph line, and the second was to build another road from Porto Velho to the Bolivian border. Properly trained students, it was thought, could help the undermanned battalion with medical care, surveying, and the design of roads and bridges.

The program was named for Rondon for multiple reasons, Choeri would explain in an oral history of the Rondon Project published in 2006. First of all, it was a way to pay homage to "the Great Pioneer of the 20th Century, the tireless trailblazer who swept across the wilderness, created the Indian Protection Service and knew Brazil" like no other. But equally important was Rondon's status as "an impeccably neutral, impartial figure" who had avoided partisan politics. By linking itself to Rondon, the man above suspicion, the program "would not bear the name of any President, nor bear the name of any politician."[12]

Darcy Ribeiro had already discovered for himself just how powerful and coalescing a factor Rondon's legacy could be. After the 1964 coup, he wrote in his memoirs, "I was jailed in a Navy barracks" as a prelude to being forced to leave Brazil, when "the officers learned that I had been a disciple, or friend and disciple, of Rondon. To them, it was inconceivable that a Communist agent, which was the image they had of me, could have lived with Indians and, above all, been close to the only hero of the Armed Forces, the uncontested hero of all of them. I had to send for my funeral eulogy . . . to show them that I had been one of Rondon's biggest friends."[13]

Despite Choeri's professed desire that the Rondon Project remain as "impeccably neutral" as Rondon himself, the program was from its very beginning identified with the most nationalist faction of the military dictatorship. The project's motto was *Integrar para não entregar*, or "Integrate so as not to have to submit" or turn over to foreign control, and that rhyming phrase was repeated over and over for decades in all of its publicity material. The military government was dominated by officers who considered themselves "developmentalists," dedicated to construction of a strong Brazilian state that would play a leading role in spurring the economic growth that would transform the country into a world power. As they saw the international scene, the established powers—not just the Soviet Union but also the West—considered Brazil's advancement a threat to their own entrenched interests, and would try to weaken this rising new force by nibbling away at Brazil's weakest points. Hence the importance of integrating outlying areas.

A major part of this program, of course, involved settling the Amazon and exploiting its resources, and an essential aspect of that effort was construction of the Trans-Amazon Highway and colonization of the jungle by impoverished peasants trucked in from the Northeast. In the words of another of the dictatorship's favorite slogans, the government intended to supply "land without men for men without land." There were obviously echoes here of the impulses that led the First Republic to assign Rondon to the region back in 1890 and prompted Vargas to launch his March to the West—the same fear of losing the Amazon to what were assumed to be covetous foreign interests, the same desire to fully incorporate it into the Brazilian nation, the same unwillingness to acknowledge this was not really "land without men." In fact, any mention of Indigenous peoples and their rights as individual ethnic groups and original inhabitants of the land was being carefully scrubbed out of consideration.

The first group of participants in the Rondon Project, transported to Rondônia in July 1967 as the dry season was underway in the Amazon and the winter college break had started in the south, consisted of two professors and thirty university students, mostly premedical, engineering, and geography majors. Quickly, the program expanded: soon, students majoring in ethnology, anthropology, and linguistics, not just those in "hard science" disciplines like geology or zoology, were also recruited, from all twenty-seven of Brazil's states and territories. So were interning architects and city planners, who were assigned to the new settlements and colonies springing up alongside the new Cuiabá–Porto Velho highway, as outgrowths of the telegraph stations Rondon had built a half century earlier.

And while the Rondon Project's initial focus was only Rondônia, its area of activity also gradually enlarged, first to include all of the Brazilian Amazon, and then other backward or ignored areas. Within a decade, it had also become a year-round program of civilian national service, rather than one that operated only during the academic vacation period, and had permanent operations in every region of the country. In all of these activities, Rondon's name and image were constantly brandished as sources of legitimacy.

During this same period, a similar process of indoctrination taking advantage of Rondon's prestige and achievements was underway among young recruits doing their obligatory military service. A fourteen-minute training film introduced in 1969, called *Rondon: The Last of the Great Pioneers*, drew on footage that Luiz Reis had shot more than fifty years before and emphasized Rondon's service in various "strategic points" along the border and his leading role in "successive phases of national integration." It was due to Rondon, new soldiers were told, that Brazil was able to "establish new criteria of national security" and "carry out the settlement of border areas." And according to the film, Rondon's final words were not religious, reflecting his lifelong Positivism, but patriotic: "Long Live the Republic!"[14]

However, during the same year the Rondon Project was launched, both the SPI and the National Council for the Protection of the Indian were abolished and replaced by a new agency, the National Indian Foundation, known by the Portuguese-language acronym FUNAI. The hard-line minister of the interior appointed in 1967— a former military engineer who early in his career had supervised construction of the Macapá-Clevelândia road Rondon had originally projected during his border-inspection tour in 1928—then ordered a sweeping investigation into reports of abuses and corruption at the two agencies. The result was a report of more than seven thousand pages that detailed appalling instances of collusion between officials of the SPI and rich landowners in the seizure of Indigenous lands, mass killings, enslavement, deliberate infection with diseases, and sexual exploitation.

The report made clear that the vast majority of these abuses occurred after Rondon's death, and that the others began only in his dotage. But FUNAI, created as the dictatorship was hardening, now had a justification to operate with a philosophy radically different from Rondon's, and for the next decade it was administered by military officers intent on doing just that. While the new agency continued to honor Rondon's name in theory, it was under orders to pursue "a policy of integration at an accelerated rhythm"[15] and "compulsory assimilation"[16] regardless of the desires or readiness of Indigenous peoples themselves. Additionally, Rondon's vision of Indian tribes as "sentinels of the frontier" was abandoned, replaced by a policy of encouraging—if not forcing—tribes to move to the interior, where they could be more easily monitored.

The Rondon Project endured for nearly a quarter century, until 1989, outlasting by four years the dictatorship that created it. Thanks to their service as "Rondonistas," more than 325,000 idealistic, aspiring young professionals from urban areas, today in late middle age or older, got their first glimpse of the "other" Brazil; many became outspoken advocates of protecting the Amazon and its peoples. But by linking Rondon's name to an authoritarian and repressive government, some damage was done to his persona and standing among ordinary Brazilians.

Nor did it help that school textbooks used during the dictatorship, written in conformity with the military's vision of a "Brasil Grande," ossified Rondon's image. He became "the modern-day flag-bearer" who opened up the interior, and was hailed as author of the "Die if you must, but kill never" policy, which became a kind of feel-good assertion of Brazil's supposed moral superiority over other countries that had treated their Indigenous peoples more harshly—this even as the Amazon was being deforested and Indians driven off their ancestral lands by ranchers, miners, and loggers supported and financed by the government.

But all of Rondon's other dimensions seemed to vanish. Certainly there was no mention of his refusal to seize power for himself or his

392 • INTO THE AMAZON

repeated rejection of military involvement in overthrows of civilian rule. "The Army should be mute" when it comes to politics, Rondon had said in one of his final interviews, "ready to sacrifice for the good of the Nation, but without intervening in petty questions of backroom intrigue and scheming."[17]

With the fall of the military dictatorship in 1985, some tentative efforts were made to reclaim aspects of Rondon's image that had been deliberately played down or ignored. In addition, followers of Rondon's philosophy, including one of the Villas-Bôas brothers, were put in charge of FUNAI and told to steer it back on course through implementation of Rondon's four principles. But a backlash came in the mid-1990s, when intellectuals who came of age during the military dictatorship, were trained in disciplines like semiotics and postmodernism, had absorbed the influence of contestatory scholars like Michel Foucault and Edward Said, and were without living memories of "the Marshal of Peace," began to take a revisionist look at Rondon and his work.

For the most part, they did not like what they thought they saw: in their view, Rondon had from the beginning been at the service of a rapacious, almost genocidal, national project, had done much to advance that process in contradiction of the lofty goals he had proclaimed, and had a hopelessly naive and incoherent view of Brazilian Indians and their needs.[18] Far from being a hero, he was a dupe and perhaps even a traitor to his own culture and people.

Some of the revisionist criticisms of specific incidents have a strong foundation in the historical record; there is no way to deny the sorry record of massacres, land seizures, and invasions to which Brazil's Indigenous peoples were subjected throughout the twentieth century. But the revisionists of the 1990s had an enormous advantage that Rondon did not: hindsight. Looking back, it is always easy to point out the errors of others on the basis of information acquired only after the events in question, and this is what the revisionists consistently did. Never mind that they offered criticisms of Rondon's activities in the field without suggesting prescriptions of their own or explaining what Rondon could or should have done differently.

In an essay published in 2009 and titled "Why I Am a Rondonian," Mércio Pereira Gomes, an anthropology professor and former president of FUNAI, provided perhaps the most effective rejoinder. "Rondon's critics habitually accuse him of only having demarcated small parcels of land," he wrote. "They purposely neglect to take into account the historical context in which the SPI emerged and operated." It is thus unjust "to expect that Rondon and the indigenous experts of his time would have a broader vision than that provided by historical evidence and anthropological studies" and equally important to remember that "the political conditions for demarcation of land for Indians were extremely adverse during that first half-century of the SPI."[19]

"In any case, what we see developed here is an ethical attitude," on Rondon's part, "that is unexpected in the moral panorama of Brazil" at that time, Pereira Gomes concluded. "This attitude is also unprecedented in other parts of the world. If only for this, there would be sufficient justification to be a follower of Rondon."[20]

Though these revisionist criticisms have continued into our own time, they are limited largely to pockets of academia and have not gained traction beyond those narrow confines. Early in 2005, for example, the Rondon Project was revived at the request of the National Union of Students, a traditionally leftist organization, and with the support of a government led by the left-wing Workers' Party. Then-president Luiz Inácio Lula da Silva took part in the ceremony that brought the program back to life, which was held in Tabatinga, just across the border from the site where Rondon had spent four long years preventing Colombia and Peru from going to war against each other. There Lula explicitly linked himself to some of the same aspects of Rondon's legacy that Darcy Ribeiro had emphasized nearly fifty years earlier, using some of the same buzzwords, and simultaneously rejected the military government's co-optation of Rondon for its policy of muscular developmentalism.

"In the past," Lula argued, "geographic utopianism saw our country as an immense pioneering front, pulling an expanding market. The road ended at the edge of the jungle. In the eyes of some, it seemed enough to push the trail ahead, and progress would do the rest. Today we know that is not the way it is. The country, essentially, is integrated" and now "it is necessary to overcome the great frontier of inequality and conquer a future that is more humane, to open roads of opportunity." This, he concluded, was a "peaceful task demanded by the country, ordained by history and placed within our reach by democracy."[21]

"Lula Relaunches Rondon Project, One of the Symbols of the Military Government,"[22] read the headline of the story that ran that day on the home page of Brazil's leading online portal. This assessment was partially true, but not entirely, for Lula's government was clearly shifting the program's focus. "We are re-creating a Rondon Project with the face of today's Brazil," he announced to an audience that included the commanders of the army, navy, and air force, members of his cabinet, Rondonistas from the program's original incarnation, and the first class of two hundred volunteers from version 2.0.

"The new Rondon is part of a gigantic effort to connect all of Brazil through the bridge of solidarity," Lula explained. "Social justice represents today that which the telegraph symbolized in the past, when Marshal Rondon roamed the country at the head of the Strategic Commission for Telegraph Lines. It was in order to conquer this new frontier that the Project has gained a new face, as a proposal to engage young people and universities in overcoming our social distances."[23]

As the rebirth of the Rondon Project suggests, the two main facets of Rondon's public image, once seen as inherently antagonistic and philosophically incompatible, are increasingly being fused into a unified whole. "All of us, military and civilians, know that Cândido Mariano da Silva Rondon—Marshal Rondon—was the first humanist and first Brazilian environmentalist to give us a true example of Brazilianness,"[24] Gen. Mendonça Bastos, a former commandant of Brazil's military academy, wrote in his introduction to the "Oral History of the Rondon Project" in 2006. For military nationalists, this constitutes a marked retreat from their previous position.

And in a Brazil in which racial and ethnic minorities are asserting their identities with ever greater pride, the notion of Rondon as a paragon of "Brazilianness" has also meant renewed attention to his mixed racial background, often in a highly idealized form. In 2014, for example, Brazil's largest television network broadcast a five-part miniseries called *Rondon: The Great Chief*, to coincide with the centennial of the Roosevelt-Rondon Scientific Expedition. In one scene, set just before the fall of the monarchy, Benjamin Constant engages the young Rondon in a conversation, clearly apocryphal, about the country's future, and exalts him as the personification of what the Estado Novo would later call the "new tropical man."

"You, cadet Rondon, have a great mission ahead of you," Benjamin Constant says. "The fatherland is in great need of you. You have coursing through your veins the blood that represents Brazil. In your body flow Indian, caboclo, white and black currents."[25]

By the 150th anniversary of Rondon's birth, in 2015, he had thus been transformed, for better or worse, into a national unanimity, his image largely cleansed of the controversies that surrounded him during important phases of his life. This has proved useful since 2019, when Jair Bolsonaro, an extreme right-wing former army captain nostalgic for the dictatorship and openly hostile to protection of Indian tribes or the Amazon, became president.[26] Just as Rondon once cited José Bonifácio, Brazil's "Patriarch of Independence," to confer legitimacy on his own policy plans, so today can Bolsonaro's critics reference Rondon, the "most profound, coherent, energetic and generous personality ever to emerge from the Brazilian people," anytime their demagogic president accuses them of serving "globalist" interests or blocking economic progress.

The presidential election of October 2022 returned Lula to power by the narrowest margin in the history of Brazilian democracy. But Mato Grosso, Rondônia, Goiás, Acre, Roraima, and other Amazon states voted overwhelmingly for Bolsonaro, whose allies not only won governor's races throughout the region, but also performed far better than Lula's coalition throughout Brazil in the vote for seats in both houses of Congress. During Lula's first two terms in office, he often made concessions to the agricultural lobby, especially soybean growers, and approved projects to build new dams and pave highways throughout the Amazon; the pressure on him to offer further compromises will be even stronger now.

So the twin battles that preoccupied Rondon throughout his life continue, and though more than sixty years have passed since his burial, he remains a combatant through the relevance of his ideas. Now, as then, advocates of Rondon's four principles sometimes fall victim to the same violent tactics of the predatory loggers, ranchers, miners, and other commercial interests who plagued Rondon in the Amazon—the shooting deaths of the Indigenous expert Bruno Araújo Pereira and the journalist Dom Phillips in June 2022 being a tragic recent example.

But thanks to the efforts of Rondon and his heirs, Brazil now has an Indigenous population that surpasses one million, including lawyers, doctors, nurses, teachers, social workers, university professors, engineers, pilots, and information-technology advisers to tribal groups—all demanding their prerogatives as citizens. It also has Indigenous members of Congress and a constitution that abandons an assimilationist perspective and, for the first time, formally recognizes Indian land rights as both "original," preceding the existence of a Brazilian state, and inalienable.[27] Lula even promised to create a new "Ministry for Original Peoples" to protect Indigenous rights.

No doubt, as presidents of Brazil and presidents of FUNAI come and go, bringing changes in policy with them, advances and retreats will continue to occur. But the humanist, nonviolent, multicultural template that Rondon created for the Amazon and its peoples will remain a shining example of the best that Brazil has to offer the world, an inspiration far into the future. "The life of Rondon is a comfort to every Brazilian who has lost faith in his country," the poet Manuel Bandeira wrote the week the "pacifist general" died. "He demonstrates that not everything is chicanery within our 3.3 million square miles."[28]

ACKNOWLEDGMENTS

THIS PROJECT WAS blessed with help and support from many individuals and institutions, in both Brazil and the United States. I'm going to start in Brazil, where this book was published in 2019 as *Rondon: Uma Biografia*. I talked for years, decades even, about writing a Rondon biography "someday," but it was my *compadre* Leonardo Haefeli who insisted I keep my word. And when I finally took the plunge, he and his wife, Ana Parrini, and his sister Mônica, offered me shelter during my research trips, as well as instantaneous feedback to my findings. The rest of the large Haefeli clan—three generations' worth!—proved equally enthusiastic and supportive.

Beyond the family orbit, I owe a great deal to two longtime journalist friends, Rosental Calmon Alves and Paulo Sotero, both of whom saw a full-scale, modern biography of Rondon as a way to enhance Brazilians' knowledge of their own history and spurred me, a foreigner hesitant to write about a national hero, forward. My agent in Brazil, Lucia Riff, also immediately recognized the relevance of a Rondon biography at a time when the Amazon and Indigenous rights remain under assault. In Luiz Schwarcz at Companhia das Letras, she found a publisher who allowed me full rein to address all of the many facets of Rondon's long and eventful life; my editors, Daniela Duarte and Marcelo Ferroni, waded through an Amazon jungle of words and ideas, opening clearings in the thicket just like scouts on one of Rondon's expeditions.

At the institutional level, I was cordially received everywhere I went, and no one questioned the audacity of an American launching his own Rondon Project; I took this as one more sign of the deep regard and esteem in which Rondon is held, in both military and civilian circles. At the Historical Archive of the Brazilian Army, I was assisted by Maj. Alcemar Ferreira, Capt. Celso Pereira Soares, and Sgt. Álvaro Alves, and at the Army Library I got valuable research tips from Maj. Wagner Alcides de Souza. At the Army Museum, Maj. João Rogério de Souza Armada and Lt. Cristiane Monteiro went out of their way to help me, and at the Marshal Rondon Cultural Space in Santo Ángelo, Lt. Col. André Luiz dos Santos Franco and Sgt. José Apolinário dos Santos did everything they were able to do in aiding my research.

In Rondon's home state of Mato Grosso, I was also welcomed with open arms. At the Public Archives in Cuiabá, the director, Waltemberg Santos, guided me through various collections and made valuable suggestions about lines of research. At the Historical and Geographic Institute of Mato Grosso, Maria Luiza Marconi was especially generous with her time. At the national film library in São Paulo, Alexandre Miyazoto guaranteed my access to all the films of Luiz Thomaz Reis and all the documentation relating to his work. And in Brasília, the chief archivist at the Darcy Ribeiro Memorial at the National University of Brasília, Margareth Barbosa, pointed me in the direction of some unexpected discoveries.

Back in Rio, the staff historian at the Benjamin Constant House and Museum, Marcos Felipe de Brum Lopes, also made me aware of resources not initially on my research list. At the Museum of the Indian, where it is easy to get lost in the vast documentation of the life of Rondon and history of the SPI, Rodrigo Piquet Saboia de Mello helped keep me on course. At the National Museum, the historian Gustavo Alves Cardoso Moreira not only knew where everything was kept but also had intriguing questions about Rondon and his associates, while at the museum's library, chief librarian Dulce Maranha Paes de Carvalho and her assistants Adriana Ornellas, Fernando Henrique de Almeida Lima, and Márcio Nunes de Miranda were happy to help. Tragically, much of this invaluable scientific and cultural heritage was destroyed on September 2, 2018, when a raging fire reduced the National Museum to ashes and rubble.

At the Getúlio Vargas Foundation's Center for Research and Documentation, archivist Nixon Marques proved an accommodating host; at the Brazilian Academy of Letters, I was hosted by Rodolfo Garcia and Lúcio de Mendonça, who helped me savor an atmosphere ideal for research. Finally, at the Association of Friends of the Temple of Humanity, Luiz Edmundo Horta Barbosa da Costa Leite and Virginia Rigot-Müller offered me a detailed orientation on the history of the Positivist Church of Brazil, its beliefs, and the role the Horta Barbosa family played in the Positivist movement and on the Rondon Commission. I hope their campaign to completely restore the temple, an important place in Brazil's history that was severely damaged in 2009, succeeds.

In the United States, my greatest debt is to the Cullman Center for Scholars and Writers, where I was fortunate enough to spend the 2015–16 academic year as a research fellow. Aside from validating my notion that a biography of a Brazilian explorer barely known in the English-speaking world was needed, the Cullman Center offered the perfect environment to read, think, and write about Rondon, with full access to the bountiful stacks of the New York Public Library. My deepest thanks to the center's then director, Jean Strouse, and her wonderful staff: Lauren Goldenberg, Paul Delaverdac, and Julia Pagnamenta. Thanks also to all fourteen of the other fellows from that year, each of whom contributed in one way or another, from asking probing questions to offering tips on useful sources.

Nor could this book have seen the light of day in the English-speaking world without the savvy, enthusiasm, and persistence of my agents, Peter and Amy Bernstein, who consistently went the extra mile on my behalf. They believed in the viability and worth of this project from the first moment, offered sage counsel and guidance as we navigated the publication process, and also displayed extraordinarily sharp editorial instincts that helped shape this book for non-Brazilian readers. At W. W. Norton, I am grateful to John Glusman for his willingness to take a risk and to Helen Thomaides for shepherding my manuscript through to completion.

Since childhood, I have always liked libraries and librarians. But in the course of this project, that admiration only grew. As regards the Roosevelt-Rondon expedition, I benefited from the knowledge of Heather Cole at the Houghton Library of Harvard University and Mai Reitmeyer at the library and archives of the American Museum of Natural History. At the Brown University library, the assistance of Patricia Figueroa, curator of the Brasiliana Collection, was fundamental in gaining access to a rich archive of material about the Brazilian Positivist Church. And at the New York Public Library, Rebecca Federman, Melanie Locay, and Rhonda Evans were always helpful and attentive, no matter how obscure the document or book I was seeking.

Finally, the most profound thanks to my wife, Clotilde Amaral Rohter, through whom I first discovered Brazil. As always when I am writing a book, she made astute observations, pertinent criticisms, and helpful suggestions, while also offering unconditional support. Also unrestricted was her patience: for years, Rondon has dominated not only my work hours but also our dinner-table conversations. Her curiosity, her desire to know more and more about Rondon, was contagious, a constant source of encouragement even when the going was at its toughest.

NOTES

Introduction

1 Cândido Mariano da Silva Rondon, *História da Minha Vida* (São Paulo: LeBooks, 2019), 506. See also Theodore Roosevelt, press conference on arrival in New York City, May 19, 1914, as per Associated Press in numerous American newspapers.

2 Léopold Boissier, "La Croix-Rouge et l'assistance aux détenus politiques," *Politique étrangère* (Paris, Centre d'Études de Politique Étrangère) 23, no. 1 (1958): 24.

3 Douglas O. Naylor, "Col. Roosevelt as His Guide Remembers Him," *New York Times*, January 6, 1929.

4 Algot Lange, *The Lower Amazon: A Narrative of Explorations in the Little Known Regions of the State of Pará on the Lower Amazon* (New York: G. P. Putnam's Sons, 1914), 403.

5 Henri Badet, *Rondon: Charmeur d'Indiens* (Paris: Nouvelles Éditions Latines, 1951), 110.

6 All citations in this paragraph are from Rondon's "Credo positivista," an appendix to Rondon, *História da Minha Vida*, 6.

Chapter I: Beyond the End of the World

1 See Lylia da Silva Guedes Galetti, *Sertão, fronteira, Brasil: Imagens de Mato Grosso no mapa da civilização* (Cuiabá: Entrelinhas/EdUFMT, 2012). See especially chapters 6 and 8, and by the same author "Mato Grosso: O estigma da barbárie e a identidade regional," *Textos de História*, Brasília 3, no. 2 (1995): 48–81.

2 William Lewis Herndon, *Exploration of the Valley of the Amazon 1851–1852* (New York: Grove Press, 2000), xviii, 311.

3 Karl von den Steinen, *O Brasil central: Expedição em 1884 para a exploração do Rio Xingu* (São Paulo: Companhia Editora Nacional, 1942), 56–57.

4 Rondon, *História da Minha Vida*, 15–16.

5 Rondon, 18.

6 Rondon, 18–19.

7 Rondon, 18.

8 Percy H. Fawcett, *Lost Trails, Lost Cities: From His Manuscripts, Letters and Other Records*, ed. Brian Fawcett (New York: Funk & Wagnalls, 1953).

9 Luiz Marcigaglia, *Os Salesianos no Brasil* (São Paulo: Escolas Profissionais Salesianas, 1955), 53.

10 "The newspaper *O Povo*, in Cuiabá, by the end of the 1870s regularly published a column called 'Echoes of Siberia.' . . . In other words, there was an appropriation of that image to indicate the isolation of the province in relation to the coastal capital and other large cities." In Francisco Bento da Silva, "Acre, a pátria dos proscritos: Prisões e desterros para as regiões do Acre em 1904 e 1910" (PhD diss., Universidade Federal do Paraná, 2010), 234–35.

11 Charles Wagley, *Amazon Town: A Study of Man in the Tropics* (New York: Alfred A. Knopf, 1964), 30, 109. The caboclo, he writes, is always seen as "uneducated, poor, backward, and generally inferior to others, especially urban folk." Thus "the Amazon caboclo exists only in the concept of the groups of higher status referring to those of lower status."

12 Galetti, *Sertão, fronteira, Brasil*, 91.

13 Galetti, 12, 203. Quotation marks in the original.

14 Rondon, *História da Minha Vida*, 18.

15 Rondon, 18.

16 Rondon, 19.

17 Amilcar Armando Botelho de Magalhães, *Rondon: Uma relíquia da pátria* (Curitiba: Guaíra, 1942).

18 Rondon, *História da Minha Vida*, 18.

19 Rondon, 18.

20 Rondon, 18.

21 Rondon, 21.

22 Rondon, 21.

23 Rondon, 21.

Chapter II: The "Furry Beast" in the Imperial City

1 Rondon, *História da Minha Vida*, 23.

2 Lúcia Maria Bastos Pereira das Neves and Humberto Fernandes Machado, *O Império do Brasil* (Rio de Janeiro: Nova Fronteira, 1999).

3 All quotes in this paragraph are from Rondon, *História da Minha Vida*, 23.

4 Botelho de Magalhães, *Rondon: Uma relíquia*, 19.

5 Rondon, *História da Minha Vida*, 22.

6 Botelho de Magalhães, *Rondon: Uma relíquia*, 19.

7 Afonso Monteiro, "Reminiscências da escola militar da Praia Vermelha," in *Cadetes e alunos militares através dos tempos (1878–1932)*, ed. Francisco de Paula Cidade (Rio de Janeiro: Biblioteca do Exército, 1961), 50.

8 Monteiro, "Reminiscências," 50.

9 Monteiro, 50.

10 Monteiro, 50.

11 Rondon, *História da Minha Vida*, 24–25.

12 Botelho de Magalhães, *Rondon: Uma relíquia*, 20.

13 Monteiro, "Reminiscências," 59.

14 Monteiro, 59.

15 Monteiro, 59.

16 Lobo Vianna, "Reminiscências da lendária escola militar da Praia Vermelha," in Cidade, *Cadetes e alunos militares*, 78.

17 Vianna, "Reminiscências," 64.

18 Monteiro, "Reminiscências," 57.
19 Rondon, *História da Minha Vida*, 26.
20 Rondon, 26.
21 Rondon, 27–28.
22 Rondon, 28.
23 Rondon, 28.
24 All citations in this paragraph from *Revista da Família Acadêmica* (Rio de Janeiro) 1 (November 1887): 2–3.
25 Rondon, *História da Minha Vida*, 31.
26 Rondon, 31.
27 Rondon, 31.

Chapter III: The Republic

1 Auguste Comte, *The Gospel of Maternal Love*, ed. Henri Dussauze (Newcastle-on-Tyne: Hedson, 1910), 42.
2 Auguste Comte, *Curso de filosofia positivista* (São Paulo: Nova Cultural, 1983).
3 Auguste Comte, *A General View of Positivism* (New York: E. P. Dutton, 1907), 1.
4 Andrew Wernick, *Auguste Comte and the Religion of Humanity: The Post-Theistic Program of French Social Theory* (Cambridge: Cambridge University Press, 2005), 1.
5 José Murilo de Carvalho, "A ortodoxia positivista no Brasil: Um bolchevismo de classe média," in *O positivismo: Teoria e prática*, ed. Hélgio Trindade (Porto Alegre: Editora da UFRGS, 2007), 179–92.
6 See Todd A. Diacon, "Cândido Mariano da Silva Rondon: One Man's Search for the Brazilian Nation," in *The Human Tradition in Modern Brazil*, ed. Peter M. Beattie (Wilmington, DE: SR Books, 2004), 113.
7 Renato Lemos, *Benjamin Constant: Vida e história* (Rio de Janeiro: Topbooks, 1999), 485.
8 Augusto Tasso Fragoso, "Revolvendo o passado," *Jornal do Commercio* (Rio de Janeiro), March 3, 1940, 5.
9 Rondon, *História da Minha Vida*, 33.
10 Rondon, 32.
11 Rondon, 33–34.
12 *O Estado* (Niterói), November 15, 1939, in Lemos, *Benjamin Constant*, 305.
13 Laurentino Gomes, *1889* (São Paulo: Globo, 2013), 263.
14 All citations in this paragraph from site of the Clube Militar: https://clubemilitar.org/historia/.
15 Letter from Deodoro da Fonseca to Clodoaldo da Fonseca, September 30, 1889, cited in Ivan Monteiro de Barros Lins, *Benjamin Constant* (Rio de Janeiro: J. R. de Oliveira, 1936), 71.
16 Document dated November 11, 1889, "Pacto de sangue," from archives of the Museu Casa de Benjamin Constant, Cândido Rondon file.
17 Rondon, *História da Minha Vida*, 38.
18 Rondon, 39.
19 Rondon, 39.
20 Rondon, 40.
21 Affonso Celso de Assis Figueiredo, *O Visconde de Ouro Preto: Excertos biográficos* (Porto Alegre: Globo, 1936).
22 Rondon, *História da Minha Vida*, 42.
23 Rondon, 43.

Chapter IV: "There Begins the Harshest of Backlands"

1 "Síntese da fé de ofício do Marechal do Exército Cândido Mariano da Silva Rondon," Arquivo Histórico do Exército, Group ii, Folder 16, Documento 27, Folio 1.

2 "Notinhas biográficas sobre a saudosa esposa do general Rondon, a exma. sra. Francisca Xavier Rondon (dona Chiquita Rondon), segundo a fala ritual do Apostolado Positivista do Brasil," Archives of the Museu Benjamin Constant, Amilcar Armando Botelho de Magalhães file.

3 Rondon, *História da Minha Vida*, 29.

4 Rondon, 29.

5 Rondon, 47.

6 Rondon, 52.

7 Alfredo d'Escragnolle Taunay, *Inocência* (São Paulo: Ática, 1986), 9.

8 Rondon, *História da Minha Vida*, 50.

9 Rondon, 59.

10 Rondon, 59.

11 Rondon, 67.

12 Rondon, 67.

13 All citations in this paragraph from Peter M. Beattie, *The Tribute of Blood: Army, Honor, Race and Nation in Brazil, 1864–1945* (Durham, NC: Duke University Press, 2001), 136.

14 Hiram Reis e Silva, "Rondon e o Conde de Lippe," *Gente de Opinião* (Porto Velho, Rondônia), July 25, 2009.

15 From the Military Penal Code.

16 Botelho de Magalhães, *Rondon: Uma relíquia*, 40.

17 Rondon, *História da Minha Vida*, 49.

18 Rondon, 49.

19 "Síntese da fé de ofício do Marechal do Exército Cândido Mariano da Silva Rondon," Arquivo Histórico do Exército, Group ii, Folder 16, Documento 27, Folio 3.

20 Rondon, *História da Minha Vida*, 47.

21 Citations for this and the previous paragraph come from Rondon, 74.

22 Simon Schwartzman, *Um espaço para a ciência: A formação da comunidade científica no Brasil* (Brasília: MCT, 2001), 97–98.

23 Rondon, *História da Minha Vida*, 75.

Chapter V: Burdensome Tasks and Forced Obedience

1 Rondon, *História da Minha Vida*, 83.

2 Rondon, 84.

3 Rondon, 84.

4 Rondon, 84.

5 Rondon, 84.

6 Rondon, 85.

7 Rondon, 85.

8 Rondon, 86.

9 Rondon, 87.

10 Rondon, 87.

11 Rondon, 87.

12 Ordem do dia no. 694 de 1895, 1089, Arquivo Histórico do Exército.

13 Ordem do dia no. 694 de 1895, 159.

14 Auguste Comte, "Social Physics (Book VI of *Cours de philosophie positive*, 1830–42)," in *Auguste Comte and Positivism: The Essential Writings*, ed. Gertrud Lenzer (New York: Harper Torchbooks, 1975), 197.

15 Cândido Rondon, Diaries, Book 010306 (December 1895–May 1896), May 13, 1896, Museu Histórico do Exército e Forte de Copacabana (MHEx/FC).

16 Euclides da Cunha, *Os sertões* (São Paulo: Ateliê Editorial, 2001), 67.

17 Rondon, *História da Minha Vida*, 91.

18 All citations in this paragraph come from: Donald F. O'Reilly, "Rondon: Biography of a Brazilian Republican Army Commander" (PhD diss., New York University, 1969), 66.

19 Miguel Lemos and Raimundo Teixeira Mendes, "Nossa iniciação no positivismo," in *Benjamin Constant*, ed. Ivan Monteiro de Barros Lins (Rio de Janeiro: J. R. de Oliveira, 1936), 501.

20 Lins, *Benjamin Constant*, 501.

21 Lins, 503.

22 Comte, *Appel aux conservateurs* (Paris: Chez V. Dalmont, 1855), 19.

Chapter VI: Article 44, Section 32

1 Cândido Mariano da Silva Rondon, *Relatório dos trabalhos realizados de 1900–1906* (Rio de Janeiro: Departamento de Imprensa Nacional, 1949), 30.

2 O'Reilly, "Rondon: Biography," 66.

3 Campos Salles cited in Raymundo Faoro, *Os donos do poder* (São Paulo: Globo, 2012), 529.

4 Cândido Rondon, Diaries, Book 010302 (January 7–September 22, 1900), MHEx/FC.

5 Cândido Rondon, Diaries, Book 010302 (January 7–September 22, 1900), MHEx/FC.

6 Cândido Rondon, Diaries, Book 010302 (January 7–September 22, 1900), MHEx/FC.

7 Rondon, *História da Minha Vida*, 101.

8 Cândido Rondon, Diaries, Book 010302 (January 7–September 22, 1900), MHEx/FC.

9 Cândido Rondon, Diaries, Book 010302 (January 7–September 22, 1900), MHEx/FC.

10 Cândido Rondon, Diaries, Book 010302 (January 7–September 22, 1900), MHEx/FC.

11 Cândido Rondon, Diaries, Book 010309 (January 6–May 27, 1901), MHEx/FC.

12 "Síntese da fé de ofício do Marechal do Exército Cândido Mariano da Silva Rondon," Arquivo Histórico do Exército, Group ii, Folder 16, Document 27, Folio 6.

13 O'Reilly, "Rondon: Biography," citing a personal interview with Hildebrando Horta Barbosa, 76.

14 Cândido Rondon, Diaries, Book 010315 (May 29–August 28, 1902), MHEx/FC.

15 Rondon, *História da Minha Vida*, 112.

16 Rondon, 20.

17 Letter of Cândido Rondon to Raimundo Teixeira Mendes, in O'Reilly, "Rondon: Biography," 79.

18 Rondon, *História da Minha Vida*, 161.

19 Cândido Rondon, Diaries, Book 010294 (1905–1907), MHEx/FC.

20 Rondon, *História da Minha Vida*, 162.

Chapter VII: "Correcting the World"

1 Rondon, *História da Minha Vida*, 176.

2 Rondon, 176–77.

3 Rondon, 177.

4 Rondon, 177.

5 Maria Fátima R. Machado, "Índios de Rondon: Rondon e as linhas telegráficas na visão dos sobreviventes Wáimare e Kaxíniti, grupos Paresí" (PhD diss., Museu Nacional/UFRJ, Rio de Janeiro, 1994), 53.

6 Machado, "Índios de Rondon," 52.

7 Antônio Pires de Campos in *Revista do Instituto Histórico e Geográfico Brasileiro*, t. 25 (1862): 443, cited in Karl von den Steinen, *Entre os Aborígenes do Brasil central* (São Paulo: Departamento de Cultura, 1940), 540.

8 Von den Steinen, *Entre os Aborígenes do Brasil central*, 540.

9 All citations in this paragraph from von den Steinen, 542ff.

10 Machado, "Índios de Rondon," 103.

11 All citations in this paragraph from Machado, 83–84.

12 Machado, 84.

13 Rondon, *História da Minha Vida*, 184.

14 Rondon, 184.

15 Rondon, 185.

16 Rondon, 185.

17 Rondon, 185.

18 Rondon, 186.

19 Rondon, 186.

20 Rondon, 186.

21 Rondon, 187.

22 Rondon, 187.

23 Both the arrow and the bandolier are now on display at the Espaço Cultural Marechal Rondon museum in Santo Ângelo, Rio Grande do Sul.

24 Rondon, *História da Minha Vida*, 188.

25 Rondon, 188.

26 Cf. entry for "Nambikwara" at the site Povos Indígenas no Brasil, of the Instituto Socioambiental: https://pib.socioambiental.org/pt/Povo:Nambikwara.

27 Rondon, *História da Minha Vida*, 201.

28 Rondon, 202.

29 Rondon, 202.

30 Rondon, 203.

31 Rondon, 206.

32 Cândido Rondon, Diaries, Book 010296 (November 4, 1908–March 9, 1909), MHEx/FC.

33 Rondon, *História da Minha Vida*, 207.

Chapter VIII: "Returning Immediately, through the Other Side"

1 All citations for this paragraph from: Cândido Mariano da Silva Rondon, *Comissão Rondon: Apontamentos sobre os trabalhos realizados pela Comissão de Linhas Telegráficas Estratégicas de Mato Grosso ao Amazonas, sob a direção do Coronel de Engenharia Cândido Mariano da Silva Rondon, de 1907 a 1915* (Brasília: Senado Federal, 2003), 100.

2 Gen. Francisco Jaguaribe de Mattos, in O'Reilly, "Rondon: Biography," 116.

3 Gen. Francisco Jaguaribe de Mattos, interviewed in O'Reilly, 116.

4 Rondon, *História da Minha Vida*, 221.

5 Gen. Francisco Jaguaribe de Mattos, in O'Reilly, "Rondon: Biography," 118.

6 Amilcar Armando Botelho de Magalhães, in O'Reilly, 119.

7 Rondon, *História da Minha Vida*, 223.

8 Rondon, 223.

9 Amílcar Armando Botelho de Magalhães, *Pelos sertões do Brasil* (Rio de Janeiro: Companhia Editora Nacional, 1941), 317–18.

10 Rondon, *História da Minha Vida*, 234.

11 Manoel Theophilo da Costa Pinheiro, *Exploração do Rio Jaci-Paraná* (Rio de Janeiro: Departamento de Imprensa Nacional, 1949), Publication #5 of the Comissão de Linhas Telegráficas Estratégicas de Mato Grosso ao Amazonas (Comissão Rondon), anexo n. 2, 174–75.

12 Rondon, *História da Minha Vida*, 228.

13 Rondon, *Comissão Rondon: Apontamentos*, 109–10.

14 Proclamation of the III International Congress of the Academy of History of Science (October 4, 1934), meeting in Porto, Portugal, as reported in *Diário de Lisboa*.

Chapter IX: "With Presents, Patience and Good Manners"

1 Claude Lévi-Strauss, *Saudades do Brasil* (São Paulo: Companhia das Letras, 1994), 22.

2 Jules Henry, *Jungle People: A Kaingáng Tribe of the Highlands of Brazil* (Richmond, VA: J. J. Augustin, 1941), 55.

3 Hermann von Ihering, "A antropologia do estado de São Paulo," *Revista do Museu Paulista* (São Paulo) 7 (1907): 215.

4 Luís Bueno Horta Barbosa, "Em defesa dos indígenas brasileiros," *Jornal do Commercio* (Rio de Janeiro), November 11, 1908, 12.

5 Hermann von Ihering, "A questão dos índios no Brasil," *Revista do Museu Paulista* (São Paulo: Typographia do Diario Official) 8 (1911): 113, 125.

6 All citations in this paragraph from von Ihering, "A questão dos índios no Brasil," 125–27.

7 On the relationship between the Bororo and the Salesians, see Sylvia Caiuby Novaes, *The Play of Mirrors: The Representation of Self Mirrored in the Other* (Austin: University of Texas Press, 1993), 70–71.

8 Von Ihering, "A questão dos índios no Brasil," 125.

9 Angus Mitchell, ed., *The Amazon Journal of Roger Casement* (London: Anaconda, 1997), 71.

10 Angus Mitchell, *Roger Casement in Brazil: Rubber, the Amazon and the Atlantic World, 1884–1916* (São Paulo: Humanitas, 2010).

11 All citations from José Bonifácio de Andrada e Silva, *Apontamentos para a civilização dos índios bravos do Império do Brasil* (Rio de Janeiro: Imprensa Nacional, 1823), 12.

12 Luciene P. C. Cardoso, "Notas sobre as origens do Escritório Central da Comissão Rondon no Rio de Janeiro," *Histórica: Revista eletrônica do Arquivo Público do Estado de São Paulo* (São Paulo) 43 (August 2010): 5.

13 Botelho de Magalhães, *Pelos sertões do Brasil*, 372.

14 The letters were also published in pamphlet form as *Em defesa dos selvagens brasileiros* (Rio de Janeiro: Tipographia da Igreja Positivista do Brasil, May 1910).

15 *Em defesa dos selvagens brasileiros*, 24–25.

16 Rondon, *História da Minha Vida*, 221.

Chapter X: Mariano's Tongue

1 Rondon, *História da Minha Vida*, 276.

2 Cândido Mariano da Silva Rondon, *Conferências realizadas em 1910 no Rio de Janeiro e em São Paulo* (Rio de Janeiro: Typographia Leutzinger, 1922), 79.

3 Rondon, *Conferências 1910*, 79.
4 Rondon, *Conferências 1910*, 81.
5 Rondon, *Conferências 1910*, 81.
6 Rondon, *Conferências 1910*, 111.
7 Rondon, *Conferências 1910*, 97.
8 Rondon, *História da Minha Vida*, 277.
9 Rondon, 277.
10 Rondon, 277.
11 Rondon, 278.
12 Rondon, 278.
13 Rondon, 278.
14 Cândido Rondon, Diaries, Book 010337 (June 10, 1910–March 12, 1912), MHEx/FC.
15 Rondon, *História da Minha Vida*, 280.
16 Rondon, 280.
17 "Homenagem dos Bororos da catequese salesiana em Mato Grosso ao Exmo. sr. ten. coronel dr. Cândido M. da S. Rondon," August 31, 1911, Archives of the Museu Nacional, Rondon folder, 2.
18 Edgar Roquette-Pinto, *Rondônia* (São Paulo: Companhia Editora Nacional, 1935), 60.
19 Rondon, *História da Minha Vida*, 282–83.
20 Rondon, 283.
21 Rondon, 283.
22 Rondon, 284.
23 Rondon, 288.
24 Rondon, 289.
25 Rondon, 174.
26 Cândido Rondon, Diaries, Book 014147 (June 9–December 21, 1913), MHEx/FC.

Chapter XI: "The Greatest Number of Unforeseen Difficulties"

1 Letter from Theodore Roosevelt to John H. Patterson, cited in Michael R. Canfield, *Theodore Roosevelt in the Field* (Chicago: University of Chicago Press, 2015), 288.
2 Canfield, *Theodore Roosevelt in the Field*, 288.
3 Joseph R. Ornig, *My Last Chance to Be a Boy: Theodore Roosevelt's South American Expedition of 1913–1914* (Baton Rouge: Louisiana State University Press, 1994), 29.
4 J. A. Zahm, *Through South America's Southland* (New York: D. Appleton, 1916), 11.
5 Morison, Elting E., ed. *The Letters of Theodore Roosevelt: Volume VIII—The Days of Armageddon, 1914–1918* (Cambridge, Mass.: Harvard University Press, 1954), 904.
6 Ornig, *My Last Chance to Be a Boy*, 32.
7 George K. Cherrie, *Dark Trails: Adventures of a Naturalist* (New York: G.P. Putnam's Sons, 1930), 248–49.
8 E. Bradford Burns, *Unwritten Alliance: Rio Branco and Brazilian-American Relations* (New York: Columbia University Press, 1966), 95.
9 Francisco Luiz Teixeira Vinhosa, ed., *Domício da Gama em Washington: Guia de pesquisa* (Rio de Janeiro: Centro de História e Documentação Diplomática, Ministério das Relações Exteriores, 2011).
10 Itamaraty-Washington, 1913, 234.2.1, Centro de História e Documentação Diplomática do Ministério das Relações Exteriores.
11 Rondon, *História da Minha Vida*, 291.
12 Itamaraty-Washington, 1913, Centro de História e Documentação Diplomática do Ministério das Relações Exteriores.

13 Cândido Rondon, Diaries, Book 014147 (June 9–December 21, 1913), MHEx/FC.
14 Leo Miller, *In the Wilds of South America* (New York: Charles Scribner's Sons, 1918), 194.
15 Theodore Roosevelt, *Through the Brazilian Wilderness* (New York: Charles Scribner & Sons, 1914), 9.
16 Cândido Mariano da Silva Rondon, *Conferências realizadas nos dias 5, 7 e 9 de outubro de 1915 pelo Sr. Coronel Cândido Mariano da Silva Rondon no Theatro Phenix do Rio de Janeiro sobre trabalhos da Expedição Roosevelt e da Comissão Telegraphica*, p. 17.
17 Roosevelt, *Through the Brazilian Wilderness*, 9.
18 Theodore Roosevelt, "A Journey in Central Brazil," *Geographical Journal* 45, no. 2 (February 1915): 98.
19 Letter from Theodore Roosevelt to Frank Chapman, November 4, 1913, in Morison, *The Letters of Theodore Roosevelt: Volume VIII*, 754.
20 Letter from Edith Roosevelt to Ethel Roosevelt Derby, October 25, 1913, in Ornig, *My Last Chance to Be a Boy*, 51.
21 Henry Fairfield Osborn, "Theodore Roosevelt, Naturalist," *Natural History: The Journal of the American Museum* (New York) 19 (January 1919): 7.
22 Frank Chapman, "Introduction," in Roosevelt, *Through the Brazilian Wilderness*, xviii.
23 Henry Fairfield Osborn, *Impressions of Great Naturalists: Reminiscences of Darwin, Huxley, Balfour Cope and Others* (New York: Charles Scribner's Sons, 1924), 180.

Chapter XII: Dismissals, Resignations, and Two Colonels

1 Rondon, *História da Minha Vida*, 293.
2 Rondon, 293.
3 Letter from Roosevelt to David Gray, cited in Edmund Morris, *Colonel Roosevelt* (New York: Random House, 2010), 64.
4 Cândido Rondon, Diaries, Book 014147 (June 9–December 21, 1913), MHEx/FC.
5 Roosevelt, *Through the Brazilian Wilderness*, 8.
6 Letter from T. Roosevelt to his son Kermit, in Morison, *The Letters of Theodore Roosevelt, Volume VIII—The Years of Armageddon, 1914–1918*, 946.
7 Arquivo Histórico do Exército, Setor de Pessoal, Fé de Ofício, pasta X-3-9, 2.
8 Arquivo Histórico do Itamaraty, Case 928.
9 Arquivo Histórico do Itamaraty, Case 935, Packet C 912/914, Dated 17.12.13.
10 Rondon, *História da Minha Vida*, 291.
11 Amílcar Armando Botelho de Magalhães, *Impressões da Comissão Rondon* (Porto Alegre: Globo, 1929), 224.
12 Rondon, *História da Minha Vida*, 300.
13 Rondon, 302.
14 Rondon, 303.
15 Rondon, 303.
16 Botelho de Magalhães, *Rondon: Uma relíquia*, 245.
17 All citations in this and previous paragraph are from: Telegrams from Rondon to Lauro Müller, Itamaraty Archives.
18 Candice Millard, *The River of Doubt: Theodore Roosevelt's Darkest Journey* (New York: Broadway, 2005), 103–4.
19 Ornig, *My Last Chance to Be a Boy*, 108.
20 Rondon, *Conferências realizadas nos dias 5, 7 e 9 de Outubro de 1915 no Theatro Fênix do Rio de Janeiro sobre trabalhos da Expedição Roosevelt e da Comissão Telegráfica* (Rio de Janeiro: Typographia do Jornal do Commercio, 1916), 43.

21 Rondon, *História da Minha Vida*, 309.

22 Morris, *Colonel Roosevelt*.

23 Cândido Rondon, Diaries, Book 014149 (January 21–March 5, 1914), MHEx/FC.

24 Canfield, *Theodore Roosevelt in the Field*, photograph on an unnumbered page.

25 Canfield, photograph on an unnumbered page.

26 George Kruk Cherrie, "George K. Cherrie's Diary of the Theodore Roosevelt Expedition to Explore the River of Doubt in Brazil, October 1913 to May 1914," transcribed by Joseph R. Ornig, November 1975, Archives of the American Museum of Natural History, 38.

Chapter XIII: Boxes and Rain

1 Cherrie, "George K. Cherrie's Diary," 338.

2 Rondon, *História da Minha Vida*, 306.

3 Rondon, 306.

4 Roosevelt, *Through the Brazilian Wilderness*, 202, 207.

5 Cândido Rondon, Diaries, Book 014149 (January 21–March 5, 1914), MHEx/FC.

6 Indian Rights Association, *19th Annual Report of the Executive Committee of the Indian Rights Association* (Philadelphia: Office of the Indian Rights Association, 1902), 3.

7 Theodore Roosevelt, *A Compilation of the Messages and Speeches of Theodore Roosevelt, 1901–1905* (Washington, DC: Bureau of National Literature and Art, 1906), 1:610; and Theodore Roosevelt, *The Works of Theodore Roosevelt: Presidential Addresses and State Papers* (New York: P. F. Collier & Sons, 1914), 2:594.

8 Roosevelt, *Through the Brazilian Wilderness*, 193.

9 Roosevelt, 157.

10 Citations in this paragraph from Roosevelt, 222.

11 All citations in this paragraph are from José Antonio Cajazeira, *Relatório apresentado ao chefe da Comissão Brasileira, coronel de Engenharia Cândido Mariano da Silva Rondon pelo médico da expedição, dr. José Antonio Cajazeira, capitão-médico do Exército, Anexo 6* (Rio de Janeiro: Typographia do Jornal do Commercio, 1915), 113.

12 Cândido Rondon, Diaries, Book 014149 (January 21–March 5, 1914), MHEx/FC.

13 Roosevelt, *Through the Brazilian Wilderness*, 204.

14 Roosevelt, 193.

15 All citations in this paragraph from Cherrie, "George K. Cherrie's Diary," 12.

16 Anthony Fiala, "The Outfit for Travelling in the South American Wilderness," in Roosevelt, *Through the Brazilian Wilderness*, Appendix B, 378.

17 Morison, *The Letters of Theodore Roosevelt: Volume VIII—The Years of Armageddon, 1914–1918*, 904–5.

18 Morison, 904–5.

19 Morison, 905.

20 All citations in this paragraph from Roosevelt, *Through the Brazilian Wilderness*, 200.

21 Roosevelt, 194.

22 Roosevelt, 234–35.

23 Roosevelt, 237.

24 Roosevelt, 236.

25 Letter from Leo Miller to Frank Chapman, February 24, 1914, Archives of the American Museum of Natural History.

26 Roosevelt, *Through the Brazilian Wilderness*, 242.

Chapter XIV: Portage, Pole, and Paddle

1 Roosevelt, *Through the Brazilian Wilderness*, 262.
2 Roosevelt, 241–42.
3 Roosevelt, 244.
4 Theodore Roosevelt, *A Book-Lover's Holidays in the Open* (New York: Charles Scribner's Sons, 1920), 162.
5 Miller, *In the Wilds of South America*, 240.
6 Miller, 242.
7 Rondon, *História da Minha Vida*, 319.
8 Rondon, 319.
9 Rondon, 319.
10 Roosevelt, *Through the Brazilian Wilderness*, 258.
11 Roosevelt, 262.
12 Roosevelt, 353.
13 See George Miller Dyott, "The Last Miles of the River of Doubt," *New York Times*, July 10, 1927, 10.
14 Cherrie, "George K. Cherrie's Diary," diary entry March 11, 1914.
15 Elsie M. B. Naumburg, with field notes by George K. Cherrie, "The Birds of Matto Grosso, Brazil: A Report on the Birds Secured by the Roosevelt-Rondon Expedition," *Bulletin of the American Museum of Natural History* 60 (1930): 12.
16 Roosevelt, *Through the Brazilian Wilderness*, 266.
17 Roosevelt, 262.
18 Cândido Mariano da Silva Rondon, "Segunda conferência: O Rio da Dúvida," in *Conferências realizadas nos dias 5, 7 e 9 de Outubro de 1915 no Theatro Fênix do Rio de Janeiro sobre trabalhos da Expedição Roosevelt e da Comissão Telegráfica* (Rio de Janeiro: Typographia do Jornal do Commercio, 1916), 70.
19 Entry by Kermit Roosevelt in his diary, March 15, 1914. From the Kermit & Belle Roosevelt Collection at the Library of Congress.
20 Rondon, *Conferências realizadas nos dias 5, 7 e 9*, 71.
21 Ordem do Dia n. 13, 28 fev. 1914, p. 1, Museu Benjamin Constant, Amílcar Armando Botelho de Magalhães Folder.

Chapter XV: Passion

1 Rondon, "Segunda conferência," in *Conferências realizadas nos dias 5, 7 e 9*, 72.
2 Rondon, "Segunda conferência," in *Conferências realizadas nos dias 5, 7 e 9*, 72.
3 Rondon, *História da Minha Vida*, 321.
4 Rondon, "Segunda conferência," in *Conferências realizadas nos dias 5, 7 e 9*, 68.
5 Roosevelt, *Through the Brazilian Wilderness*, 276.
6 Cherrie, *Dark Trails*, 291.
7 Rondon, *História da Minha Vida*, 325.
8 Roosevelt, *Through the Brazilian Wilderness*, 290.
9 Roosevelt, 302–3.
10 Roosevelt, 303.
11 Rondon, "Segunda conferência," in *Conferencias realizadas nos dias 5, 7 e 9*, 90.
12 Rondon, *História da Minha Vida*, 325.
13 Rondon, 320.
14 Cherrie, "George K. Cherrie's Diary," 55.

15 Cândido Rondon, Diaries, Book 010323 (March 7–April 7, 1914), MHEx/FC.
16 Rondon, *História da Minha Vida*, 321.
17 Rondon, 322.
18 Rondon, 322.
19 Rondon, 311.
20 Associated Press account, published on September 4, 1902, in publications ranging from the *San Francisco Call* and *Indianapolis Journal* to the *Street Railway Review*, all on page 1.
21 Millard, *The River of Doubt*, 98.
22 Millard, 98.
23 Cherrie, "George K. Cherrie's Diary," diary entry on March 27, 1914.
24 Roosevelt, *Through the Brazilian Wilderness*, 317.
25 Vilhjalmur Stefansson, ed., "Theodore Roosevelt: Memorial Meeting at the Explorers Club," *Bulletin of the New York Explorers Club* (March 1919): 25.
26 Cherrie, "George K. Cherrie's Diary," diary entry for April 2, 1914, 63.
27 Cherrie, *Dark Trails*, 308–9.
28 Stefansson, "Theodore Roosevelt: Memorial Meeting," 26.
29 Cajazeira, *Relatório apresentado*, 113.
30 Cajazeira, 113–14.
31 Cherrie, *Dark Trails*, 307–8.
32 Kermit Roosevelt diary entry, March 30, 1914.
33 Roosevelt, *Through the Brazilian Wilderness*, 312.

Chapter XVI: Expedition in Peril

1 Roosevelt, *Through the Brazilian Wilderness*, 313.
2 Kermit Roosevelt diary entry, April 7, 1914.
3 Rondon, *História da Minha Vida*, 325.
4 Rondon, 325.
5 All citations from this and previous paragraph: Rondon, 325–26.
6 Rondon, *Conferências realizadas nos dias 5, 7 e 9*, 90.
7 Rondon, "Segunda conferência," 92.
8 Rondon, *Comissão Rondon: Apontamentos*, 418.
9 Rondon, *História da Minha Vida*, 327.
10 Rondon, 327.
11 Kermit Roosevelt, *The Long Trail* (New York: Review of Reviews/Metropolitan Magazine, 1921), 161–62.
12 Kermit Roosevelt diary entry, April 5, 1914.
13 Cherrie, *Dark Trails*, 315.
14 Rondon, *História da Minha Vida*, 326.
15 Botelho de Magalhães, *Rondon: Uma relíquia*, 176–77.
16 Edilberto Coutinho, *Rondon e a integração da Amazônia* (São Paulo: Arquimedes, 1968), 18.
17 Rondon, *História da Minha Vida*, 327.
18 Rondon, 327.
19 Rondon, 327.
20 Kermit Roosevelt diary entry, April 6, 1914.
21 Cherrie, "George K. Cherrie's Diary," diary entry, April 8, 1914.
22 Cherrie, diary entry, April 8, 1914.
23 Cherrie, diary entry, April 8, 1914.

24 Cherrie, diary entry, April 9, 1914.
25 Cherrie, diary entry, April 11, 1914.
26 Cherrie, diary entry, April 12, 1914.
27 Kermit Roosevelt diary entry, April 13, 1914.
28 Stefansson, "Theodore Roosevelt: Memorial Meeting," 24.
29 Rondon, *Conferências realizadas nos dias 5, 7 e 9*, 100.
30 Kermit Roosevelt diary entry, April 17, 1914.
31 Kermit Roosevelt diary entry, April 18, 1914.
32 Roosevelt, *Through the Brazilian Wilderness*, 322.
33 Cherrie, "George K. Cherrie's Diary," diary entry, April 21, 1914.
34 Roosevelt, *Through the Brazilian Wilderness*, 337.
35 Roosevelt, 327.
36 Douglas O. Naylor, "Col. Roosevelt as His Guide Remembers Him," *New York Times*, January 6, 1929.
37 Roosevelt, *Through the Brazilian Wilderness*, 393.
38 All citations in this paragraph from: Ordem do dia n. 21, 1 maio 1914, 1–2, in "Cópias das ordens do dia da Expedição Científica Roosevelt-Rondon," Museu Benjamin Constant, Amílcar Botelho de Magalhães folder.
39 Ordem do dia n. 21, 1 maio 1914, 1–2.
40 Rondon, *História da Minha Vida*, 330.

Chapter XVII: "Shifts and Contrivances Available in Wild Countries"

1 Naylor, "Col. Roosevelt."
2 Theodore Roosevelt interview with Associated Press, published in various American newspapers on May 7, including the *New York World*.
3 Ornig, *My Last Chance to Be a Boy*, 335.
4 Rondon, *História da Minha Vida*, 331.
5 Rondon, 331.
6 All citations for this paragraph from Rondon, 331.
7 Rondon, 331.
8 "Fé de ofício do tenente-coronel médico dr. José Antonio Cajazeira," Arquivo Histórico do Exército, Document X-3-9.
9 Excerpted from a Theodore Roosevelt interview published by Associated Press and published in various American newspapers on May 7, 1914, including the *New York World*.
10 Ibid.
11 John Keay, *Explorers Extraordinary* (London: John Murray/British Broadcasting Corporation, 1985).
12 Arnold Henry Savage-Landor, *Across Unknown South America* (Boston: Little, Brown, 1913), 1:72.
13 Savage-Landor, *Across Unknown South America*, 1:77.
14 Savage-Landor, 1:245.
15 Savage-Landor, 1:15.
16 All citations for this paragraph from Savage-Landor, 1:228.
17 Savage-Landor, 1:191.
18 Roosevelt, *Through the Brazilian Wilderness*, 359.
19 Millard, *The River of Doubt*, 338.
20 Millard, 338.
21 *New York Times*, May 27, 1914.
22 Roosevelt, "A Journey in Central Brazil," 108.

23 Roosevelt, 97.

24 The letter is in French: "À Paris, j'ai publié, dans Le Matin, le texte entier de votre lettre au sujet des 'explorations' de Savage-Landor et je pense que j'ai définitivement arreté qu'on prenne en considération sérieuse ses prétensions comme explorateur, du moins pour tous ceux qui sont d'une certaine compétence, comme observateurs et témoins." Cited in Rondon, *História da Minha Vida*, 333.

25 William J. Wharton and Douglas Freshfield, eds. *Hints to Travellers: Scientific and General* (London: Royal Geographic Society, 1893), 109. (Galton's original edition dates from 1855.)

26 Francis Galton, *The Art of Travel, or Shifts and Contrivances Available in Wild Countries* (London: Phoenix Press, 2000), 309.

27 David Grann, *The Lost City of Z: A Tale of Deadly Obsession in the Amazon* (New York: Doubleday, 2009), 176–77.

28 Percy H. Fawcett, *Exploration Fawcett* (London: Century, 1988), 115.

29 Hermes Leal, *Coronel Fawcett: A verdadeira história do Indiana Jones* (São Paulo: Geração Editorial, 1996), 68.

30 Grann, *Lost City of Z*, 177.

31 Fawcett, *Exploration Fawcett*, 11.

32 Letter to Sir John Scott Keltie, director of the RGS, on February 15, 1915, in Percy Fawcett, *Lost Trails, Lost Cities*, 228.

33 Fawcett, *Exploration Fawcett*, 209.

34 Brian Fawcett, *Ruins in the Sky* (London: Hutchinson, 1958), 231.

35 P. Fawcett, cited in Grann, *Lost City of Z*, 186.

36 B. Fawcett, *Ruins in the Sky*, 231.

37 *A Noite*, January 1920, in Leal, *Coronel Fawcett*, 122.

38 Antônio Callado, *Esqueleto na lagoa verde: Um ensaio sobre a vida e o sumiço do Coronel Fawcett* (Rio de Janeiro: Departamento de Imprensa Nacional, 1953), 90.

39 B. Fawcett, *Ruins in the Sky*, 231.

Chapter XVIII: "Is He a General Yet?"

1 Miller, *In the Wilds of South America*, 251–52.

2 Botelho de Magalhães, *Rondon: Uma relíquia*, 48.

3 "Síntese da fé do Marechal Cândido Mariano da Silva Rondon" Arquivo Histórico do Exército, Group ii, Folder 16, Document 27, Folio 26.

4 Alcides Maia, "Rondon," *O Paiz*, Rio de Janeiro, October 26, 1915, 1.

5 Botelho de Magalhães, *Rondon: Uma relíquia*, 41–42.

6 "O Caso de Matto Grosso—A Opinião do Sr. Coronel Rondon," *O Imparcial* (Rio de Janeiro), November 26, 1917, 3.

7 "Viagem do cel. Theodore Roosevelt ao Brasil. Excursão ao estado de Mato Grosso," Unnumbered folder 1912–14, November 21, 1913, Arquivo Histórico do Itamaraty.

8 Rondon, *História da Minha Vida*, 354.

9 Darcy Ribeiro, "Parecer sobre a extinção do SPI," pasta dr/spi 1910.00.00, v. 2.85, 7, and "Dotações orçamentárias ao SPI para auxílios aos índios" [undated], Arquivos Memorial Darcy Ribeiro, Universidade Nacional de Brasília.

10 Samuel Paiva and Sheila Schvarzman, eds., *Viagem ao cinema silencioso do Brasil* (São Paulo: Azougue, 2011), 266.

11 Paiva and Schvarzman, *Viagem ao cinema silencioso*, 267.

12 Paiva and Schvarzman, 267–68.

13 Paiva and Schvarzman, 268.

14 Paiva and Schvarzman, 277–78.
15 Paiva and Schvarzman, 271.
16 Paiva and Schvarzman, 280–81.
17 Rondon, *História da Minha Vida*, 349.
18 Rondon, 350.
19 Rondon, 351.

Chapter XIX: Jack of All Trades

1 Contained in Alípio Bandeira, *Rondon*, 19–20 (pamphlet without publisher information or date, in the collection of the Biblioteca Nacional in Rio de Janeiro).
2 All citations in this paragraph from: Bandeira, *Rondon*, 19–20.
3 Rondon, *História da Minha Vida*, 357.
4 Rondon, 357.
5 Tristão de Athayde, *Pandiá Calógeras na opinião de seus contemporâneos* (São Paulo: Typ. Siqueira, 1934), 161.
6 Maurice Gamelin, "Le Général Rondon et ses explorations au Brésil," *France-Amérique* 112 (April 1921): 81.
7 Gamelin, "Le Général Rondon," 83.
8 Coutinho, *Rondon e a integração*, 30.
9 Rondon, *História da Minha Vida*, 375–85.
10 Rondon, 387.
11 "Obras do Nordeste: Resposta da Comissão de Inspeção ao dr. Epitácio Pessoa," CPDOC/Fundação Getúlio Vargas, Isidoro Simões Lopes Folder, ISL 58-F, 14.
12 "Injurioso e ultrajante," *Correio da Manhã* (Rio de Janeiro), October 9, 1921, 2.
13 "A famosa carta injuriosa ao Exército" *O Imparcial* (Rio de Janeiro), October 25, 1921, 1.
14 "Continua no mesmo pé o caso da carta" *O Imparcial* (Rio de Janeiro), October 27, 1921, 1.
15 Rondon, *História da Minha Vida*, 375.
16 See Botelho de Magalhães, *Rondon: Uma relíquia*, 93–94.
17 Rondon, *História da Minha Vida*, 375.
18 Rondon, 375.
19 Rondon, 375.
20 Rondon, 376.
21 Rondon, 376.
22 Rondon, 376.
23 "Síntese da fé de ofício do Marechal do Exército Brasileiro Cândido Mariano da Silva Rondon," July 15, 1922, Group ii, Folder 16, n. de ordem 27, Folio 30, Arquivo Histórico do Exército.
24 Ibid.
25 Cândido Rondon, Diaries, Book 010380 (April–October 1922), MHEx/FC.

Chapter XX: Catanduvas

1 Rondon, *História da Minha Vida*, 389.
2 Comte, *Appel aux conservateurs*, 105.
3 Rondon, *História da Minha Vida*, 390.
4 Rondon, 391.
5 Rondon, 390.

6 O'Reilly, "Rondon: Biography," 206.

7 Capt. Hugh Barclay to Lt. Col. N. E. Margetts (Chief, M. I. 5, G-2), Rio de Janeiro, April 14, 1925, 2052–106, War Dept., General Staff, Military Intelligence Division, rg 165.

8 Ibid.

9 Rondon, *História da Minha Vida*, 391.

10 Cândido Rondon, Diaries, Book 010373 (October 1924), MHEx/FC.

11 Rubens Massena. "Rondon Entrevistado." *A Defesa Nacional* 52, no. 607 (May/June 1966): 35–36.

12 Rondon, *História da Minha Vida*, 391.

13 Rondon, 393.

14 Domingo Meirelles, *As Noites das grandes fogueiras: Uma biografia da Coluna Prestes* (Rio de Janeiro: Record, 1995), 328.

15 Rondon, *História da Minha Vida*, 393.

16 Jorge Amado, *O cavaleiro da esperança: A vida de Luís Carlos Prestes* (Rio de Janeiro: Record, 1979), 107–8.

17 Daniel Aarão Reis, *Luís Carlos Prestes: Um revolucionário entre dois mundos* (São Paulo: Companhia das Letras, 2014), 58.

18 Reis, *Luís Carlos Prestes*, 58.

19 Reis, 59.

20 Meirelles, *As noites das grandes fogueiras*, 369.

21 Meirelles, 373.

22 Capt. Hugh Barclay to the War Dept., General Staff, Military Intelligence Division.

23 Gen. Maurice Gamelin, from site of the Academia da História Militar Terrestre do Brasil: http://www.ahimtb.org.br/rondon.htm.

24 Rondon, *História da Minha Vida*, 393.

25 Rondon, 393.

26 Rondon, 394.

27 Rondon, 394.

28 Rondon, 395.

Chapter XXI: Back in the Field

1 Rondon, *História da Minha Vida*, 400.

2 Rondon, 427.

3 Rondon, 406.

4 Rondon, 407.

5 Rondon, 407.

6 Everard im Thurn, "The Ascent of Mount Roraima," *Proceedings of the Royal Geographical Society and Monthly Record of Geography* (London) 7, no. 8 (August 1885): 497–521.

7 George Henry Hamilton Tate, "Through Brazil to the Summit of Mount Roraima," *National Geographic*, November 1930, 587.

8 Tate, "Through Brazil to the Summit of Mount Roraima," 586–87.

9 Tate, 587.

10 Tate, 589.

11 Tate, 589.

12 Rondon, *História da Minha Vida*, 417.

13 Rondon, 419.

14 José Luiz de Andrade Franco and José Augusto Drummond, "Alberto José Sampaio: Um botânico brasileiro e o seu programa de proteção à natureza," *Varia história*, no. 33 (January 2005): 133.

15 Alberto José Sampaio, "O problema florestal no Brasil em 1926," *Archivos do Museu Nacional* 28 (March 1926).

16 Gastão Cruls, *A Amazônia que eu vi: Óbidos-Tumucumaque* (Rio de Janeiro: Companhia Editora Nacional, 1938), 167.

17 Rondon, *História da Minha Vida*, 426.

18 Rondon, 429.

19 Cruls, *A Amazônia que eu vi*, 163, 166.

20 Rondon, *História da Minha Vida*, 430.

21 Cruls, *A Amazônia que eu vi*, 166.

22 Rondon, *História da Minha Vida*, 430.

23 Rondon, 431.

24 Rondon, 431.

25 Rondon, 434.

26 Cruls, *A Amazônia que eu vi*, 251.

Chapter XXII: *"I Think It Advisable the General Not Continue His Journey"*

1 Rondon, *História da Minha Vida*, 440.

2 Rondon, 442.

3 Rondon, 443.

4 Rondon, 443.

5 O'Reilly, "Rondon: Biography," 242.

6 Cândido Rondon, Diaries, Book 010440 (1929–1930), MHEx/FC.

7 Rondon, *História da Minha Vida*, 451.

8 Rondon, 453.

9 James Stuart Olson, *The Indians of Central and South America: An Ethnohistorical Dictionary* (New York: Greenwood, 1991), 277.

10 Rondon, *História da Minha Vida*, 453.

11 Cândido Rondon, Diaries, Book 010443, (1930), MHEx/FC.

12 Rondon, *História da Minha Vida*, 455.

13 Reis, *Luís Carlos Prestes*, 138.

14 "Como se deu a prisão de general Rondon, em Marcelino Ramos," *O Jornal* (Rio de Janeiro), November 1, 1930, 5.

15 "Como se deu a prisão," 5.

16 João Neves da Fontoura, *Memórias: A aliança liberal e a revolução de 1930* (Rio de Janeiro: Globo, 1963), 2:444.

17 Fontoura, *Memórias*, 2:444.

18 "Tudo fizemos pela Paz," *Diário Carioca* (Rio de Janeiro), October 29, 1930, 2.

19 Rondon, *História da Minha Vida*, 458.

20 All citations in this paragraph are from Rondon, 459.

21 Cândido Rondon, Diaries, Book 10386 (October 25, 1930–May 4, 1932), MHEx/FC.

22 Rondon, *História da Minha Vida*, 459.

23 Laura Antunes Maciel, *A nação por um fio: Caminhos, práticas e imagens da Comissão Rondon* (São Paulo: PUC-SP/Fapesp, 1998), 22.

24 Rondon, *História da Minha Vida*, 459.

25 Cândido Rondon, Diaries, Book 10386 (October 25, 1930–May 4, 1932), MHEx/FC.

26 Ibid.

27 Edilberto Coutinho, *Rondon: O salto para o desconhecido* (São Paulo: Companhia Editora Nacional, 1987), 98.

28 Cândido Rondon, Diaries, Book 10386 (October 25, 1930–May 4, 1932), MHEx/FC.

Chapter XXIII: In the Wilderness

1 Rondon, *História da Minha Vida*, 460.

2 Rondon, 460.

3 Rondon, 460.

4 *Gazeta de Notícias* (Rio de Janeiro), August 24, 1939, 1.

5 *Gazeta de Notícias*, 1.

6 *Gazeta de Notícias*, 1.

7 All citations from this paragraph and the previous two: letter of Father Joseph Audrin to the SPI, 1931. Arquivo do SPI/Memorial Darcy Ribeiro, Brasília, DRr/SPI 1910.00.00 VI/21.

8 Claude Lévi-Strauss, *Tristes trópicos* (São Paulo: Companhia das Letras, 1996), 288–89.

9 Cândido Rondon, Diaries, Book 10386 (October 25, 1930–May 4, 1932), MHEx/FC.

10 Rondon, *História da Minha Vida*, 14.

11 Constitution of 1934, Article 10, Clause iii.

12 Rondon, *História da Minha Vida*, 463.

13 Rondon, 464.

14 Article III of the Protocol of Friendship and Cooperation between the Republic of Colombia and the Republic of Perú.

15 Article VI of the Protocol of Friendship and Cooperation between the Republic of Colombia and the Republic of Perú.

16 Rondon, *História da Minha Vida*, 476.

17 Rondon, 476.

18 Rondon, 469.

19 Rondon, 470.

20 Rolf Blumberg interview in O'Reilly, "Rondon: Biography," 266.

21 Rondon, *História da Minha Vida*, 470.

22 Rondon, 471.

23 All citations in this paragraph from Rondon, 472.

Chapter XXIV: Old Rondon versus the "New State"

1 Personal communication from Maria Cecilia Rondon Amarante, September 3, 2019.

2 From Benjamin Costallat, cited in Botelho de Magalhães, *Rondon: Uma relíquia*, 34.

3 Suely Braga da Silva, ed., *Luiz Simões Lopes: Fragmentos de memória* (Rio de Janeiro: FGV, 2006), 95.

4 Braga da Silva, *Luiz Simões Lopes*, 97.

5 João de Lira Neto, *Getúlio: Do governo provisório à ditadura do Estado Novo (1930–1945)* (São Paulo: Companhia das Letras, 2013), 378.

6 Decree-Law no. 1736, of November 3, 1939, subordinating the Indian Protection Service to the Ministry of Agriculture.

7 Cândido Mariano da Silva Rondon, "Benjamin Constant e o problema republicano," *Jornal do commercio* (Rio de Janeiro), November 19, 1939, 4.

8 Rondon, *História da Minha Vida*, 477.

9 Rondon, 477.

10 Niccolò Machiavelli, *The Prince*, chap. 20, subsection 5.

11 Darcy Ribeiro, "Dotações orçamentárias ao Serviço de Proteção aos Índios para auxiliar os Índios," DR/SPI 1910.00.00, v.2/85, 7, Memorial Darcy Ribeiro, UNB, Brasília.

12 Mércio Pereira Gomes, "Por que sou rondoniano," *Estudos avançados* (São Paulo) 23, no. 65 (2009): 180–81.

13 Cândido Mariano da Silva Rondon, *Rumo ao oeste* (Rio de Janeiro: Laemmert Biblioteca Militar, 1942).

14 Botelho de Magalhães, *Rondon: Uma relíquia*, 203–4.

15 Rondon, *Rumo ao Oeste*, 14.

16 Ibid., 21.

17 Letter from Father Hipólito Chovelon to Getúlio Vargas, titled "Relatório de 1937 da Missão Salesiana entre os Índios Xavante, Mato Grosso," annex of Hipólito Chovelon, Francisco Fernandes, and Pedro Sbardellotto, *Do primeiro encontro com os Xavante à demarcação de suas reservas: Relatórios do Pe. Hipólito Chavelon* (Campo Grande: Missão Salesiana de Mato Grosso, 1996), 130.

18 Ibid.

19 Orlando Villas-Bôas and Cláudio Villas-Bôas, *A marcha para o oeste* (São Paulo: Globo, 1994), 11.

20 Orlando Villas-Bôas, Roda Viva, December 10, 1999. Interview text available at site of Projeto Memoria Roda Viva da Fapesp: https://rodaviva.fapesp.br/.

21 Ibid., December 4, 1987.

22 Ibid.

23 Ibid.

24 Ibid., December 10, 1999.

25 Ibid.

26 Ibid., December 4, 1987.

27 Sociedade Civil Amigos da América, *Estatutos, regimento interno e regulamento das filiais* (Rio de Janeiro: Editora Henrique Velho, 1944), 32 and 15, respectively. See the Osvaldo Aranha Collection at CPDOC/FGV.

28 Ari Franco, "Mandado de Segurança. Fechamento da Sociedade Amigos da América. Denegação. Tribunal de Apelação do Distrito Federal, 27 jul. 1945," *Revista de Direito Administrativo* 6 (October 1946): 162.

29 Larry Rohter, "Natal Journal: A Has-Been Wonders How to Honor What Was," *New York Times*, June 20, 2001, 4.

30 Lira Neto, *Getúlio*, 450.

Chapter XXV: The Gandhi of Brazil

1 "Os índios Xavante rondam o acampamento," *O Radical* (Rio de Janeiro), September 16, 1944, 1, 4.

2 Darcy Ribeiro, *Confissões* (São Paulo: Companhia das Letras, 1997), 151.

3 Ribeiro, *Confissões*, 150.

4 Letter from Rondon to Odorico Ribeiro dos Santos Tocantins, November 27, 1949, cited in Ivan Echeverria and Aecim Tocantins, *Cartas do Marechal Cândido Mariano da Silva Rondon: Relíquias do telegrafista Tocantins* (Cuiabá: KCM Editores, 2013), 113.

5 Ibid.

6 Cândido Rondon, Diaries, Book 010448 (November 1–5, 1949), MHEx/FC.

7 Cândido Rondon, Diaries, Book 010448 (November 1–5, 1949), MHEx/FC.

8 Darcy Ribeiro, cited in an introductory panel to the permanent exhibition of the Memorial Darcy Ribeiro at the Universidade Nacional de Brasília, written by Isa Grinspum Ferraz, in which she cites a letter written by Darcy Ribeiro.

9 Ibid.

10 Ibid.

11 Ibid.

12 "Rondon recebeu no Congresso as insígnias de marechal," *Correio da Manhã*, May 6, 1955, 8, 14.

13 "Rondon recebeu no Congresso."

14 Albert Einstein, letter of May 22, 1925, quoted in Abraham Pais, *Subtle Is the Lord: The Science and the Life of Albert Einstein* (London: Oxford University Press, 1982), 514.

15 Emily Greene Balch, *Nomination of Cândido Mariano da Silva Rondon* (1953), https://www.nobelprize.org/prizes/peace/1946/balch/nominations/.

16 Ibid.

17 Jardel P. Arruda, "AML fará cerimônia de gala para comemorar centenário da expedição Roosevelt-Rondon," *Olhar direto*, May 5, 2014.

18 From "Full Text of Alfred Nobel's Will," translated by Jeffrey Ganellen, 2018. Nobel Prize Database, "The Nobel Prize—Alfred Nobel's Will," https://www.nobelprize.org/alfred-nobel/full-text-of-alfred-nobels-will-2/.

19 For Lester B. Pearson, The Nobel Peace Prize 1957, NobelPrize.org, https://www.nobelprize.org/prizes/peace/1957/summary/. For Adolfo Pérez Esquivel, see press release of October 27, 1980, https://www.nobelprize.org/prizes/peace/1980/press-release/. "Work for the Rights of Indigenous Peoples: Rigoberta Menchú Tum," Nobel Prize Nomination Database, https://www.nobelprize.org/prizes/peace/1992/summary/.

20 Edilberto Coutinho, *Piguara, senhor do caminho: A saga do defensor dos Índios e pioneiro das comunicações* (Rio de Janeiro: Lê, 1993), 9.

21 Coutinho, *Piguara*, 9.

22 Ribeiro, *Confissões*, 151.

Chapter XXVI: Battle over a Legacy

1 "Sepultado com todas as honras o marechal Rondon," *Correio da Manhã* (Rio de Janeiro), January 21, 1958, 1, 10.

2 Ibid.

3 Citations for this paragraph come from: Darcy Ribeiro, *Uirá sai à procura de Deus: Ensaios de etnologia e indigenismo* (Rio de Janeiro: Paz e Terra, 1974), 159–60.

4 Citations for this and the two paragraphs preceding come from: Ribeiro, *Uirá*, 161–62.

5 Carlos Drummond de Andrade, *A vida passada a limpo* (São Paulo: Companhia das Letras, 2013), 37–39. Translation of "Pranto Geral dos Índios" by Larry Rohter.

6 Citations for this and the preceding paragraph come from Manuel Bandeira, "Rondon," *Jornal do Brasil*, January 22, 1958.

7 Teixeira did not share that enthusiasm. "To Anísio," Ribeiro would write in his memoirs, "Rondon was a kind of half-mad military man, a priest who reigned by preaching to the Indians, a kind of apostle in uniform," or a "Positivist zealot." See Ribeiro, *Confissões*, 223.

8 Ceremony at the Universidade de Espirito Santo, May 5, 1965.

9 Law 4743, July 16, 1965.

10 Aricildes de Moraes Motta, ed., *Projeto Rondon: Integrar para não entregar* (Rio de Janeiro: Biblioteca do Exército, 2006), 35.

11 Gen. Ivan de Mendonça Bastos, in Motta, *Projeto Rondon*, 8.

12 Motta, 38.

13 Ribeiro, *Confissões*, 151–52.

14 In the film archive at the Marechal Rondon Cultural Space in Santo Ângelo, Rio Grande do Sul, Brazil.

15 Gen. Oscar Jerônimo Bandeira de Mello, president of FUNAI between June 1970 and March 1974, in Carlos Alberto Ricardo, ed., *Povos Indígenas do Brasil 85/86* (Brasília: Centro Ecumênico de Documentação e Informação, 1986), 27.

16 From a speech by the minister of the interior, Maurício Rangel Reis, inaugurating Gen. Ismarth Araújo de Oliveira as president of FUNAI, March 1974, in Ricardo, *Povos Indígenas do Brasil.*

17 Marshal Cândido Mariano da Silva Rondon, quoted in Edilberto Coutinho, *Rondon: O civilizador da última fronteira* (Rio de Janeiro: Civilização Brasileira, 1975), 90.

18 See, for example, Antônio Carlos de Souza Lima, *Um grande cerco de paz: Poder tutelar, indianidade e formação do estado no Brasil* (Petrópolis: Vozes, 1995).

19 Gomes, "Por que sou rondoniano."

20 Gomes, 180.

21 Speech by President Luiz Inácio Lula da Silva at the refounding of the Rondon Project, Tabatinga, Brazil, January 19, 2005. From "Discurso do Presidente da República, Luiz Inácio Lula da Silva, na cerimônia de relançamento do Projeto Rondon Tabatinga/AM, 19 de janeiro de 2005," Biblioteca da Presidência.

22 UOL Notícias, January 19, 2005, notícias.uol.com.br/ultnot/reuters/2005/01/19.

23 Citations in this and preceding paragraph from "Discurso do Presidente da República."

24 Gen. Ivan Mendonça Bastos, in Motta, *Projeto Rondon*, 7.

25 Transcription of dialogue from episode 2 (minute 29) of *Rondon, O grande chefe.*

26 See, for example, Bolsonaro's speech delivered in Cuiabá, Rondon's hometown, on November 13, 2015, as reported by *O Globo*: "We have an area larger than the entire Southeast set aside for the Indians, who ought to be integrated among us. . . . We are losing the entire Northern region because of people who don't want to take note of the risk we run of having Indian presidents with warclubs in their hands." He added that "environmental policy in our country is awful" because "the quantity of Indian land" off-limits to commercial development is so large that it "inflicts harm on agribusiness. . . . We have to put an end to this Shiite policy that is suffocating Brazil." http://g1.globo.com/mato-grosso/noticia/2015/11/em-cuiaba-bolsonaro-se-diz-contra-terra-para-indios-e-cota-para-negros.html.

27 Brazilian constitution of 1988, Article 231.

28 Manuel Bandeira, "Rondon," *Jornal do Brasil*, January 22, 1958, 3.

SELECT BIBLIOGRAPHY

Books

Abreu, Alzira Alves de, ed. *Dicionário histórico-biográfico Brasileiro pós-1930*. 5 vols. Rio de Janeiro: Editora da Fundação Getúlio Vargas, 2001.

———. *Dicionário histórico-biográfico da Primeira República 1889–1930*. Rio de Janeiro: Editora da Fundação Getúlio Vargas, 2015.

Amado, Jorge. *O cavaleiro da esperança: Vida de Luís Carlos Prestes*. Rio de Janeiro: Editora Record, 1979.

Amarante, João. *Major Amarante: Sua vida*. Rio de Janeiro: Departamento de Imprensa Nacional, 1972.

Araripe, Tristão de Alencar. *Tasso Fragoso: Um pouco de história do nosso exército*. Rio de Janeiro: Biblioteca do Exército Editora, 1960.

Athayde, Tristão de. *Pandiá Calógeras na opinião de seus contemporâneos*. São Paulo: Typ. Siqueira, 1934.

Badet, Henri. *Le Général Rondon: Charmeur d'Indiens*. Paris: Nouvelles Éditions Latines, 1951.

Bastos Filho, Jayme de Araújo. *A missão militar Francesa no Brasil*. Rio de Janeiro: Biblioteca do Exército Editora, 1994.

Beattie, Peter M. *The Tribute of Blood: Army, Honor, Race, and Nation in Brazil, 1864–1945*. Durham, NC: Duke University Press, 2001.

———., ed. *The Human Tradition in Modern Brazil*. Wilmington, DE: SR Books, 2004.

Bigio, Elias dos Santos. *Cândido Rondon: A integração nacional*. Rio de Janeiro: Contraponto, 2000.

Borges, Tadeu de Miranda, and Maria Adenir Peraro, eds. *Brasil e Paraguai: Uma releitura da guerra*. Cuiabá: Entrelinhas/EdUFMT, 2012.

Braudeau, Michel. "Le télégraphe positiviste de Candido Rondon." In *Le rêve amazonien*. Paris: Gallimard, 2004.

Buarque de Holanda, Sérgio. *Marechal Rondon: 1865–1958*. São Paulo: Editora Abril, 1973.

Burns, E. Bradford. *Unwritten Alliance: Rio Branco and Brazilian-American Relations*. New York: Columbia University Press, 1966.

Callado, Antônio. *Esqueleto na lagoa verde: Um ensaio sobre a vida e o sumiço do Coronel Fawcett.* Rio de Janeiro: Departamento de Imprensa Nacional, 1953.

Calmon, Pedro. *Gomes Carneiro: O general da república.* Rio de Janeiro: Editora Guanabara, 1933.

Canfield, Michael R. *Theodore Roosevelt in the Field.* Chicago: University of Chicago Press, 2015.

Carone, Edgard. *A república velha.* 8 vols. São Paulo: Difel, 1974.

Casement, Roger. *The Amazon Journal of Roger Casement.* Edited by Angus Mitchell. London: Anaconda Editions, 1997.

Castelnau, Francis de. *Expedição às regiões centrais da América do Sul.* São Paulo: Companhia Editora Nacional, 1949.

Castro, Celso. *Os militares e a república: Um estudo sobre cultura e ação política.* Rio de Janeiro: Jorge Zahar Editor, 1995.

Chalhoub, Sidney. *Visões da liberdade: Uma história das últimas décadas da escravidão na corte.* São Paulo: Companhia das Letras, 1990.

Cherrie, George K. *Dark Trails: Adventures of a Naturalist.* New York: G. P. Putnam's Sons, 1930.

Churchward, Robert. *Wilderness of Fools: An Account of the Adventures in Search of Lieut. Colonel P. H. Fawcett, D.S.O.* London: George Routledge & Sons, 1936.

Cidade, Francisco de Paula, ed. *Cadetes e alunos militares através dos tempos (1878–1932).* Rio de Janeiro: Biblioteca do Exército Editora, 1961.

Comte, Auguste. *Appel aux conservateurs.* Paris: Chez V. Dalmont, 1855.

———. *Curso de filosofia positivista.* São Paulo: Nova Cultural, 1983.

———. *A General View of Positivism.* New York: E. P. Dutton, 1907.

———. *The Gospel of Maternal Love.* Edited by Henri Dussauze. Newcastle-on-Tyne: Hedson, 1910.

———. *Introduction to Positivist Philosophy.* Indianapolis: Hackett, 1988.

Corrêa, Valmir Batista. *Coronéis e bandidos em Mato Grosso.* Campo Grande: Editora UFMS, 1995.

Costa, João Cruz. *A History of Ideas in Brazil: The Development of Philosophy in Brazil and the Evolution of National History.* Berkeley: University of California Press, 1964.

Coutinho, Edilberto. *Piguara, senhor do caminho: A saga do defensor do Índio e pioneiro das comunicações.* Belo Horizonte: Editora Lê, 1993.

———. *Rondon e a integração da Amazônia.* São Paulo: Editora Arquimedes, 1968.

———. *Rondon e a política indigena no século vinte.* Rio de Janeiro: Editora PUC, 1978.

———. *Rondon: O civilizador da última fronteira.* Rio de Janeiro: Civilização Brasileira, 1975.

———. *Rondon: O salto para o desconhecido.* São Paulo: Companhia Editora Nacional, 1987.

Cruls, Gastão. *Amazônia que eu vi: Óbidos-Tumucumaque.* Rio de Janeiro: Editora Cisne, 1930.

Cunha, Euclides da. *Os sertões: Campanha de Canudos.* Rio de Janeiro: Laemmert, 1905.

Diacon, Todd A. *Stringing Together a Nation: Cândido Mariano da Silva Rondon and the Construction of a Modern Brazil, 1906–1930.* Durham, NC: Duke University Press, 2004.

Drummond de Andrade, Carlos. *A vida passada a limpo.* São Paulo: Companhia das Letras, 2013.

Dyott, George M. *Man-Hunting in the Jungle.* Indianapolis: Bobbs-Merrill, 1930.

Enders, Armelle. *Os vultos da nação: Fábrica de heróis e formação dos brasileiros.* Rio de Janeiro: Editora Fundação Getúlio Vargas, 2014.

Faoro, Raymundo. *Os donos do poder.* São Paulo: Globo, 2012.

Fawcett, Brian. *Ruins in the Sky.* London: Hutchinson, 1958.

Fawcett, Percy H. *Exploration Fawcett.* London: Century, 1988.

———. *Lost Trails, Lost Cities: From His Manuscripts, Letters, and Other Records, Selected and Arranged by Brian Fawcett.* New York: Funk & Wagnalls, 1953.

Figueiredo, Affonso Celso de Assis. *O Visconde de Ouro Preto: Excertos biográficos.* Porto Alegre: Globo, 1936.

Figueiredo, Luiza Vieira Sá de. *Das comissões telegráficas ao Serviço de Proteção ao Índio: Rondon, o agente público e político.* Curitiba: Editora CRV, 2013.

Freundt, Erich, and Herbert Baldus. *Índios de Mato Grosso.* São Paulo: Edições Melhoramento, 1947.

Galetti, Lylia da Silva Guedes. *Sertão, fronteira, Brasil: Imagens de Mato Grosso no mapa da civilização.* Cuiabá: Entrelinhas/EdUFMT, 2012.

Galton, Francis. *The Art of Travel, or Shifts and Contrivances Available in Wild Countries.* London: Phoenix Press, 2000.

Garfield, Seth. *Indigenous Struggle at the Heart of Brazil: State Policy, Frontier Expansion and the Xavante Indians, 1937–1988.* Durham, NC: Duke University Press, 2001.

Goes Filho, Synesio Sampaio. *Navegantes, bandeirantes, diplomatas: Um ensaio sobre a formação das fronteiras do Brasil.* Rio de Janeiro: Martins Fontes/Biblioteca de Exército Editora, 2000.

Gomes, Laurentino. *1889.* Rio de Janeiro: Editora Globo, 2013.

Gomes, Mércio Pereira. *The Indians and Brazil.* Gainesville: University of Florida Press, 2000.

Grann, David. *The Lost City of Z: A Tale of Deadly Obsession in the Amazon.* New York: Vintage/Random House, 2005.

Guerra, Flávio. *Rondon, o sertanista.* Rio de Janeiro: Distribuidora Record, 1970.

Hecht, Susanna R. *The Scramble for the Amazon and the Lost Paradise of Euclides da Cunha.* Chicago: University of Chicago Press, 2013.

Henry, Jules. *Jungle People: A Kaingáng Tribe of the Highlands of Brazil.* Richmond: J. J. Augustin Press, 1941.

Herndon, William Lewis. *Exploration of the Valley of the Amazon, 1851–1852.* New York: Grove Press, 2000.

Horta Barbosa, Luiz Bueno. *O problema indígena do Brasil.* Rio de Janeiro: Imprensa Nacional, 1947.

Jaguaribe de Mattos, Francisco. *Rondon merecia o Prêmio Nobel de Paz.* Rio de Janeiro: Departamento de Imprensa Nacional, 1958.

Keay, John. *Explorers Extraordinary.* London: John Murray/British Broadcasting Corporation, 1985.

Korda, Michael. *Hero: The Life and Legend of Lawrence of Arabia.* New York: Harper, 2010.

Lange, Algot. *The Lower Amazon: A Narrative of Explorations in the Little Known Regions of the State of Pará, on the Lower Amazon.* New York: G. P. Putnam's Sons, 1914.

Lasmar, Denise Portugal. *O acervo imagético da Comissão Rondon no Museu do Índio, 1890–1938.* Rio de Janeiro: Museu do Índio, 2011.

Leal, Hermes. *Coronel Fawcett: A verdadeira história do Indiana Jones.* São Paulo: Geração Editorial, 1996.

Lemos, Miguel. *O positivismo e a escravidão moderna.* Rio de Janeiro: Sociedade Positivista, 1884.

Lemos, Renato. *Benjamin Constant: Vida e história.* Rio de Janeiro: Topbooks, 1999.

Lenzer, Gertrud, ed. *Auguste Comte and Positivism: The Essential Writings.* New York: Harper Torchbooks, 1975.

Lévi-Strauss, Claude. *The Raw and the Cooked.* Chicago: University of Chicago Press, 1990.

———. *Saudades do Brasil.* São Paulo: Companhia das Letras, 1994.

———. *Tristes Trópicos.* São Paulo: Companhia das Letras, 1996.

Lima, Antônio Carlos de Souza. *Um grande cerco de paz: Poder tutelar, indianidade e formação do estado no Brasil.* Petrópolis: Editora Vozes, 1995.

Lins, Ivan Monteiro de Barros. *Benjamin Constant.* Rio de Janeiro: J. R. de Oliveira, 1936.

———. *História do positivismo no Brasil.* Brasília: Edições do Senado Federal, 2009.

Lira Neto, João de. *Getúlio.* 3 vols. São Paulo: Companhia das Letras, 2012.

Maciel, Laura Antunes. *A nação por um fio: Caminhos, práticas e imagens da "Comissão Rondon."* São Paulo: Editora da PUC, 1998.

Magalhães, Amilcar Armando Botelho de. *Impressões da Comissão Rondon.* Porto Alegre: Livraria do Globo, 1929.

———. *Pelos sertões do Brasil.* São Paulo: Companhia Editora Nacional, 1941.

———. *Rondon: Uma relíquia da pátria.* Curitiba: Editora Guaíra, 1942.

Malan, Alfredo Souto. *Missão militar Francesa de instrução junto ao Exército Brasileiro.* Rio de Janeiro: Biblioteca do Exército Editora, 1988.

Marcigaglia, Luiz. *Os Salesianos no Brasil.* São Paulo: Escolas Profissionais Salesianas, 1955.

McCann, Frank D. *Soldiers of the Patria: A History of the Brazilian Army, 1889–1937.* Palo Alto, CA: Stanford University Press, 2004.

Meirelles, Domingos. *As noites das grandes fogueiras: Uma história da Coluna Prestes.* Rio de Janeiro: Editora Record, 1995.

Mello-Leitão, Cândido de. *História das expedições científicas no Brasil.* São Paulo: Companhia Editora Nacional, 1941.

Millard, Candice. *The River of Doubt: Theodore Roosevelt's Darkest Journey.* New York: Anchor Books, 2005.

Miller, Leo E. *In the Wilds of South America.* New York: Charles Scribner's Sons, 1918.

Mitchell, Angus. *Roger Casement in Brazil: Rubber, the Amazon and the Atlantic World, 1884–1916.* São Paulo: Ed. Humanitas, 2010.

Moreno, Gislaene. *Terra e poder em Mato Grosso: Política e mecanismos de burla 1892–1992.* Cuiabá: Entrelinhas/EdUFMT, 2007.

Morgan, Zachary R. *Legacy of the Lash: Race and Corporal Punishment in the Brazilian Navy and the Atlantic World.* Bloomington: Indiana University Press, 2014.

Morison, Elting E., ed. *The Letters of Theodore Roosevelt: Volume VIII—The Days of Armageddon, 1914–1918.* Cambridge, Mass.: Harvard University Press, 1954.

Morris, Edmund. *Colonel Roosevelt.* New York: Random House, 2010.

Motta, Aricildes de Moraes, ed. *História oral do Projeto Rondon: Integrar para não entregar.* 4 vols. Rio de Janeiro: Biblioteca do Exército Editora, 2006.

Motta, Jehovah. *Formação do oficial do exército: Currículos e regimes na academia militar 1810–1944.* Rio de Janeiro: Editora Companhia Brasileira de Artes Gráficas, 1976.

Müller, Cristina, Luiz Octavio Lima, and Moisés Rabinovici. *O Xingu dos Villas-Boas.* São Paulo: Agência Estado/Metalivros, 2002.

Needell, Jeffrey D. *A Tropical Belle Epoque: Elite Culture and Society in Turn-of-the-Century Rio de Janeiro.* Cambridge: Cambridge University Press, 1987.

Neves, Lúcia Maria Bastos Pereira das, and Humberto Fernandes Machado. *O Império do Brasil.* Rio de Janeiro: Nova Fronteira, 1999.

Neves da Fontoura, João. *Memórias: A aliança liberal e a revolução de 1930.* 2 vols. Rio de Janeiro: Editora Globo, 1963.

Novaes, Sylvia Caiuby. *The Play of Mirrors: The Representation of Self Mirrored in the Other*. Austin: University of Texas Press, 1993.

Ornig, Joseph R. *My Last Chance to Be a Boy: Theodore Roosevelt's South American Expedition of 1913–1914*. Baton Rouge: Louisiana State University Press, 1994.

Osborn, Henry Fairfield. *Impressions of Great Naturalists: Reminiscences of Darwin, Huxley, Balfour, Cope and Others*. New York: Charles Scribner's Sons, 1924.

Pais, Abraham. *Subtle Is the Lord: The Science and the Life of Albert Einstein*. London: Oxford University Press, 1982.

Paiva, Samuel, and Sheila Schvarzman, eds. *Viagem ao cinema silencioso do Brasil*. São Paulo: Azougue, 2011.

Prestes, Luís Carlos. *Documentos de Luís Carlos Prestes*. Buenos Aires: Ediciones Nuevos Tiempos, 1947.

———. *Prestes com a palavra: Uma seleção das principais entrevistas do líder comunista*. Campo Grande: Letra Livre Editora, 1997.

———. *Prestes por ele mesmo*. São Paulo: Editora Martin Claret, 1995.

Reis, Daniel Aarão. *Luís Carlos Prestes: Um revolucionário entre dois mundos*. São Paulo: Companhia das Letras, 2014.

Ribeiro, Darcy. *Confissões*. São Paulo: Companhia das Letras, 1997.

———. *Os Índios e a civilização: A integração dos povos indígenas no Brasil moderno*. Petrópolis: Editora Vozes, 1977.

———. *Uirá sai à procura de Deus: Ensaios de etnologia e indigenismo*. Rio de Janeiro: Editora Paz e Terra, 1974.

Ricardo, Carlos Alberto, ed. *Povos Indígenas do Brasil 85/86*. Brasília: Centro Ecumênico de Documentação e Informação, 1986.

Rocha, Leandro Mendes. *A política indigenista no Brasil: 1930–1967*. Goiânia: Editora UFG, 2003.

Rondon, Cândido Mariano da Silva. *Apontamentos sobre os trabalhos realizados pela Comissão de Linhas Telegráficas Estratégicas de Mato Grosso ao Amazonas, sob a direção do Coronel Cândido Mariano da Silva Rondon, de 1907 a 1915*. Brasília: Edições do Senado Federal, 2003.

———. *História da Minha Vida*. São Paulo: LeBooks Editora, 2019.

Rondon, Frederico. *Na Rondônia ocidental*. São Paulo: Companhia Editora Nacional, 1938.

———. *Pelos sertões e fronteiras do Brasil sob as ordens de Rondon, o civilizador*. Rio de Janeiro: Reper Editora, 1969.

Roosevelt, Kermit. *The Long Trail*. New York: Review of Reviews/Metropolitan Magazine, 1921.

Roosevelt, Theodore. *A Book-Lover's Holidays in the Open*. New York: Charles Scribner's Sons, 1920.

———. *Through the Brazilian Wilderness*. New York: Charles Scribner & Sons, 1914.

Roquette-Pinto, Edgar. *Rondônia*. São Paulo: Companhia Editora Nacional, 1938.

Santos, Roberto. *História econômica da Amazônia 1800–1920*. São Paulo: T. A. Queiroz Editora, 1980.

Savage-Landor, Arnold Henry. *Across Unknown South America*. 2 vols. New York: Hodder & Stoughton, 1913.

———. *Everywhere: The Memoirs of an Explorer*. 2 vols. New York: Frederick A. Stokes, 1924.

Schwartzman, Simon. *Um espaço para a ciência: A formação da comunidade científica no Brasil*. Brasília: Ministério de Ciência e Tecnologia, 2001.

Silva, Francisco Bento da. *Acre, a Sibéria tropical: Desterros para a região do Acre em 1904–1910*. Rio Branco: Edições UFA, 2013.

Simões Lopes, Luiz. *Fragmentos de memória*. Rio de Janeiro: Editora FGV, 2006.

Steinen, Karl von den. *Entre os Aborígenes do Brasil central*. São Paulo: Departamento de Cultura, 1940.

———. *O Brasil central: Expedição em 1884 para a exploração do Rio Xingu*. São Paulo: Companhia Editora Nacional, 1942.

Tacca, Fernando de. *A imagética da Comissão Rondon*. Campinas: Papirus Editora, 2001.

Taunay, Alfredo d'Escragnolle. *Inocência*. São Paulo: Ática, 1986.

Tocantins, Aecim, and Ivan Echeverria. *Cartas do Marechal Cândido Mariano da Silva Rondon: Relíquias do telegrafista Tocantins*. Cuiabá: KCM Editora, 2013.

Trindade, Hélgio, ed. *O Positivismo: Teoria e prática*. Porto Alegre: Editora da UFRGS, 2007.

Villas-Boas, Orlando, and Cláudio Villas Boas. *A marcha para o oeste: A epopéia da expedição Roncador-Xingu*. São Paulo: Editora Globo, 1994.

Wagley, Charles. *Amazon Town: A Study of Man in the Tropics*. New York: A. Knopf, 1964.

Weinstein, Barbara. *The Amazon Rubber Boom, 1850–1920*. Palo Alto, CA: Stanford University Press, 1983.

Werneck Sodré, Nelson. *A história militar do Brasil*. Rio de Janeiro: Editora Civilização Brasileira, 1979.

Wernick, Andrew. *Auguste Comte and the Religion of Humanity: The Post-Theistic Program of French Social Theory*. Cambridge: Cambridge University Press, 2001.

Wharton, William J., and Douglas Freshfield, eds. *Hints to Travellers: Scientific and General*. London: Royal Geographic Society, 1893.

Zahm, John Augustine. *Through South America's Southland, with an Account of the Roosevelt Scientific Expedition to South America*. New York: D. Appleton, 1916.

Archives

Academia Brasileira de Letras (Rio de Janeiro)
American Museum of Natural History (New York)
Arquivo Histórico do Exército (Rio de Janeiro)
Arquivo Histórico e Mapoteca Histórica do Itamaraty (Rio de Janeiro)
Arquivo Público do Estado de Mato Grosso (Cuiabá)
Biblioteca Nacional (Rio de Janeiro)
Brown University Library, Brasiliana Collection of Positivist Pamphlets (Providence, Rhode Island)
Cinemateca Brasileira (São Paulo)
Espaço Cultural Marechal Rondon (Santo Ângelo)
Fundação Getúlio Vargas, Centro de Pesquisa e Documentação (Rio de Janeiro)
Instituto Histórico Geográfico Brasileiro (Rio de Janeiro)
Instituto Histórico Geográfico de Mato Grosso (Cuiabá)
Harvard University, Houghton Library (Cambridge, Massachusetts)
Library of Congress (Washington, DC)
Memorial Darcy Ribeiro, Universidade Nacional de Brasília (Brasília)
Museu Casa de Benjamin Constant (Rio de Janeiro)
Museu das Telecomunicações Marechal Rondon (Ji-Paraná)
Museu Histórico do Exército e Forte de Copacabana (Rio de Janeiro)
Museu Nacional (Rio de Janeiro)
New York Public Library (New York)
Observatório Nacional, Núcleo de Informação e Documentação (Rio de Janeiro)

Reference Works, Dictionaries, and Encyclopedias

Hoehne, Frederico Carlos. *Índice bibliográfico e numérico das plantas colhidas pela Comissão Rondon 1908–1923*. São Paulo: Secretaria de Agricultura, 1951.

Lobo Vianna, José Feliciano. *Guia militar para o anno de 1898 (Abrangendo os annos de 1893–1897)*. Rio de Janeiro: Imprensa Nacional, 1897.

Marsh, Ernest. "The Salesian Society." In *The Catholic Encyclopedia*. New York: Robert Appleton, 1912.

Olson, James Stuart. *The Indians of Central and South America: An Ethnohistorical Dictionary*. New York: Greenwood, 1991.

Roosevelt, Theodore. *A Compilation of the Messages and Speeches of Theodore Roosevelt, 1901–1905*. Washington, DC: Bureau of National Literature and Art, 1906.

———. *The Works of Theodore Roosevelt: Presidential Addresses and State Papers*. New York, P. F. Collier & Sons, 1914.

Spiller, G., ed. *Papers on Inter-Racial Problems: A Record of the Proceedings of the First Universal Races Congress*. London: P. S. King & Son, 1911.

Vinhosa, Francisco Luiz Teixeira, ed. *Domício da Gama em Washington: Guia de pesquisa*. Rio de Janeiro: Centro de História e Documentação Diplomática, Ministério das Relações Exteriores, 2011.

Documents, Diaries, and Official Reports

Andrada e Silva, José Bonifácio. *Apontamentos para a civilização dos índios bravos do Império do Brasil*. Rio de Janeiro: Imprensa Nacional, 1823.

Câmara dos Deputados. *Marechal Cândido Mariano da Silva Rondon: Homenagem*. Rio de Janeiro: Departamento de Imprensa Nacional, 1958.

Centro de Sciências, Letras e Artes de Campinas. *A questão indígena: Appello dirigido à opinião pública do Brazil pela Comissão Promotora da Defesa dos Índios*. Campinas: Typ. Livro Azul, 1909.

Cherrie, George Kruk. *George K. Cherrie's Diary of the Theodore Roosevelt Expedition to Explore the River of Doubt in Brazil, October 1913 to May 1914*. Transcribed by Joseph R. Ornig, November 1975. Archives of the American Museum of Natural History.

Comissão da Linha Telegraphica Estratégica Mato Grosso ao Amazonas (CLTEMA). *A Comissão Rondon e o Museu Nacional*, by Alípio de Miranda Ribeiro. Rio de Janeiro: CLTEMA/Luiz Macedo, 1916.

CLTEMA. *Annexo no. 3: Levantamento e locação do trecho comprehendido entre os Rios Zolaharuiná (Burity) e Juruena*, by Emmanuel Silvestre do Amarante. Rio de Janeiro: Papelaria Macedo, 1909.

———. *Annexo no. 4: Relatório dos trabalhos realizados durante o anno de 1908*, by Alípio de Miranda Ribeiro. CLTEMA Publicação No. 27. Rio de Janeiro: 1916.

———. *Expedição Scientífica Roosevelt-Rondon: Annexo no. 2, Botânica*, by Frederico Carlos Hoehne. Rio de Janeiro: CLTEMA, 1914.

———. *Expedição Scientífica Roosevelt-Rondon: Annexo no. 5, Relatório*, by Amilcar Armando Botelho de Magalhães. Rio de Janeiro: CLTEMA, 1916.

———. *Expedição Scientífica Roosevelt-Rondon: Annexo no. 6: Relatório apresentado ao chefe da Comissão Brasileira, Coronel de Engenharia Cândido Mariano da Silva Rondon pelo médico da expedição*, by José Antonio Cajazeira. Rio de Janeiro: Typ. do Jornal do Commercio, 1916.

———. *Exploração do Rio Ikê (1912–1913)*, by Julio Caetano Horta Barbosa. Publicação no. 29, Annexo no. 2. Rio de Janeiro: CLTEMA, 1916.

————. *História natural (botânica): Parte X, Lauráceas de Matto-Grosso e duas novas espécies da Amazônia,* by Alberto José de Sampaio. Publicação no. 56, Annexo no. 5. Rio de Janeiro: CLTEMA, 1917.

————. *Memorial dedicado ao governo da república e aos srs. membros do Congresso nacional,* by Amilcar Armando Botelho de Magalhães. Rio de Janeiro: Papelaria Macedo, 1919.

————. *O Serviço de Protecçaõ aos Índios e a "História da colonisação do Brazil,"* by Luis Bueno Horta Barbosa. Rio de Janeiro: Typ. do Jornal do Commercio, 1919.

————. *Relatórios diversos: Projectos, orçamentos, medições, observações meteorológicas, etc.* Publicação no. 27, Annexo no. 4. Rio de Janeiro: Papelaria Luiz Macedo, 1910.

Conselho Nacional de Proteção aos Índios (CNPI). *Exploração e levantamento do Rio Culuene, principal formador do Rio Xingu,* by Ramiro Noronha. Comissão Rondon, Publicação no. 75. Rio de Janeiro: Departamento de Imprensa Nacional, 1952.

CNPI. *Pelo Índio e pela sua proteção oficial,* by Luis Bueno Horta Barbosa. Rio de Janeiro: Imprensa Nacional, 1947.

————. *Exploração e levantamento dos Rios Anarí e Machadinho,* by Nicolau Bueno Horta Barbosa. CLTEMA Publicação no. 48, Anexo no. 2, 2a edição. Rio de Janeiro: Imprensa Nacional, 1945.

————. *Exploração do Rio Jaci-Paraná e diário de viagem,* by Manoel Theophilo da Costa Pinheiro and Amilcar Armando Botelho de Magalhães. Comissão Rondon Publicação no. 5, Anexo no. 2. Rio de Janeiro: Departamento de Imprensa Nacional, 1949.

Fernandes, Francisco, and Pedro Sbardellotto, eds. *Do primeiro encontro com os Xavante à demarcação de suas reservas: Relatórios do Pe. Hipólito Chovelon.* Cuiabá: Missão Salesiana de Mato Grosso, 1996.

Franco, Ari. *Mandado de Segurança—Fechamento da "Sociedade Amigos da América"— Denegação.* Tribunal de Apelação do Distrito Federal (July 27, 1945), 137–73.

Indian Rights Association. *19th Annual Report of the Executive Committee of the Indian Rights Association.* Philadelphia: Office of the Indian Rights Association, 1902.

Ministério da Guerra. "Atas da sessão do Club Militar de 9 de Novembro de 1889: Coleção de pactos de sangue e mensagens recebidos por Benjamin Constant." Rio de Janeiro: Gab. Fotocartográfico do Min. da Guerra, 1939.

Protocol of Friendship and Cooperation between the Republic of Colombia and the Republic of Perú. Signed in Rio de Janeiro, May 24, 1934.

Rondon, Cândido Mariano da Silva. *Comissão de Linhas Telegraphicas Estratégicas de Matto Grosso ao Amazonas, Annexo no. 5, História natural: Ethnografia Índios Parecis.* Rio de Janeiro: Papelaria Luiz Macedo, 1911.

————. *Conferências realizadas em 1910 no Rio de Janeiro e em S. Paulo.* (Publicação n. 68 CLTEMA.) Rio de Janeiro: Typographia Leuzinger, 1922.

————. *Conferências realizadas nos dias 5, 7 e 9 de Outubro de 1915 no Teatro Phenix do Rio de Janeiro e referentes a trabalhos executados sob sua chefia pela Expedição Scientífica Roosevelt-Rondon e pela Comissão Telegraphica.* Rio de Janeiro: Typ. do Jornal do Commercio, 1916.

————. "Diários 1892–1954." 79 volumes. Museu Histórico do Exército e Forte de Copacabana (MHEx/FC), Rio de Janeiro.

————. *Homenagem a José Bonifácio no 88° anniversario da independência do Brasil—Inauguração do Serviço de Protecção dos Índios.* Rio de Janeiro: Ministério da Agricultura, 1910.

————. *Índios do Brasil.* 3 vols.: *Vol. 1: Índios do centro, do noroeste e do sul de Mato Grosso; Vol. II: Índios das cabeceiras dos Rios Xingu, Araguaia e Oiapoque; Vol. III: Norte do Rio Amazonas* (CNPI Publicação no. 98). Rio de Janeiro: Imprensa Nacional, 1953.

————. *Pelos nossos Aborígenes: Appello ao Congresso Nacional.* Rio de Janeiro: Papelaria Macedo, 1915.

————. *Relatório apresentado à directoria geral dos telegraphos e à Divisão de Engenharia do Departamento da Guerra (2° Volume): Construcção 1907–1910* (CLTEMA Publicação no. 39). Rio de Janeiro: Papelaria Macedo, 1919.

————. *Relatório apresentado à Divisão de Engenharia (G5) do Departamento da Guerra e à Directoria Geral dos Telegraphos: 3° Volume, Correspondente aos Annos de 1911 e 1912.* Rio de Janeiro: CLTEMA, 1915.

————. *Relatório dos trabalhos realizados de 1900–1906.* (CNPI Publicação no. 69/70.) Rio de Janeiro: Departamento de Imprensa Nacional, 1949.

Rondon, Cândido M. S., and João Barbosa de Faria. *Esboço gramatical e vocabulário da língua dos Índios Bororo.* Rio de Janeiro, 1948.

————. *Esboço gramatical, vocabulário, lendas e canticos dos Índios Ariti (Parici).* Rio de Janeiro, 1948.

Rondon, Cândido, Paulo de Moraes Barros, and Isidoro Simões Lopes. *Obras do nordeste: Resposta da Comissão de Inspecção ao Dr. Epitácio Pessoa.* Rio de Janeiro: s/n, 1924.

Rondon, General. *Rumo ao oeste.* (Biblioteca Militar, Volume Avulso.) Rio de Janeiro: Gráfica Laemmert, 1942.

Rondon, Joaquim. *O Índio como sentinela das nossas fronteiras: Conferência realizada no colégio militar.* Rio de Janeiro: Departamento de Imprensa Nacional, 1948.

Roosevelt, Kermit. "Diary 1913–1914." Box 1, Kermit and Belle Roosevelt Papers, Library of Congress, Washington, DC.

Roquette-Pinto, Edgard. *Note sur la situation sociale des Indiens du Brésil: Monographie présentée a le Congrès Universel des Races, dans l'Université de Londres, en 1911.* Rio de Janeiro: Departamento de Imprensa Nacional, 1955.

Sociedade Civil Amigos da América. *Estatutos, regimento interno e regulamento das filiais.* Rio de Janeiro: Editora Henrique Velho, 1944.

Tratado de Límites y Navegación Fluvial Entre Colombia y El Perú, 24 de marzo de 1922.

Theses, Dissertations, and Academic Articles

American Geographical Society. "Award of the David Livingstone Centenary Medal to Colonel Rondon." *Geographical Review* 5, no. 6 (June 1918): 496–503.

————. "Presentation of the David Livingstone Centenary Medal to Colonel Theodore Roosevelt." *Geographical Review* 3, no. 4 (April 1917): 253–57.

Boissier, Léopold. "La Croix-Rouge et l'assistance aux détenus politiques." *Politique Étrangère* 23, no. 1 (1958): 5–24.

Bordin, Marcelo. "A guerra de trincheiras esquecida em Catanduvas, Paraná (1924–1925): Aspectos geohistóricos." *Geographia opportuno tempore* 1, no. 1 (January/June 2014): 57–67.

Cabeda, Coralio Bragança Pardo. "A sombra do Conde de Lippe no Brasil: Os artigos de guerra." *História militar terrestre do Brasil.*

Cardoso, Luciene P. C. "Notas sobre as origens do escritório central da Comissão Rondon no Rio de Janeiro." *Histórica—revista eletrônica do arquivo público do estado de São Paulo* 43 (August 2010).

Correia Neto, Jonas de Morais. "Missão militar Francesa." *DaCultura* 5, no. 8 (2005): 34–39.

Cunha, Eliaquim Timoteo da. "'Quando esse tal de SPI' chegou: O Serviço de Proteção aos Índios na formação de Rondônia." Master's thesis, Universidade Federal do Amazonas, 2016.

Diacon, Todd A. "Candido Mariano da Silva Rondon and the Politics of Indian Protection in Brazil." *Past & Present* 177 (November 2002): 157–94.

———. "Searching for a Lost Army: Recovering the History of the Federal Army's Pursuit of the Prestes Column in Brazil, 1924–1927." *The Americas* 54, no. 3 (January 1998): 409–36.

Domingues, César Machado. "A Comissão de Linhas Telegráficas do Mato Grosso ao Amazonas e a integração do noroeste." *Encontro regional da Anpuh-Rio: Memória e patrimônio* (July 2010).

Duarte, Regina Horta. "Pássaros e cientistas no Brasil: Em busca de proteção, 1894–1938." *Latin American Research Review* 41, no. 1 (2006): 3–26.

Dyott, G. M. "The Search for Colonel Fawcett." *Geographical Journal* 74, no. 6 (December 1929): 513–42.

Franco, José Luiz de Andrade. "A Primeira Conferência Brasileira de Proteção à Natureza e a questão da identidade nacional." *Varia história* 26 (January 2002).

Franco, José Luiz de Andrade, and José Augusto Drummond. "Alberto José Sampaio: Um botânico brasileiro e o seu programa de proteção à natureza." *Varia história* 33 (January 2005).

———. "Frederico Carlos Hoehne: A atualidade de um pioneiro no campo da proteção à natureza no Brasil." *Ambiente & sociedade* 8, no. 1 (January/June 2005).

Gamelin, Maurice. "Le Général Rondon et ses explorations au Brésil." *France-Amérique* 112 (April 1921).

Garfield, Seth. "A Nationalist Environment: Indians, Nature and the Construction of the Xingu National Park in Brazil." *Luso-Brazilian Review* 41, no. 1 (2004): 139–67.

———. "'The Roots of a Plant That Today Is Brazil': Indians and the Nation-State under the Brazilian Estado Novo." *Journal of Latin American Studies* 29, no. 3 (October 1997): 747–68.

Gomes, Mércio Pereira. "Por que sou Rondoniano." *Estudos avançados* 23, no. 65 (2009): 173–91.

Gregório, Maria do Carmo. "Eu também sou amigo da América!" *Anais do XXVI Simpósio Nacional de História*, July 1–8, 2011.

Guimarães, Heitor Velasco Fernandes. "Os Índios na história do Brasil republicano: O território étnico-indígena Paresi e o território Indigenista Utiarity." *Anais do XXVI Simpósio Nacional de História*, July 2011.

Ihering, Hermann von. "The Anthropology of the State of S. Paulo, Brazil, Written on the Occasion of the Universal Exhibition of S. Luiz." *Diario oficial*, 1906.

———. "A antropologia do estado de São Paulo." *Revista do Museu Paulista* 7 (1907).

———. "A questão dos Índios no Brasil." *Revista do Museu Paulista* 8 (1911).

im Thurm, Everard. "The Ascent of Mount Roraima." *Proceedings of the Royal Geographical Society and Monthly Record of Geography* 7, no. 8 (August 1885): 497–521.

Instituto Histórico e Geográfico de São Paulo. "Recepção e posse do General Rondon: Discursos proferidos na sessão extraordinária de 25 de março de 1939." São Paulo: IHGSP, 1939.

Klever, Lucas de Oliveira. "Passado e presente: Projeto político e escrita da história na marcha para oeste." *III Encontro de Pesquisas Históricas PPGH-PUCRS* (2016).

Laroque, Luís Fernando da Silva. "Fronteiras geográficas, étnicas e culturais envolvendo os Kaingang e suas lideranças no sul do Brasil (1889–1930)." *Pesquisas antropológicas do Instituto Anchietano*, no. 64 (2007).

Leite, Jurandyr Carvalho Ferreira. "Proteção e incorporação: A questão Indígena no pensamento político do positivismo ortodoxo." *Revista de antropologia* 30/32 (1987–1989): 255–75.

Lévi-Strauss, Claude. "The Name of the Nambikwara." *American Anthropologist*, n.s., 48, no. 1 (January–March 1946): 139–40.

Lobato, Ana. "Da exibição dos filmes da Comissão Rondon." *Documentos on-line* 18 (September 2015): 300–322.

Machado, Maria Fátima Roberto. "Índios de Rondon: Rondon e as linhas telegráficas na visão dos sobreviventes Waimare e Kaxiniti, grupos Paresi." PhD diss., Museu Nacional da Universidade Federal do Rio de Janeiro, 1994.

———. "Quilombos, Cabixis e Caburés: Índios e Negros em Mato Grosso no século XVIII." Associação Brasileira de Antropologia, 2006.

Maestri, Mário. "Os positivistas ortodoxos e a Guerra do Paraguai." *Estudos históricos CDHRP* 3, no. 6 (July 2011): 1–23.

Martins Junior, Carlos. "Expedição Científica Roosevelt-Rondon: Um aspecto das relações Brasil-EUA e da consolidação do mito Rondon." *Revista de história* 1, no. 1 (January/June 2009): 25–54.

Massena, Rubens. "Rondon entrevistado." *A Defesa Nacional* 52, no. 607 (May/June 1966): 27–37.

McCann, Frank D. "The Brazilian General Staff and Brazil's Military Situation, 1900–1945." *Journal of Interamerican Studies and World Affairs* 25, no. 3 (August 1983): 299–324.

Mialhe, Jorge Luis. "O contrato da missão militar Francesa de 1919: Direito e história das relações internacionais." *Cadernos de direito* 19, no. 18 (January/June 2010): 80–119.

Miranda Ribeiro, Alípio. "Ao redor e através do Brasil." *Kosmos* 5, nos. 9, 11, 12 (1908).

Moreira Bento, Cláudio. "Gírias de cadetes do exército da Academia Militar das Agulhas Negras." *História militar terrestre do Brasil* (2007).

———. "O Clube Militar e a proclamação da república." *Revista do Instituto Histórico e Geográfico do Rio Grande do Sul* (1990).

———. "O exército na época da proclamação da república: Organização, equipamento, instrução/ensino, motivação, emprego." *Revista do Clube Militar, edição histórica do centenário* 280, no. 26–27 (June 1987): 1–44.

Nascimento, Marcio Luis Ferreira. "Rondon, Einstein's Letter and the Nobel Peace Prize." *Ciência e sociedade* 4, no. 1 (2016): 27–35.

Naumburg, Elsie M. B., with field notes by George K. Cherrie. "The Birds of Matto Grosso, Brazil: A Report on the Birds Secured by the Roosevelt-Rondon Expedition." *Bulletin of the American Museum of Natural History* 60 (1930).

Novaes, Sylvia Caiuby, Edgar Teodoro Cunha, and Paul Henley. "The First Ethnographic Documentary? Luiz Thomaz Reis, the Rondon Commission and the Making of *Rituais e festas Bororo* (1917)." *Visual Anthropology* 30, no. 2 (February 2017): 105–45.

O'Connor, Thomas F. "John A. Zahm, C.S.C.: Scientist and Americanist." *The Americas* 7, no. 4 (April 1951): 435–62.

O'Reilly, Donald F. "Rondon: Biography of a Brazilian Republican Army Commander." PhD diss., New York University, 1969.

Osborn, Henry Fairfield. "Theodore Roosevelt, Naturalist." *Natural History, The Journal of the American Museum* 19 (January 1919).

Pereira, Edmundo, and Gustavo Pacheco. "Rondônia 1912: Gravações históricas de Roquette-Pinto." CD booklet. Coleção Documentos Sonoros, Rio de Janeiro: Museu Nacional.

Regina, Adriana Werneck. "A Ponte de Pedra, travessia para outros mundos." *Historia oral* 2, no. 14 (July–December 2011): 89–106.

Rodrigues, João Carlos. *Major Luiz Thomaz Reis: O cinegrafista de Rondon*. Rio de Janeiro: Embrafilme, 1982.

Roosevelt, Theodore. "A Journey in Central Brazil." *Geographical Journal* 45, no. 2 (February 1915).

Saake, Guilherme. "A aculturação dos Bororo do Rio São Lourenço." *Revista de antropologia* 1, no. 1 (1953): 43–52.

Sampaio, Alberto José de. "Flora do Rio Cuminá: Resultados botânicos da Expedição Rondon à Serra Tumac-Humac em 1928." *Archivos do Museu Nacional* 35 (1933): 9–206.

———. "O problema florestal no Brasil em 1926." *Archivos do Museu Nacional* 28 (March 1926).

Santos, Margaret Ferreira dos. "A destruição da natureza e os arautos do conservacionismo Brasileiro nas primeiras décadas do século XX." *Revista uniara* 21/22 (2008–9): 30–49.

Selegny, Thomas. "The Franco-Brazilian Border: Historical Territorial Dispute, Arbitral Resolution and Contemporary Challenges." *ResearchGate* (March 2016): 1–25.

Silva, Hiram Reis e. "Rondon e o Conde de Lippe." Available online at Roraima em Foco and Amazônia Nossa Selva.

Stauffer, David H. "The Origin and Establishment of Brazil's Indian Service: 1889–1910." PhD diss., University of Texas at Austin, 1955.

Stefansson, Vilhjalmur, ed. "Theodore Roosevelt: Memorial Meeting at the Explorers Club." *Bulletin of the New York Explorers Club* (March 1919).

Tate, George Henry Hamilton. "Through Brazil to the Summit of Mount Roraima." *National Geographic*, November 1930.

Vangelista, Chiara. "Missões Católicas e políticas tribais na frente de expansão: Os Bororo entre o século XIX e o século XX." *Revista de antropologia* 39, no. 2 (1996): 165–97.

W.L.G.J. "Col. Roosevelt's Exploration of a Tributary of the Madeira." *Bulletin of the American Geographical Society* 46, no. 7 (1914): 512–19.

Zarur, George de Cerqueira Leite. "O herói e o sentimento: Rondon e a identidade Brasileira." Brasília: Câmara dos Deputados, 1998. www.georgezarur.com.br.

Newspapers and Magazines

A Defesa Nacional
A Noite
Careta
Correio da Manhã
Correio do Povo
Diário Carioca
Diário da Noite (Rio de Janeiro)
Folha de S. Paulo
Fon-Fon 1907–1958
Gazeta de Noticias
Jornal do Brasil
Jornal do Commercio (Rio de Janeiro)
Kosmos 1904–1909
Manchete
New York Times 1913–1914, 1929
New York World 1913–1914
O Cruzeiro 1928–1985
O Estado de São Paulo

O Globo
O Imparcial
O Jornal
O Radical
Renascença
Revista da Semana 1900–1962
Revista da Família Acadêmica 1887–1889
Revista Ilustrada 1876–1898
Última Hora

Sites and Discography

Brasiliana Collection of Positivist pamphlets: https://library.brown.edu/create
  /brasiliana/positivism/
Centro de Pesquisa e Documentação de História Contemporânea do Brasil: http://
  www.fgv.br/cpdoc/acervo/arquivo
Povos Indígenas no Brasil: https://pib.socioambiental.org/pt/Página_principal
"Rondônia 1912: Gravações históricas de Roquette-Pinto": https://soundcloud.com
  /nimuendaju/sets/rondonia

INDEX